Coercion and Wage Labour

WORK AROUND THE WORLD: STUDIES IN GLOBAL LABOUR HISTORY

Series Editors
KARIN HOFMEESTER (IISH and University of Antwerp)
and ULBE BOSMA (IISH and Vrije Universiteit Amsterdam)
Executive Editor AAD BLOK (IISH)

Over the past six hundred years an increasingly connected and competitive global economy has had tremendous consequences for how people have made a living. It has brought unprecedented opportunities for many, but also massive dispossession of livelihoods and natural habitats to this very day. People have moved towards agricultural frontiers and industrial centres in growing numbers and over increasing distances for work. Slavery and other coerced labour regimes have shaped persistent social inequalities, racial discrimination and exclusion. Confronted with exploitation, disenfranchisement, gender inequalities, racism and xenophobia, workers have tried to improve their position either individually or collectively.

Drawing on core research at the International Institute of Social History in Amsterdam, this series explores the connectivity between changes in work and shifting labour relations, evolving social and economic inequalities that result from or are connected to these changes, and individual as well as collective responses to these inequalities. Situating these historical dynamics within the context of an unfolding global economy that externalizes social and environmental costs, the series aims for global comparisons across time, space and scale to bring out how evolving social inequalities are connected to the development of work and labour relations, and how these histories may help to understand the causes of inequalities in the present. By combining broad diachronic, transnational and transcontinental comparisons, synthetic overviews and exemplary case studies, the series offers a conversant global perspective on how work and the social and economic relations and contexts in which it is performed, has shaped and defined our world.

Series advisers
Carlos Illades Aguiar, Universidad
Autónoma Metropolitana, Mexico City, Mexico
Görkem Akgöz, Humboldt Universität, Berlin, Germany
Asef Bayat, University of Illinois at Urbana Champaign, Chicago, USA
Akua Opokua Britwum, University of Cape Coast, Ghana
Paulo Drinot, UCL, UK
Omar Gueye, Université Cheikh Anta Diop de Dakar (UCAD), Dakar, Senegal
Peyman Jafari, Princeton University and IISH, Amsterdam, The Netherlands
Marcel van der Linden, IISH, Amsterdam, The Netherlands
Leo Lucassen, IISH, Amsterdam and Leiden University, The Netherlands
Christine Moll-Murata, Ruhr-Universität Bochum, Germany
Samita Sen, University of Cambridge, Cambridge, UK
Paulo Cruz Terra, Universidade Federal Fluminense, Niterói, Rio de Janeiro, Brazil

Coercion and Wage Labour

Exploring work relations through history and art

Edited by Anamarija Batista, Viola Franziska Müller and Corinna Peres

First published in 2024 by
UCL Press
University College London
Gower Street
London WC1E 6BT

Available to download free: www.uclpress.co.uk

Collection © Editors, 2024
Text © Contributors, 2024
Images © Contributors and copyright holders named in captions, 2024

The authors have asserted their rights under the Copyright, Designs and Patents Act 1988 to be identified as the authors of this work.

A CIP catalogue record for this book is available from The British Library.

Any third-party material in this book is not covered by the book's Creative Commons licence. Details of the copyright ownership and permitted use of third-party material is given in the image (or extract) credit lines. If you would like to reuse any third-party material not covered by the book's Creative Commons licence, you will need to obtain permission directly from the copyright owner.

This book is published under a Creative Commons Attribution-Non-Commercial 4.0 International licence (CC BY-NC 4.0), https://creativecommons.org/licenses/by-nc/4.0/. This licence allows you to share and adapt the work for non-commercial use providing attribution is made to the author and publisher (but not in any way that suggests that they endorse you or your use of the work) and any changes are indicated. Attribution should include the following information:

Batista, A., Müller, V. and Peres, C. (eds). 2024. *Coercion and Wage Labour: Exploring work relations through history and art*. London: UCL Press. https://doi.org/10.14324/111.9781800085381

Further details about Creative Commons licences are available at https://creativecommons.org/licenses/

ISBN: 978-1-80008-540-4 (Hbk.)
ISBN: 978-1-80008-539-8 (Pbk.)
ISBN: 978-1-80008-538-1 (PDF)
ISBN: 978-1-80008-541-1 (epub)
DOI: https://doi.org/10.14324/111.9781800085381

This publication is based upon work from COST Action *Worlds of Related Coercions in Work* (WORCK CA18205), supported by COST (European Cooperation in Science and Technology).

COST (European Cooperation in Science and Technology) is a funding agency for research and innovation networks. Our Actions help connect research initiatives across Europe and enable scientists to grow their ideas by sharing them with their peers. This boosts their research, career and innovation.

www.cost.eu

Contents

List of figures — xi
List of diagrams — xiii
List of contributors — xv
Acknowledgements — xxi

Introduction

1 Coercion and wage labour in history and art — 1
   Anamarija Batista, Viola Franziska Müller and Corinna Peres

Part I: Binding the workforce

Chapter frontispieces – collages © Tim Robinson, 2021

2 In the name of order: (im)mobilising wage labour for the Ottoman naval industry in the nineteenth century — 22
   Akın Sefer

3 Contracts under duress: work documents as a matter and means of conflict in the Habsburg Monarchy/Austria in the late nineteenth and early twentieth centuries — 47
   Sigrid Wadauer

4 Working for the enemy: civil servants in occupied Serbia, 1941–1944 — 79
   Nataša Milićević and Ljubinka Škodrić

5 Exploitation and care: public health aspirations and the construction of the working-class body in the Budapest Museum of Social Health, 1901–1945 — 107
   Eszter Őze

Part II: Confronting coercion

Chapter frontispieces – digital drawings with watercolours
© Dariia Kuzmych, 2021

6	Subdued wage workers: textile production in Western and Islamic sources (ninth to twelfth centuries) *Colin Arnaud*	141
7	'One gets rich, one hundred more work for nothing': German miners in Medici Tuscany *Gabriele Marcon*	165
8	Entangled dependencies: the case of the runaway domestic worker Emine in late Ottoman Istanbul, 1910 *Müge Özbek*	185
9	The dilemma of being a 'good worker': cultural discourse, coercion and resistance in Bangladesh's garment factories *Mohammad Tareq Hasan*	201
10	Border plants: globalisation as shown to us by the women living at its leading edge *Eva Kuhn*	225

Part III: Manipulating labour relations

Chapter frontispieces – graphic novel © Monika Lang, 2021–2022

11	Negotiating the terms of wage(less) labour: free and freed workers as contractual parties in nineteenth-century Rio de Janeiro *Marjorie Carvalho de Souza*	249
12	Constructing debt: discursive and material strategies of labour coercion in the US South, 1903–1964 *Nico Pizzolato*	272
13	Obligatory contributions to society: student foreign-language guides as seasonal wage workers in socialist Bulgaria, 1970s–1980s *Ivanka Petrova*	301
14	To put a human face on the question of labour: photographic portraiture and the Australian-Pacific indentured labour trade *Paolo Magagnoli*	331

Afterword

15 Word and image in communication: 'translation loop' as a means of historiographical research 357
Anamarija Batista

Chapter endpieces – graphic novel © Monika Lang, 2021

Index 377

List of figures

5.1	Poster of the First International Exhibition of Occupational Safety and Labour Welfare of 1907.	122
5.2	Leaflet of the Museum of Social Health used in propaganda against emigration from the villages after 1928: 'Don't emigrate to the cities, don't leave your home.'	128
5.3	Exhibition poster on the topic of social health protection of the year 1932.	129
10.1	Factory worker Carmen Durán in the film *Maquilápolis: City of Factories*, directed by Vicky Funari and Sergio De La Torre, 2006.	226
10.2	Factory workers in the film *Maquilápolis: City of Factories*, directed by Vicky Funari and Sergio De La Torre, 2006.	227
10.3	Teresa Loyola and other factory workers display the components they assemble, in *Maquilápolis: City of Factories*, directed by Vicky Funari and Sergio De La Torre, 2006.	228
10.4	Lupita Castañeda films a video diary as part of the film *Maquilápolis: City of Factories*, directed by Vicky Funari and Sergio De La Torre, 2006.	234
10.5	The toxic waste site left behind by Metales y Derivados, a battery recycling factory; from the film *Maquilápolis: City of Factories*, directed by Vicky Funari and Sergio De La Torre, 2006.	238
11.1	Philippe Benoist and Jean-Victor Frond, *Encaissage et pesage du sucre*, 1861. Lithograph on paper, 63.5 × 47.9 cm. Frond's photograph engraved by Benoist portrays slave and freed workers weighing and boxing sugar in the streets of Rio de Janeiro, distinguished by the use or lack of shoes, an iconographic sign of social distinction. Public domain, reproduced courtesy of Biblioteca Nacional Digital of Brazil.	254
14.1	Dylan Mooney, *Stop and Stare*, 2018 (showing one of the two images forming the artwork). Pencil and charcoal on paper.	333

14.2 Jasmine Togo–Brisby, South Sea Islanders with sugar plantation owner, from the series *The Past is Ahead, Don't Look Back*, 2019. Collodion on glass. This work was one of three photographs by the artist displayed in the exhibition Plantation Voices at the State Library of Queensland, 16 February–8 September 2019. — 334

14.3 Harriett Pettifore Brims (1864–1939), untitled, late 1890s, negative glass. Taken in Ingham, north Queensland, this portrait shows an anonymous South Sea Islander wearing a pearl necklace, feathers and other traditional ornaments. — 340

14.4 F. C. Wills, 'Kanakas Planting Cane (Bingera)', *Queensland Agricultural Journal*, 1 September 1897, 248. The photograph depicts a gang of Melanesian workers in a sugar cane field. While those in the background are inactive, those in the foreground seem to have been instructed by the operator to ignore the cameraman. — 343

14.5 D. McFarlane, 'South Sea Islanders', *North Queensland Register*, 21 December 1892, 41. This double portrait depicts a South Sea Islander man and woman wearing Western clothing and posing for the camera. — 345

14.6 D. McFarlane, 'South Sea Islanders', *North Queensland Register*, 21 December 1892, 44. These portraits show the same Melanesian couple as in Figure 14.5, this time dressed in their 'authentic' traditional costumes. — 345

14.7 'Before the Exodus: A Kanaka Wedding', *The Sydney Mail*, 31 October 1906, 563. Part of a feature narrating the experience of a Christian wedding among South Sea Islanders, the article includes various portraits of assimilated Melanesians accompanied by sneering captions. — 347

14.8 'The Evolution of the Plantation Kanaka', *The Queenslander*, 23 March 1901, 563. Drawing on the photographs published by the *North Queensland Register* a decade earlier, the article arranges collective and individual portraits of Melanesians in a sequential manner to suggest the benign effects of coerced labour. — 349

List of diagrams

3.1 Matters of dispute at trade courts in Vienna, 1898–1914   58
3.2 Workers' concerns brought forward to trade inspectors, 1894–1900   59

List of contributors

Colin Arnaud is a lecturer at the University of Münster. He studied history and literature at the universities of Bielefeld, Germany; Paris 7 Denis Diderot, France; and Bologna, Italy. He wrote his doctoral thesis at the Humboldt-Universität zu Berlin, Germany, about the social topography of Bologna and Strasbourg around 1400. He is now working on a research project about male weavers in the Middle Ages in Europe and the Middle East.

Anamarija Batista is an experienced interdisciplinary researcher and curator working at the intersection of art, architecture and economics. As Assistant Professor at the Institute for Art Theory and Cultural Studies, Academy of Fine Arts, Vienna, she has been exploring socialist perspectives on leisure time within the project 'Collective Utopias of Post-War Modernism: The Adriatic Coast as a Leisure and Defence Paradise', funded by the PEEK programme of the Austrian Science Fund. She coedited the book *Rethinking Density: Art, Culture and Urban Practices*, published in 2017 by Sternberg Press in the series of the Academy of Fine Arts in Vienna. She is also the editor of the anthology *Notions of Temporalities in Artistic Practice* (Berlin and Boston: De Gruyter, 2022). She teaches at the University Mozarteum in Salzburg.

Marjorie Carvalho de Souza is a PhD candidate in Global History and Governance at the Scuola Superiore Meridionale, Italy. She holds a graduate degree in Labour Law from the Pontifical Catholic University of Rio Grande do Sul, Brazil, a master's degree in Global History from the Federal University of Santa Catarina, Brazil, and a bachelor's degree in Law from the same institution.

Mohammad Tareq Hasan is Associate Professor at the Department of Anthropology, University of Dhaka, Bangladesh. After initial training in Anthropology from the University of Dhaka, he pursued an MPhil in Anthropology of Development (2014) and a PhD in Social Anthropology (2018) from the University of Bergen (UiB), Norway. He also completed a postdoctoral research fellowship (2021) at the International Institute for Asian Studies (IIAS), Leiden University, the Netherlands.

His research interests include the anthropology of work, state formation, political economy and egalitarianism. He is the author of *Everyday Life of Ready-made Garment* Kormi *in Bangladesh: An Ethnography of Neoliberalism* (Cham: Palgrave Macmillan, 2022).

Eva Kuhn is an art and film scholar, currently working as a research associate at the Faculty of Humanities at the Leuphana University Lüneburg (Professorship for Contemporary Art). Previously, she was a visiting professor at the University of the Arts, Berlin, and a research associate at the Institute of Art History at the University of Basel. Her fields of research are the intersection of arts and cinema, (queer-)feminist and postcolonial criticism and experimental film. She is currently working on a guest edition of *Frauen und Film*: 'Feminist economies and temporalities', and on a book project entitled 'Maintenance (Art-)Work and the Production of Presence'.

Dariia Kuzmych is a Ukrainian artist. She currently lives and works in Kyiv and Berlin. After finishing her bachelor's degree in monumental painting at the Fine Art Academy in Kyiv, Kuzmych completed the master's programme in media art at the Berlin University of Arts. She works in various techniques, such as installation, drawing, video and text. A central point that connects these multimedia practices is that they capture times of transition in a society and explore how these impact individuals. In her current projects, she is engaged with various aspects of experiencing trauma and the perception of time. https://dariiakuzmych.com/

Monika Lang graduated from the Faculty of Applied Arts in Belgrade, Department of Illustration and Book Design. She works as an independent illustrator and graphic designer, chiefly on culture-related projects and publishing. Lang is cofounder and member of the 'Turbotomorrow' designer group established in 2006. In addition to illustration and print design, she also researches screen printing techniques, mural painting and other media of visual expression. http://www.behance.net/monikalang; http://monikalang.com/

Paolo Magagnoli is Senior Lecturer in Art History at the University of Queensland. He holds a PhD in Art History from UCL, and he was previously an honorary associate in the Department of Art History at the University of Sydney. His research is focused on the history and theory of photography and artists' cinema. His essays have appeared in the *Oxford Art Journal*,

Third Text, *Photography and Culture* and *Philosophy of Photography*. He is the author of *Documents of Utopia: The Politics of Experimental Documentary* (Wallflower/Columbia University Press, 2015).

Gabriele Marcon is Lecturer in European History (1450–1750) at Durham University, UK. His research lies at the intersection of labour history and the history of science, and currently focuses on mining activities in Europe and the Iberian world. He recently received his PhD in History from the European University Institute (Florence, Italy) with a thesis titled 'The Movements of Mining: German Miners in Renaissance Italy (1450–1560)'. Marcon is the co-convenor of the European Labour History Network working group 'Labour in Mining' and editor of the online series 'The Young Mining Historians' Corner'.

Nataša Milićević is a research associate at the Institute for Recent History of Serbia. Her main field of interest is the social history of Serbia and Yugoslavia in the twentieth century, with a special focus on the history of the Serbian middle class, the intelligentsia, relations between the authorities and social groups, and everyday life, as well as the history of historiography. She has recently focused particularly on the history of Serbian society in occupied Serbia during the Second World War. Milićević has coedited two books (2011, 2020) and she is the author of the monograph *Yugoslav Authority and Serbian Middle Class 1944–1950* (originally *Југословенска власт и српско грађанство 1944–1950*, Београд: ИНИС, 2009), for which she received an award from the Ministry of Science and Technological Development of the Republic of Serbia for a special contribution in the field of the Social Sciences and Humanities for the year 2009.

Viola Franziska Müller is a historian and postdoctoral researcher at the Bonn Centre for Dependency and Slavery Studies at the University of Bonn, Germany. She is the author of *Escape to the City: Fugitive Slaves in the Antebellum Urban South* (Chapel Hill: University of North Carolina Press, 2022) and coeditor of *Moving Workers: Historical Perspectives on Labour, Coercion and Im/Mobilities* (Berlin and Boston: De Gruyter, 2023).

Müge Özbek is Assistant Professor in the Core Program at Kadir Has University, Istanbul, Turkey. Özbek completed her PhD at Boğaziçi University in 2018 with a dissertation entitled 'Single, Poor Women in Istanbul, 1850–1915: Prostitution, Sexuality, and Female Labor'. Her research focuses on the themes of the everyday lives of lower-class women, urban life, labour and im/mobility in the late Ottoman Empire.

Eszter Őze is an art historian and a research fellow in the Historical Avant-garde Research Program at the Museum of Fine Arts – Central European Research Institute for Art History Budapest. She completed her PhD in Philosophy, Film, Media and Cultural Theory at Eötvös Loránd University, Budapest. Her research field is museology in the interwar period: she analyses public health and social museums in Europe and the workers' culture in Central and Eastern Europe. Since 2020 she has taught in the Department of Art Theory and Curatorial Studies at the Hungarian University of Fine Arts, before which she was a lecturer at Eötvös Loránd University.

Corinna Peres is a PhD candidate and university assistant at the Department of Economic and Social History at the University of Vienna, Austria. She received her Master of Arts degree with distinction in History and Romance Philology (Italian) from Ruhr University Bochum, Germany. In 2022, she held a research grant from the German Historical Institute in Rome, Italy. Her research interests lie in the history of labour, slavery and the slave trade in the Mediterranean, with a special focus on Tuscan merchant networks in the late Middle Ages.

Ivanka Petrova is Associate Professor at the Institute of Ethnology and Folklore Studies with Ethnographic Museum at the Bulgarian Academy of Sciences. Since 1998 she has worked in the Department of Ethnology of Socialism and Post-socialism. Her major fields of research are the culture of labour, entrepreneurship and entrepreneurial culture, everyday culture in socialism and post-socialism, cultural heritage and urban culture. Petrova has published over 70 articles on these topics in national and international journals and books. She has worked on 15 research projects and published the book *World of Labor and Ethnology* (Sofia, 2010).

Nico Pizzolato is Associate Professor in Global Labour Studies at Middlesex University, London, UK. He is the author of *Challenging Global Capitalism: Labor Migration, Radical Struggle and Urban Change in Detroit and Turin* (New York: Palgrave Macmillan, 2013) and of numerous articles that focus on the interplay between labour migration, race and ethnic relations, working-class self-activity and social movements. His work has appeared in journals such as the *American Historical Review*, the *International Review of Social History* and *Labor History*. He has coedited *Antonio Gramsci: A Pedagogy to Change the World* (Cham: Springer, 2017). His most recent work is on unfree and precarious labour in the twentieth-century United States.

Tim Robinson is a conceptual collage artist who uses traditional elements along with digital imagery to produce evocative editorial illustration. He first had his work published when working for Milton Glaser's design studio in New York City. Since then, his illustrations have been reproduced in books, magazines and newspapers worldwide. Clients include the *New York Times*, *The Nation*, the *Wall Street Journal*, the *New Republic*, *NPR*, *Conde Nast*, the *Boston Globe* and many more. http://timrobinsonstudio.blogspot.com/

Akın Sefer is a postdoctoral research fellow at Koç University's Department of History in Istanbul, Turkey. He received his PhD in History in 2018 from Northeastern University. Currently (between 2021 and 2024), he is the principal investigator of a research project on shipbuilding and labour migration in the Black Sea Coast and Istanbul in the nineteenth century. His research focuses on labour, migration and modernisation in the late Ottoman Empire.

Ljubinka Škodrić is a senior research associate at the Institute of Contemporary History in Belgrade. She earned her PhD in Yugoslav history at Belgrade University. She is the author of the monographs *Ministry of Education and Religion in Serbia 1941–1944*: *The Fate of the Institution under Occupation* (originally *Ministarstvo prosvete i vera u Srbiji 1941–1944: Sudbina institucije pod okupacijom*; Beograd: Arhiv Srbije, 2009) and *Women in Occupied Serbia 1941–1944* (originally *Žena u okupiranoj Srbiji 1941–1944*; Beograd: Institut za savremenu istoriju, Arhipelag, 2020). Her research areas are the gender and social history of Serbia, the history of education and the history of the Serbian archival service.

Sigrid Wadauer is a historian at the University of Vienna, Austria. Her publications deal with topics such as work, livelihood and mobility, crafts and trades, autobiography and the life course, and street level bureaucracy from the late eighteenth to the early twentieth centuries, with a regional focus on Central Europe. She has worked as a researcher and taught at the universities of Salzburg and Vienna. Wadauer has held various grants and fellowships in Austria, Germany and the USA, including an ERC Starting Grant ('The Production of Work'). Currently she is working in the Austrian Science Fund project 'Co-Producing and Using Identity Documents'.

Acknowledgements

This publication is based upon work from the COST Action 'Worlds of Related Coercions in Work' (WORCK), CA18205 (2019–2024), supported by COST (European Cooperation in Science and Technology). WORCK is a European network of labour historians and social scientists, led by Juliane Schiel and Johan Heinsen. The network is committed to recontextualising work in history with the aim of more deeply understanding 'the mechanisms of coercion in all work relations throughout history' (see www.worck.eu). The idea for this book emerged in the aftermath of WORCK's virtual conference Reconceptualising Wage Labour, hosted by the Central European University in Budapest, Hungary, in September 2020. Additional financial support for the publication of this book was kindly provided by the Mozarteum Salzburg, as well as by the Doctoral School and Faculty of Historical and Cultural Studies, both at the University of Vienna.

The editors would like to thank the illustrators Dariia Kuzmych, Monika Lang and Tim Robinson for their collaboration and the stunning artwork they created for this book. We extend our gratitude to Juliane Schiel for her support and encouragement in the preparation of this project and throughout its course. Laura Šukarov-Eischer, grant holder manager of the COST Action, impressively manoeuvred this project through several challenges. At UCL Press, we were lucky in being able to count on Pat Gordon-Smith and her team for their fantastic work. Jillian Bowie deserves special mention for her exceptional copy-editing work. We are grateful to the blind reviewers of the book proposal and to the reviewer of the manuscript for their valuable critique and suggestions. Thanks also go to Christine Brocks for her rigorous language editing. David de Boer, Christian De Vito and Johan Heinsen provided important feedback on earlier drafts of the introduction, which is very much appreciated. Lastly, we thank the contributors to this book, whose patience, reliability and commitment within a tight schedule have made this project possible.

Introduction

1
Coercion and wage labour in history and art

Anamarija Batista, Viola Franziska Müller and Corinna Peres

This book explores the manifold ways in which coercion has occurred in and through remunerated labour. Covering a variety of historical periods and places brought together for the first time, it does so in a unique way by mobilising an interdisciplinary dialogue. Texts by historians and social scientists are accompanied by a series of images specifically created by illustrators that visualise and interpret the main messages. Other chapters written by art scholars draw on image material such as photographic portraits, film and exhibition posters to discuss how coercion in wage labour has been constructed and reflected in artistic practice. This book thus offers three means of knowledge production and reception: 1) through the academic text, which develops its argument successively word by word; 2) through the image, which develops the argument simultaneously and spatially; and 3) through the collaboration of image and text, which develops the argument in a hybrid way.

Two main purposes stand central. First, this book challenges the juxtaposition of wage labour and coerced labour by showing that different mechanisms of coercion have been used in combination with wages over the centuries. Most of the chapters deal with the nineteenth and twentieth centuries, when wage labour became the dominant form of labour relations in industrialised societies, such as Brazil, the Ottoman Empire, Hungary, Bulgaria, Serbia, North America and contemporary Bangladesh. And yet, wages are an age-old phenomenon, as the chapters on the medieval Frankish empire and Fatimid Egypt and on early modern Tuscany demonstrate. By assembling areas as diverse as textile production, mining, naval and war industries, civil service, domestic work and agriculture, we attempt to renew the scholarly attention to wage labour, which has conceptually been largely separated from coerced labour. To do so, *Coercion and Wage Labour* scrutinises anew, with a trans-epochal perspective, this 'traditional' subject of labour history through the lenses of global labour history.[1]

The second intervention departs from the fact that narrating history in academic disciplines usually takes place in textual form. To challenge this conventional approach, the book places written histories in dialogue with artistic illustrations. This dialogue has two dimensions: the illustrations were created out of the text, while the chapters, in turn, also integrate and reflect on the illustrations. This hybridity of image and text makes it possible to accentuate different aspects. The text weaves dense information about coercion into its argumentation lines, including historical causes, consequences and possible ambiguities. The illustrators, by contrast, selected central aspects of the argument capable of carrying significant parts of the narrative. The direct links between the two media activate diverse interpretations and can draw unexpected parallels between work in past centuries and now.

Current debates on wage labour in capitalism

The understanding of work in industrialised countries has been greatly informed by the impact of labour movements and the advent of labour markets in which labour power is traded for wages.[2] This characteristic, that labour power is bought rather than the products of work or workers themselves, makes wage labour truly unique – yet not new. Today, social and economic inequality and exploitation have become the cornerstones of debates about work,[3] and the question of whether and to what extent wage labour is a constitutive part of capitalism stirs the minds of scholars from disciplines such as economics, development theory, history, political theory and sociology.[4] Although the answers to this question diverge, there is a consistent tendency in the argumentation: wage labour is the dominant form of work in modern industrial societies, and capitalism is compatible with both so-called 'free' and 'unfree' forms of labour.[5] While far from disagreeing with these imperatives, we aim to strike a different path by breaking open the dichotomy between 'free' and 'unfree' labour.

In times of pandemic and inflation, remuneration is becoming a global 'hot topic'. Skyrocketing living costs combined with higher energy bills are overshadowing tariff negotiations in many work sectors. Debates on minimum wages are looming in nation-state policy-making. At the same time, the rising global trend of deteriorating working conditions is not only about low and stagnating wages, also but has many pillars such as precariousness, overtime work and lack of access to social security.[6] To stress this hyper-exploitative nature that remunerated labour can assume in different political and economic systems, the notion of 'modern slavery' has been mobilised in both scholarly and public discourse.[7] The definition of modern slavery – albeit vague – diverges from earlier institutionalised forms of slavery and emphasises extreme coercion in a world of allegedly 'free' wage work.[8] In this politicised context, historical and present-day attention to slavery have come to mutually inform one another. A new research strand on the historical significance of slavery for global – and especially European and US – economic development has emerged, and a whole 'new debate on the relationship between capitalism, freedom, and democracy has been reopened'.[9]

On the basis of these discussions, scholarship has been able to more firmly move away from the teleological master narrative of linear, and hardly overlapping, labour relations that evolved from 'bonded forms' to free wage work.[10] The basic element of this view has been that '[v]arious coercive labour practices – slavery, serfdom, indenture, vassalage – are regarded' as having given 'way to free but commodified forms of labour'. This has particularly been related to the 'expansion of capitalist modernity, free contract, and wage work', as historians Christian De Vito and Alex Lichtenstein have outlined.[11] 'Coercive labour practices' came to be seen as mere anachronisms from older times, because – at least in institutionalised forms – they gradually disappeared in favour of unconstrained labour relations.[12] This view, just like the spread of wage labour itself, was accelerated by the positive changes it accompanied in Europe after the World Wars. Rapid economic development enabled steeply rising incomes and wider access to education and culminated in the establishment of the welfare state.[13]

The idea of fading labour coercion, however, has to be rethought. The modern industrial societies postulated after the Second World War that freedom of labour correlated with freedom of consumption. It was precisely 'secured' and ever-growing consumption that was crucial for the stability of the nation-state and its economy. Based on the premise that everyone could equally shape the market with their subjective preferences, it was assumed that the production side of the economy and its labour relations were democratised through the act of consumption. This implied that consumerism would not only improve the quality of life of a 'freely acting' working individual, but also contribute to the regulation of potential market crises.[14] Depending on the political-economic setting, this ideology could manifest itself in varying ways, from 'the right to work' to 'the duty to work' or even 'being human through consumption'. Think here, for example, of the long-running advertisement by a German drug store, which claims that shopping is a fundamental facet of being human.[15]

At the same time, in socialist countries such as Yugoslavia, attempts were made to link the freedom of labour with the question of property, and to introduce forms of self-management in factories. This turned workers into collective owners, who partook in the factory collective and provided infrastructure for the common good and consumption. Their competition with other factory collectives was envisioned to boost the productivity of all labour processes.[16] The meaning of freedom in wage work also features prominently in the nineteenth-century writings of Karl Marx. He conceptualised wage workers as 'doubly free' because they were free to sell their labour power on the labour market (unlike 'unfree' workers, they were neither the property of someone else nor bound to the land), and they were free from access to the means of production or subsistence.

We should take from these examples that the issue of freedom of labour cannot be considered outside its historical context, and cannot be disconnected from other economic factors, such as consumption, credit, interest rates and social infrastructures. These aspects significantly influence the experience of employment, especially the 'decisions' on its start, duration and ending.[17] In this line, and offering a broad historical perspective, this book shows that wage work has taken different shapes and played diverse roles in combination with other forms of labour across the centuries.[18]

Coercion in and through remunerated work

In recent publications, wage labour is increasingly conceptualised alongside coerced labour.[19] In particular, the new research agenda of the history of work breaks with empirically untenable dichotomies, aiming to show 'that the coexistence, entanglement, and overlapping of diverse labour relations has been the rule throughout history'.[20] But what exactly is the relation between wage labour and coercion? The International Labour Organization (ILO) has been working to understand this for a long time in its fight against 'forced labour'; the Global Estimates of Modern Slavery represent only one measure in this process. In its endeavour, the ILO also acknowledges, for example, deception about payments and indebtedness through advance wages as coercive elements.[21]

This recognition of remuneration not only as intrinsic to labour coercion but also as an essential *tool* of coercion is paramount.

Yet, wages can take on many forms; the most prevalent form today is money – paid either by the day or in regular intervals like a salary. Remuneration can be based on a fixed time frame, on the completion of certain tasks or on the concrete products of work. In labour relations that do not abstract the produced output of work from the worker, piece rates are a dominant form of payment.[22] The quantity and quality of remuneration depends on the contemporary understanding of labour, labour market structures and the worker's individual profile. Remunerated labour relations can be informal, formalised by law involving written contracts or oral agreements, and even produced under high pressure, but they are always a product of negotiations.[23] All negotiations necessarily emerge out of asymmetrical power relations, which manifest themselves in the quality of working conditions and the level of wages. Studying these aspects enables us to deduct conclusions about the power relations between employers and employees. A telling example is the case of the German-speaking miners in Gabriele Marcon's chapter in this volume, whose high wages did not prevent them from forced relocation between different mines in sixteenth-century Tuscany.

Negotiations can go beyond the realm of work and include all social interactions that make a person work. Think of an enslaved woman in Richmond, Virginia, who pleaded with her hirer that 'her friends and favourites' had to be allowed to visit her.[24] Successfully resisting commodification and accentuating her humanity through the insistence on having a private life, this woman brought the broader social context of her work to the negotiating table. Others took bargaining to the collective level, most successfully during the 'golden age' of the welfare state, when negotiations went far beyond the modalities of wages – their form, conditions and rhythms of payment – to include other benefits, such as transportation to work, housing, pensions and protection from inflation.

Contracts are manifestations of negotiations, but they are not their end point. The historian Jairus Banaji has discussed how contracts were fundamental to the idea of wage labour in modern history, and he makes a strong point claiming that a contract is 'probably never' voluntary.[25] This is obvious in the case of indentured Pacific Islanders who came to work on Australian sugar plantations and whose employers demanded to record 'voluntariness' in the labour contracts, as Paolo Magagnoli shows in his contribution to this volume. Due to the absence of alternatives in a situation of economic hardship, a situation aggravated by their position in a racist colonial system, the legal authority to sign contracts did not empower workers to access property but only brought the possibility of selling their labour power.

At the same time, wage earners were not only impacted by the market. In the nineteenth century, institutionalised slavery and various forms of bound servitude were in the process of abolition. The challenge of the day was to move workers into the mushrooming factories, which involved a set of legal, political and social pressures. New forms of coercion were introduced to achieve the transformation of the economy. This required, as historian Sven Beckert puts it, 'a lopsided distribution of power that allowed statesmen and capitalists to dominate the lives of individuals and families in [unprecedented] ways'.[26] In the case of industrial workers, this domination reached into interfering with their bodies, habits and reproduction, as the chapter by Eszter Őze shows for the Hungarian case. Preceded by fundamental transformations of the countryside, labour coercion in modern industrial societies was 'increasingly accomplished by the state, its bureaucrats and judges, and not by lords and masters'.[27] In short, governments created new legal frameworks to regulate labour relations. Marjorie Carvalho de Souza and Sigrid Wadauer's respective contributions illustrate these developments for Brazil and Habsburg Austria, where states enforced work contracts by penalising their infringement with high fines.

Studying remuneration in combination with coercion provides new insights into power relations on different levels and allows us to understand the prevalence of wages as intrinsic to the history of work. But we need to know more about how coercion was constructed, applied and operated. This is especially important when we look at work that might not take place against the worker's will per se. In the Bangladeshi textile industry, for example, employers deliberately build on cultural discourses of solidarity, as Mohammad Tareq Hasan demonstrates in his chapter, to increase the workers' commitment. Coercion, it becomes clear, can take very different shapes and forms. Sometimes, coercion in remunerated work was very visible, foremost when the workers had a legally unfree status. Hired-out enslaved workers (who, in some cases, could keep a part of their payment) are the prime example of this, as well as landlords in Asia and Europe who stipulated their subjects to work for a wage they set.[28] In these cases where lords or governments set the level of wages, the payment was often significantly low, such as in medieval Western Europe and Egypt, as Colin Arnaud's contribution emphasises, but also in the nineteenth-century Ottoman naval industry, as Akın Sefer argues in his chapter. But legally free workers, like domestic servants after the abolition of Ottoman slavery in Müge Özbek's chapter, could also be caught in discernibly coercive structures.

At other times, coercive acts were overshadowed by remuneration tactics, for example by using low wages to increase dependency situations when alternatives were largely absent, or by justifying them through forms of liability. The former is dealt with by Nataša Milićević and Ljubinka Škodrić, who show that coercion was not even straightforward when Serbia and its civil servants were under the occupation of Nazi Germany in the Second World War. The latter is the topic of Nico Pizzolato's study on African American and Mexican agricultural workers in the US, who were immobilised through accumulated debts. At other times again, coercion was hardly perceivable at all, namely when it appeared under the disguise of 'care' for the workers, or when the alternatives were perceived as much worse so that the employees even developed a certain gratitude. Ivanka Petrova argues that this happened with students in socialist Bulgaria who 'had to volunteer' as tourist guides to be spared other types of compulsory labour. Independently of whether it occurs in the past or in the present, coercion is often literally invisible when it receives no attention. In this vein, Eva Kuhn highlights the medium of film and its powerful potential to convey the precarities and struggles of those who labour at the edge of our globalised world: women in Mexican sweatshops. The central question that all contributions deal with is how forms of coercion can be detected and understood in the context of paid employment.

Interdisciplinary and intermedial dialogue

With coercion taking such a prominent role in the human experience of labour, *Coercion and Wage Labour* employs textual and visual ways of understanding. To this end, the historical, anthropological and sociological contributions in this book partner with illustrations that were produced in close collaboration between the artists, authors and curators. Created by Monika Lang, Dariia Kuzmych and Tim Robinson, the illustrations are based on key scenes of the chapters which the curators Anamarija Batista and Corinna Peres have extracted, while the chapters themselves also feed back to the visual interpretations. The abstraction of the body is typically very strong in textual scholarship, and the three artists differ in visual strategies to bring the physical (back) into the picture to encourage a discussion of how images themselves can shape the perception of history.[29]

'Reading' a text and 'looking at' an image are complex processes that depend on the readers' comprehension skills. While the former demands making sense of a chain of letters on black and white ground (*lógos*, the 'merely thinkable'), the latter requires making sense of a composition of forms and colours (*aísthesis*, the 'sensually perceptible').[30] A historical text, however, usually offers interpretations in an already more structurally determined way while illustrations invite people to create their own walkthroughs of history.

In taking this approach of combining two media to tell one story, this book does not have many peers. But an important one is *Art and Public History* by Rebecca Bush and Tawny Paul, which explores how art can be part of public history telling – that is, history is neither done exclusively *by* historians, nor exclusively *for* historians.[31] While the focus is on museum exhibitions, Bush and Paul likewise engage a 'more active and intensive collaboration between' art and history with the goal being to 'yield new meanings, new stories and new forms of engagement with the public'.[32] In our case, illustrations, because they rely on individual interpretations, can mobilise a more direct relation with the recipient to increase their subjective understanding of coercion in wage labour. The presentation of coercion, then, draws on individual and collective experiences and scopes of knowledge.

This book tells of historical cases from different, interwoven angles. The authors and illustrations refer to one other and 'translate' the interpretation of the respective other into their own medium. The aim of this 'translation loop', which is explained in more detail in the afterword by Anamarija Batista, is to shift, intensify and expand on the historical narrative by including spatial and corporeal aspects. While telling the same story, text and image can complement and challenge each other. Take, for example, the illustration by Dariia Kuzmych and the text by Müge Özbek in this book. They deal with the case of a young domestic worker in late Ottoman Istanbul. Kuzymch visually brings the worker's will to leave her employers' household into the foreground by positioning her on a door threshold in which a piece of her clothing is wedged. Although she is physically outside the house, this symbolically keeps her from entering the urban space, which we can glimpse in the background. We can interpret her being bound to the house as forced immobilisation. We can make informed guesses at her motivations and the location, and we can observe and imagine the struggle of the young woman who wants to escape, including how coercion might have felt for her. In her text, Özbek links the city to its surroundings by singling out socioeconomic inequality and patriarchal discourses as conditions for the relocation of young girls from rural areas into Istanbul households as domestic workers. In this case, image and text add meaning to each other by emphasising diverse mechanisms and dimensions of coercion through different techniques of abstraction and focalisation. We can speak in this sense of a medial collaboration to transmit historical knowledge. Text and image also challenge each other by highlighting both the worker's powerlessness and the worker's resistance. This shows that this new approach can complement and shift meanings with the hope of tackling rigid dichotomies in academic history telling.

With the linguistic and cultural turns of the 1980s, as well as postmodern influences, the question of 'how to narrate' experienced a boom in both artistic practice and historical studies.[33] This concern stresses that an engagement with the past is not only a question of *what* we decide to study, but also of *how* best to communicate or present our findings if we want to make the recipients of our message curious to engage with our ideas and thoughts.[34] Initially inspired by narrative approaches to history provocatively formulated by Hayden White and Paul Ricoeur, current debates in the fields of intermediality, public history (especially visual history), global history and historical theory have picked up these older debates around the two levels of narration, emphasising the premise that '[h]istory is about content *and* form'.[35]

Artistic practice, too, has become a relevant field to explore how genealogies – the ways in which history writing is composed and organised – and subjectivity feature in historical narratives. Braco Dimitrijević, Anna Artaker, Elizabeth Price and Anna Daučíková, to name just a few, have assembled images such as archive photography or video recordings, visually introduce historical actors whose names are unknown to us, and combine history with fictitious elements to reinterpret historical writing.[36] It becomes apparent that those who provide historical knowledge inevitably encounter narrative choices that are dependent on both the genre and the chosen medium. The material side of the medium – such as paper and ink, or screens and digital pencils – and the ways the messages are conveyed, for example through words, signs, pictures, colours, determine both the constraints and possibilities of their endeavours.[37]

Our current times are full of diverse media forms, and many of these media take a stake in narrating the past, such as films, magazine articles, novels, public lectures, comics, illustrations and academic texts.[38] Taking seriously these claims of telling history, we want to encourage a re-evaluation of the academic-historiographical 'unbroken fixation on the text'.[39] Reversely, engagement with the possibilities that the illustrations provide can galvanise historians and social scientists into re-exploring the different ways texts can be written as well. Think of the choice of words, textual structure, narrative techniques, the position of the author, implementation of visuals and the place of individual historical actors.

We integrate modes of intermedial narration in our explorations of coercion in remunerated labour relations. Placing scholarly texts alongside illustrations, contrasting and combining them, as well as involving artistic works and exhibition practices, demonstrates different ways of dealing with the past and opens up new spaces for communication and reflection.[40] Yet, it is challenging to build historical narratives, and interpreting labour coercion holds room for ambiguities.[41] This does not only concern the illustrators, authors and editors of this book, but also its readers, who are encouraged to develop their own interpretations of and reflections on coercion in and through labour relations.

Chapter overview: binding, confronting, manipulating

In order to shift the attention to tools and mechanisms of coercion, this book goes beyond categories such as slavery, indentureship, convict work, corvée labour, tributary service and other types of work to which it is relatively easy to attach a 'label of coercion'. Coming from multidisciplinary scholarly backgrounds, the contributors in this book consult and redevelop categories of analysis, such as punishment and debt, the state as a constraining employer, immobility as a tool of coercion, and discipline as an 'educational' measure. They historicise their cases in a broader nexus of work incentives, labour supply and demand, and social relations that shaped experiences of coercion.[42] In some chapters, wages play a very central role, while others focus on factors structuring remuneration, such as contracts, legal status or group belonging. As they collectively show, depending on the political, legal, social and economic considerations at play, employers could bind, control and exploit workers at any time through and under the guise of remuneration.

The book is divided into three parts, each focusing on the key parties involved in the world of work: 1) the state, 2) the workers and 3) the employers. The first part, 'Binding the workforce', looks at legal and institutional frameworks conceptualised by the state for the organisation of labour and the control of labour relations. Akın Sefer shows how, during intensive Ottoman reform programmes targeting the military and naval industry, the government not only used the prospect of regular wage payments to legitimise coercive recruitment practices, but also used the delay of wage payments to strategically restrict the mobility of workers. Sigrid Wadauer discusses how labour booklets, which were obligatory identity papers for people in search of regular employment, were instrumented to control workers in the Habsburg Empire in the late nineteenth and early twentieth centuries. In the context of Nazi-occupied Serbia, Nataša Milićević and Ljubinka Škodrić argue that wages too low to cover living costs, combined with a constant fear of losing one's job, exacerbated civil servants' economic fears and ideological-political dilemmas and made them comply with the orders of the occupier.

These three chapters are accompanied by a set of collages by Tim Robinson, who connects material fragments from the historical sources of the respective chapters with pictorial elements and colour filters on different spatial levels. The fourth contribution in this section, by Eszter Őze, explores how the Budapest Museum of Social Health created a 'class body' of industrial wage workers in the early twentieth century. Analysing four exhibitions and the corresponding posters, Őze exposes institutionalised state care as a new scientific way of disciplining workers. The chapters in this part attest that wages can be promised, deferred, denied, reduced and transformed in the contexts of state processes of modernisation, industrialisation and war. Governmental initiatives promoted wage work as an effective instrument to draft, bind and control the workforce.

The second part, 'Confronting coercion', centres on the workers' experiences of and reactions to coercion. Among different groups of workers that Colin Arnaud discusses in his chapter on textile production in medieval Western Europe and Egypt, those working as cooperative subcontractors enjoyed high autonomy. Being remunerated for the end product, they were able to avoid supervision during the production process and mitigate coercion.[43] This adaptation strategy of working as self-employed also drove German men and women into the silver mines of sixteenth-century Tuscany, as Gabriele Marcon lays out, yet they were quickly turned into dependent wage earners. Extreme dependence is likewise the context of Müge Özbek's chapter on early twentieth-century Istanbul. Forced to hand over her wages to her father and highly controlled in the urban space, a female domestic worker was, against all odds, capable of taking legal actions against her exploitation, Özbek shows. Mohammad Tareq Hasan explores a different kind of resistance, focusing on small acts of sabotage as well as organised collective action in the garment factories of current-day Bangladesh. For each of these four chapters, Dariia Kuzmych created a watercolour illustration with striking contrasts and alternations of hard and fluid stroke lines. The last chapter of this section, by Eva Kuhn, discusses how workers themselves employ the medium of film to document and capture their own coercive working conditions. Slipping into an active role as narrators and directors, they turn the viewers into witnesses of their activism along the Mexican and US border.

This section shows that while fighting for higher or due wages, workers also strove for better working conditions, including social security and decision-making powers in the production process. Resistance, importantly, emerges here not as a way out but as an attempt to improve an existing situation. In the Foucauldian 'battlefield of a microphysics of powers'[44] at the labour site, workers and employers switched the roles of actors and reactors. While doing so, their practices and behaviours were constantly linked to the realm outside of work – and often enough, coercion was too. To the extent that workers were individually and collectively part of a society, the quality and quantity of remuneration for work became tied to social status and opportunities for social mobility, especially in the case of labour migration.

'Manipulating labour relations', as the third part, addresses employers' strategies to ensure the efficiency of the workforce. While some of these studies reveal an entanglement of labour with debt, migration and the threat of punishment that employers used to their advantage, others expose contractual wage labour arrangements as promoters of ideologies and power inequalities. The first three chapters partner with a series of illustrations by Monika Lang, who employs digital drawing techniques with bold colours. Marjorie Carvalho de Souza centres the debts of European immigrants and formerly enslaved workers in nineteenth-century Rio de Janeiro as an entry point into exploitative labour contracts. Mechanisms of indebtment to recruit and control workers are also part of Nico Pizzolato's chapter on Black Americans and, some decades later, Mexican migrant workers in the US cotton economy. He combines a historical narrative with his subjective perspectives as a researcher. By focusing on ethnic minorities and foreigners, both contributions clearly show that debt – and its redemption – was more than an economic tool and had far-reaching social implications.

The Bulgarian students in Ivanka Petrova's chapter also found themselves indebted, namely morally to a state that provided them with education and spared them physical work. Exploring working norms, duties and the relevance of wages in an ideologically loaded socialist context, Petrova shows how the perception of coercion was fundamentally shaped by the existing alternatives. Paolo Magagnoli concludes this section with a study of the wage negotiations of South Sea Islanders in Australia. Analysing late nineteenth-century photographic portraits alongside twenty-first-century exhibition practices, Magagnoli emphasises how social discourses and presentations of civilisation and race informed labour relations and continue to shape perceptions of work and workers.

By exploring a wide spectrum of labour regimes, this book demonstrates that wage labour and coerced labour did not contradict each other either in theory or in practice. Rather, they were frequent historical phenomena, occurring side by side. Even more, the chapters stress that remuneration did not protect workers from coercion. Rather, remuneration mirrors the distribution of power in labour relations, can emotionally and physically separate the employer from the employee, and can disguise exploitation and coercion. Thereby, coercion and wages often appear as mutually constitutive.

***

Looking at the manifold ways in which coercion is produced raises the question of whether production is really the main concern of those who run the economy. This book shows that wages are not only the basis for remunerating workers for their work but are, historically, an effective instrument for controlling the workforce in contexts of social and economic asymmetry. This ties in with the bold claim of economic historian Jeffrey Sklansky that the struggle over the means of payment, rather than over the means of production, might be the real class conflict.[45] While we do not intend to make this thesis a new master narrative, the research undertaken in the case studies supports the historical and contemporary potential for conflict around wages. Absent wages, withheld wages, promised wages, forfeited wages and indebting wages are practices that can exert legal, physical and social coercion on workers across time and space.

Emphasising the human experience of coercion, this book situates labour history within a larger spectrum of interdisciplinary works. It brings scholars and illustrators together in the attempt to increase our understanding of remunerated work. *Coercion and Wage Labour* thereby makes history more accessible for audiences with a variety of backgrounds, serves as an innovative and creative tool for teaching and raises awareness of the fact that narrating history is always contingent on the medium chosen and its inherent constraints and possibilities.

Notes

1. On the trajectory of labour history, see Zemon Davis, 'Decentering History', 2011; Alexander, 'On the Road to Global Labour History – via Comparison'; De Vito, 'Labour Flexibility and Labour Precariousness'.
2. Eckert, 'Why all the Fuss about Global Labour History?', 3.
3. See Piketty, *Capital and Ideology*; Fraser, 'Behind Marx's Hidden Abode', 2014; Beckert, *Empire of Cotton*; Kocka and van der Linden, *Capitalism*; Magubane, *Making of a Racist State*; Rama et al., *Addressing Inequality in South Asia*; Milanovic, *Measuring International and Global Inequality*.
4. Welskopp, 'Kapitalismus und Konzepte von Arbeit', 2017, 199. See, for example, the debate between the sociologist Gerhard Hauck and the political scientist and economist Heide Gerstenberger, in Hauck, 'Zwangsarbeit, Lohnarbeit, Kapitalismus', 2019, esp. 473. Theories and definitions of capitalism are numerous; see, for example, Kocka, 'Introduction', 2–5; Fraser, 'Behind Marx's Hidden Abode', 2014, esp. 57–8.
5. Hauck, 'Zwangsarbeit, Lohnarbeit, Kapitalismus', 2019, 487; Fudge, '(Re)Conceptualising Unfree Labour', 2019, 111; van der Linden, 'Introduction', 6; van der Linden, 'Why "Free" Wage Labor?', 39; Beckert, 'Revisiting Europe and Slavery', 2021, 173; Banaji, 'Historical Arguments for a "Logic of Deployment" in "Precapitalist Agriculture"', 110.
6. Martin, 'Cost of Living: "Costs going up but finances stagnant"'; OECD Report on 'Average Annual Hours Actually Worked per Worker'; Aljazeera, 'South Africa's Transnet, Unions in Wage Deadlock as Strike Looms'.
7. For example, BBC Yorkshire, 'Seven Held in Modern Slavery Investigation in Sheffield'; *Guardian*, 'Brazilian Woman Forced into Domestic Slavery and Marriage Freed after 40 Years'; Aljazeera, 'Seafood Slaves'; Bales, *Blood and Earth*; Bales, *Disposable People*.
8. See Bales, *Understanding Global Slavery*. For a discussion of continuities and divergences of 'traditional slavery' and 'modern slavery' from a business perspective, see Crane et al., 'Confronting the Business Models of Modern Slavery', 2022.
9. Kocka, 'Introduction', 4. See also Beckert, 'Revisiting Europe and Slavery', 2021; Beckert, *Empire of Cotton*; Fudge, '(Re)Conceptualising Unfree Labour', 2019, 108; LeBaron, Pliley and Blight (eds), *Fighting Modern Slavery and Human Trafficking*.
10. De Vito et al., 'From Bondage to Precariousness?', 2020, 644.
11. De Vito and Lichtenstein, 'Writing a Global History of Convict Labour', 49. For a similar approach, see Banaji, 'Historical Arguments for a "Logic of Deployment" in "Precapitalist Agriculture"', 106–7; Müller, 'Introduction', 2019, 865.
12. See, for example, Engerman, 'Coerced and Free Labour', 1992.
13. van der Linden, 'Why "Free" Wage Labor?', 40.
14. See, for example, Keynes, *General Theory of Employment, Interest, and Money*.
15. The slogan by DM reads 'Here I am human, here I do my shopping' ('Hier bin ich Mensch, hier kauf' ich ein').
16. See, for example, Horvat et al., *Self-Governing Socialism*.
17. van der Linden, 'Dissecting Coerced Labor', 297.
18. See van der Linden, *Workers of the World*, 40–8. On a global scale, scholars have shown that wage labour was the exception rather than the norm, and that self-subsistence, the putting-out system and various forms of dependency were much more common. For Finley Moses' conceptualisation of wage labour as the 'peculiar institution', see Finley, 'A Peculiar Institution?', 1976, 819–21. See also Eckert, 'Von der 'freien Lohnarbeit', 2017, 298, 304; Eckert, 'Why all the Fuss about Global Labour History?', 4; Welskopp, 'Kapitalismus und Konzepte von Arbeit', 2017, 197. Moreover, recent research has stressed the constitutive link between wage labour and reproductive labour, as '[w]age labour could not exist in the absence of housework, child-raising … and a host of other activities which help to produce new generations of workers and replenish existing ones'; Fraser, 'Behind Marx's Hidden Abode', 2014, 61. For a historiographical overview on the link between feminist studies and labour history, see Grama and Zimmermann, 'The Art of Link-Making in Global Labour History', 2018. Note that also in the family economy it was possible that all members – women, men and children – worked for wages simultaneously. For a critique of the application of 'the male breadwinner model with husband/father as the sole source of earnings' for the early modern period, see Horrell et al., 'Beyond the Male Breadwinner', 2022, esp. 531, 554.

19 For example, Hauck, 'Zwangsarbeit, Lohnarbeit, Kapitalismus', 2019; Bonazza and Ongaro, *Libertà e Coercizione*.
20 De Vito et al., 'From Bondage to Precariousness?', 2020, 645.
21 ILO, *Cost of Coercion*; Walk Free Foundation, International Labour Organization, International Organization for Migration, 'Global Estimates of Modern Slavery, Forced Labour and Forced Marriage', 2022.
22 For a study on terms, composition and value of wages in the Middle Ages, see Beck et al., *Rémunérer le travail au Moyen Âge*.
23 On negotiations in master–servant relations in premodern times, see Sarti, 'Can Historians Speak?', 353.
24 Müller, *Escape to the City*, 39.
25 Banaji, 'The Fictions of Free Labour', 2003.
26 Beckert, *Empire of Cotton*, 179–82.
27 Beckert, *Empire of Cotton*, 182.
28 Martin, *Divided Mastery*; van der Linden, 'Why "Free" Wage Labor?', 43.
29 See the Afterword by Batista. To consult the webpages of the illustrators, see https://dariiakuzmych.com/; https://monikalang.com/; https://www.behance.net/TimRobinsonCollage.
30 Youngs, 'Understanding History through the Visual Images in Historical Fiction', 2012; Krämer, 'Über die Rationalisierung der Visualität', 50.
31 Allowing and even enabling a variety of relationships with the past is the core of public history, and art has been part and parcel of public history for a long time. For the emergence and development of public history and historical culture in Germany and the United States, see Zumhof, 'Historical Culture, Public History, and Education'.
32 Bush and Paul, 'Introduction: Art and Public History', 2.
33 Middell, 'Weltgeschichte erzählen', 101.
34 In narratology, there are two levels: the *histoire*, which consists of the happenings, and the *discours*, which concentrates on the way the happenings are presented; see Rajewsky, 'Von Erzählern', 2007, 35.
35 Munslow, 'Narrative Works in History', 2016, 123; Bunnenberg, 'Bewegte Bilder', 2020, 9; Lingelbach, *Narrative und Darstellungsweisen der Globalgeschichte*. For some insights into the debate about 'fiction' and 'factuality', see, for example, Fludernik and Ryan, 'Factual Narrative', 12. For the 'classical' reference works in this context, see White, *Metahistory*; Ricoeur, *Temps et récit*.
36 Peyer-Heimstätt, 'Braco Dimitrijević Looking Beyond the Canon'; Artaker and Gleim, *Atlas of Arkadia*; Hofer, 'Sonic Assemblies: Artistic Historiography, Video Sound, and Representation in the Woolworths Choir of 1979'; Hoffner. 'With and Against Contemporaries: Anna Daučiková's 33 Scenes'.
37 Ryan, 'On the Theoretical Foundation of Transmedial Narratology', 20. On conventions and stylistic trends in the historiography of the present, see, for example, Fulda, 'Historiographic Narration', 230; Lingelbach, *Narrative und Darstellungsweisen der Globalgeschichte*; Jaeger, 'Factuality in Historiography', 341.
38 Rajewsky, 'Von Erzählern', 2007, 35; Rajewsky, 'Percorsi transmediali', 2018; Munslow, 'Narrative Works in History', 2016, 121.
39 Bunnenberg et al., 'SocialMediaHistory', 2021, 273. See also Munslow, 'Narrative Works in History', 2016, 110–11.
40 On 'multimodality', see Stöckl, 'Sprache-Bild-Texte lesen', 50. For a similar approach to the analytical potentials of 'visual sources', see Griesse et al., 'Introduction', 6. For a definition of media combination, see Rajewsky, 'Intermedialität', 15.
41 Munslow, 'Narrative Works in History', 2016, 110; Weible, 'Defining Public History'.
42 See LeBaron, 'Unfree Labour Beyond Boundaries', 2015, 14.
43 See Lucassen, *Story of Work*, 302–3.
44 Sarti, 'Can Historians Speak?', 353.
45 Sklansky, 'Labor, Money, and the Financial Turn', 2014.

Bibliography

Alexander, Peter. 'On the Road to Global Labour History – via Comparison'. In *On the Road to Global Labour History: A Festschrift for Marcel van der Linden*, edited by Karl Heinz Roth, 187–202. Leiden/Boston: Brill, 2018.

Aljazeera. 'Seafood Slaves'. Accessed 7 October 2022. https://www.aljazeera.com/program/fault-lines/2016/3/9/seafood-slaves.

Aljazeera. 'South Africa's Transnet, Unions in Wage Deadlock as Strike Looms'. Accessed 7 October 2022. https://www.aljazeera.com/news/2022/8/26/s-africas-transnet-unions-in-wage-deadlock-as-strike-looms.

Artaker, Anna and Gleim, Meike S. *Atlas of Arkadia*. Wien: Walther König, 2021.

Bales, Kevin. *Understanding Global Slavery: A Reader*. Berkeley/Los Angeles/London: University of California Press, 2005.

Bales, Kevin. *Disposable People: New Slavery in the Global Economy*. Berkeley, CA: University of California Press, 2012.

Bales, Kevin. *Blood and Earth: Modern Slavery, Ecocide, and the Secret to Saving the World*. New York: Spiegel & Grau (Random House), 2016.

Banaji, Jairus. 'The Fictions of Free Labour: Contract, Coercion, and the so-called Unfree Labour', *Historical Materialism* 11/3 (2003): 69–95.

Banaji, Jairus. *Theory as History: Essays on Modes of Production and Exploitation*. Leiden/Boston: Brill, 2010 (esp. 'Modes of Production in a Materialist Conception of History', 45–101, 'Historical Arguments for a "Logic of Deployment" in "Precapitalist" Agriculture', 103–16, and 'The Fictions of Free Labour', 131–54).

BBC Yorkshire. 'Seven Held in Modern Slavery Investigation in Sheffield'. Accessed 7 October 2022. https://www.bbc.com/news/uk-england-south-yorkshire-62151747.

Beck, Patrice, Bernardi, Philippe and Feller, Laurent (eds). *Rémunérer le travail au Moyen Âge. Pour une histoire sociale du salariat*. Paris: Picard, 2014.

Beckert, Sven. *Empire of Cotton: A New History of Global Capitalism*. London: Penguin Books, 2015.

Beckert, Sven. 'Revisiting Europe and Slavery', *Slavery & Abolition* 42/1 (2021): 165–78.

Bonazza, Giulia and Ongaro, Giulio (eds). *Libertà e coercizione. Il lavoro in una prospettiva di lungo periodo*. Palermo: NDF Editore, 2018.

Bunnenberg, Christian. 'Bewegte Bilder, bewegende Bilder, Bewegung in Bildern – Gedanken zur Einführung in den Themenschwerpunkt', *Zeitschrift für Geschichtsdidaktik* 19/1 (2020): 4–14.

Bunnenberg, Christian, Logge, Thorsten and Steffen Nils. 'SocialMediaHistory. Geschichtemachen in Sozialen Medien', *Historische Anthropologie* 29/2 (2021): 267–83.

Bush, Rebecca and Paul, Tawny K. 'Introduction. Art and Public History: Opportunities, Challenges, and Approaches'. In *Art and Public History: Opportunities, Challenges, and Approaches*, edited by Rebecca Bush and K. Tawny Paul, 1–19. Lanham/London: Rowman & Littlefield, 2017.

Crane, Andrew, LeBaron, Genevieve, Phung, Kam, Behbahani, Laya and Allain, Jean, 'Confronting the Business Models of Modern Slavery', *Journal of Management Inquiry* 31/3 (2022): 264–85.

De Vito, Christian G. 'Labour Flexibility and Labour Precariousness as Conceptual Tools for the Historical Study of the Interactions among Labour Relations'. In *On the Road to Global Labour History: A Festschrift for Marcel van der Linden*, edited by Karl Heinz Roth, 219–40. Leiden/Boston: Brill, 2018.

De Vito, Christian G. and Lichtenstein, Alex. 'Writing a Global History of Convict Labour'. In *Global Histories of Work*, edited by Andreas Eckert, 49–89. Berlin/Boston: De Gruyter, 2016.

De Vito, Christian G., Schiel, Juliane and van Rossum, Matthias. 'From Bondage to Precariousness? New Perspectives on Labor and Social History', *Journal of Social History* 54/2 (2020): 644–62.

Eckert, Andreas. 'Why all the Fuss about Global Labour History?'. In *Global Histories of Work*, edited by Andreas Eckert, 3–22. Berlin/Boston: De Gruyter, 2016.

Eckert, Andreas. 'Von der ‚freien Lohnarbeit' zum ‚informellen Sektor'? Alte und neue Fragen in der Geschichte der Arbeit', *Geschichte und Gesellschaft* 43 (2017): 297–307.

Engerman, Stanley L. 'Coerced and Free Labor: Property Rights and the Development of the Labor Force', *Explorations in Economic History* 29 (1992): 1–29.

Finley, Moses I. 'A Peculiar Institution?', *Times Literary Supplement* 3877 (1976): 819–21.

Fludernik, Monika and Ryan, Marie-Laure. 'Factual Narrative: An Introduction'. In *Narrative Factuality: A Handbook*, edited by Monika Fludernik and Marie-Laure Ryan, 1–26. Berlin/Boston: De Gruyter, 2020.

Fraser, Nancy. 'Behind Marx's Hidden Abode: For an Expanded Conception of Capitalism', *New Left Review* 86 (2014): 55–72.

Fudge, Judy. '(Re)Conceptualising Unfree Labour: Local Labour Control Regimes and Constraints on Workers' Freedoms', *Global Labour Journal* 10/2 (2019): 108–22.

Fulda, Daniel. 'Historiographic Narration'. In *Handbook of Narratology*, Volume 1, Second Edition, edited by Peter Hühn, Jan Christoph Meister, John Pier and Wolf Schmid, 227–40. Berlin/Boston: De Gruyter, 2014.

Grama, Adrian and Zimmermann, Susan. 'The Art of Link-Making in Global Labour History: Subaltern, Feminist and Eastern European Contributions', *European Review of History: Revue européenne d'histoire* 25/1 (2018): 1–20.

Griesse, Malte, Barget, Monika and de Boer, David. 'Introduction: Revolts and Political Violence in Early Modern Imagery'. In *Revolts and Political Violence in Early Modern Imagery*, edited by Malte Griesse, Monika Barget and David de Boer, 1–17. Leiden/Boston: Brill, 2022.

Guardian. 'Brazilian Woman Forced into Domestic Slavery and Marriage Freed after 40 Years'. Accessed 7 October 2022. https://www.theguardian.com/world/2020/dec/21/brazilian-woman-forced-into-domestic-slavery-and-marriage-freed-after-40-years.

Hauck, Gerhard. 'Zwangsarbeit, Lohnarbeit, Kapitalismus. Eine Auseinandersetzung mit Heide Gerstenberger', *Peripherie* 156/39 (2019): 472–89.

Hofer, Kristina Pia. 'Sonic Assemblies: Artistic Historiography, Video Sound, and Representation in the Woolworths Choir of 1979'. In *Notions of Temporalities in Artistic Practice*, edited by Anamarija Batista, 153–69. Berlin: De Gruyter 2022.

Hoffner, Ana. 'With and Against Contemporaries: Anna Daučiková's 33 Scenes'. In *Notions of Temporalities in Artistic Practice*, edited by Anamarija Batista, 67–80. Berlin: De Gruyter, 2022.

Horrell, Sara, Humphries, Jane and Weisdorf, Jacob. 'Beyond the Male Breadwinner: Life-Cycle Living Standards of Intact and Disrupted English Working Families, 1260–1850', *The Economic History Review* 75 (2022): 530–60.

Horvat, Branko, Marković, Mihailo and Supek, Rudi. *Self-Governing Socialism: Historical Development, Social and Political Philosophy*. New York: International Arts and Sciences Press, 1975.

International Labour Organization. *The Cost of Coercion: Global Report under the follow-up to the ILO Declaration on Fundamental Principles and Rights at Work*. Genf: International Labour Office, 2009.

Jaeger, Stephan. 'Factuality in Historiography/Historical Study'. In *Narrative Factuality: A Handbook*, edited by Monika Fludernik and Marie-Laure Ryan, 335–49. Berlin/Boston: De Gruyter, 2020.

Keynes, John Maynard. *The General Theory of Employment, Interest, and Money*. London: Palgrave Macmillan, 2018.

Kocka, Jürgen and van der Linden, Marcel (eds). *Capitalism: The Reemergence of a Historical Concept*. London/New York: Bloomsbury Academic, 2016.

Krämer, Sybille. 'Über die Rationalisierung der Visualität und die Visualisierung der Ratio. Zentralperspektive und Kalkül als Kulturtechniken des „geistigen Auges"'. In *Bühnen des Wissens. Interferenzen zwischen Wissenschaft und Kunst*, edited by Helmar Schramm, 50–67. Berlin: Dahlem University Press, 2003.

LeBaron, Genevieve. 'Unfree Labour Beyond Boundaries: Insecurity, Social Hierarchy and Labour Market Restructuring', *International Feminist Journal of Politics* 17/1 (2015): 1–19.

LeBaron, Genevieve, Pliley, Jessica R. and Blight, David W. (eds). *Fighting Modern Slavery and Human Trafficking: History and Contemporary Policy*. Cambridge: Cambridge University Press, 2021.

Lingelbach, Gabriele (ed.). *Narrative und Darstellungsweisen der Globalgeschichte*. Berlin/Boston: De Gruyter, 2022.

Lucassen, Jan. *The Story of Work: A New History of Humankind*. New Haven/London: Yale University Press, 2021.

Magubane, Bernard. *The Making of a Racist State: British Imperialism and the Union of South Africa, 1875–1910*. Trenton, NJ: Africa World Press, 1996.

Martin, Jonathan D. *Divided Mastery: Slave Hiring in the American South*. Cambridge, MA/London: Harvard University Press, 2004.

Martin, Paul. 'Cost of Living: "Costs going up but finances stagnant"'. Accessed 7 October 2022. https://www.bbc.com/news/uk-wales-60215495.

Middell, Matthias. 'Weltgeschichte erzählen. Das Beispiel der "Cambridge World History"'. In *Narrative und Darstellungsweisen der Globalgeschichte*, edited by Gabriele Lingelbach, 101–25. Berlin/Boston: De Gruyter, 2022.

Milanovic, Branko. *Worlds Apart: Measuring International and Global Inequality*. Princeton: Princeton University Press, 2005.

Müller, Viola Franziska. 'Introduction: Labour Coercion, Labor Control, and Workers' Agency', *Labor History* 60/6 (2019): 865–68.

Müller, Viola Franziska. *Escape to the City: Fugitive Slaves in the Antebellum Urban South*. Chapel Hill: University of North Carolina Press, 2022.

Munslow, Alun. 'Narrative Works in History', *Narrative Works: Issues, Investigations & Interventions* 6/1 (2016): 108–25.

Organisation for Economic Co-operation and Development. 'Average Annual Hours Actually Worked per Worker'. Accessed 07 October 2022. https://stats.oecd.org/index.aspx?DataSetCode=ANHRS.

Peyrer-Heimstätt, Flora. 'Braco Dimitrijević Looking Beyond the Canon'. In *The Common Which No Longer Exists*, edited by Anamarija Batista and Majda Turkić, 124–35. Vienna: Künstlerhaus, 2012.

Piketty, Thomas. *Capital and Ideology*. Translated by Arthur Goldhammer. Cambridge, MA: Harvard University Press, 2020.

Rajewsky, Irina O. 'Intermedialität – eine Begriffsbestimmung'. In *Intermedialität im Deutschunterricht*, edited by Marion Bönnighausen and Heidi Rösch, 8–30. Baltmannsweiler: Schneider Verlag, 2004.

Rajewsky, Irina O. 'Von Erzählern, die (nichts) vermitteln. Überlegungen zu grundlegenden Annahmen der Dramen-Theorie im Kontext einer transmedialen Narratologie', *Zeitschrift für französische Sprache und Literatur* 117/1 (2007): 25–68.

Rajewsky, Irina O. 'Percorsi transmediali. Appunti sul potenziale euristico della transmedialità nel campo delle letterature comparate', *Between* Vol. VIII/16 (2018): 1–30.

Rama, Martín, Béteille, Tara, Li, Yue, Mitra, Pradeep K. and Newman, John Lincon. *Addressing Inequality in South Asia*. Washington: World Bank Group, 2015.

Ricoeur, Paul. *Temps et récit*. Vols. 1–3. Paris: Seuil, 1983–1985.

Ryan, Marie-Laure. 'On the Theoretical Foundation of Transmedial Narratology'. In *Narratology beyond Literary Criticism: Mediality, Disciplinarity*, edited by Jan Christoph Meister, 1–24. Berlin: De Gruyter, 2005.

Sarti, Raffaella. 'Can Historians Speak? A Few Thoughts and Proposals on a Possible Global History of Domestic Service/Work'. In *Servants' Pasts: Sixteenth to Eighteenth Century, South Asia*, edited by Nitin Sinha, Nitin Varma and Pankaj Jha, 345–70. New Delhi: Orient BlackSwan, 2019.

Sklansky, Jeffrey. 'Labor, Money, and the Financial Turn in the History of Capitalism', *Labor: Studies in Working-Class History of the Americas* 11/1 (2014): 23–46.

Steinfeld, Robert J. and Engerman, Stanley L. 'Labour – Free and Coerced? A Historical Reassessment of Differences and Similarities'. In *Free and Unfree Labour: The Debate Continues*, edited by T. Brass and M. van der Linden, 107–26. Berlin: Lang, 1997.

Stöckl, Hartmut. 'Sprache-Bild-Texte lessen. Bausteine zur Methodik einer Grundkompetenz'. In *Bildlinguistik. Theorien, Methoden, Fallbeispiele*, edited by Hajo Diekmannshenke, Michael Klemm and Hartmut Stöckl, 45–70. Berlin: Erich Schmidt Verlag, 2010.

van der Linden, Marcel. *Workers of the World: Essays towards a Global Labour History*. Leiden: Brill, 2008 (esp. 'Introduction', 1–14, and 'Why "Free" Wage Labor?', 39–61).

van der Linden, Marcel. 'Dissecting Coerced Labour'. In *On Coerced Labor: Work and Compulsion after Chattel Slavery*, edited by Marcel van der Linden and Magaly Rodríguez García, 293–322. Leiden: Brill, 2016.

van der Linden, Marcel. 'The Promise and Challenges of Global Labor History'. In *Global Histories of Work*, edited by Andreas Eckert, 25–48. Berlin/Boston: De Gruyter, 2016.

Weible, Robert. 'Defining Public History: Is it Possible? Is it Necessary?', *Perspectives on History*, 1 March 2008. Accessed 28 June 2022. https://www.historians.org/publications-and-directories/perspectives-on-history/march-2008/defining-public-history-is-it-possible-is-it-necessary.

Welskopp, Thomas. 'Kapitalismus und Konzepte von Arbeit. Wie systemisch zentral ist „freie Lohnarbeit" für den Kapitalismus?', *Geschichte und Gesellschaft* 43 (2017): 197–216.

White, Hayden. *Metahistory: The Historical Imagination in Nineteenth Century Europe*. Baltimore: Johns Hopkins University Press, 1973.

Youngs, Suzette. 'Understanding History through the Visual Images in Historical Fiction', *Language Arts* 89/6 (2012): 379–95.

Zemon Davis, Natalie. 'Decentering History: Local Stories and Cultural Crossings in a Global World', *History and Theory* 50/2 (2011): 188–202.

Zumhof, Tim. 'Historical Culture, Public History, and Education in Germany and the United States of America: A Comparative Introduction to Basic Concepts and Field of Research'. In *Show, Don't Tell: Education and Historical Representation on Stage and Screen in Germany and the USA*, edited by Tim Zumhof and Nicholas K. Johnson, 15–30. Bad Heilbrunn: Julius Klinkhardt, 2020.

Part I
Binding the workforce

Collages © Tim Robinson, 2021

IN THE NAME OF ORDER 23

2
In the name of order: (im)mobilising wage labour for the Ottoman naval industry in the nineteenth century

Akın Sefer

In the long nineteenth century, the Ottoman state launched reforms to (re)install order (*nizam*) under the banners of the Nizam-ı Cedid (New Order) and the Tanzimat (Reordering/Reorganisation).[1] One of the main goals of these reforms was to form a competitive army and navy in the face of the increasing military gap between European powers and the Ottoman Empire. As industrialisation accelerated the transformation of European navies, particularly with the growing use of steam and iron in shipbuilding, the continuous reorganisation of the Ottoman navy to catch up with these transformations became critical. In addition to successive wars and naval threats faced by the Ottomans in this period, the traumatic naval disasters wielded by the Russians, first in 1770 and then in 1827, placed naval modernisation at the centre of the Ottoman reform efforts.[2] These naval reforms had to be implemented in a context marked by internal rebellions and revolutions, ongoing military/naval competition and confrontations, deepening integration with global capitalism, and an increasingly radical bureaucratic and military reform programme, as well as dramatic technological transformations in global shipbuilding catalysed by industrialisation.

It was in this period that irregular forms of labour relations, which concerned occasionally and flexibly employed workers, became increasingly inconsistent with the idea of *nizam* in the eyes of bureaucratic-military authorities, who followed European armies and navies in reorganising labour in military production and the field of war.[3] Beginning with the late eighteenth century, in parallel with the efforts to create a modern and disciplined corps in the army utilising conscripts, irregular workers became targets of reform in military worksites due to the association of being irregular with being unskilled (that is, without sufficient artisanal knowledge and experience in the respective crafts), unproductive and unruly. The political debates and proposals on military reform revolved around the conception of orderliness, highlighting discipline and drilling as the basis of efficiency in warfare.[4]

In what follows, I will discuss how Ottoman policies towards production and labour in the state-run military-industrial establishments essentially reflected the ideological association between order and efficiency throughout the reform era. A core target that emanated from this mentality, I will argue, was creating regimes of labour immobility at the worksite. Ottoman administrators used remuneration as an instrument to establish and secure these regimes for maintaining a stable workforce in the long nineteenth century. The mobilisation of labour for naval production was characterised by Ottoman efforts to bind individuals, and at times communities, to specific worksites and by struggles between the state and its subjects over the mobility of labour. I will demonstrate such characteristics by examining how the Ottoman officials employed wage payment as a discursive and practical tool to justify coercion in the recruitment process and how they tried to maintain the coercive relations of production through special efforts to restrict workers' mobility.

I will discuss this crucial dimension of the transforming relationship between the Ottoman state and the working classes by focusing on two worksites that served the Ottoman navy and the illustrations that represented them.[5] The Imperial Arsenal (Tersane-i Amire) in Istanbul, the central shipyard of the Ottoman state from the sixteenth century, was perhaps the most important among state-run industrial establishments, becoming a bedrock (and a showcase) of Ottoman industrial transformation in the nineteenth century. Located right across from it on the Golden Horn was another worksite, which manufactured yarn and ropes primarily for naval vessels. The Imperial Yarn Factory (İplikhane/Riştehane-i Amire), established in 1827, was a worksite characterised by diverse labour relations, similar to the Imperial Arsenal. Unlike the latter, however, the specific conditions of production increasingly pushed it to rely almost exclusively on conscripts and convicts as workers before its closure in the early 1870s.

The discussion below will primarily draw on documents produced through bureaucratic correspondence and official regulations of the Ottoman state, which makes a study on labour coercion particularly challenging. Especially in the context of the Tanzimat, when forced labour became increasingly illegitimate, bureaucratic authorities made a special effort to normalise it as a 'service' to the state or underline that these workers were hired 'by their own will'. A critical perspective to such discourses, however, will keep us cautious against the hasty conclusion that these workers were recruited from a wage labour market characterised by 'free labour'. In an era riven by naval confrontations, these worksites continuously needed highly skilled and experienced workers for efficient and competitive production. Remuneration became a central issue in this context, especially to tackle widespread reluctance to work in military worksites for long periods. Highlighting remuneration, official sources might have ignored, repressed or dismissed any references to labour coercion or denied it when the issue came to the fore. However, analysing how the state drafted workers and restricted their mobility reveals the coercive dimension of workers' recruitment and employment at these worksites.

'Gedik' as a binding tool

The key concept that bureaucratic discourses most frequently employed and evoked highlighted the idea behind Ottoman military reforms and the banners associated with them: order (*nizam*). In a line of thinking that increasingly became popular among bureaucratic classes throughout the nineteenth century, the making and maintenance of discipline in the corps were to be the core of any meaningful transformation. The Ottoman troops, including the elite Janissary corps, which was the core standing unit of the army, proved far from competitive in wars, lacking skill, discipline and even the willingness to join the war efforts. In this context, Ottoman reformists saw the creation of a new military corps, consisting of regularly trained soldiers whose everyday life would largely be restricted to the barracks, as critical to making a modern (and thus competitive) army and navy.[6]

This mindset seems to have been actively employed when the Ottoman state made efforts to reorganise the military worksites, first and foremost the Imperial Arsenal. Throughout the eighteenth century, workers at this worksite consisted mainly of men employed without a contract or status by which they would be bound on a long-term basis. Many of them, including those employed in the construction of ships, worked in return for daily wages, and they were often released when their respective tasks ended. In addition, the manufacture of materials and tools necessary for ships (ranging from sailcloth to items in wood, iron or copper) was often outsourced and paid in piecework. As naval modernisation in the 1790s aimed at boosting efficiency and productivity in shipbuilding, naval bureaucrats increasingly considered the employment of such irregular workers as a significant problem in the Imperial Arsenal. They saw the prevalence of such casual relations at the workplace as incompatible with the reformist goal of giving 'order' to the production process. In their eyes, this goal required a labour force consisting of regularly employed, skilled and disciplined workers who would ideally accept working for lower wages than they would receive elsewhere.

Skilled shipbuilding workers were already present in the arsenal. The challenge now was to increase their number and secure their regular attendance and long-term employment at the worksite. This changing perspective is attested by a regulation issued through an edict of Sultan Selim III in 1794, which reorganised the main body of shipbuilding workers, carpenters (*marangoz*) and hole-borers (*burgucu*) into regular corps. It justified this policy by referring to the inefficiency of the workforce: those employed in shipbuilding were leaving their jobs to work elsewhere whenever they were offered higher wages by other employers (including facilities or constructions financed by other state institutions), and they had to be brought back by force.[7] As a result, the text argued, their numbers always remained insufficient, and they did not work willingly. In response to these concerns, the edict stated that, besides a slight increase in wages, these workers would be given regular slots in the arsenal in the form of '*gedik*', an institution that served to protect guildsmen from the competition by restricting the right to enter the trade from outside.[8] These *gedik*s would provide them with a salary, paid every three months, in return for full-time employment and job security. Although their income would still remain lower than the market average for these craftsmen, naval bureaucrats hoped that their possession of *gedik*s would discourage them from attempting to run away from their jobs.[9]

Nevertheless, it is striking that the edict justified these measures not in reference to any possible demands by workers for such recognition. Rather, it did so by highlighting how these measures would curb workers' mobility and bind them to their workplace, as those with regular slots would not be allowed to work elsewhere. In effect, the regulation acknowledged that wages for these workers were too low, and even after specific improvements in payments, the state could not compete with the market due to budget constraints. Recognising the workers as regular employees with permanent slots and salaries served as much to provide a legitimate framework to forcefully bond these workers to their worksites as to attract skilled labour to work in the arsenal. In this way,

Ottoman authorities attempted to transform *gedik*, an institution that functioned to protect craftsmen, into a tool of labour management that would reduce the latter's ability to re-commodify their labour power in the market, restricting their exit from work.

A similar regulation in the same period concerning caulkers testifies to how *gedik* was seen as a legitimate instrument to tie workers to the worksite. In an effort to increase the quality of the caulking process, which was critical for ships to operate longer without requiring frequent maintenance, the administration decided to form a regular corps by bringing caulkers from Alexandria, who were known for their distinctive skills in caulking, to replace caulkers in the capital to whom the job was outsourced. Although these caulkers were not to receive salaries, and thus would not officially have *gedik*s, the regulation underlined that they were to be considered equivalent to *gedik* holders: they were required to be present and working in the arsenal 'day and night', also referring to the special barracks built to accommodate these corps.[10]

Negotiating coercion

This, however, was far from sufficient to satisfy the need for a regular labour force in the arsenal, which did not consist only of workers employed in ship construction and repair. The demand for other craftsmen and day labourers grew consistently, parallel to the dramatic increase in naval production. Such growth owed much to technological modernisation and the construction of several new workshops and shipbuilding facilities, which gradually marginalised the role of outsourcing in the production of tools and materials.[11] Thus, along with the *gedik* arrangement in the 1790s, the state also sought to decrease its dependence on migrant workers, who had been occasionally recruited from provincial towns outside Istanbul, mostly as day labourers. It obliged the guilds in Istanbul to send an assigned number of their men as workers on a daily basis. These workers were remunerated through a combination of fixed daily wages paid by the arsenal and mandatory donations (*iane*) collected within their respective guilds.[12]

Throughout the four decades this regulation remained in action, the capital's guilds did not stop showing their discontent about the arrangement: they failed to send the required numbers assigned to them, often sent youngsters who had little skills or experience, and continuously petitioned for exemptions due to a range of excuses, from financial distress to frequent catastrophic incidents such as fires. In 1837, this type of labour obligation was finally replaced with a tax to be paid in cash, for which the state essentially blamed the guilds. A bureaucratic report highlighted how such resistance by the guilds failed the state's initial expectation for increased productivity, as the young men sent by guilds proved to have neither the skill and experience nor the motivation to work, a major reason for which was that they could not receive their donations, as obliged by the state, due to embezzlement by the guilds' elders. As a result, the administration decided to hire wage labourers in their place, financed by the tax.[13]

The abolition of the obligation to send workers, in effect, demonstrated the administration's acknowledgement that the labour arrangements of the New Order were not sufficient to address the needs of (re)building a competitive navy. Thus, the reformist naval administrations devised a new scheme in the 1830s: they started to systematically introduce military labour into the production process by organising naval conscripts (or civilian workers given military status) under the 'labour/industrial battalions' (*esnaf/sanayi taburları*). These conscripts would be trained in specific skills and kept under constant supervision and discipline at work, and were obliged to serve for long periods (initially 10 years) at a cost much lower than their civilian counterparts. Thus it was thought to be the ideal solution to create an efficient labour force. Although the subsequent administrations continued to push for this path for the rest of the century, the dream of forming an entirely militarised labour force never came true, thanks to the effective resistance of Muslim and non-Muslim subjects against military conscription.[14] As a result, naval authorities remained dependent on employing civilian workers and coercing them to work, which required the authorities to devise new techniques and discourses.

In the early nineteenth century, aside from the regular craftsmen and labourers sent by the guilds in the capital, many workers continued to be drafted from the provincial districts around Istanbul or along the Black Sea and the Mediterranean coast. From the sixteenth century, in case of labour shortage, an imperial decree was sent to the judge or the administrator of a district to round up the required number of men with certain occupational qualifications and send them to Istanbul. The Imperial Arsenal utilised this source especially in wartime, marked by persistent demand for labour, primarily for shipbuilding workers.[15] While the orders usually emphasised that workers should be selected from among skilled, young and healthy volunteers, the district officials often had to resort to coercion. As they were obliged to meet the assigned number of men, these officials sometimes did not shy away from sending whomever they could draft, regardless of skill or age, or imprisoning those who resisted the draft. As a result, desertion was neither rare nor unexpected, especially when men had to give up their agricultural tasks to sustain their families or when they were able to earn more than the meagre wages offered by the arsenal.[16]

The coercive nature of the recruitment process became more apparent and controversial, particularly after the edict of 1839, which officially launched the Tanzimat reforms that would substantially transform state–society relations for the rest of the century. In particular, the proclamation opened a discursive space for Ottoman subjects to raise their voices against the forced labour draft. In addition to the sultan's commitment to the guarantees for the protection of life, honour and property as well as for the equality of both Muslim and non-Muslim subjects, the edict also promised that taxes would be reassessed and collected in cash, and no further exaction would be requested from the subjects.[17] These promises corroborated an earlier edict that intended to abolish the practice of *angarya* (corvée) in the Balkan provinces, which had recently led to social unrest due to the serfdom-like conditions of non-Muslim peasants, who were forced by their Muslim landlords into bondage to the soil.[18]

Following the edict's proclamation, the labour draft for the arsenal became increasingly contested by Ottoman subjects, and in a seemingly unprecedented way. The draft decrees preceding the 1839 edict refrained from naming the practice as *angarya*, a term often used in reference to compulsory and unpaid work either in the fields owned by other landowners or for local public enterprises, including road construction and repair.[19] Ottoman bureaucrats were aware of the widespread resentment against this practice: in the sixteenth century, for example, the state had actively used this knowledge as it often decreed against *angarya* in the newly conquered areas to consolidate its legitimacy among local populations.[20] Such institutional memory might have had a role in the official reluctance to call the draft *angarya*, which otherwise could have injured the already challenging efforts to mobilise labourers.[21] Another reason might have been the officials' hope, expectation or implicit assumption that there would be no need to forcefully recruit workers due to the payment of wages (even if lower than the market level): similar to the decrees for the mobilisation of soldiers, some orders for labour draft were explicit enough regarding the centre's preference for workers' consent, which would save the central authorities from dealing with potential runaways.[22]

Moreover, state elites were tempted to assume that, even when workers were not paid wages, other forms of remuneration (for instance, tax exemptions or monthly allowances paid to a worker's family during his employment) justified the extraction of their labour on a consensual basis. This assumption led the authorities to expect such consent to continue when tax exemptions were abolished and replaced with wage payments during the Tanzimat era. In 1840, the tax collector (*muhassıl*) of a village on the Aegean island of Chios, which used to send 18 sawyers and replace them every six months, asked the centre to abolish this obligation since the villagers would 'obviously' not want to pay their taxes as long as the obligation to send workers continued. The government, however, rejected this request as the arsenal still needed their labour, underlining that the workers would be paid their due wages from now on.[23]

The emphasis on paid labour in the state's response heralded the future approach of the Tanzimat administrations regarding the disagreements between the state and its subjects over how *angarya* should be defined and understood. These disagreements suggest that, by *angarya*, the Ottoman ruling elites primarily understood unpaid labour. They acknowledged that it was a form of forced labour only because work was not compensated monetarily as wages. Thus, when the imperial edicts referred to the abolition of *angarya* at the beginning of the Tanzimat era, the imperial bureaucracy interpreted this as the abolition of the practice of unpaid employment. However, the confrontations over the draft of provincial workers for the arsenal during this period demonstrate that *angarya* was not defined merely as unpaid employment but also by coercion in the popular mind. In other words, at least for some Ottoman subjects, it seems that *angarya* referred to any involuntary service even when the service was financially compensated, regardless of whether those serving worked for the central state, landlords or other local powerholders.

The mobilisation process of workers with wages after the Tanzimat highlights the state's struggle to impose its own definition on the popular mind by claiming a contradiction between remuneration and coercion. In 1848, the government again sent orders to mobilise workers for shipbuilding to coastal areas, including the province of Trabzon, an important source of shipbuilding labour on the Black Sea coast.[24] Writing back to the capital to get its approval for the local administration's coercive measures in drafting these workers, the province's governor admitted that using physical force was unjust and that many people were running away to escape the draft. Yet, the Grand Admiral, referring the case to the High Council (*Meclis-i Vâlâ*), argued that the subjects were 'not justified' in refusing to work in the arsenal since the latter would pay them for their labour. In its ruling, the High Council accepted this rationale and argued that it was likely that their desertion was 'due to the fear of *angarya*, which was practised in some affairs before the Tanzimat'.[25] Thus, it urged the local administrators to encourage and persuade the subjects by explaining to them clearly that they would not be used as *angarya* but be paid and employed only for a limited period of time. However, continued the council's ruling, in case some still resisted the draft, this should be seen as a refusal 'to serve the Sublime State', and thus, after leaving out the ones with serious health problems, the required number of workers should be drafted and sent to the arsenal immediately, 'disregarding their lame excuses (*a'zar-ı vahiyesine bakılmayarak*)'.[26]

Petitions written by provincial subjects on labour recruitment throughout the Tanzimat era contained complaints about physical violence and corruption used in the draft process, about deserted towns and villages as many young men ran away, and about the increasing poverty of the families left behind as a result. For these people, the recruitment for the arsenal did not really differ from the *angarya* practice of earlier times. Official responses to such petitions, however – albeit warning administrators not to use violence but rather 'encouraging' methods in drafting these workers – likewise dismissed the petitions' complaints on the basis of wage payment.[27] According to the official line of argument, payment of service made resistance to employment unjustified and disproved the accusations that this was a form of corvée. Unlike the state elites, however, these petitions put forward an alternative definition, implying that *angarya* happened when workers were forcefully drafted, paid lower than the market rate and, in many cases, bound to a worksite and a task unfamiliar to them for long periods. Such hidden traces of alternative angles in the archives inspire us to explore new perspectives and research questions, which we will do with the help of illustrations.

Shifting the perspective from state to workers

In the first collage by Tim Robinson (p. 22), images of workers at the arsenal and outside in a coffeehouse are placed between the figures of two reformist statesmen, Mehmed Emin Âli Pasha (on the left) and Sadık Rıfat Pasha (on the right), whose gazes are highlighted. The presence of these two figures in this scene is not due to a particular role they played individually in the cases discussed above, but rather to the political class they represented: both belonged to the

Western-oriented reformist state elites of the mid-nineteenth century and served, on various appointments, in several institutions established throughout the reform era.[28] Among these institutions was the High Council they served throughout the 1840s, which played a crucial role in the reorganisation of state–subject relations in this period through its decisions, including those on the above-discussed cases over *angarya*. In the lower part of the illustration are two images referring to the two aspects of Ottoman modernisation in the context of our discussion: a scene from the modernised arsenal and an excerpt of the Tanzimat Edict of 1839.

At first sight, one may argue that the illustrative collage follows the still-dominant perspective in historiography that highlights the central role the state authorities played, through their institutions, policies and discourses, in Ottoman modernisation and the accompanying transformation of the state's relations with the working classes in this process. From this perspective, the direct impact of the top-down reforms on labour relations at these sites may even be self-evident for the present cases, which are mainly concerned with naval worksites. Such a state-centric view is also corroborated by visual evidence in the archives regarding the Imperial Arsenal. Most of the images of the arsenal were shot on behalf of more extensive efforts for Ottoman state propaganda addressing Western public opinion in the late nineteenth century, which aimed at representing the Ottoman state and society as 'modernised' in European ways. Consisting overwhelmingly of human-free images of public institutions, worksites and urban landscapes, the state-sponsored photographic albums of this period often depicted the Ottoman subjects, including workers or conscripts in the military worksites, in an orderly fashion – the way reformist statesmen wanted them to become and to be seen.[29] In short, the illustration conveys the impression that this discussion confirms the centrality of state policies and elites in nineteenth-century modernisation processes.

But this is only one side of our narrative. Perhaps we might interpret Robinson's choice to place workers' images at the centre of his collage, and in particular, his emphasis on the individual figures of workers at the arsenal in red circles, as the artist's own way of expressing the questions that this research aims to raise concerning the bigger narratives of Ottoman reform: questions about how working-class individuals experienced these transformations, in what ways they might have shaped them or what 'Ottoman modernity' meant from the perspective of the relations of production. Such questions could indeed point to possibilities of alternative narratives in which the working classes played roles at least as central as the state authorities. Seen in this way, the discussion above could offer some clues about what archival evidence offers us to pursue such interrogations for a more comprehensive understanding of Ottoman transformations in the nineteenth century.

One significant dynamic that such questions concerning archival sources may highlight is what seems to be an internal relation between Ottoman reform and labour coercion. As creating and maintaining coercive regimes at work was central to the Ottoman agendas for naval modernisation, bureaucratic discourses of the reform era tried to conceal the coercive characteristics of the labour relations by underlining wage payment, with an implicit reference to modern capitalist discourses that associate wages with freedom of labour. The struggles of working-class subjects, such as running away from work or employing discourses of reform to resist the labour draft, produced the written sources revealing how coercion characterised the modernisation attempts at these worksites.

The image of the coffeehouse at the top of the collage, where workers sit side by side with officers, deserves a particular note in this regard. Thanks to these struggles, the forced labour schemes of reformist statesmen failed to eliminate dependence on hiring workers for wages. As a result, the latter, consisting mostly of migrants from the Black Sea and Eastern Anatolia, dominated the workforce of the arsenal in the second half of the nineteenth century. In the face of this, new mechanisms had to be developed not only to discipline the labour process at the worksite (for example, by time discipline and division of labour) but also to control the everyday spaces of the working classes, due to the perceived threat of their presence, lifestyle and mobility to urban elites, especially in the capital. Coffeehouses and other public spaces where such migrant working-class subjects gathered and sometimes were accommodated became particularly important in such efforts.[30] Indeed, such spaces could be central to the formation of workers' strikes and protests in this period, which largely emanated from their inability to receive wages regularly: a problem that linked wage payment to processes of immobility.

Following commodities and materials

Let us turn to the second collage by Tim Robinson (p. 23), which largely uses themes connected to the process by which cotton was spun into yarn, used in manufacturing sailcloth for naval vessels. Unlike the first one, where Robinson chose exclusively from among the Ottoman-era images sent by the author, here he makes two exceptions by introducing two generic images of his own choice, a paddle steamer and, connected to its rigging, some cotton yarn. In the foreground, we see peasant men, women and children picking cotton. Below is an 'orderly' scene of child conscripts and their officers posing in front of the barracks of the Riştehane, the Imperial Yarn Factory. In a distinct frame, Robinson puts two images side by side: a petition written in 1847 by the Greek community in the Black Sea province of Trabzon against the draft for the Imperial Arsenal, and a scene of a ship in the making, highlighting the internal connections between modernised shipbuilding, coercion and the historical agency of Ottoman subjects.[31]

The paddle steamer in the background, a transitional type between sailing vessels and full steamers in the early nineteenth century, is likely a reference to the era in which the Riştehane was established, its operations starting in 1827. With its sails lowered down, the image is perhaps a saluting gesture at the age of steamships, implying the ironic characteristic of this investment: launched as a spinning mill with the primary aim of increasing the production of yarn for sail-making, as well as for military uniforms, the Riştehane was founded in an age when the demand for sailcloth would gradually diminish in the navy. Although the initial plan was to employ civilian wage workers, management problems and the low profitability of the initiative pushed the Ottoman authorities to increasingly resort to forced labour.[32]

In the early 1830s, the factory largely utilised non-Muslim children who were forcefully drafted from Anatolia and worked under 'perishing' conditions, according to an Ottoman edict.[33] However, as discussed earlier, it was in this period that such forced labour draft, being considered *angarya* by Ottoman subjects, became increasingly antithetical to the promises of the Tanzimat. Thus, almost simultaneously with the Imperial Arsenal, the Riştehane turned towards military labour in the early years of the Tanzimat, as the Ottoman navy began to conscript (mostly non-Muslim) workers to the 'Riştehane battalions'. In parallel with the decreasing profitability of yarn production as well as the failures in forming these battalions due to popular resistance to conscription, the factory was likely seen as more functional to serve as a prison, as by the end of the 1860s, it was exclusively used for ropemaking by convicts.[34]

Then, there is the 'yarn'. Let us look at the artist's introduction of this generic image in the collage as a token raising possible questions: did the cotton thread connect different worksites, with diverse characteristics of relations of production and coercion, to each other? Can we think of the cotton fields of Anatolia, the manufacturing worksites of Constantinople and the naval vessels sailing through Ottoman waters as different scenes of the same narrative? Or, more generally, can we see the transformation of a commodity from an agricultural to an industrial product as a process that mobilised different forms of labour, activating diverse types of coercive relations? If so, how could the characteristics of a commodity shape the formation of these relations?

Considering that scholars of global history have successfully revealed the ways in which commodities and materials connected distinct socioeconomic and political formations, such questions indeed inspire and encourage us to form new and exciting agendas for research in Ottoman history.[35] Besides cotton, we may take the artist's use of an image of wooden ship construction in the arsenal next to the petition as a plea for a focus on how coercive labour relations connected different phases of the procurement of timber. Indeed, certain districts in Ottoman Anatolia and the Balkans, particularly along coastal areas, were obliged to fell trees, process them into timber and transport them to the closest docks to be sent to the arsenal by sea. The same districts were also required to send the assigned numbers of shipwrights when requested, not only for the Imperial Arsenal but also for the provincial shipyards that produced ships for the navy. The entire process, from felling trees to constructing wooden ships, entailed a wide range of actors: a non-exhaustive list would include village communities, nomadic populations, animals, regional notables and their militias, rural and urban craftsmen, naval conscripts and officers, seafarers and judicial and administrative officials.[36] The transformation of the tree into pieces of timber ending up in wooden shipbuilding, in other words, was a process characterised by connected (and, in most cases, established) sets of labour relations and practices spanning distinct villages, towns and cities.

Restrictions on workers' mobility

One thread that might connect different worksites across diverse sectors (for example, agricultural, industrial and service sectors), weaving a significant pattern of Ottoman transformations in the long nineteenth century, concerns the immobilisation of labour. Research on Ottoman agricultural estates, the *çiftlik*s, has already highlighted how notables controlling these estates tried to maintain or reimpose restrictions to labour mobility and increase their control over the labour force in the production process, within the context of commodification and market competition.[37] Reminiscent of the *çiftlik*-holders' quest for bonded labour, the Ottoman state had to use diverse methods for binding workers to its worksites in order to curtail workers' ability to leave for better jobs during a period when maintaining a regular and productive labour force was essential to meet the increasingly competitive demands of naval production.

For this purpose, the Ottoman state utilised certain means to prevent workers from running away from its worksites, some of which it had already been familiar with from earlier periods. For workers drafted from the provinces or Istanbul, one reliable restriction method was communal obligation. When the central administration required a district or community to send a certain number of workers to the arsenal, responsibility to address this demand was levied not on individual subjects but rather on the official representatives of districts or religious communities. Such an obligation on communities secured the replacement of workers whenever one or more of them deserted from the draft, ran away during work or needed to be replaced due to problems ranging from workers' skills or health to job accidents. In most cases, these workers were drafted to work in the construction of specific vessels, and they were released when these tasks were completed. Thus, in most orders, we see a reference to the construction of a specific warship, as well as a rather general reference to 'the increasing number of tasks' in the arsenal.[38]

However, when the construction process took too long to keep an individual worker at the worksite or when labourers were needed continuously, the districts were obliged to replace workers on a regular basis. These replacement periods were most likely decided according to the district's proximity to the capital, often ranging from one to six months, with some exceptions including Armenian boys in the Yarn Factory, who were replaced after 12 years of service in the 1840s.[39] Since the obligation was levied on the entire district or sometimes on a Christian religious community (*millet*) rather than on individuals, the district or community had to complete the missing number of workers when labourers deserted or did not arrive.[40] As a result, a worker who deserted would most likely face the threat of alienation from his own community or at least from those who had to replace him and their families. Furthermore, since it was the community leaders or district officials who were held responsible for sending workers, the unwanted prospect of antagonising local or communal powerholders might also have played a role in discouraging workers from running away, thus cementing immobilisation at the worksite.

In addition to communal obligation and tracking down workers and retrieving them by force when they escaped,[41] the state also took physical measures to prevent desertion when workers arrived. Provincial workers were often accommodated in the same inn close to their worksites; the doors of these inns were locked at night, and at times tax receipts of non-Muslims (obliged to pay poll tax) were not given back until their release.[42] Such measures had to be complemented by additional ones to prevent their flight across different worksites in the city. Tax officials were required to note down on the tax receipts the worksite that the labourers were assigned to, with the intention of at least curbing the competition for skilled labourers among different worksites owned by the state, including the Imperial Arsenal and the Yarn Factory.[43]

Such measures were supplemented by more institutional methods of spatial control in the nineteenth century. A core aspect of military reform was the construction of barracks where soldiers were kept under continuous surveillance, discipline and training. Soon, Ottoman authorities used such spatial control for similar efforts to create a regular and skilled labour force in the naval worksites, with the construction of barracks for workers and conscripts inside these worksites. In the 1790s, when skilled caulkers from Alexandria, Egypt, were brought to create a regular corps, they were accommodated in barracks constructed specifically for them in the Imperial Arsenal.[44] Similarly, barracks were built throughout the century for the conscripts employed in the arsenal or the Riştehane (as seen in the second illustration). A barracks, in other words, was considered a physical tool of labour control and a prerequisite for a regular workforce, a symbol of order in production, in the age of Ottoman reform.

A very important way of restricting workers' mobility was the cancellation or withdrawal of wages for months, with payments made in instalments. The Tanzimat era reforms aimed to shift the obligation for taxes and conscription from communities to individuals.[45] In harmony with these efforts, the Naval Council decided in the 1840s to sanction individual runaways by denying them their right to claim outstanding wages for the time they had worked in the arsenal.[46] The decision demonstrates that the naval authorities saw unpaid wages as an instrument to prevent provincial draftees from running away. The official documents always justified the delays in payment through financial problems, which was not entirely wrong: budget constraints led to failures in many state industries in the mid-nineteenth century.[47] However, these delays also served to keep the labour force working more regularly. In effect, it is not a coincidence that such payment problems marked the relations between workers and the state throughout the mid-to-late nineteenth century when the arsenal desperately needed a more regular and experienced labour force. Such delays, prompting several strikes and demonstrations, particularly in the 1870s, became an important dimension of working-class formation in this period.[48]

Besides Ottoman workers, this was particularly the case with foreign (mostly British) mechanics and shipbuilders employed during the mid-century industrialisation campaign. As they initially came under short-term contracts, at the end of which they were entitled to leave, the administration delayed their payments for long periods. These delays gave the Ottoman administration the chance to keep skilled and experienced workers as long as possible in a time of massive investments in naval production throughout the 1860s and 1870s. Such long delays in payments were made when huge amounts of money were spent on mechanisation, building new factories and workshops in the arsenal, and buying new steamships and ironclads for the navy.[49] In short, capital expansion in the naval worksites owed very much to such delays, both by bonding the skilled labour necessary to run these factories and enabling the administrators to fund this expansion through the money temporarily withdrawn from local and foreign workers in the arsenal.

Conclusion

Ottoman bureaucratic documents on the Imperial Arsenal and the Imperial Yarn Factory refer, for each site, to a workforce marked by a diversity of labour relations, consisting of different groups with distinct relations to the state, ranging from salaried craftsmen and mechanics with contracts to enforced guildsmen, provincial draftees, conscripts and convicts. However, such documents often remain either silent or in denial about the coercive nature of these relations. The discussion here highlights the fact that the diversity in the profiles of the labour force at each site was in itself a product of decades-old struggles between the Ottoman state and its working-class subjects over the former's attempts to reorganise labour relations for the sake of *nizam* in the production process. Not only that, it also shows how the official emphasis on remuneration could disguise a range of coercive relations with the help of the ideological association of wage labour with freedom in the modern mind. What these struggles in the nineteenth century show, among other things, is the necessity of considering remuneration in an analytical framework where we examine different relations of labour alongside various forms of payment and coercion. In this sense, these struggles remind us that wage labour is an abstraction that consists of, and could easily be used as a cover for, complicated histories of coercive relations and processes.

This chapter explored research questions and analytical possibilities related to the history of labour in the Ottoman naval industry through a dialogue with artistic illustrations, which in turn were based on the initial draft of this chapter. Focusing in this way on the relations of production in a worksite highlights what might be a significant dynamic of Ottoman reform policies: to create an efficient labour force, these policies used wage relations as a means of bondage, both in discourse and in practice, in the context of the state's struggle to expand industrial capital and survive against military threats in the nineteenth century. Wage payment was used not only as a cover to forcefully mobilise workers to the worksite but also as a tool to immobilise workers at the worksite. Research on different worksites and from the perspective of relations of production could, thus, lead us to a wider pattern in understanding a possibly central component of 'modernity' in the nineteenth-century Ottoman Empire.

Notes

1 The Nizam-ı Cedid refers to the reform programme under the rule of Sultan Selim III (r.1789–1807), whereas the Tanzimat refers to the bureaucratic reform process officially launched with a reform edict in 1839. See Shaw, *Between Old and New*, 71–208; Quataert, 'The Age of Reforms, 1812–1914'.
2 Panzac, 'Un Prologue Aux Tanzimat', 2002.
3 In state worksites, casual or irregular workers, who were also called *muvakkat* ('temporary') in official categorisation, referred to those who were hired or drafted for specific tasks (or shipbuilding projects) in return for daily wages and/or tax exemptions. The regular workers, often called *daimi* (permanent) or *yerlu* (local), consisted mostly of skilled craftsmen who were kept employed without a definitive length of employment, often receiving salaries and/or other benefits (for example accommodation and clothing) in addition to daily wages.
4 Yaycıoğlu, *Partners of the Empire*, 41–2.
5 Two illustrations, collated by Tim Robinson from Ottoman photographs and documents dated back to the nineteenth century and based on the scenarios by Anamarija Batista and Corinna Peres, accompany this paper, an initial draft of which was presented at the Worlds of Related Coercions in Work (WORCK) annual conference in 2019, under the title of 'The Mobilization of Wage Labour for Ottoman State Factories in the 19th Century'. As I hope to demonstrate by engaging in an active dialogue with them, the illustrations will contribute to this discussion by going beyond a mere description of specific scenes regarding the cases that involve workers, worksites and state authorities. Rather, I will attempt to use the artistic creations of Robinson, perhaps at the risk of overinterpretation, as a space to discuss some of the historically important questions and connections these creations highlight, pointing also to the scope of possibilities in understanding and explaining the historical relations between the Ottoman state and the working classes in the nineteenth century. Besides Tim Robinson, I owe

special thanks to the editors, Anamarija Batista, Viola Müller and Corinna Peres, each of whom provided extensive comments and suggestions to develop the paper, and to the other authors and illustrators of this volume, for making this space possible.

6 On the modernisation of the naval corps in the late eighteenth century, see Shaw, *Between Old and New*, 150–66.
7 Vak'anüvis Halil Nuri Bey, *Nûrî Tarihi*, 375–8. The text explained desertion to other worksites by underlining that in the latter they were paid an amount five times higher than that paid by the arsenal, and sometimes more.
8 Although it had often been used for administrative and military officials earlier, the concept started to refer mostly to the rights of artisans and traders in the eighteenth century; see Akarlı, 'Gedik: A Bundle of Rights', 170. Still, serving as both occupational licenses and financial instruments, the meaning of *gedik* and what it referred to remained ambiguous at the time of its practice and in historiography. For a comprehensive analysis, see Yıldırım and Ağır, 'Gedik: What's in a Name?'.
9 Vak'anüvis Halil Nuri Bey, *Nûrî Tarihi*, 375–8.
10 Presidency State Archives of the Republic of Turkey (hereafter, BOA). BOA.C.BH.59-2754.
11 On technological transformation in the late eighteenth-century Imperial Arsenal, see Zorlu, *Innovation and Empire in Turkey*.
12 On Ottoman artisans and their guilds, see Faroqhi, *Artisans of Empire*.
13 BOA.C.BH.53/2491.
14 Sefer, 'From Class Solidarity to Revolution', 2013, 403–4.
15 For the mobilisation of such irregular workers for the Imperial Arsenal in the seventeenth century, see Bostan, *Osmanlı Bahriye Teşkilâtı*, 71–81.
16 For examples from the eighteenth century, see Aydın, *Sultanın Kalyonları*, 106–7.
17 For an English translation of the edict by Halil İnalcık, see Khater, *Sources in the History of the Modern Middle East*, 11–14.
18 Inalcık, 'Application of the Tanzimat', 1973, 105. See also Kaya, 'Were Peasants Bound to the Soil'.
19 *Angarya*, originally a Greek word, means 'compulsory service'. For seafarers on board, any extra work assigned in addition to the regular work was described by this term. Kahane and Tietze, *The Lingua Franca in the Levant*, 476.
20 Inalcık, 'Balkanlar'da Osmanlı Fetihleri'nin Sosyal Koşulları', 2011, 7; Shaw, *The Financial and Administrative Organization*, 20.
21 Indeed, it was this bureaucratic memory that prompted the Egyptian authorities in the early nineteenth century to put special efforts into encouraging the population towards conscription by highlighting in their orders that conscription had nothing in common with corvée, which was particularly ill-famed in the popular mind. See Fahmy, *All the Pasha's Men*, 98.
22 See, for example, BOA.HAT. 1243/48301B.
23 BOA.C.BH.105/5080.
24 BOA.A.MKT.MVL.9-17.
25 BOA.İ.MVL.119-2972.
26 BOA.İ.MVL.119-2972.
27 For examples, see BOA.HR.MKT.197/46; BOA.A.MKT.MHM.126/95; BOA.A.MKT.48-5.
28 For Ottoman bureaucracy and bureaucrats in the reform era, see Findley, *Ottoman Civil Officialdom*.
29 Deringil, *The Well-Protected Domains*, 151. A version of the photographic albums sponsored by the state during the reign of Abdulhamid II is preserved at the Library of Congress, accessible online. See 'Abdulhamid II Collection', Library of Congress, Prints & Photographs Division, accessed 5 October 2022. http://www.loc.gov/pictures/collection/ahii/
30 Kırlı, 'Coffeehouses'.
31 For the petition, see BOA.İ.MVL.103/2269.
32 Öztürk, 'XIX. Yüzyılda Osmanlı Imparatorluğu'nda Sanayileşme',1990.
33 Kabadayı, 'Working for the State', 35.
34 Naval Museum Archives, Istanbul (hereafter, DMA). ŞUB.51/139a.
35 Beckert, *Empire of Cotton*; Mintz, *Sweetness and Power*.
36 On the provision process of timber and other raw materials for the Ottoman navy in different periods, see Düzcü, *Yelkenliden Buharlıya Geçişte Osmanlı Denizciliği*; Aydın, *Sultanın Kalyonları*.

37 See Kaya, 'Were Peasants Bound to the Soil'.
38 For examples, see BOA.A.MKT.MHM.70/3 and A.MKT.MHM.126/95.
39 BOA.C.BH.209/9756; C.BH.3/131; A.DVN.21/90.
40 This was the case when six men, sent by a village on the island of Chios, which was normally supposed to send 18 sawyers to the arsenal every six months, deserted in 1829. BOA.C.BH.3/136.
41 Vak'anüvis Halil Nuri Bey, *Nûrî Tarihi*, 375.
42 Faroqhi, 'Labor Recruitment and Control', 24–5.
43 BOA.C.ML.15/652.
44 Beydilli and Şahin, *Mahmud Raif Efendi*, 224.
45 Rogan, *Frontiers of the State*, 13; Aytekin, 'Tax Revolts during the Tanzimat Period', 2013, 314.
46 DMA.Env.341/28.
47 Clark, 'The Ottoman Industrial Revolution', 1974, 73.
48 Sefer, 'From Class Solidarity to Revolution', 2013.
49 Sefer, 'British Workers and Ottoman Modernity', 2021.

Bibliography

Akarlı, Engin Deniz. 'Gedik: A Bundle of Rights and Obligations for Istanbul Artisans and Traders, 1750–1840'. In *Law, Anthropology, and the Constitution of the Social: Making Persons and Things*, edited by A. Pottage and M. Mundy, 166–200. Cambridge: Cambridge University Press, 2004.
Aydın, Y. Alperen. *Sultanın Kalyonları: Osmanlı Donanmasının Yelkenli Savaş Gemileri (1701–1770)*. Istanbul: Küre Yayınları, 2011.
Aytekin, E. Attila. 'Tax Revolts during the Tanzimat Period (1839–1876) and before the Young Turk Revolution (1904–1908): Popular Protest and State Formation in the Late Ottoman Empire', *Journal of Policy History* 25/3 (2013): 308–33.
Beckert, Sven. *Empire of Cotton: A Global History*. New York: Alfred A. Knopf, 2014.
Beydilli, Kemal and Şahin, İlhan. *Mahmud Raif Efendi ve Nizâm-ı Cedîd'e Dair Eseri*. Ankara: Türk Tarih Kurumu Basımevi, 2001.
Bostan, İdris. *Osmanlı Bahriye Teşkilâtı: XVII. Yüzyılda Tersâne-i Âmire*. Ankara: Türk Tarih Kurumu Basımevi, 1992.
Clark, Edward C. 'The Ottoman Industrial Revolution', *International Journal of Middle East Studies* 5/1 (1974): 65–76.
Düzcü, Levent. *Yelkenliden Buharlıya Geçişte Osmanlı Denizciliği (1825–1855)*. İstanbul: Doğu Kütüphanesi, 2016.
Fahmy, Khaled. *All the Pasha's Men: Mehmed Ali, His Army, and the Making of Modern Egypt*. Cairo: The American University in Cairo Press, 2002.
Faroqhi, Suraiya. 'Labor Recruitment and Control in the Ottoman Empire (Sixteenth and Seventeenth Centuries)'. In *Manufacturing in the Ottoman Empire and Turkey, 1500–1950*, edited by D. Quataert, 13–57. Albany, NY: SUNY Press, 1994.
Faroqhi, Suraiya. *Artisans of Empire: Crafts and Craftspeople under the Ottomans*. London/New York: I.B. Tauris, 2009.
Findley, Carter Vaughn. *Ottoman Civil Officialdom: A Social History*. Princeton, NJ: Princeton University Press, 2014.
İnalcık, Halil. 'Application of the Tanzimat and Its Social Effects', *Archivum Ottomanicum* 5 (1973): 99–127.
İnalcık, Halil. 'Balkanlar'da Osmanlı Fetihleri'nin Sosyal Koşulları', *Adam Academy Journal of Social Sciences* 1/1 (2011): 1–10.
Kabadayı, M. Erdem. 'Working for the State in a Factory in Istanbul: The Role of Factory Workers' Ethno-Religious and Gender Characteristics in State-Subject Interaction in the Late Ottoman Empire'. Unpublished PhD diss., Ludwig Maximilian University of Munich, 2008.
Kahane, Henry, Kahane, Renée and Tietze, Andreas, *The Lingua Franca in the Levant: Turkish Nautical Terms of Italian and Greek Origin*. Urbana: University of Illinois Press, 1958.
Kaya, Alp Yücel. 'Were Peasants Bound to the Soil in the Nineteenth-Century Balkans? A Reappraisal of the Question of the New/Second Serfdom in Ottoman Historiography'. In *Working in

Greece & Turkey: A Comparative Labour History from Empires to Nation-States, 1840–1940, edited by L. Papastefanaki and M. E. Kabadayı, 61–112. New York/Oxford: Berghahn Books, 2020.

Khater, Akram Fouad. *Sources in the History of the Modern Middle East*. Boston: Houghton Mifflin, 2004.

Kırlı, Cengiz. 'Coffeehouses: Public Opinion in the Nineteenth-Century Ottoman Empire'. In *Public Islam and the Common Good*, edited by A. Salvatore and D. Eickelman, 75–97. Leiden, The Netherlands: Brill, 2004.

Mintz, Sidney W. *Sweetness and Power: The Place of Sugar in Modern History*. New York, NY: Viking, 1985.

Öztürk, Nazif. 'XIX. Yüzyılda Osmanlı İmparatorluğu'nda Sanayileşme ve 1827'de Kurulan Vakıf İplik Fabrikası', *Vakıflar Dergisi* 21 (1990): 23–80.

Panzac, Daniel. 'Un Prologue Aux Tanzimat: La Modernisation Des Forces Navales Ottomanes, Empire, Maghreb, Egypte (Fin XVIIIe – Début XIXe Siècle)', *Journal of Mediterranean Studies* 12/2 (2002): 435–50.

Quataert, Donald. 'The Age of Reforms, 1812–1914'. In *An Economic and Social History of the Ottoman Empire, 1300–1914*, edited by H. İnalcık and D. Quataert, 759–946. Cambridge: Cambridge University Press, 1994.

Rogan, Eugene L. *Frontiers of the State in the Late Ottoman Empire: Transjordan, 1850–1921*. Cambridge: Cambridge University Press, 2002.

Sefer, Akın. 'From Class Solidarity to Revolution: The Radicalization of Arsenal Workers in the Late Ottoman Empire', *International Review of Social History* 58/3 (2013): 395–428.

Sefer, Akın. 'British Workers and Ottoman Modernity in Nineteenth-Century Istanbul', *International Labor and Working-Class History* 99 (2021): 147–66.

Shaw, Stanford J. *The Financial and Administrative Organization and Development of Ottoman Egypt, 1517–1798*. Princeton, NJ: Princeton University Press, 1962.

Shaw, Stanford J. *Between Old and New: The Ottoman Empire under Sultan Selim III, 1789–1807*. Cambridge, MA: Harvard University Press, 1971.

Vak'anüvis Halil Nuri Bey. *Nûrî Tarihi*, edited by Seydi Vakkas Toprak. Ankara: Türk Tarih Kurumu Basımevi, 2015.

Yaycıoğlu, Ali. *Partners of the Empire: The Crisis of the Ottoman Order in the Age of Revolutions*. Stanford, CA: Stanford University Press, 2016.

Yıldırım, Onur, and Seven Ağır. 'Gedik: What's in a Name?'. In *Bread from the Lion's Mouth: Artisans Struggling for a Livelihood in Ottoman Cities*, edited by S. Faroqhi, 217–36. Oxford: Berghahn Books, 2015.

Zorlu, Tuncay. *Innovation and Empire in Turkey: Sultan Selim III and the Modernisation of the Ottoman Navy*. London/New York: IB Tauris, 2008.

CONTRACTS UNDER DURESS

3
Contracts under duress: work documents as a matter and means of conflict in the Habsburg Monarchy/ Austria in the late nineteenth and early twentieth centuries

Sigrid Wadauer

Controversial depictions

In the Habsburg Monarchy of the nineteenth and early twentieth centuries, specific identity documents (*Arbeitsbuch, Dienstbotenbuch*) were mandatory for labourers and servants, and they were a precondition for legal employment and travelling.[1] It was argued by authorities, employers and their political representatives in favour of these documents that they were necessary to protect order, provide security and enforce the work contract. At the same time, such papers were supposed to enable labourers and servants to prove their identity and skills, search for work and move freely[2] – in other words, to meet the demands of the labour market. From the perspective of contemporary critics, however, these papers manifested legal, social and political inequality. They were seen as a tool of control and coercion, a symbol of humiliation. 'The labour booklet', as a parliamentary motion of social democratic representatives put it, 'is the mark of slavery, of bondage, the yellow badge, which is attached to anyone who is regarded as outcast, as inferior, as in need of control.'[3] Only streetwalkers, servants and workers, it was maintained, required such papers.[4] 'The dogs on the streets have to wear a mark, otherwise they will be caught by the flayer,' as it was phrased in an article published in the social democratic newspaper *Arbeiterwille* of 1909. That article continues:

> [T]he worker has to show a labour booklet, otherwise he has no right to work and life. ... In times of slavery, the slave-owner had

his name burned into the body of the slave with a red-hot iron. The Austrian authorities, however, issue a wanted poster for the life-long worker that stamps him as a slave. If today a young person leaves school and starts an apprenticeship, he needs a labour booklet. As long as he does not have one, he has no right to be exploited. Only when he possesses that booklet, which marks him as a subject of exploitation, does he have the right to be exploited by others.[5]

The 'free worker', a social democratic lawyer wrote, was forced to carry around such papers all the time inasmuch as his freedom and life depended on the possession and the contents of them.[6] No other civilised country at the time, as was claimed by critics, knew such a disgraceful institution that patronised the worker and left him defenceless against an employer's abuse of these documents.[7]

Nevertheless, even workers who presented their situation in such a manner as 'wage slaves' would still regard themselves as free in comparison to 'real slaves', serfs or servants.[8] Such controversial depictions of labour booklets, the pointed characteristics and equations, were apparently an element of political struggles to justify or challenge the legitimacy of regulations and remedies – that is, political propaganda. The involved parties tried to ideologically and practically move the boundaries between legitimate and illegitimate practices, to define or redefine 'free' and 'unfree' labour conditions. Notions of freedom and constraints – as Robert J. Steinfeld and Stanley Engerman have argued – are complex and underlie historical change; they are not a fixed, essential attribute of labour relations but context-bound and a matter of interpretation and struggle.[9] The evolution of such categories, distinctions and hierarchies of work has become a prominent topic of historiography in the last decades.[10] Global labour history has highlighted the persistence of exploitation practices and forms of coercion that do not seem to fit so well into long-established images of the features and trajectories of modern capitalism.[11] Such debates can lead us to discover and re-evaluate fairly neglected practices and aspects of labour in European labour history as well. Even wage labour now does not look so 'free' anymore.[12] Apart from the most apparent economic constraints of wage labour, one can find various forms of non-economic, legal or illegal, subtle or manifest forms of coercion as well. This chapter reflects the possibilities of coercion linked to labour booklets in the Austrian part of the Habsburg Empire in the late nineteenth and early twentieth centuries. (I will only marginally address the documents of servants here.[13]) At the outset, I will describe some aspects of the history of such identity papers, including the basic regulations and design of these documents. I will then focus on the question of how they might be practically used (or abused) to establish, categorise, negotiate or enforce work contracts within remunerated labour relations.

Historical developments, context and source material

Written documents as proof of the orderly termination of a work engagement and as a legal precondition for further employment were certainly not an invention of the nineteenth century. Such documents were repeatedly stipulated already in the eighteenth-century Habsburg monarchy apparently with limited efficacy. In the course of the nineteenth century, however, identity papers and documentation of work became more and more regulated and a matter of state policy and public administration.[14] Additionally, the requirement of possessing such documents was extended to include ever-greater shares of workers and servants. In the early nineteenth century, *Kundschaften*, certificates that had been issued by guilds, were replaced by travelling journeymen's *Wanderbücher* which were then issued by local authorities.[15] The Trade Law of 1859, which abolished guilds, stipulated *Arbeitsbücher* (translated as 'labour booklets' or 'labour books', 'workman's passports' or 'worker's booklets'), quite similar in form,[16] for all journeymen and for all skilled workers (*Gehilfen*) employed in workshops and factories, both men and women, regardless of whether they were travelling or not.[17] Subsequently, labour booklets became mandatory for miners and then for all regularly employed workers in trades and industries above the age of 16, along with apprentices and railroad construction-workers.[18] Hence, labour booklets referred to an ever more general and abstract category of worker in distinction to agricultural labourers and domestic servants (who were required to have a servants' employment book, a *Dienstbotenbuch*),[19] to sailors (who needed a *Seedienstbuch*), or to higher employees and employees in sales (who required work certificates, albeit not in the form of a booklet). At the same time, the regulations distinguished the 'lowest' category of wage work, meaning (formally) unskilled casual workers or day labourers, who did not need such papers.

Such documents were not a unique institution of the Habsburg Empire; similar papers can be found in other countries like France, Belgium or Germany.[20] Robert Steinfeld also points out comparable conflicts and sanctions for violation of labour agreements in Britain and the United States. The history of wage labour in all these countries, he argues, is quite diverse, yet the general pattern followed was surprisingly similar in this respect.[21] It does not lie within the scope of this paper to provide a comparison of labour policies in these countries. Nonetheless, there is one obvious difference between the Habsburg Empire and those other countries: whereas such papers had been fully abolished or restricted to juvenile workers in France or Germany in the course of the nineteenth century, the Habsburg Empire generalised and maintained the papers, an institution that was not abolished before the end of the Monarchy. In 1919, the Republic of Austria eliminated labour booklets.[22] Servants' booklets were abolished in 1920 in communities with more than 5,000 inhabitants and in 1926 generally.[23] However, this was not a linear and irrevocable development. Just a few years later, labour booklets were reintroduced in some provinces for agricultural labourers. The National Socialist regime established mandatory labour booklets again and more broadly as a tool to control labourers and the labour market.[24]

Are such papers thus a mere anachronism or do they persist in age-old repression, as the Austrian labour movement's press indicated? Neither was entirely the case, as I will explicate. Whereas such papers undoubtedly could be and were used in repressive ways, the manifold sources available on this topic also illustrate how in the nineteenth century new notions of work were emerging and being institutionalised. Conflicts reveal workers' claims; the sources also manifest their new (however unequal and fragmentary) political rights, their opportunities to organise and represent their interests and demands, as well as to file complaints and legal actions. To be sure, this was no automatic, linear and uncontested development, nor did such new rights and entitlements apply to all labour relations equally. Hence, the workers' complaints that the obligatory labour booklet would put them on the same level as slaves, servants (a larger share of whom were women) and prostitutes also evoked a hierarchy of work, revealing differences in possibilities, status and entitlements. Much of the existing, limited literature on this topic focuses on legal regulations, political debates or theoretical questions, especially on the overall character of the work contract.[25] Yet, as the result of the developments and struggles I have outlined, there is a broad variety of source material available. It ranges from reports of trade inspectors[26] and trade court decisions,[27] to statistics, numerous labour and servants' booklets[28] and archival records, and finally to autobiographical accounts. All these sources allow us to reconstruct and differentiate the various ways in which the involved parties used, abused, accepted or avoided these papers – certainly not always in accordance with the regulations or with ideological positions. As I will show, neither authorities, nor workers, nor employers were homogeneous or acted uniformly, as had been suggested in political debates.[29]

Labour booklets and the labour contract

Labour booklets were issued by the municipalities, serving as a precondition for any regular employment. The type of document defined the labour relation and categorised its holder as a worker, juvenile worker or apprentice.[30] The booklets likewise contained personal data, describing the individual's appearance and his or her occupation, education and occupational training. Those used as travel documents included an official permit designating provinces or countries open to such travel for a certain period. Labour booklets of juveniles had to document the father's or legal warden's consent to the employment. Booklets of apprentices additionally specified the basic terms of their apprenticeship, such as the duration, payment and who was in charge of boarding and lodging. Finally – and this was the most contested aspect – the booklets included a consecutive documentation of a person's employment history, that is, work certificates that had to be verified by police, municipality or trade association.[31] These certificates contained an assessment on the kind of employment and the worker's skills, diligence and faithfulness. Examples of such certificates are displayed in the collages by Tim Robinson. Some of the booklets I found in archives[32] show additional entries on support received by relief stations for work-seeking wayfarers (*Naturalverpflegsstationen*) or on hospital care. Some include stamps referring to the population census or to railway stations. In some, there are notes or numbers – likely concerning wages or advances. The common allegation that these papers were 'wanted posters' referred to such a documentation of employment and conduct. In addition, the handling of these papers implied – depending on the incidence of job change and mobility – more or less frequent interactions with authorities and police.

However, authorities and employers' representatives rejected the notion that the labour booklets were exclusively a matter of surveillance and control. They maintained that these booklets were not only indispensable for the employer in identifying a person and assessing her or his experience, diligence and reliability. Rather they were also convenient for the worker, a handy combination of all the relevant documents necessary for finding a suitable position. It was emphasised that the papers had multiple functions and documented both the rights and obligations of workers.[33] (Booklets also contained respective chapters of the Trade Law.)

To establish a legal work contract, the labour booklets had to be handed over to the employer, who was supposed to keep them – like a pawn[34] – during the period of employment. After termination of the working relationship, the employer was obliged to enter a work certificate and return it to the worker.[35] It was prohibited to employ a worker who had no booklet or whose certificates indicated that she or he had not terminated previous employment in accordance with mutually negotiated and stipulated terms. 'The purpose of labour booklets', a contemporary author wrote, 'is to secure the work contract against any single-sided arbitrary act, whether by the worker or employer, and to engrain in young persons the liabilities to which they committed themselves through the work contract.'[36] Workers, it was claimed, wished to be completely free,[37] like a bird on a twig.[38] They were frequently changing their jobs, breaching their contracts or 'running away' without notice, before the agreed-upon period was over or before they had fulfilled their work assignments. The labour booklet was thus intended to prohibit such things.[39]

From a legal perspective, the work contract was an oral or written agreement between employer and worker regarding work assignments, working hours, payment, work conditions, shop rules, period of employment, the modalities of termination and so on.[40] Such a contract was a matter of civil law, yet at the same time it was a matter of the trade law (or, in other cases, regulations concerning servants or commercial law) which defined the legal framework and what was regarded as customary or appropriate if there was no explicit individual agreement. In addition, the 1859 Trade Law defined eligible reasons that allowed the worker or employer to terminate a work contract or apprenticeship *before* the agreed-upon time. Legitimate reasons for an employer to dismiss a worker in such a way were, for example, work incapacity or inability to work,[41] illegal acts or insubordination, breach of trust, and sideline earnings. A worker could quit, for example, if the work endangered her or his health, or in case of physical abuse or libel. Other lawful grounds were the employer's attempts to seduce the worker to conduct immoral or illegal acts, undue retention of wages or any other substantial violations of the work agreement, and an employer's bankruptcy or inability to pay the wages. An apprentice could also quit if the employer neglected his or her duties, abused the right to castigate or moved to another place. She or he could give notice and leave after two weeks if she or he wanted a change of vocation.[42]

The breach of such a contract was analogously a matter of civil law, according to which employers or workers could be forced to provide monetary compensation. For example, employers had to compensate for the wage loss of the worker and workers could be liable for damages or payments for substitute workers. Breach of contract also constituted a violation of the Trade Law. According to § 135 of the 1859 Trade Law,[43] any violations committed by the employer were subject to monetary fines, or loss of the trade permit or of the right to train apprentices. Offences by a worker could result in arrest of up to three months. From 1907,[44] monetary fines were defined as the general norm also for workers. However, in the case of repeated offences and/or inability to pay the fines, time in prison could be ordered. In case workers left their workplace without an orderly termination (this means without explicitly quitting, without legitimate reason and/or without staying for the period of notice), the employer could request compensation for economic harm (for example higher wages for replacement), punishment[45] and/or that the worker be forced by the police to return and work until the agreed-upon time and period of notice was over.[46] (Up to the early twentieth century, servants were additionally threatened with physical caning by their employer.)[47] Collective breaches of contracts – that is, strikes – were also a violation of the criminal law until freedom of coalition was granted in 1870.[48] Hence, civil law, trade law and penal code were interrelated and complementary.[49]

The work contract – and this seemed a consensus among all parties – was obviously not like any other contract.[50] It was not, or not exclusively, a private matter but one of public concern.[51] It not only implied submission by one party (the worker),[52] but was also a contract between unequal parties, who faced unequal consequences when one or the other failed to fulfil their obligations (to work or to pay a particular wage, and so on). Isidor Ingwer, a social democratic lawyer, questioned whether the work contract could be perceived as a contract in the sense of the civil law at all, since this would require that the involved parties were acting on free will:

> ... the work contract is not free and it is impossible to create legal relationships between entrepreneur and worker in the capitalist order of economy, relationships that even come close to a contract. The owner of the means of production, whose final aim is to make a profit, has the power to prescribe work conditions to the owner of labour power, who is isolated from all other means of production, who is not able to produce without means of production and who

knows he has to starve if he does not produce. Driven by the will to live, he has to obey the terms of work.[53]

Hence, such a contract should not have a binding character for the worker, who had no alternatives to wage labour and few possibilities to negotiate the terms of the contract (wages, terms of payment, working hours, obligations and so on), according to some. The starving party, it was argued from this perspective, should not be obliged to fulfil the contract.[54]

Use, abuse and avoidance of labour booklets

The labour booklets undoubtedly gave further power to the employer,[55] opening up various possibilities for use and abuse. This topic was frequently addressed in conflicts documented by trade courts.[56] Additionally, numerous workers' complaints were brought to trade inspectors, a set of positions created in 1883 to supervise the enforcement of labour regulations in trade and industry.[57] There was only a small number of trade inspectors charged with supervising the enforcement of the Trade Law in numerous factories and workshops in all the Austrian lands.[58] Nevertheless, their annual reports, together with the published trade court decisions,[59] supply a vivid picture of possible violations of the regulations involving the labour booklet. The largest share of the recorded conflicts was related to the beginning, continuation and termination of employment[60] (see Diagrams 3.1 and 3.2).

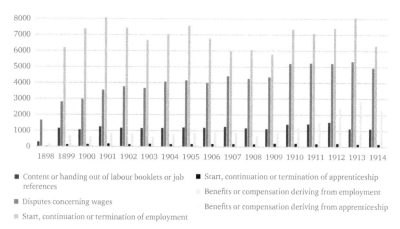

Diagram 3.1 Matters of dispute at trade courts in Vienna, 1898–1914. (Selected topics. Cases could concern more than one topic.)[61]

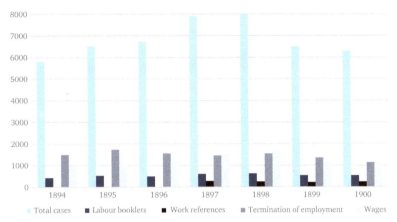

Diagram 3.2 Workers' concerns brought forward to trade inspectors, 1894–1900. (Selected topics according to the inspectors' annual reports.)[62]

A common complaint was that the employer kept the booklet and did not return it to the worker if the contract was not fulfilled, or if it was not terminated in an orderly way[63] individually or collectively (for example by a strike). Some employers were depositing the booklets at local authorities or police offices. Among lawyers, the legitimacy of this was questioned.[64] Anyway, in such a case the worker was not able to take on another position – at least formally – until in possession of his or her papers again. It is difficult to know to what extent employers exhausted other possibilities for enforcing a labour contract,[65] such as their right to request the return of the worker.[66] I could find only very few such cases in the published trade court decisions. Some contemporary authors argue that this was rather exceptional and a mere threat since employers did not have any interest in the return of a worker who was noncompliant or who was likely to cause discord.[67] It is also very difficult to find numbers on cases in which a breach of contract was penalised with arrest.[68] In Vienna, for example, one worker was arrested on such grounds in 1880; 76 were detained in 1881. The annual report of the Viennese police reports 14 cases of cessation of work in 1879, 23 in 1880, 43 in 1881, 60 in 1882, 297 in 1883[69] and 68 in 1885. Between 1877 and 1892, on average 512 charges per year were filed against apprentices and 219 against servants[70] for 'escaping' an apprenticeship or situation.[71] Hence, these numbers are overall very small in relation to the numbers of workers or work contracts. However, penal sanctions for strikes in particular could also be subsumed under other categories of the law, such as incitement, violence, intimidation or violations of the public order.

Numerous documented conflicts involved the request of monetary compensation for untimely termination.[72] The period of termination could be arranged between employer and worker; a two-week term was regarded as customary. Nonetheless, such claims against workers could be substantive, especially when work contracts concerned piecework or were made for a longer period and included putative commercial damages. Consider the following exemplary cases intended to provide an idea of such conflicts at trade court and the ratio between wage and compensation claims.

In 1902, a tailor journeyman requested a termination of employment by the trade court because of a conflict with his employer, a milliner in Cracow.[73] The trade court rejected this and arranged for his return, as requested by his employer. The journeyman obeyed and continued to work for the milliner. After another argument with the employer, he again requested a termination of employment because he felt his honour had been impugned. The employer now also requested termination and, additionally, a compensation of 100 K (*Kronen*). She argued that the journeyman had finished two jackets with garnishment in four weeks instead of four jackets, as he used to do before the conflict. Consequently, she would be forced to employ another tailor for considerably higher wages (12 K more per week). The journeyman insisted that he had worked at the same pace, but working to completely new models had consumed more time. The trade court ruled that the employment was terminated – after all, a wish expressed by both parties – and the employer had to return the booklet. All compensation claims were rejected.[74]

In another court case of 1901 at the trade court of Brünn (Brno), the company requested a 500 K (*Kronen*) fine for breaching a contract for two years from a weaver who had not taken up the unredeemable position in a wool factory at the agreed-upon date.[75] This fine was part of a contract between the weaver and the wool factory which had been made orally, but the parties had decided that it should subsequently be put in writing. However, this did not happen, and in front of the court, the weaver tried to present his meeting with the company's representatives as preliminary, noncommittal negotiations. Yet, with a letter, written immediately after the meeting, in which he asked the company to dismiss him from his obligations, the weaver had implicitly confirmed the binding character of the oral agreement. Accordingly, the trade court acknowledged the factory's claim for monetary compensation. Still, the company's claims were regarded as excessive since the worker only had a monthly wage of 150 K in his current position and was deemed easy to replace. The worker lost the case and was required to provide a compensation of 50 K.

However the court decided, in such cases of conflict, workers breaching contracts individually or by striking faced a risk of losing much or all of what they owned. This threat, the lawyer Ingwer maintained, not only endangered the workers' existence but was also being used to undermine political rights and harm the unions.[76]

Breach of contract by untimely termination could certainly be committed by *both* parties to the contract – a fact easily overlooked since breach of contract by the *worker* figured so prominently in these debates.[77] It is not easy to determine the share of cases that concern termination by workers or by employers. The available statistics from the trade court decisions in Vienna did not make such distinctions. However, cases brought forward to the arbitrational board of trade associations in Vienna from 1896 to 1898 concerned 9 to 13 times more cases in which a worker was dismissed before the agreed-upon time compared with cases of workers leaving.[78] Furthermore, almost all cases at the trade court for machine and metalware industries on termination of employment from 1894 to 1897 were filed by workers against employers and not conversely.[79] (In a case where an employer dismissed a worker before the agreed date, only compensation for wage loss was at stake.[80]) Such evidence – however patchy it may be – indicates that employers used labour booklets and related regulations quite flexibly and according to their needs. They tried to tie down workers when they needed their labour, when other workers were not available or when substitute workers were more expensive. They tried to get rid of them at short notice, for example when they were not needed or not fulfilling expectations.

Apart from conflicts over the start and termination of the contract and the transfer of the booklets, disputes also frequently concerned the work certificates.[81] These had to contain the dates of employment and the name and address of the employer, as well as brief remarks on the kind of employment and on the worker's loyalty, morality, diligence and skills. Employers were not allowed to enter explicitly negative statements, thereby creating obstacles to further employment.[82] Hence, certificates in labour booklets – which it was a worker's right to receive – were usually quite short. Larger companies even used stamps with the required dates and phrases. (Examples of such certificates are displayed in Diagram 3.1, p.58, and Diagram 3.2, p. 59.) Additionally, more elaborate certificates could be handed out separately from the booklet, and workers could request a more elaborate certificate in the booklet.

Because of these restrictions and common practices, employers often complained that certificates were mostly insignificant or worthless. The only useful information for assessing a worker's character was the length of employment and the frequency of job changes. A decent, diligent worker – it was maintained – had nothing to fear and could be proud of his references.[83] Yet even this limited information was ambiguous and a matter for interpretation, as was pointed out by politically organised workers.[84] Employment over a longer time could indicate either dependability or a deficit of ambition. A negative assessment could still be suggested by phrasing or by not explicitly mentioning reliability, diligence or 'utter' satisfaction. Employers were also accused of entering 'secret' signs – numbers or characters – into the booklets so as to brand a worker as lazy or incompetent, or as a drinker, agitator and so on.[85] Terminating a job on 1 May, for instance, indicated – particularly when written in red ink – that a person was engaged in the labour movement.[86] (Moreover, striking workers or socialists were said to be blacklisted.)[87] To be sure, such 'secret' signs were explicitly prohibited, and there was no agreement on how often these signs were actually used, something that cannot be determined definitively. Trade inspectors pointed out that many complaints were simply based on labourers' fundamental mistrust towards employers.[88]

From the perspective of the workers, it seems obvious that the labour booklets – from which one could not remove a page legally – were an odious institution exposing them to arbitrariness and malice by employers. Yet at the same time, trade inspectors' reports indicate that the booklets were an effective disciplinary measure only to a limited extent. The use of the booklets certainly did not prevent breaches of contract or unorderly terminations, either by workers or by employers.[89] There are various reasons for that, as discussed below.

Firstly, the implementation of the Trade Law of 1859 was rather inconsistent. In fact, large numbers of workers did not possess the mandatory documents at all. Administrative statistics from Vienna and trade inspectors' reports indicate that labour booklets were not issued in significant numbers before the 1890s. Even in the first decades of the twentieth century, we find frequent complaints about missing documents, and enforcement varied greatly in respect to branches and regions. (The same can be said about servants' booklets.)[90] The most astonishing reason for this was that many municipalities, badly informed and/or incompetent, often did not issue papers, particularly in the late nineteenth century.[91] Some communities did not have enough blank forms available to meet the demand. Others feared that issuing papers would also mean assigning rights of residency to strangers. Some local authorities denied papers to residents, or to juvenile workers or to women inasmuch as it seemed unnecessary to provide them. They also seemed to act on gender-specific notions of work or labour relations. Women, whatever jobs they had, often received documents for servants' booklets instead of those for workers.[92]

Secondly, employers, who in political debates unanimously insisted that such papers were inalienable, frequently employed persons without labour booklets and without registering them, as requested by the Trade Law. Year after year, trade inspectors pointed out numerous cases that concerned mostly trades and industries with seasonal work, high labour turnover and changing labour demand, such as the sugar industry, brickmaking and tourism. They likewise concerned trades with subcontractors (such as construction work) or areas with a greater share of foreign workers from countries not belonging to the Habsburg Empire. To be sure, booklets were not the only documents that could be used to identify working persons, and foreign workers often brought specific documents.

Not registering workers or wrongly categorising them as servants or casual labourers could be a pretext for denying them basic rights defined in the Trade Law and social insurances linked to formal employment and the status of a worker, who was in a better position vis-à-vis her or his employer than a servant, who was seen as part of a household and subordinated to the head of the household.[93] Up to the interwar period, servants had no entitlement to insurance for sickness or work accidents.[94] Conflicts on the distinctions between trade and household, servants and workers can be found, for example, in regard to (predominantly female) workers in laundries, inns or hotels.[95]

Labour booklets were also not the only remedy for employers to enforce labour contracts in trade and industries.[96] Some employers requested deposits while others kept larger amounts of payments and only paid smaller advances until the task was completed, the contract ended or the period of notice was over. Payment practices, the employers' handling of documents, their bureaucratic organisation, the use of written documentation, the willingness to fulfil or violate legal requirements – all of these varied, depending on the type of business or branch, economic cycle, availability and demand: whether for labour that was skilled and specifically qualified or easy to replace and rather exchangeable.[97]

At the same time, we can find differences in workers' attitudes, vulnerabilities and practices. Certainly, a high share of workers' complaints to trade inspectors and a large number of trade court cases involved labour booklets. Yet, overall, these numbers of complaints were still small in relation to all workers in trade and industries who theoretically needed or possessed such documents. Not every worker was willing or had the necessary resources to turn to a trade inspector or file a formal complaint for a bad certificate and wait for a trade court decision to fix it. Not every worker was equally dependent on papers. Those who had ambitions and expectations of betterment in position or wage, those who envisaged a probable career as a self-employed master artisan were probably more susceptible to blackmailing by certificates or even more inclined to adopt such constraints. This might explain why many workers who breached a contract or had a disadvantageous work record or unfavourable certificates simply left behind their documents, 'misplaced' or destroyed them. Large numbers of abandoned identity documents were held in storage by companies or authorities. We can additionally find many documents marked or registered as 'duplicates' or 'triplicates'. Obviously, it was not very difficult to apply for new documents or to find casual employment without a booklet.[98] Nevertheless, lack of documents or documents without a decent work record were a risk, in particular for workers without employment and on the move.

Benefits, ambivalences and (in)differences

Most of the autobiographical accounts dealing with labour booklets refer to the use of these papers in the context of job search and tramping.[99] Up to the early twentieth century, finding employment commonly implied mobility in a larger area – as in tramping or by 'looking around' at workshops or factories (*Umschau*).[100] In this context, labour booklets were frequently requested. They not only served as travel documents but also defined the person as a work-seeker, thereby enabling access to public support, such as price reduction on train tickets or lodging, board and labour exchanges at relief stations for work-seeking wayfarers. Those were established in the most industrialised provinces from the 1880s on, the aim being to support, organise and control the job search and travels of work-seekers, while at the same time distinguishing and separating them from the allegedly workshy vagrants or from people without any papers, work certificates or means of subsistence. Hence, papers, public support or support by trade associations and unions allowed journeymen or formally skilled workers (rather than formally unskilled workers) to move and to search for work for some time and accept employment on a selective basis (at least for a limited period of time). In this respect, one author even called the papers 'the workers' palladium of freedom'.[101] Yet this also required them to demonstrate the willingness to work and to take on work eventually, even on unfavourable terms.[102] The Austrian book printer Karl Steinhardt (who later became a founding member of the communist party) outlined the possible sanctions and emphasised the coercive aspects of this tramping system:[103]

> The organisation of book printers cared well for its travelling members ... They paid a viaticum ... A network of hostels relieved the travelling fellow from the pressure to find shelter at the police's relief stations.[104] A night in those stations, which were visited by decent journeymen only in greatest distress and which were polluted by dirt and bugs, regularly included some hours of forced work. In exchange, one received a workhouse gruel and a small piece of bread. ... The police clamped down on so-called vagabonds. ... One was then treated to arrest in the local prison, transfer to a forced-labour institution or forced removal. If we who received support from our organisations were caught begging, the punishment was more severe. Nonetheless, we all begged.[105]

Obviously, Steinhardt's memoirs – with a title translating as 'A Viennese Worker's Memoirs' – tried to exemplify, describe and explain an institutional landscape and practices of the past to an audience of the 1950s.[106] In his youth, as he put it, tramping had still been a common practice.[107] It seems safe to assume that contemporary wayfarers were familiar with both the opportunities to receive support and the threats of being arrested, removed or sentenced to forced labour in a forced labour institution. He also shows that they had more or less means and resources available to deal with such risks. He presented himself as better off. Nevertheless, like access to relief stations, support provided by trade associations or unions was neither unconditional nor unlimited, as Steinhardt explained: 'When I started my first journey in 1894, after working 3 weeks in Vienna, I had planned to see the largest part of the monarchy and a part of Bavaria. ... Yet the organisation's regulations required that the traveller had to accept a job offer.' The consequences here, however, were less severe: 'If he refused, he lost travel support.' Steinhardt only made it to Upper Austria, where he had to accept a post.[108] 'In April 1895', he continued, 'I started my second journey. This time I avoided all the tribulations of work. I wandered through larger parts of the monarchy and returned in October of the same year to Vienna.' On his travels, he became acquainted with the lives and working conditions of farmers and agricultural labourers. 'So I came home richer in insights and positive knowledge. Yet my wanderlust demanded more.'[109]

Such accounts – mostly written by politically organised, educated and formally skilled male workers or journeymen – demonstrate the hardships of tramping. The writers depict the frequent interactions with police, the risks of being arrested for vagrancy and the pressure to accept work on undesirable terms. Yet they *also* describe how they successfully managed the fragile balance between their wish to travel and to avoid work or unfavourable posts, and their economic need and legal obligation to work. They highlight acts of insubordination, as well as ways to avoid sanctions, break the rules, find loopholes in the system and use papers for their own purposes. In what follows, I outline some variations in the ways that this was addressed.[110]

Julius Deutsch, an Austrian book printer journeyman and later a social democratic representative and politician, described how a fellow journeyman forged a work certificate for him that allowed him to travel unbothered by the police through Germany and back home.[111] Wenzel Holek – German-Bohemian worker, social democrat and later educator – was dismissed after attending a meeting on 1 May. After some unsuccessful attempts to find new employment with a labour booklet, which now marked him as an organised worker, he destroyed it and applied for a new one.[112] Ignaz Danzinger's manuscript describes how he made a work contract from a distance, becoming a foreman at a sawmill in Sarajevo. When he arrived with his family, he had already spent almost the entire advance he had received from the employer, who turned out to be brutal and difficult to satisfy. The requirements seemed too high and the workers too labile, always asking for wage raises. Danzinger was desperate but the employer, as he wrote, 'had all my work references and had me in his hands'. He left anyway, terrified, without papers, without any money and without saying goodbye to his family, 'like a hounded deer'.[113]

In contrast to that, the baker journeyman and social democrat Josef Jodlbauer, who also frequently referred to the labour booklet, described an open and violent confrontation with a master baker who seemed particularly rude and disrespectful. The situation escalated when the employer ordered him to work in the vineyards. Jodlbauer quit and asked for his labour booklet and five days' wages, yet the master refused to pay an 'idler'; he laughed at and spat on Jodlbauer, who threatened to file complaints at the Gendarmerie. Finally, Jodlbauer threatened the master with a solid stick and fled.[114] Ferdinand Hanusch, later the secretary for social welfare in the Republic of Austria, described how he and another fellow pushed a drunk policeman, who wanted to arrest them, to the ground. Then they took back their booklets, locked him up and ran away.[115] Alfons Petzold's accounts take a rather ironic or cynical tone in describing negotiations on the meaning of his patchy work record with potential employers.[116] What Jodlbauer and Petzold have in common, though, is that they frequently use the term 'slavery' to describe the constraints of their situation.[117] 'I toiled like a Negro slave,' Alfons Petzold noted in his diary. The inaccuracy of these notions is apparent: 'I am cursed by any work; I will only take on my employment until Monday. People might say I am lazy. I don't care.'[118] Unlike in his autobiographical novel, Petzold did not mention the labour booklet so much in the behind-the-scenes account of his diary. Similarly, Adelheid Popp elaborates the constraints related to the servants' booklets in her book *Hausklavinnen*[119] but neglects this topic in her own autobiographical account of her life as a factory worker.[120] Several other authors – particularly those who make no explicit reference to political parties – mention labour booklets randomly or not at all. Avoidance or termination of employment did not always result in conflicts. 'Because I didn't like to remain so close to home,' the shoemaker journeyman Landerl wrote about his first day on the tramp, which unexpectedly and unintentionally resulted in a post, 'I asked the master for my labour booklet the next day'[121] – and then continued on his journey.

Conclusion

Labour booklets opened up various possibilities to legally or illegally exert coercion, which challenges simplified notions of 'free wage labour' in late nineteenth- and early twentieth-century Europe. They could be used and abused as a tool to urge people into employment and accepting unfavourable labour conditions, to discipline them at the workplace, and to hinder them from quitting and simply 'running away' before the contract ended or before the period of notice was over.[122] Denying or withholding papers, negative certificates, secret signs or blacklisting could exclude a person from regular or adequate employment. Such threats or measures could be used to prevent or sanction undesired behaviour or political action. Hence, labour booklets were often seen as a symbol of inequality and (political) oppression. Did such papers and regulations thus constitute a prison, as the first illustration by Tim

Robinson (p. 47) suggests? In order to assess the forms of coercion related to such papers, we need to reflect on the effectiveness of such measures and investigate how the involved parties actually made use of papers and regulations.

When social democratic representatives argued for the abolition of the labour booklets in early twentieth-century Austria, they did not only stress the repressive, odious or humiliating aspects of these papers. Trying to establish a consensus, they also emphasised the expendability and dysfunctionality of such papers for all parties involved: employers, authorities and workers. They pointed out that this institution had largely failed as a reliable tool for identifying persons and exerting effective control, while at the same time it was causing an immense bureaucratic effort and constantly evoking antagonism between classes.[123] Nevertheless, '[t]o the shame of the majority of Austrian workers', as Isidor Ingwer wrote, 'one has to say that they never seriously fought against the labour booklet, the infamy of which they should have felt every day.'[124] When the Social Democratic Party finally succeeded in 1919 and labour booklets were replaced by a new type of document (an identity card for workers, which remained with the worker and which did not include certificates), many workers reportedly kept using their old booklets. After all, some identity papers and work records were still requested and useful in various situations. Unlike the criticism, protest and conflicts that are documented in multiple sources, such pragmatism and indolence – albeit an essential aspect – is elusive.

Despite all political attempts to mobilise, organise and represent themselves, workers – as well as employers or authorities – did not act uniformly. The use and perception of labour booklets varied and could be ambiguous; it had manifold facets and was context-bound.[125] Labour booklets were not the employers' only means of coercion, nor were they always requested. Employers acted flexibly, according to their needs and situation. Law enforcement remained fairly inconsistent, and many workers did not own the required documents. Even workers' autobiographical accounts show how papers – despite all the risks involved – could be destroyed, manipulated and also used for their own purposes. These papers certified one's identity and the status of a worker or work-seeker, allowed mobility and evidenced qualifications and work experiences, and they could give access to support. Various sources – the narratives, officially documented conflicts and political debates over the labour booklets – reveal not simply or exclusively repression, but also attempts and possibilities to challenge rules, to redefine, negotiate and shift distinctions between legitimate and illegitimate obligations and constraints of the work contract. They illustrate the (not linear and not uncontested) emergence of a state social policy in which *certain* formalised categories of work and labour relations were linked to new social and political rights, entitlements and obligations. The 1919 abolition of the booklets and related forms of sanctions for breach of contract in Austria was conceived as an act of liberation and as a success of the labour movement. Even so, it did not signal a retreat by the state but rather the beginning of a new period in which its involvement in labour relations became more effective.[126]

Acknowledgements

My research on the subject of identity papers was funded initially by the Gerda-Henkel-Stiftung (AZ 52/V/18) and is currently funded by the Austrian Science Fund (FWF, project no. P32226-G29). I would like to thank Theresa Wobbe, Léa Renard and Nicola Schalkowski for discussion and exchange of ideas. I would also like to thank the editors for their comments.

Notes

1. See, for example, Mayerhofer, *Handbuch*, Vol. 3, 536–82; Heller, *Das österreichische Gewerberecht*, 604–27; on the controversy, see Ebenhoch and Pernerstorfer (eds), *Stenographisches Protokoll*.
2. Ertl, 'Bericht der k. k. Gewerbeinspektoren', 1886, 56.
3. 'Antrag des Abgeordneten Smitka, Palme und Genossen', 3. The quotes from German source material in this text were translated by the author.
4. Ingwer, *Zwei Fesseln des Koalitionsrechtes*, 3; *Bericht der k. k. Gewerbe-Inspektoren über ihre Amtstätigkeit, 1886*, 22; *1888*, 56; *1909*, CXXff; these annual reports are available on https://anno.onb.ac.at/; 'Das Arbeitsbuch', 1911, 1.
5. 'Weg mit dem Arbeitsbuch', 1909, 7.
6. Ingwer, *Der sogenannte Arbeitsvertrag*, 24.
7. Ingwer, *Zwei Fesseln des Koalitionsrechtes*, 14; 'Arbeitsbücher und Schwarze Listen', 1910, 8.
8. See, for example, Steinfeld, *Coercion, Contract and Free Labor*, 13; Engerman, 'Institutional Change', 2012; Patterson and Zhuo, 'Modern Trafficking', 2018; Eiden-Offe, '"Weisse Sclaven"', 2014.
9. Engerman, 'Introduction', 9–19; Steinfeld, Engerman, 'Labour – Free or Coerced?', 107–26.
10. E.g. Wobbe et al., 'Deutungsmodelle von Arbeit', 2023.
11. See, for example, Eckert (ed.), *Global Histories of Work*.
12. Engerman, 'Institutional Change', 2012, 599.
13. Regulations and labour relations differ in various respects, yet distinctions between the status of a worker, journeyman or servant were contested, in flux and often blurred in practice. I address the consequences of such a categorisation below. See Richter, *Die Produktion besonderer Arbeitskräfte*; Wadauer, 'Kategorisierung, Kontrolle, Vertrauen?'.
14. On the history of identity papers in the Habsburg Empire, see Heindl and Saurer (eds), *Grenze und Staat*.
15. 'Patent vom 24. Februar 1827', 231–32.

16 *Wanderbücher* remained valid; see 'Der Magistrat der Stadt Wien', 1860, 108. Ehmer stresses the continuities between guilds and trade associations after 1859. Ehmer, 'Zünfte in Österreich', 126.
17 Reichsgesetzblatt (hereafter RGBl.) 1859/227, § 74 and appendix.
18 RGBl. 1885/22; RGBl. 1902/156.
19 On servants' booklets, see Morgenstern, *Österreichisches Gesinderecht*, 120–28; Ehrenfreund and Mráz, *Wiener Dienstrecht*; Pierson, *Das Gesinde*; Vormbaum, *Politik und Gesinderecht*.
20 See, for example, Stieda, 'Arbeitsbuch'; Marchet, 'Zur Reform der österreichischen Gewerbe-Gesetzgebung', 1878; Keiser, *Vertragszwang und Vertragsfreiheit*; Landriani, 'Rethinking the Livret d'ouvriers', 2019; Stanziani, 'The Legal Status of Labour', 2009; Gerstenberger, *Markt und Gewalt*; for a comparison of the French *livret ouvrier* and workers' booklets in a colonial context, see Ricciardi, 'Categorizing Difference', 336–9.
21 Steinfeld, *Coercion, Contract and Free Labor*, 10; Böninger, *Die Bestrafung des Arbeitsvertragsbruchs*; Van den Eeckhout, 'Giving Notice'; Steinmetz, *Begegnungen vor Gericht*.
22 Staatsgesetzblatt (hereafter StGBl.) 1919/106.
23 StGBl. 1920/101, StGBl. 1920/144; Bundesgesetzblatt (BGBl.) 1926/72.
24 Linne, 'Von der Arbeitsvermittlung zum "Arbeitseinsatz"'.
25 Apart from contemporary and historical writings I have already quoted above, see, for example, Becker, 'The Practice of Control', which focuses on social sorting and authorities' attempts to use these documents for migration control. Lichtenberger describes labour booklets as mere tools of (political) repression: see Lichtenberger, 'Überbleibsel', 2020.
26 *Bericht der k. k. Gewerbe-Inspektoren über ihre Amtstätigkeit*, 1884–1916.
27 K.k. Justizministerium (ed.), *Sammlung von Entscheidungen der (k. k.) Gewerbegerichte*, 1900–1918 (in 1919 the title changed to Bundesministerium für Justiz (ed.), *Sammlung von Entscheidungen der Gewerbegerichte und Einigungsämter*).
28 Such documents can be found in many Austrian archives, for example in the Wiener Stadt- und Landesarchiv (in the *Dokumentensammlung* as well as in the sources of the *Versorgungshaus Mauerbach*, A6 Arbeitsbücher); in the Burgenländisches Landesarchiv (Gemeindearchiv Nord Pöttelsdorf etc.) and in the Oberösterreichisches Landesarchiv (Stadtarchiv Freistadt, Alte Registratur).
29 Ebenhoch and Pernerstorfer (eds), *Stenographisches Protokoll*, 415.
30 I am referring to the form of 1885: see RGBl. 1885/69.
31 RGBl. 1859/227, Anhang; Heller, *Das österreichische Gewerberecht*, 604–27.
32 See, for example, the documents in the Wiener Stadt- und Landesarchiv, *Dokumentensammlung* or *Versorgungshaus Mauerbach*, A6 Arbeitsbücher.
33 'Gewerbeordnung. Regierungsvorlage', 111–14.
34 Ebenhoch and Pernerstorfer (eds), *Stenographisches Protokoll*, 391.
35 Heller, *Das österreichische Gewerberecht*, 609–15.
36 Marchet, 'Zur Reform der österreichischen Gewerbe-Gesetzgebung', 1878; Heilinger, *Österreichisches Gewerberecht*, 525–27.
37 Ebenhoch and Pernerstorfer (eds), *Stenographisches Protokoll*, 156.
38 Schmoller, 'Die Natur des Arbeitsvertrages', 1874, 468.
39 'Gewerbeordnung. Motive', 112.
40 Verkauf, 'Arbeitsvertrag'; Přibram, 'Die juristische Struktur', 1904; Schreiber, 'Der Arbeitsvertrag', 1887/7, 49–51; Landgraf, *Die Sicherung des Arbeits-Vertrages*.
41 Self-inflicted inability to work or inability to work for more than four weeks. Apprentices could be dismissed if they were sick for more than six weeks; see Trade Law RGBl. 1859/222 § 78 and § 96.
42 Trade Law RGBl. 1859/222 § 78, § 96 and § 97.
43 RGBl. 1859/227.
44 RGBl. 1859, § 135.
45 RGBl. 1859/222, § 80; see also Heller, *Das österreichische Gewerberecht*, 674–712.
46 Caspaar, 'Zur praktischen Anwendung des § 80 der Gewerbe-Ordnung', 1883, 33–34; 'Verhaltung von Arbeitern zur Rückkehr in die Arbeit', 1909, 4–5. 'This recalls times of slavery', Ingwer wrote, 'when the slave who ran away was returned to the slave owner by public authority, and times of serfdom, when the serf who ran away was forcibly returned to his master'; Ingwer, *Zwei Fesseln des Koalitionsrechtes*, 6.

47 Morgenstern, *Gesindewesen und Gesinderecht*, 35; see also Richter, *Die Produktion besonderer Arbeitskräfte*, 49–52.
48 RGBl. 1870/43.
49 'Gewerbeordnung. Motive', 113–14.
50 Verkauf, 'Arbeitsvertrag', 150. On the problem of the 'incomplete contract' in sociology, see Hirsch-Kreinsen, 'Arbeit', 35.
51 Pfersche, *Das gewerbliche Arbeitsverhältnis*, 17; Schmoller, 'Die Natur des Arbeitsvertrages', 67 and 472.
52 Schmoller, 'Die Natur des Arbeitsvertrages', 451.
53 Ingwer, *Der sogenannte Arbeitsvertrag*, 32; see also Schmoller, 'Die Natur des Arbeitsvertrages', 470.
54 'Bergarbeiter aufgepasst!', 1892, 4.
55 Schmoller, 'Die Natur des Arbeitsvertrages', 490. 'Ist das Arbeitsbuch ein Machtmittel in der Hand des Unternehmers?', 1903, 6538.
56 Trade courts were established in 1869 and included both elected representatives of employers and workers, all laymen. In 1898 they were subdued to state district courts. RGBl. 1869/63; RGBl. 1896/218; Ingwer, *Rechtsstreitigkeiten*.
57 RGBl. 1883/117.
58 At that time, there was no similar supervision of work relations in domestic service or in agriculture; see Richter, *Die Produktion besonderer Arbeitskräfte*, 46.
59 (K. k.) Justizministerium (ed.), *Sammlung von Entscheidungen der (k. k.) Gewerbegerichte* 1900–1920.
60 van der Linden, 'Dissecting Coerced Labour'.
61 The available statistics provide numbers on topics and not on overall court cases. *Statistisches Jahrbuch der Stadt Wien* 1898–1914; available at https://www.wienbibliothek.at/.
62 The statistics of trade inspectors concern complaints or requests both by workers and by employers. This figure concerns only those brought forward by workers. Between 1894 and 1900, concerns related to labour booklets represented on average 8 per cent of all concerns, those related to wages 18 per cent, and those related to termination of employment 22 per cent. Other concerns related to insurances, work conditions, work time, apprenticeship, strike, work regulations etc. After 1900, the reports do not indicate the topics anymore. *Bericht der k. k. Gewerbe-Inspektoren über ihre Amtstätigkeit* 1894–1900. Reports are available at https://www.onb.ac.at/.
63 On such problems, see also Van den Eeckhout, 'Giving Notice'.
64 Verkauf, 'Arbeitsvertrag', 182; a different position is taken by Ingwer, *Das Arbeitsverhältnis nach öffentlichem Recht*, 188.
65 An article in *Die Arbeit* – a periodical representing employers – complained that the employers neglected their legal options. 'Entschädigungspflicht des Arbeiters wegen Kontraktbruchs', 1907, 8256.
66 Verkauf, 'Arbeitsvertrag', 181.
67 *Bericht der k. k. Gewerbe-Inspektoren über ihre Amtstätigkeit*, 1884, 217. Particularly in case of a strike, see 'Die Gewerbenovelle', 1896, 163.
68 Heilinger, *Gewerberecht*, 777; Pfersche, *Das gewerbliche Arbeitsverhältnis*, 94; Ingwer, *Zwei Fesseln des Koalitionsrechtes*, 6.
69 This number is probably related to the strike of baker journeymen in that year.
70 These were on average 0.14 per cent of all recorded newly started employments.
71 K. k. Polizei-Direction (ed.): *Die Polizeiverwaltung Wiens* 1877–1892, available at https://www.wienbibliothek.at/.
72 Verkauf, 'Arbeitsvertrag', 181.
73 K. k. Justizministerium (ed.), *Sammlung von Entscheidungen der k. k. Gewerbegerichte* 1904, Gewerbegerichtsentscheidung no. 829.
74 K. k. Justizministerium (ed.), *Sammlung von Entscheidungen der k. k. Gewerbegerichte* 1904, Gewerbegerichtsentscheidung no. 829.
75 K. k. Justizministerium (ed.), *Sammlung von Entscheidungen der k. k. Gewerbegerichte* 1905, Gewerbegerichtsentscheidung no. 901.
76 Ingwer, *Zwei Fesseln des Koalitionsrechtes*, 11–12.
77 'Wochenschau', 1889, 304–5.
78 *Statistisches Jahrbuch der Stadt Wien 1889*, 646.

79 *Statistisches Jahrbuch der Stadt Wien 1889*, 650.
80 On the uneven consequences, see Ingwer, *Der sogenannte Arbeitsvertrag*, 15; Soušek, *Der rechtliche Charakter der Arbeitskonflikte*.
81 Brichta, 'Das Dienstzeugnis', 1906.
82 Heilinger, *Gewerberecht*, 530.
83 Ebenhoch and Pernerstorfer (eds), *Stenographisches Protokoll*, 209–10, 306, 390.
84 Stieda, 'Arbeitsbuch', 599.
85 Heilinger, *Gewerberecht*, 531; Ebenhoch and Pernerstorfer (eds), *Stenographisches Protokoll*, 255.
86 See Ebenhoch and Pernerstorfer (eds), *Stenographisches Protokoll*, e.g. 86, 154–5, 209, 211, 283, 306, 391–2, 416–17; K. k. Justizministerium (ed.), *Sammlung von Entscheidungen der k. k. Gewerbegerichte*, Gewerbegerichtsentscheidung no. 164 (1899), no. 791 (1903), no. 934 (1901).
87 'Arbeitsbücher und Schwarze Listen', 1910, 8–9.
88 *Bericht der k. k. Gewerbe-Inspektoren über ihre Amtstätigkeit*, 1893, 23.
89 Marchet, 'Zur Reform der österreichischen Gewerbe-Gesetzgebung', 1878, 174.
90 Morgenstern, *Österreichisches Gesinderecht*, 126.
91 *Bericht der k. k. Gewerbe-Inspektoren über ihre Amtstätigkeit*, 1891, 306; 1892, 394.
92 *Bericht der k. k. Gewerbe-Inspektoren über ihre Amtstätigkeit*, 1899, LVII.
93 On this status, see Richter, *Die Produktion besonderer Arbeitskräfte*, 41.
94 Tálos and Wörister, *Soziale Sicherung im Sozialstaat Österreich*.
95 *Bericht der k. k. Gewerbe-Inspektoren über ihre Amtstätigkeit*, 1913, CLXXV–CLXXVI. The distinction between household and trade was not indisputable; see Richter, *Die Produktion besonderer Arbeitskräfte*.
96 Steinfeld, *Coercion, Contract and Free Labor*.
97 Ebenhoch and Pernerstorfer (eds), *Stenographisches Protokoll*, 325, 391. Schmoller called the complaints on breach of contract a distress call from small trades; see Schmoller, 'Die Natur des Arbeitsvertrages', 526.
98 Ebenhoch and Pernerstorfer (eds), *Stenographisches Protokoll*, 212.
99 See Wadauer, *Die Tour der Gesellen*.
100 Wadauer, 'Tramping in Search of Work'.
101 'Natural-Verpflegsstationen in Niederösterreich', 1888, 1.
102 See Jodlbauer, *Ein Mensch zieht in die Welt*, 118.
103 On this system, see Wadauer, *Der Arbeit nachgehen?*; Wadauer, 'Establishing Distinctions', 2011.
104 In fact, relief stations were run by municipalities; see Wadauer, *Der Arbeit nachgehen?*, 55–66.
105 Steinhardt, *Lebenserinnerungen*, 110.
106 Steinhardt, *Lebenserinnerungen*, 83.
107 Steinhardt, *Lebenserinnerungen*, 110.
108 Steinhardt, *Lebenserinnerungen*, 111.
109 Steinhardt, *Lebenserinnerungen*, 113.
110 On such sources and narratives in general, see Wadauer, *Die Tour der Gesellen*.
111 Deutsch, *Ein weiter Weg*, 49. The German baker Karl Ernst mentioned in his autobiographical account that a fellow 'corrected' the occupation in his documents from 'apprentice' to his actual status of a journeyman; see *Aus dem Leben eines Handwerksburschen. Erinnerungen von Karl Ernst*, 114–16.
112 Holek, *Lebensgang eines deutsch-tschechischen Handarbeiters*, 248.
113 *Die Geschichte zweier Leben*, 13–14.
114 Jodlbauer, *Ein Mensch zieht in die Welt*, 120.
115 Hanusch, *Auf der Walze*, 37.
116 Petzold, *Das rauhe Leben*.
117 Kirschner, *Die Tagebücher Alfons Petzolds*, vols. 1, 8, 10, 20, 27.
118 Kirschner, *Die Tagebücher Alfons Petzolds*, vols. 1, 8, 10.
119 Popp, *Haussklavinnen*, 19, 26, 31.
120 Popp, *Die Jugendgeschichte einer Arbeiterin*, 76.
121 Landerl, *Mein Lebenslauf*, 3.
122 They helped to establish 'contractual discipline', as Ricciardi put it; see Ricciardi, 'Categorizing Difference', 339.

123 'Gewerbeordnung, Motive'.
124 Ingwer, *Der sogenannte Arbeitsvertrag*, 25.
125 On such questions in a colonial context, see Tiquet, 'Connecting the "Inside" and the "Outside"', 2019; Tiquet, 'Challenging Colonial Forced Labor? Resistance, Resilience, and Power in Senegal (1920s–1940s)', 2018.
126 Steinfeld, *Coercion, Contract and Free Labor*, 321.

Bibliography

'Antrag des Abgeordneten Smitka, Palme und Genossen, betreffend die Beseitigung der Arbeitsbücher (Entlaßscheine, Seedienstbücher)', *Stenographische Protokolle über die Sitzungen des Hauses der Abgeordneten des österreichischen Reichsrathes*, XXI Session, Beilage 70. Wien: Kaiserlich-königliche Hof- und Staatsdruckerei, 1911.
'Arbeitsbücher und Schwarze Listen', *Arbeiter Zeitung* 22 (19.3.1910) 77: 8–9.
Aus dem Leben eines Handwerksburschen. Erinnerungen von Karl Ernst, 3rd ed. Neustadt im Schwarzwald: Karl Wehrle, 1912.
Becker, Peter. 'The Practice of Control and the Illusion of Evidence: Passports and Personal Identification in Cities of Habsburg Austria.' In *Migration Policies and Materialities of Identification in European Cities: Papers and Gates, 1500s to 1930s*, edited by Hilde Greefs and Anne Winter, 217–42. New York/London: Routledge, 2019.
'Bergarbeiter aufgepasst!', *Arbeiterwille* 3 (17.11.1892) 22: 3–5.
Bericht der k. k. Gewerbe-Inspektoren über ihre Amtsthätigkeit. Wien: Druck und Verlag der kaiserlich-königlichen Staatsdruckerei, 1884–1916, available at https://anno.onb.ac.at/.
Böninger, Alfred. *Die Bestrafung des Arbeitsvertragsbruchs der Arbeiter. Insbesondere der gewerblichen Arbeiter*. Tübingen: Laupp, 1891.
Brichta, Rudolf. 'Das Dienstzeugnis. Eine gewerbepolitische Studie', *Juristische Blätter* XXXV (1906) 10: 109–112 and 11: 121–24.
Bundesgesetzblatt (BGBl.).
Caspaar, Moriz. 'Zur praktischen Anwendung des § 80 der Gewerbe-Ordnung (Vorzeitiger Austritt.)', *Zeitschrift für Verwaltung* XVI (1.3.1883) 9: 33–4.
'Das Arbeitsbuch', *Salzburger Wacht* 12 (16.8.1911) 184: 1.
'Der Magistrat der Stadt Wien', *Wienerzeitung* (3.5.1860) 27: 108.
Deutsch, Julius. *Ein weiter Weg. Lebenserinnerungen*. Zürich/Leipzig/Wien: Amaltea, 1960.
Die Geschichte zweier Leben von Ignaz und Karl Danzinger. Nach Original Aufzeichnungen geschrieben von Helga Köhler. Typescript, Dokumentation lebensgeschichtlicher Aufzeichnungen, University of Vienna, 1994.
'Die Gewerbenovelle', *Die Arbeit* 3 (5.4.1896) 83: 162–3.
Ebenhoch, Alfred and Pernerstorfer, Engelbert (eds). *Stenographisches Protokoll der Gewerbe-Enquête im österreichischen Abgeordnetenhause sammt geschichtlicher Einleitung und Anhang*. Wien: Kaiserlich-königliche Hof- und Staatsdruckerei, 1893.
Eckert, Andreas (ed). *Global Histories of Work*. Berlin/Boston: De Gruyter, 2016.
Ehmer, Josef. 'Zünfte in Österreich in der frühen Neuzeit'. In *Das Ende des Ancién Regimes. Zünfte in Europa um 1800*, edited by Heinz-Gerhard Haupt, 87–126. Göttingen: Vandenhoeck & Ruprecht, 2011.
Ehrenfreund, Edm. O. and Mráz, Franz. *Wiener Dienstrecht*. Wien: Manz, 1908.
Eiden-Offe, Patrik. '"Weisse Sclaven", oder: Wie frei ist die Lohnarbeit? Freie und unfreie Arbeit in den ökonomisch-literarischen Debatten des Vormärz'. In *Geld und Ökonomie im Vormärz*, edited by Jutta Nickel, 183–214. Bielefeld: Aisthesis, 2014.
Engerman, Stanley L. 'Introduction'. In *Terms of Labor. Slavery, Serfdom, and Free Labor*, edited by Stanley Engerman, 9–19. Stanford: Stanford University Press, 1999.
Engerman, Stanley. 'Institutional Change', *Journal of Comparative Economics* 40 (2012) 4: 596–603.
'Entschädigungspflicht des Arbeiters wegen Kontraktbruchs. Die Anwendung des Gesetzes', *Die Arbeit* 14 (14.4.1907), 965: 8256.
Ertl, Moriz. 'Bericht der k. k. Gewerbeinspektoren über ihre Amtsthätigkeit im Jahre 1884. Wien 1885', *Statistische Monatsschrift* 12 (1886): 54–9.

Gerstenberger, Heide. *Markt und Gewalt. Die Funktionsweise des historischen Kapitalismus*. Münster: Westfälisches Dampfboot, 2018.

'Gewerbeordnung. Regierungsvorlage. Motive'. In *Stenographische Protokolle über die Sitzungen des Hauses der Abgeordneten des österreichischen Reichsrathes* XI, Beilage 253. Wien: Kaiserlich-königliche Hof- und Staatsdruckerei, 1881.

Hanusch, Ferdinand. *Auf der Walze*. Wien: Selbstverlag, 1907.

Heilinger, Alois. *Österreichisches Gewerberecht*. Wien: Manz, 1909.

Heindl, Waltraud and Saurer, Edith (eds). *Grenze und Staat. Paßwesen, Staatsbürgerschaft, Heimatrecht und Fremdengesetzgebung in der österreichischen Monarchie (1750–1867)*. Wien: Böhlau, 2000.

Heller, Emil. *Das österreichische Gewerberecht mit Berücksichtigung der Gewerbenovelle vom 5. Februar 1907, RGBl. Nr. 26*. Wien: Manz, 1908.

Hirsch-Kreinsen, Hartmut. 'Arbeit'. In *Handbuch Soziologie*, edited by Nina Baur et al., 33–53. Wiesbaden: VS Verlag für Sozialwissenschaften, 2008.

Holek, Wenzel. *Lebensgang eines deutsch-tschechischen Handarbeiter*. Mit einem Vorwort herausgegeben von Paul Göhre. Jena: Diederichs, 1909.

Ingwer, Isidor. *Der sogenannte Arbeitsvertrag. Eine sozialpolitische Studie*. Wien: Verl. d. "Österreichischen Metallarbeiter", 1895.

Ingwer, Isidor. *Die Rechtsstreitigkeiten vor dem Gewerbegerichte*. Wien: Konegen, 1899.

Ingwer, Isidor. *Das Arbeitsverhältnis nach öffentlichem Recht. Eine systematische Darstellung*. Wien: Brand, 1905.

Ingwer, Isidor. *Zwei Fesseln des Koalitionsrechtes*. Wien: Österr. Metallarbeiterverband, 1912.

'Ist das Arbeitsbuch ein Machtmittel in der Hand des Unternehmers?', *Die Arbeit* 10 (25.9.1903) 750: 6538.

Jodlbauer, Josef. *Ein Mensch zieht in die Welt/Ein Mensch sieht die Welt. Selbstbiographie eines Altösterreichers*. Typoskript 1947–1948, Dokumentation lebensgeschichtlicher Aufzeichnungen, University of Vienna.

K. k. Justizministerium (ed). *Sammlung von Entscheidungen der (k. k.) Gewerbegerichte*. Wien: Kaiserlich-königliche Hof- und Staatsdruckerei, 1900–1918. (In 1919 the title changed to: Bundesministerium für Justiz (ed.). *Sammlung von Entscheidungen der Gewerbegerichte und Einigungsämter*. Wien: Österreichische Staatsdruckerei.)

K. k. Polizei-Direction (ed). *Die Polizeiverwaltung Wiens*. Wien: Hölder, 1877–1892, available at https://www.digital.wienbibliothek.at/wbrobv/periodical/titleinfo/1440552.

Keiser, Thorsten. *Vertragszwang und Vertragsfreiheit im Recht der Arbeit von der frühen Neuzeit bis in die Moderne*. Frankfurt am Main: Vittorio Klostermann, 2013.

Kirschner, Elfriede. *Die Tagebücher Alfons Petzolds 1904–1922. Nach den Originalhandschriften und den Teildrucken herausgegeben, kommentiert, mit einer Bibliographie und einer revidierten Lebensbeschreibung versehen*. Unpublished PhD thesis, University of Innsbruck, 1884, Vol. 1.

Landerl, Adolf. *Mein Lebenslauf*. Manuscript 1936, Dokumentation lebensgeschichtlicher Aufzeichnungen, University of Vienna.

Landgraf, F. *Die Sicherung des Arbeits-Vertrages. Eine juridisch-ökonomische Studie*. Berlin: Lüderitz, 1873.

Landriani, Martino Sacchi. 'Rethinking the Livret d'ouvriers: Time, Space and "Free" Labor in Nineteenth Century France', *Labour History* 60 (2019) 6: 854–64.

Lichtenberger, Sabine, '"Überbleibsel aus längst vergangenen Tagen" – Bemerkungen zur Geschichte des Verbotes von schwarzen Listen, geheimen Zeichen und Arbeitsbüchern in Österreich', *Das Recht der Arbeit (DRdA)* 3 (2020) 388: 271–77.

Linden, Marcel van der. 'Dissecting Coerced Labour'. In *On Coerced Labor: Work and Compulsion after Chattel Slavery*, edited by Marcel van der Linden and Magaly Rodriguez Garcia, 291–322. Leiden: Brill, 2016.

Linne, Karsten. 'Von der Arbeitsvermittlung zum "Arbeitseinsatz". Zum Wandel der Arbeitsverwaltung 1933–1945'. In *Arbeit im Nationalsozialismus*, edited by Marc Buggeln and Michael Wildt, 53–70. Berlin/Boston: De Gruyter, Oldenbourg, 2014.

Marchet, Gustav. 'Zur Reform der österreichischen Gewerbe-Gesetzgebung', *Österreichische Zeitschrift für Gesetzgebung und Rechtsprechung* 2 (1878) 3 and 4: 157–227.

Mayerhofer, Ernst. *Handbuch für den politischen Verwaltungsdienst in den im Reichsrathe vertretenen Königreichen und Ländern mit besonderer Berücksichtigung der diesen Ländern gemeinsamen Gesetzen und Verordnungen*, Vol. 3. Wien: Manz, 1897.

Morgenstern, Hugo. *Gesindewesen und Gesinderecht in Österreich*. Wien: Hölder, 1902.
Morgenstern, Hugo. *Österreichisches Gesinderecht*. Wien: Hölder, 1912.
'Natural-Verpflegsstationen in Niederösterreich und ihre Wirksamkeit', *Tagespost* XXIV (26.1.1888) 21: 1–2.
'Patent vom 24. Februar 1827. Aufhebung der Kundschaften, Zeugnisse, Wanderpässe für Handwerksgesellen und Arbeiter. Einführung der Wanderbücher'. In *Seiner k. k. Majestät Franz des Ersten politische Gesetze und Verordnungen für sämmtliche Provinzen des Österreichischen Kaiserstaates, mit Ausnahme von Ungarn und Siebenbürgen*, 231–2. Wien: k. k. Hof- u. Staats-Aeralial-Druckerei, 1829.
Patterson, Orlando and Zhuo, Xiaolin. 'Modern Trafficking, Slavery and Other Forms of Servitude', *Annual Review of Sociology* 44 (2018): 407–39.
Petzold, Alfons. *Das rauhe Leben. Der Roman eines Menschen*. Berlin/Weimar: Aufbau-Verlag, 1985.
Pfersche, Emil. *Das gewerbliche Arbeitsverhältnis nach österreichischem Rechte mit Einschluß der Unfall- und Krankenversicherung der Arbeiter*. Wien: Manz, 1892.
Pierson, Thomas. *Das Gesinde und die Herausbildung moderner Privatrechtsprinzipien*. Frankfurt am Main: Vittorio Klostermann, 2016.
Popp, Adelheid. *Haussklavinnen. Ein Beitrag zur Lage der Dienstmädchen*. Wien: Brand, 1912.
Popp, Adelheid. *Die Jugendgeschichte einer Arbeiterin*. 3rd ed. München: Ernst Reinhardt, 1927.
Přibram, Karl. 'Die juristische Struktur des gewerblichen Abeitsverhältnisses nach österreichischem Recht', *Zeitschrift für das Privat- und Öffentliche Recht der Gegenwart* 31 (1904): 695–730.
Reichsgesetzblatt (RGBl.).
Ricciardi, Ferruccio. 'Categorizing Difference: Labor and the Colonial Experience (French Empire, First Half of the 20th Century)'. In *Decentering Comparative Analysis in a Globalizing World*, edited by Olivier Giraud and Michel Lallement, 326–46. Leiden/Boston: Brill, 2021.
Richter, Jessica. *Die Produktion besonderer Arbeitskräfte. Auseinandersetzungen um den häuslichen Dienst in Österreich (Ende des 19. Jahrhunderts bis 1938)*. Unpublished PhD thesis, University of Vienna 2017.
Schmoller, Gustav. 'Die Natur des Arbeitsvertrages und der Kontraktbruch', *Zeitschrift für die gesamte Staatswissenschaft* 30 (1874) 3–4: 449–527.
Schreiber, Karl. 'Der Arbeitsvertrag nach heutigem österreichischem Privatrecht. (Fortsetzung)'. In *Allgemeine österreichische Gerichts-Zeitung* XXXVIII (NF XXIV) (15.2.1887) 7: 49–51.
Soušek, Jakob. *Der rechtliche Charakter der Arbeitskonflikte. Wege zur Sicherung rechtlicher Zustände auf dem Gebiete des Arbeitsvertrages*. Wien: Perles, 1914.
Staatsgesetzblatt (StGBl.).
Stanziani, Alessandro. 'The Legal Status of Labour from the Seventeenth to the Nineteenth Century: Russia in a Comparative European Perspective', *International Review of Social History* 54 (2009) 3: 359–89.
Statistisches Jahrbuch der Stadt Wien 1898–1914, available at https://www.wienbibliothek.at/.
Steinfeld, Robert J. *Coercion, Contract and Free Labor in the Nineteenth Century*. Cambridge: Cambridge University Press, 2001.
Steinfeld, Robert J. and Engerman, Stanley L. 'Labour – Free or Coerced? A Historical Reassessment of Differences and Similarities'. In *Free and Unfree Labour: The Debate Continues*, edited by Tom Brass and Marcel van der Linden, 107–26. Bern/Berlin/New York/Paris: Peter Lang, 1997.
Steinhardt, Karl. *Lebenserinnerungen eines Wiener Arbeiters*, edited by Manfred Mugrauer. Wien: Alfred Klahr Gesellschaft, 2013.
Steinmetz, Willibald. *Begegnungen vor Gericht. Eine Sozial- und Kulturgeschichte des Englischen Arbeitsrechtes. (1850–1925)*. München: Oldenbourg, 2002.
Stieda, Wilhelm. 'Arbeitsbuch'. In *Handwörterbuch der Staatswissenschaften*, edited by J. Conrad et al., Vol. 1, 598–604. Jena: Fischer, 1890.
Tálos, Emmerich and Wörister, Karl. *Soziale Sicherung im Sozialstaat Österreich. Entwicklung – Herausforderungen – Strukturen*. Baden-Baden: Nomos, 1994.
Tiquet, Romain. 'Connecting the "Inside" and the "Outside" World: Convict Labour and Mobile Penal Camps in Colonial Senegal (1930s–1950)', *International Review of Social History* 64 (2019): 473–91.
Tiquet, Romain. 'Challenging Colonial Forced Labor? Resistance, Resilience, and Power in Senegal (1920s–1940s)', *International Labor and Working-Class History* 93 (2018): 135–50.
Van den Eeckhout, Patricia. 'Giving Notice: The Legitimate Way of Quitting and Firing (Ghent, 1877–1896)'. In *Experiencing Wages: Social and Cultural Aspects of Wage Forms in Europe*

since 1500, edited by Peter Scholliers and Leonard Schwarz, 81–109. New York/Oxford: Berghahn, 2003.

'Verhaltung von Arbeitern zur Rückkehr in die Arbeit', *Architekten- und Baumeister-Zeitung*, XVIII (31.10.1909) 44: 4–5.

Verkauf, Leo. 'Arbeitsvertrag'. In *Österreichisches Staatswörterbuch. Handbuch des gesamten österreichischen öffentlichen Rechtes*, edited by Ernst Mischler and Josef Ulbrich, 2nd ed., Vol. 1, 149–87. Wien: Hölder, 1905.

Vormbaum, Thomas. *Politik und Gesinderecht im 19. Jahrhundert (vornehmlich in Preußen 1810–1918)*. Berlin: Duncker & Humblot, 1980.

Wadauer, Sigrid. *Die Tour der Gesellen. Mobilität und Biographie im Handwerk vom 18. bis zum 20. Jahrhundert*. Frankfurt am Main/New York: Campus, 2005.

Wadauer, Sigrid. 'Establishing Distinctions: Unemployment Versus Vagrancy in Austria from the Late Nineteenth Century to 1938', *International Review of Social History* 56 (2011) 1: 31–70.

Wadauer, Sigrid. 'Tramping in Search of Work: Practices of Wayfarers and of Authorities (Austria 1880–1938)'. In *The History of Labour Intermediation: Institutions and Finding Employment in the Nineteenth and Early Twentieth Centuries*, edited by Sigrid Wadauer, Thomas Buchner and Alexander Mejstrik, 286–334. New York/Oxford: Berghahn, 2015.

Wadauer, Sigrid. *Der Arbeit nachgehen? Auseinandersetzungen um Lebensunterhalt und Mobilität (Österreich 1880–1938)*. Wien/Köln/Weimar: Böhlau, 2021.

Wadauer, Sigrid. 'Kategorisierung, Kontrolle, Vertrauen? Arbeits- und Identitätsdokumente im 19. und frühen 20. Jahrhundert'. In *Sicherheit und Differenz in historischer Perspektive. Security and Difference in Historical Perspective*, edited by Sigrid Ruby and Anja Krause, 265–91. Baden Baden: Nomos, 2022.

'Weg mit dem Arbeitsbuch', *Arbeiterwille* 20 (11.7.1909) 188: 7–8.

Wobbe, Theresa, Renard, Léa, Schalkowski, Nicola and Braig, Marianne. 'Deutungsmodelle von Arbeit im Spiegel kolonialer und geschlechtlicher Dimensionen: Kategorisierungsprozesse von "Zwangsarbeit" während der Zwischenkriegszeit (Interpretative Models of Work in the Mirror of Colonial and Gender Dimensions: Categorization Processes of "Forced Labour" during the Interwar Period)', *Zeitschrift für Soziologie* 52/2 (2023): 172–90. https://doi.org/10.1515/zfsoz-2023-2014.

'Wochenschau', *Juristische Blätter* XVIII (1889) 26: 304–5.

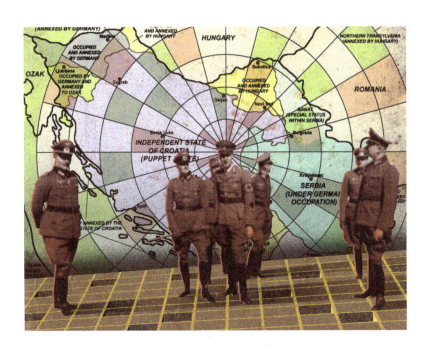

4
Working for the enemy: civil servants in occupied Serbia, 1941–1944
Nataša Milićević and Ljubinka Škodrić

The Nazi occupation of Serbia that began in the spring of 1941 had a great impact on the state administration. Germany and its allies attacked, defeated and then divided the Kingdom of Yugoslavia at the beginning of April 1941.[1] Serbia, which was an integral part of Yugoslavia, was reduced to its narrowest borders (central Serbia, Banat and the northern part of Kosovo) and occupied by German military forces.[2] The Germans labelled the Serbs and Serbia as the main causes of 'European disorder',[3] when, following a military coup on 27 March 1941, they rejected the earlier signed Tripartite Pact in a move that was supported by the population with mass demonstrations. Serbia was subsequently invaded and punished by the imposition of a strict regime of German military occupation.[4]

With the occupation of the Kingdom of Yugoslavia, the Yugoslav civil service apparatus became divided between different areas: annexed areas, areas under occupation and seemingly sovereign areas.[5] Civil servants of Serbian origin were expelled and forced to leave the other territories of the former Yugoslav state and move to occupied Serbia. Their number is difficult to estimate, as well as the number of civil servants who were taken as prisoners of war after the April War.[6] According to some data, the total number of refugees was approximately 400,000,[7] while about 100,000 people from the territory of occupied Serbia were prisoners of war.[8] This created two important problems for both the occupation and domestic authorities, which, at first sight, seem contradictory: first, it made it impossible for certain public services to function because large parts of their staff were taken as prisoners of war. And second, it increased pressure on the civil servant labour market by the influx of new candidates to existing jobs.

Before the Second World War, civil servants represented some kind of elite due to the small number of literate people in the country. In 1931, 40.96 per cent of the population in Serbia was literate.[9] This was not reflected in salaries, which, except for those of the highest-ranking civil servants (about 20,000 men), were insufficient to lead a decent life.[10] However, in a country heavily dependent on agriculture and livestock, and which was still suffering from the repercussions of the Great Depression,[11] civil servant work provided relatively secure income, opportunities for advancement, reputation and influence.[12]

In this chapter we examine the complex and contradictory dynamics of the work of civil servants in the conditions of wartime occupation. Civil service, on the one hand, provided civil servants with a certain financial security. On the other hand, however, it forced them to become an integral part of the war machine. Therefore, the question arises of what kind of options the civil servants had. What types of coercive measures were used in relation to the work of the civil servants? What was the relationship between their salary and the demands and expectations of the occupation as well as collaborationist authorities? Did salary become a means of coercion or even a strategic instrument of war?

In contrast to coercion in the work of labourers and other civilians,[13] researchers have only sporadically mentioned coercion in the work of civil servants.[14] The dynamics of ideological, political and economic factors of coercion and their influence on the work and salary of civil servants have thus remained outside the focus of researchers. In our analysis, we understand the coercion exerted by the occupation regime not only as a way to discipline civil servants but also as a means to ensure their loyalty. This was done by threats that caused fear for work and income, by curtailing political and civic rights, by not allowing them to quit work and by giving positive incentives to loyal civil servants.[15] While earlier there had been a tendency to depoliticise civil service, during war and occupation ideological and political suitability and loyalty became the most important aspects of this work. In addition to the coercive mechanisms stipulated, which weakened their own status and remuneration, civil servants were forced to carry out new decrees issued by the occupation and collaboration authorities. This meant that they themselves had to enforce coercion against the population. For example, they had to apply violent measures to collect grain from the peasants, and for that work they guaranteed 'not only with their position, but if necessary with their lives'.[16] As this chapter will show, during the occupation the government's supervision of civil servants acquired the character of coercion because it was disproportionately strengthened and expanded. Control extended far beyond the quality of work and into the very person of the civil servant whose ideological and political traits came under supervision. Keeping the job – and with it the salary and the opportunity to make ends meet in wartime – correlated strongly with the notion of loyalty.

This chapter is based on the analysis of archival sources created by the occupation and collaborationist authorities. They include legal regulations (orders, decrees, notifications and so on), statements, petitions, appeals, dismissals, statistics, and lists of 'unreliable' civil servants and their political orientation, as well as reports on resistance and coercive tools.[17] A certain limitation in the research occurs due to insufficient statistical data related to the precise number of employed, dismissed and punished civil servants, as well as the salaries of various professions within the civil service. However, the strengths of this study are the preserved statistics on the purchasing power and average incomes of civil servants, which allow us to explore their socioeconomic position.[18]

The archival sources offer insights into different types of coercion as well as the mechanisms by which coercion was exercised. In the following, we argue that coercion in the case of civil servants in occupied Serbia was carried out by means of job retention and payment strategies. The relationship of occupiers and collaborators with civil servants was marked by ideological pressure, lack of trust and the occupation authorities' constant need for the work performed by civil servants.

Occupation, collaboration and administration

In addition to those who performed standard administrative tasks, civil servants in occupied Serbia included employees in education, health care, public transportation and the police. As during the interwar period (1918–1941), this group included civil servants employed at all levels of government, from the highest government representatives to local structures. There were three basic categories of civil servants subdivided into ten salary grades, with I being the highest grade: 1) higher (university education, grades I to VIII), 2) middle (completed high school, grades V to IX) and 3) lower (incomplete high school, grades VII to X).[19] They received regular monthly salaries which depended on the salary grade and were determined by the governmental budget. Salary grades were calculated based on qualifications, experience and title. Salaries also included allowances for children and periodic raises.

The civil servants had social insurance, the right to a pension after a certain number of years in the service and the right to a holiday.[20] They were subdivided into 'real civil servants' (career civil servants), contractual (part-time) civil servants and daily civil servants, according to the type of contract. Unlike 'real civil servants', the other two types of civil servants did not receive a salary, but remuneration in the form of an occasional or regular allowance.[21]

The working status of civil servants in occupied Serbia was based on the prewar Civil Servants Act, which, like most other acts, was retained by the occupation authorities.[22] It was not easy to secure the collaboration of the civil service of the state which was abolished by force. Therefore an emphasis was placed, at least initially, on fear of punishment rather than on willing collaboration. As early as 14 April 1941, the German authorities ordered civil servants to continue their work, promising the same remuneration as before.[23] Eight days later, on 22 April 1941, they introduced their wartime military legislation, which penalised any kind of disobedience to German orders.[24] During the occupation, the Serbian administration, under the supervision of the Germans, passed numerous decrees, orders and bans that changed some prewar regulations of the employment of civil servants, the duration of their work, the required nationality and ideological and political orientation of civil servants, salaries and the conditions for the termination of the civil service.

Under German pressure, Serbian civil servants had little choice. Not reporting for duty and refusing to work could be interpreted as a failure to comply with orders and, hence, as a hostile act, which in turn meant they could stand trial according to the recently introduced German criminal code.[25] Apart from the fact that they had to work as their livelihood depended on their salary, no one able to work was allowed to be out of work under the conditions of the wartime economy and the occupation. Those who refused to work and earn a livelihood, or lost their jobs through no fault of their own, risked being labelled 'idlers'. Such identification as a non-worker entailed penalties that often took the form of forced labour, which meant, for example, having to work for a certain period in a sector determined by the occupation authorities.[26] In some cases, people were afraid to leave their homes due to the news that the Germans were taking citizens off the streets for various types of work.[27] A physician, for example, who had retired in his early fifties, feared in 1943 that 'he might be taken to another place to work, and to perform different tasks'.[28] Civil servants could, in theory, change their profession and leave the government sector, but due to the German control of economic and social life, they had a narrow choice.[29]

The Germans did not have direct access to individual civil servants. Instead, control took place through the restored Serbian authorities in accordance with the structure of the Serbian administration. Thus, the supreme German authority (Administrative Staff, *Verwaltungsstab*) supervised the work of the collaborationist ministries, while the lower bodies of the German administration (field commands, *Feldkommandantur*, and district commands, *Kreiskommanadantur*) controlled the work of the lower district and county bodies of the Serbian administration. Additionally, there were special German officials in charge of monitoring the work of all public services. However, the German control bodies were not visible, which created the appearance of an independent Serbian administration. Instead of governing, the Serbian authorities became implementers of German policy. At the same time, the Germans established an intelligence apparatus and a branched network of informants through which they accessed intelligence about the entire administrative apparatus as well as about Serbian society more broadly.[30] This allowed them not only to keep full control over the work of the administration but also to act against all those who opposed the occupation regime.

German occupation thus relied on old hierarchies of power, but introduced new rules of governance and created new relationships. After the division of Yugoslavia and its political reorganisation, civil servants received a new employer and new working conditions. Instead of the Yugoslav state, which ceased to exist, it was now the Serbian collaborationist government that, under the supervision of the German military administration, 'managed' the civil service apparatus.

As in other occupied countries, the German authorities in Serbia primarily relied on anti-communist, conservative and pro-German oriented individuals. They were few but they were willing to cooperate. Thus, Milan Aćimović, the prewar Belgrade police chief and Minister of the Interior, became the president of the Council of Commissioners, the first collaborationist government, which functioned until the end of August 1941. After that, a new government headed by General Milan Nedić, the prewar Chief of General Staff and Minister of the Army and Navy, was created, remaining in office until the end of the occupation. Both collaborationist governments had very limited powers.[31] The Germans expected their Serbian collaborators to maintain what they perceived as order. They also expected them to keep up the wartime economy by making sure people continued to work. Because of that, their basic duty was to ensure a sufficiently reliable and loyal civil service which would carry out orders without resistance and implement the goals of the German occupation.

However, the creation of such an apparatus was not an easy undertaking, a fact of which the Serbian collaborationists and the Germans were aware. The Serbian collaborationists expected a war victory of the Third Reich and wanted to provide Serbia with the most favourable position in the 'German New Order'. They thought it necessary to convince the Germans of this and bring the civil servants over to their side. To that end, Serbian collaborationists chose two approaches: the first was related to changing the previous German perception of Serbs as unreliable partners, and the second was to create their own ideological concept intended to be attractive enough to be supported by the population, especially the civil servants. This concept rested on the renunciation of the Kingdom of Yugoslavia as a negative experience that had had a disastrous effect on the Serbian people, leading them to their current bleak position. At the same time, it emphasised the importance of preserving Serbian lives and the restoration of Serbia and its statehood, which would, due to the economic importance of the rural sector, rely on the peasantry.[32]

The issue of (dis)trust

The Germans, however, had no confidence in the Serbian collaborationist administration, the population or the civil service. That distrust stemmed from racial, historical and political factors, as well as the sheer fact that they had violently invaded the country. The Serbs, as a Slavic people, were near the bottom of the Nazi racial hierarchy of peoples.[33] For the Germans, the area inhabited by the Serbs was a 'supplementary economic area', intended to be an area of peace and safe traffic connections to the south of Europe, but also a source of cheap labour, agricultural products and mineral resources.[34] Foreign civil servants who came as occupiers, especially those from Austria, also harboured historical hostility towards Serbia and the Serbian people, who were considered the main culprits for causing the First World War and the final downfall of the Austro-Hungarian Monarchy and the German Empire in 1918.[35]

These reasons for mistrust were strengthened by the view that, due to the rejection of the Tripartite Pact and the coup of 27 March 1941, Serbs and Serbia were enemies of the Third Reich. The previous Yugoslav government, which after long negotiations had signed the Tripartite Pact, had been overthrown two days later, to the great disapproval of the Nazis. Germany not only blamed the Serbian military and political elite for the coup but also the entire Serbian people. Furthermore, civil servants had participated in protests against joining the Tripartite Pact or fought against the German forces as conscripts.[36] Perhaps the best, and at the same time the most unusual, example of civil servants' anti-German attitude was the case of Svetolik Dragačevac, the retired head of Paraćin county. Although legally obliged to protect the reputation of the service and the state,[37] Dragačevac sent an insulting letter to Adolf Hitler in which he expressed his anti-fascism and willingness to resist. On 27 March, he organised a celebration which – not coincidentally – took place on the same day as the coup, only to be arrested immediately after the German occupation and later sent to the Mauthausen concentration camp, where he died in 1942.[38]

The entire nation was under the suspicion of the German occupation authorities as a nation of rebels and opponents of the Germans. That is why rigorous measures of punishment, such as public hangings, burning of villages, intimidation, taking hostages and executions, were adopted as preventive measures and initially applied in response to some attacks on the German authorities. Nevertheless, large parts of the Serbian population resisted the occupation, encouraged by libertarian traditions, an anti-fascist mood and the German attack on the Soviet Union. During the summer and autumn of 1941, resistance movements (both communist and royalist) were organised and an uprising took place. Almost one third of occupied Serbia, with around one million inhabitants, was temporarily liberated.[39] The Germans suppressed the uprising with the most brutal measures and approximately 30,000 inhabitants were killed.[40] Of particular note were the reprisals in Kragujevac, on 20–21 October 1941, in which, according to current knowledge, 2,381 people were shot. Among them were about 200 civil servants (professors, teachers, doctors, judges and administrative officers) and about 240 high school students.[41]

The uprising was followed by a new examination of all civil servants' behaviour, especially in the regions that were the hotbeds of the uprising. If they had helped the insurgents, many civil servants were transferred to other regions, and those who had directly participated not only lost their jobs but also their already limited political rights, or they were put in prison and often lost their lives.[42]

Despite their mistrust, the German authorities needed civil servants. Due to the attack on the Soviet Union and the necessary engagement of as many military forces as possible on the Eastern Front, the German government sought to control occupied Serbia with as few people as possible.[43] However, most civil servants were anti-German.

By the nature of their work, they were forced to implement decrees that deprived those considered enemies of the Nazi 'New Order' of their rights, means of livelihood and property. Among other things, this influenced the weakening of their motivation to work and reduced their authority among the population. In addition, they were convinced of the temporary nature of the occupation and therefore did not want to stand out and compromise.[44]

Laying off and hanging on

The first interventions aimed at creating an obedient administration were related to the dismissal of 'unnecessary' civil servants. This referred to two types of redundancy: one concerned civil servants who were, in the opinion of the collaborationist authorities, not sufficiently 'nationally reliable'. This was also labelled 'purge'. The other was related to a 'real' excess of employed civil servants. According to Prime Minister Milan Aćimović's estimates, the number of civil servants was twice the number necessary for the reduced territory and jurisdiction.[45] The exact size is difficult to establish, but according to some of our estimates, together with the exiled civil servants, it was probably around 100,000.[46]

The first set of measures, common even in peaceful times, included the dismissal of civil servants based on several intersecting criteria, including the cessation of the need for their work and their age, gender, marital status and qualifications. Additionally, with the beginning of the occupation, some services, such as foreign affairs, foreign trade exchange and military affairs, passed into the hands of the occupiers. This ended the need for the work of the civil servants in these sectors. In other cases, civil servants lost their jobs in institutions that were abolished or had the scope of their work reduced, such as the Presidency of the Council of Ministers, the Senate and the National Assembly. The jurisdictions of these institutions, as well as a small number of civil servants who were considered reliable and necessary by the collaborationist authorities, were taken over by the newly created governments under occupation. Thus, salary and job security only applied to those considered loyal and indispensable. Others were simply fired or forced into early retirement, which reduced the size of their pensions.[47]

Female civil servants became the first victims of the reduction of civil servants, since the collaborationist authorities did not approve of the employment of women in general due to their conservative views promoting the man as the sole 'breadwinner of the family'. Among those laid off as part of the reduction, the first were women who were judged to have enough income to support themselves with their parents or spouse and therefore not to need to work. From May 1941 onwards, the dismissal of female civil servants correlated with the level of education and the subsistence minimum set by the Ministry of Finance.[48] Over time, these measures were partially mitigated due to the fact that the subsistence level proved insufficient and more workforce was needed. That was why some of the dismissed female civil servants returned to service. However, their income from working in the service remained insufficient for supporting the family or, for example, sending packages to relatives who were prisoners of war.[49]

The measure of 13 June 1941 put additional pressure on the work and salaries of civil servants, causing numerous layoffs and considerable upheaval. Senior civil servants were the most affected. According to this regulation, all those who had completed 30 years of civil service were retired, and all those who were over 60 years of age and did not have enough years of service to receive a pension were dismissed.[50] Thus, experienced civil servants, who also remembered the Austro-Hungarian occupation during the First World War, were removed from service. Contracts with civil servants (male and female) who were not permanently employed but engaged part-time were also terminated.[51] Subsequently, these measures were gradually eased because it turned out that some institutions would otherwise not be able to function. This concerned, for example, the National Theatre, the Academy of Music and the Academy of Fine Arts.[52]

The second group of measures was typical of the Second World War and the German occupation, being marked by coercion based on racial and ethnic categories. This included the dismissal of civil servants of Jewish and Roma origin. It was carried out under special orders of the German authorities, which the Serbian authorities were forced to implement.[53] The 'racial purity check', which was conducted in conjunction with this measure, required all employed civil servants to sign declarations confirming that they were not Jewish and had no Jewish relatives.[54] In addition, the Serbian authorities, following a similar pattern, tried to dismiss non-Serb civil servants, except those who were married to Serbs. It was thought that members of other nationalities 'did not wish Serbia well'.[55] In practice, the dismissal of non-Serb civil servants was not consistently enforced as a racial purity measure.[56] In its application, selectivity gave local decision-makers more power to influence the fate of individual civil servants, their work and salary.

Two decrees, which entered into force at the beginning of August 1941, had a major impact on the work, labour relations and lives of civil servants in occupied Serbia: the 'Decree on the Systematisation of Jobs in the Civil and Self-Governing Service' and the 'Decree on the Removal of Nationally Unreliable Civil Servants'.[57] The first was supposed to come into force within two months, but was in fact not fully implemented during the entire occupation. The aim of this regulation was to determine the specific needs of individual departments and dismiss redundant employees. It subdivided civil servants into five categories: 1) those who remained in service, 2) those who were dismissed as 'nationally unreliable', 3) those who were due to retire or be removed for any reason, 4) those who were financially secure officials, and 5) civil servants who were not of Serbian nationality.[58] Essentially, this measure only strengthened the previous reduction measures, increasing the insistence on their wider implementation. Considering the slowness of its implementation, the job systematisation measure allowed many civil servants to keep their job and pay. However, at the same time, it also made civil servants constantly worry about their jobs being insecure. The constant fear of losing one's job can be seen as a very intense and devastating coercive mechanism.

The assessment and application of 'national unreliability' or 'national reliability' caused even more intense alarm, fear and discontent. According to the decree, 'nationally unreliable' civil servants were communists and freemasons, as well as those who spread false news, showed propensity for corruption, were careless or irresponsible, or harboured anti-German sentiments.[59] Civil servants who participated in the uprising on the side of the communists also fell under its provisions. The regulation itself was imprecise and vague and therefore interpreted arbitrarily. This led to errors and abuses, which were especially pronounced at lower levels of government.[60]

'Nationally unreliable' civil servants did not have the right to a pension,[61] and many were fired, not only because of their political views but also because of their family ties or friendships with members of the resistance movement.[62] This happened, for example, to Nataša Vasić and Desanka Knežević (both civil servants), the wives of two prominent members of the royalist resistance movement, Dragiša Vasić and Radoje Knežević. Both were dismissed during 1942 due to the political activities of their husbands.[63] The assessment of 'national reliability' included combined moral and political qualifications, personal qualities and quality of work during the service period. In the beginning, the measure also had a punitive function because civil servants dismissed for being 'unreliable and dangerous to public order and peace' not only lost their salary or pension but could also end up in work camps.[64] Nevertheless, the majority of ministers used the more favourable Civil Servants Act from 1931 for the dismissal of civil servants, rather than the Decree on the Removal of Nationally Unreliable Civil Servants.[65] In this way, they not only preserved the civil servants' incomes but also saved them from more serious consequences. And yet, according to some estimates, primarily by the extraordinary commissioner for personnel affairs, Tanasije Dinić, about 10,000 civil servants were dismissed between 1941 and 1944.[66]

Coercion through salaries

Civil servants' salaries were low and remained so. As early as the beginning of the occupation, the Germans prohibited the increase of civil servants' salaries, which were already insufficient to live on for an individual, let alone a family. It was stipulated that they were not to exceed the level they were at on 6 April 1941.[67] Shortly afterwards, in June 1941, Serbian authorities banned all new appointments, promotions and periodic raises.[68] This second measure particularly affected younger civil servants, who, after training, expected to get a job or receive a salary increase through promotion. Freezing prices, wages and salaries by general decree was a measure typical of the economy of the Third Reich.[69] By controlling salaries in occupied Serbia, the Germans achieved several goals: they slowed down the growth of inflation, saved funds for the support of their occupying forces and initiated coercive measures on the economic and social status of civil servants.[70]

It is important to understand the relationship between salary and cost of living, and how salary affected the work of civil servants. At the beginning of the occupation, the average monthly salary of a civil servant with a university degree, two children and 10 years of service on salary grade VI amounted to 2,839.40 dinars. An unmarried civil servant trainee with a university degree on salary grade VIII earned 1,596.37 dinars, and a civil servant with a complete high school education who was married with two children and 10 years of service on salary grade VII received 2,539.37 dinars. Their salaries covered only about 56 per cent of the total cost of living. At the end of 1942, the regular income and expenses of civil servants showed an absolute decline in their standard of living. At that time, the average regular income of civil servants covered only 10 per cent of the actual needs of a family. Civil servants were in a slightly worse position than industrial workers, with an average salary of almost half the salary of such workers. Industrial workers played a more significant role in the war economy and had a better, although often insufficient, supply of food. This relationship is best seen in average annual earnings. In December 1942, including periodic raises, it was 52,072.80 dinars for civil servants on the above-mentioned salary grade VI, and 93,600.00 dinars for workers.[71] Civil servants became completely dependent on the regime because they could hardly ever find a better-paid job with better conditions. Furthermore, working in the civil service provided certain legally guaranteed benefits.

Salaries were losing value with shortages of consumer goods and rising inflation – which was becoming rampant despite German attempts to keep it in check. However, the Serbian government tried to economically stimulate the work of civil servants. It managed to circumvent the ban on salary increases by reintroducing monthly allowances that became permanent over time.[72] Therefore, the average monthly salary of civil servants in 1943 increased by about 30 per cent, compared to 1941.[73] In a way, this salary increase was ironic because by that time, inflation had reached high levels. Prices of products on the black market had risen by up to 1,600 per cent and on the regular market by up to 300–400 per cent.[74] This is why the Serbian government introduced aid for civil servants in the form of food, clothing and firewood. Most people lived by selling valuable items from home or bartering them for food. Some civil servants were even forced to use their children for begging.[75]

Only those civil servants in the highest positions received financial and other forms of privileges. The highest civil servants in the rank of ministers had salaries that were almost five times higher (around 19,000 dinars) than that of the average civil servant at the end of 1942. The salary of the head of the Directorate for Supplying the Population of the City of Belgrade (DIRIS) was more than seven times higher (30,000 dinars). Various other benefits, such as secured food supply, cigarettes and clothes, were added on top of this.[76]

High prices and food shortages, combined with low incomes, led to problems in maintaining discipline, poor quality of work, widespread corruption and a constant search for alternative sources of income. At the same time, the working conditions of civil servants were not favourable. Most of them spent their working hours in offices that were not heated in the winter. Despite the relentless orders and threats, it was difficult to get civil servants to stay disciplined in such conditions. They did not come to the office on time, left work before the end of working hours or did private business during working hours.[77] Many, however, did so out of necessity, as they were forced to search for food and other basic needs. Delays, lack of enthusiasm, corruption and fraud were widespread.

The occupiers and collaborationist authorities insisted on quality work while depreciating civil servants by criticising and disrespecting them in public. They stressed their inappropriate attitude towards the clients and their superiors, a rhetoric which they used to demand a certain polite attitude from civil servants, fit for employees in state service.[78] Bureaucratic apathy, slowness and inefficiency, which had been dominant traits in the prewar period, intensified and became more visible during the war. Given the circumstances of the war, civil servants found it pointless to work with diligence and discipline. This also showed a lack of support for the collaborationist government's policies, which could be seen as a kind of silent sabotage.

The combination of the above factors, as well as the scarcity of opportunities to find new, more profitable and legal jobs, influenced various officials to turn to illegal activities on the black market. This type of activity was quite common among heads of the counties and municipal presidents, who were powerful in their areas. Some, like the head of the county in Mladenovac, sold at high prices various goods that had been appropriated during the war, or pardoned punishments – usually of wealthier people such as merchants – for money. Others, like the president of the municipality in Leskovac, used blackmail and physical violence to obtain material goods.[79] Many of them enjoyed the protection of the occupation and collaborationist authorities and were not punished for corruption or were given light sentences.[80] Such a situation caused the social role, prestige and authority of civil servants to decline not only among the population but also within the class itself.

From ideological coercion to forced labour

Ideological conformity stood at the heart of the system, and political motivations informed not only layoffs but also hiring decisions. The latter were carried out despite the restrictions and, basically, concerned two categories of new hires. The first were civil-servant refugees from other former Yugoslav territories. The collaborationist government believed these refugees would make better and more loyal civil servants thanks to the help given to them in time of need. Also, their employment solved a serious social problem that would have been caused by massive unemployment among refugees.[81] The second category included those that the occupation and collaborationist authorities considered ideologically desirable and necessary. The employment of both categories created a division into 'old' and 'new' civil servants. The 'old' ones, who made up the majority, hardly did more than what they had to do, while the 'new' ones, by German approval and in order to support the occupation regime, had higher incomes (between 4,000 and 7,000 dinars), were more active and tended to try to prove and impose themselves.[82]

The two groups, 'old' and 'new', perceived their own attitude towards work and participation in the politics of the collaborationist authorities differently, which also brought discord between them. Each of them considered their own activity as correct, justified and patriotic. The 'old' civil servants looked at the 'new' employees with fear, suspicion, mistrust and insufficient appreciation. The 'new' civil servants, in turn, complained that they were exposed to 'endless chicanery by their superiors', who usually were of the 'old' group and who thought that the national work of 'new' civil servants was in fact 'policing, espionage, etc.'. This was partially true because some of the 'new' officers worked for police service as informants.[83]

Among the 'new' civil servants, the members of the pro-fascist movement 'Zbor', who were most often employed in propaganda jobs (writing articles, giving lectures and public speeches, etc.), stood out. A telling example is Borivoje Karapandžić, a member of the Zbor movement and the newly hired head of the propaganda department of the district administration in Valjevo. He criticised the work of civil servants from this district administration, describing them as communists and defeatists who ridiculed the work of the government. He even publicly accused his prewar professor Momčilo Mihailović of spreading communism among students. Soon after the accusation, the professor was arrested, deported to a camp and ultimately shot.[84]

Visible forms of ideological coercion included requests to civil servants to sign declarations of loyalty to the measures of the Serbian collaborationist authorities. They were also common in other occupation regimes, for example in France.[85] One such declaration of loyalty was requested at the end of 1942 from both active and retired civil servants. All civil servants were required to pledge to fight those who threatened peace and order, especially communists and freemasons, and to actively support the course and policy of the collaborationist government. There could be serious consequences for those who refused or failed to sign the declaration. Even after signing, their income or pension could still be taken away if the superior who vouched for them refused to give them a guarantee.[86] Depending on the interpersonal relationships between civil servants, this could be used for revenge or blackmail and for exerting additional pressure.

Civil servants were also exposed to ideological coercion outside their workplace. They were expected to attend propaganda lectures and exhibitions, to be actively involved in anti-communist propaganda, to support occupation and collaborationist policies, and pave a 'new path for Serbia' within Nazi Europe.[87]

Unlike these visible examples of ideological coercion, there were also invisible forms. It was expected of civil servants, especially heads of departments, to report anyone who associated with communists or helped them, or carried out any kind of anti-German and anti-Nedić propaganda.[88] For example, Mihailo Avramović, a well-known prewar ideologist of the cooperative movement, who became the president of the Privileged Agrarian Bank in 1943, refused to report communist civil servants despite being aware this could be perceived as sabotage. As Avramović later stated, an additional contribution to the resistance was that he refused to speak German, although he knew it very well, which the Germans deeply resented.[89]

For civil servants in less esteemed positions than Avramović, such behaviour could translate to severe suspicion, which often led to arrest and, possibly, mandatory or forced labour. These were, in contrast to ideological coercion, obvious forms of coercion, not unusual in conditions of war. In fact, Serbian civil servants were not infrequently required to carry out additional mandatory work alongside their public service.

At the beginning of the occupation, civil servants had not been subjected to any form of state-organised coerced labour unless they were of Jewish origin.[90] However, due to developments on the fronts, the demand for workers grew. While being occasionally included in those forms of work from 1942 onward, civil servants became more severely exploited the following year as they were required to participate in various types of public works. One of them was '*kuluk*', a practice that dates back to the time of Ottoman rule (the fifteenth to sixteenth centuries).[91] *Kuluk* referred to short-term mandatory duties of public importance for the local community (for example, repair of municipal roads, maintenance of streets, roads, railways and telephone lines or securing citizens' safety, works arranged by the German authorities).[92] Those who were summoned by local or occupation authorities to carry out mandatory duties worked for a few days while continuing to live in their own homes, and in some cases they received remuneration.

As in interwar Yugoslavia, *kuluk* included the opportunity to buy oneself out of the obligation by cash payment. The amount varied and was determined by local authorities based on the size of the salary prescribed for this type of work in a given region or district. However, it also happened that persons who had already paid the ransom were again called to work due to the lack of manpower.[93] Although civil servants as well as some other residents were exempted from this type of work, local authorities seem to have applied it to them from 1943 onwards, and civil servants, recruited under *kuluk*, cleared snow from the streets, for example.[94] During the year of 1943, the Municipality of the City of Belgrade, by order of the occupation authorities, provided 500 municipal civil servants per month for public works assigned to them by the occupier. They were to work for three days; non-compliance was to be punished under the Regulation on Mandatory Work and they were sent to labour sites outside of Belgrade.[95] Civil servants also participated in the clearing of ruins created after the Allied bombing of Serbian cities in 1944.[96]

Work in seasonally organised service units at the local level, which were formed due to insufficient manpower, was another type of *kuluk*. For example, in 1943, the employees of the Municipality of the City of Belgrade had to work on the municipal land near Belgrade instead of in the office, regardless of their gender and position. The order was issued by the President of the Municipality of Belgrade. Civil servants were required to work six hours a day for a total of six days during the agricultural work season. For this period, they received the same salary as for their office work.[97] Additionally, the Belgrade Municipality rewarded them in kind by handing out flour, potatoes and beans for their 'commitment'.[98]

In late 1941, the Regulation on Mandatory Work and Restriction of Freedom of Employment of Manual Workers in Mines introduced 'mandatory work'.[99] Initially, civil servants were not included in its coverage, but as the war proceeded, the total mobilisation of the economy for the needs of the Third Reich led to new measures, which declared that each resident of Serbia could face mandatory work placement and even be sent to work in Germany.[100] This was a much more severe measure than *kuluk*, since the civil servants had to work for several months outside their place of residence without the possibility of leave. The working period usually lasted for six months, and civil servants, again, received the same salaries as if they were performing their office work.[101] The punishment for those who did not comply or who helped others called to mandatory labour to avoid it was imprisonment or forced labour in a camp for a period from three months to one year.[102] Civil servants sentenced to forced labour were treated as prisoners:

they stayed in labour camps and were taken to work under guard. Forced labour was a form of punishment for disobedience and disloyalty in the case of civil servants, and the working and living conditions were deliberately made harsh and exhausting.[103]

Conclusion

When considering what civil servants had to endure during the occupation of Serbia in order to keep their jobs and receive their salaries, it is necessary to take into account the complexity of the occupation system, the relationship between different levels of government and the existence of a strong anti-fascist mood in the occupied country.

In a climate of existential fear and suspicion about loyalty, civil servants were exposed to intimidation and coercion on various levels. Job retention was closely related to the right to work in civil service. This can best be seen from the measures of reduction and 'purge' of the civil service apparatus. If job reduction was common even in peaceful times, a 'purge' was not. With this second measure, anti-German and communist-oriented civil servants as well as those deemed 'racially and nationally unfit' (Jews, Roma, non-Serbs) lost their right to work. These measures, in addition to the obvious financial rationalisation, were intended to ensure an ideologically and politically reliable and loyal administrative apparatus.

Civil servants found themselves in a difficult position: they could not give up employment and work as they had to provide for their families, but their work also enabled the functioning of the authorities and was conditioned by them. In this sense, their service during the occupation was not mainly an economic but more an ideological and political issue. The Serbian public saw their work as a form of support of the occupation system, and the coercion exerted on them was often aimed to strengthen their attachment to the occupation system. This is why civil servants, although they could work and earn money, were in constant fear of being accused as collaborators after the war. At the same time, preservation of existence was crucial within the compromises of life under occupation. From the perspective of everyday life, employment was a matter of survival. However, while the systems and forms of coercion were constantly expanded, the value of earnings increasingly declined.

Disciplining the apparatus was carried out by a combination of three types of coercion: ideological coercion, (the threat of) various forms of coerced labour in camps, and salaries at such a low level that people were hardly able to survive or effectively search for employment elsewhere. With the continuation of the war and as a result of the Reich's ever-growing war needs and the lack of workforce, civil servants became increasingly drawn into labour arrangements from which they were originally excluded. This started with *kuluk*, a short-term obligatory community service for seasonal demands, but was quickly extended to mandatory labour for long periods in sectors that were important for the war economy.

By the end of the war, civil servants had lost their authority in the eyes of the population, as had the government itself. The wider population morally condemned them for having worked in the interest of the occupiers instead of the country. This study, however, has shown that the reality was much more nuanced than this. Like many other occupation groups, civil servants realistically assessed their situation, were worried about making ends meet and tried to survive the turbulent times of war and occupation. The fact that the collaborationist government paid their salaries generally did not improve their situation. Rather, job insecurity loomed large and, being at the centre of the administrative apparatus which was run by a hostile foreign oppressor, civil servants as individuals were under constant supervision and coercion.

Notes

1. The country was split into more parts than any other country in Europe. The central parts of Yugoslavia (today's Croatia and Bosnia and Herzegovina) were formed into a new satellite state, the Independent State of Croatia, where two million Serbs were persecuted; see Mazower, *Hitler's Empire*, 133; Petranović, *Srbija u Drugom svetskom ratu*, 124–5.
2. Petranović, *Srbija u Drugom svetskom ratu*, 111–15; Janjetović, 'Jugoslovenski Banat 1941'.
3. Pavlović, *Srbija*, 172.
4. Pavlowitch, *Hitler's New Disorder*, 17–19; Petranović, *Srbija u Drugom svetskom ratu*, 111–47.
5. Zundhauzen, *Istorija Srbije*, 338.
6. This war did not last long: from 6 to 17 April 1941. It shocked contemporaries because they expected strong resistance from the Yugoslav army, which had inherited the famous tradition of resistance of the First World War Serbian army. Germany waged the war under the label of 'Punishment' with the aim of punishing not Yugoslavia but Serbia. Among other things, German troops carried out the massive bombing of Belgrade and other Serbian areas. The capitulation was signed in Belgrade on behalf of the Yugoslav army, not the state, whose representatives (king and government) had left the country and continued the resistance in exile. The breakdown of the army was caused, among other things, by the abandonment of military units composed of Croats and Slovenes, which Hitler encouraged by offering them better treatment after the war; see Miletić (ed.), *Aprilski rat 1941*; Petranović, *Srbija u Drugom svetskom ratu*, 97–110.
7. Milošević, *Izbeglice i preseljenici na teritoriji okupirane Jugoslavije*, 306.
8. Janjetović, *Collaboration and Fascism*, 30.
9. Isić, *Pismenost u Srbiji*, 57.
10. Dimić, *Kulturna politika*, III, 289–90; Janićijević, *Stvaralačka inteligenicija*, 33.

11 Čalić, *Socijalna istorija*, 381.
12 Grol, *Današnji razgovori o reformama*, 19.
13 Many authors have written about forced labour in the territory of occupied Serbia during the Second World War. For a selection, see Aleksić, 'Prinudni rad u Srbiji u Drugom svetskom ratu'; Pajić, *Prinudni rad i otpor u logorima Borskog rudnika*; Rutar, 'Employment of Labour in Wartime Serbia'; Janjetović, *'U skladu sa nastalom potrebom …'*; Janjetović, 'Dobrovoljni radnici iz Srbije u Nemačkoj', 2019; Schmid and Pisari (eds), *Prinudni rad u Srbiji: proizvođači, korisnici i posledice prinudnog rada*.
14 See, for instance, Borković, *Kontrarevolucija u Srbiji*; Kerkez, *Društvo Srbije u Drugom svetskom ratu*; Aleksić, 'Prinudni rad u Srbiji u Drugom svetskom ratu'; Škodrić, *Ministarstvo prosvete i vera u Srbiji 1941–1944*; Milićević, 'Činovnici u okupiranoj Srbiji 1941–1944', 2018.
15 Janjetović, *'U skladu sa nastalom potrebom …'*, 20–1.
16 Aleksić, *Privreda Srbije*, 270.
17 These sources are kept in the State Archives of Serbia, the Historical Archives of Belgrade and the Military Archives in Belgrade.
18 The statistical data mainly come from the archives of the Commissariat for Prices and Wages (State Archives of Serbia), which was specialised in monitoring prices and wages under the occupation.
19 Lower-category civil servants started their service in salary grade X. They could advance up to salary grade VII during their years of service. Their salary grades partly overlapped with those of higher civil servants. Higher-category civil servants could advance to salary grade I.
20 Civil servants had the right to a full pension after 35 years of service and after they had reached the age of 65, and the right to a personal pension after 10 years of active service; in case of injury in the service and inability to continue working as a result, they could get 10 years of service as if they were still employed.
21 *Službene novine Kraljevine Jugoslavije*, 1 April 1931.
22 Aleksić, *Privreda Srbije*, 140.
23 *Opštinske novine*, 24 April 1941, 2.
24 *Opštinske novine*, 24 April 1941, 3.
25 *Opštinske novine*, 24 April 1941, 3.
26 Milićević, 'Srpsko građanstvo u okupiranoj Srbiji 1941–1944', 161; Janjetović, *'U skladu sa nastalom potrebom …'*, 64.
27 Milićević and Nikodijević (eds.), *Svakodnevni život pod okupacijom*, 668.
28 Vojni arhiv (Military Archives, Belgrade) – VA, Nedićeva arhiva (Nda), 68-3-6, 10 March 1943.
29 For example, immediately after the occupation of the country, a civil servant decided to become a merchant. Although in peaceful times trade was a profitable business, it was not under occupation, unless business was conducted on the 'black market'; see *Novo vreme*, 19 June 1941, 3.
30 Kreso, *Njemačka okupaciona uprava*, 233–4; Božović, *Beograd pod komesarskom upravom*, 42–3.
31 Pavlowitch, *Hitler's New Disorder*, 58–9.
32 Janjetović, *Collaboration and Fascism*, 441.
33 Connelly, 'Nazis and Slavs', 1999; Ristović, *Nemački 'novi poredak' i Jugoistočna Evropa*, 22–47; Koljanin, 'Srbija u nemačkom "novom poretku" 1941–1942', 2011, 66.
34 Koljanin, 'Srbija u nemačkom "novom poretku" 1941–1942', 2011, 67; Lukač, *Treći Rajh i zemlje Jugoistočne Evrope*, I, 279.
35 Shepherd, *Terror in the Balkans*, 36.
36 *Politika*, 28 March 1941, 7–11; *Ratni dnevnik Lazara Trklje 1941–1944*, 36; Petranović and Žutić (eds), *27. mart 1941. Tematska zbirka dokumenata*; Petranović, *Srbija u Drugom svetskom ratu*, 70–110.
37 Retirement did not completely separate civil servants from their previous job. According to the Civil Servants Act, they could even lose their pension 'for serious damage to the reputation of their work done in retirement'; see *Službene novine Kraljevine Jugoslavije*, 1 April 1931.
38 *Moderna srpska država 1804–2004*, 253.
39 Dević, *Partizani u Srbiji 1941*, 142.
40 Dević, *Partizani u Srbiji 1941*, 303.

41 The principal of the high school in Kragujevac, Lazar Pantelić, refused to be spared the fate of his students. He is said to have uttered on that occasion: 'Shoot, I'm still teaching'; see Brkić, *Ime i broj*, 64.
42 Istorijski arhiv Beograda (Historical archives of Belgrade) – IAB, Uprava grada Beograda (UgB), Tehničko odeljenje, k. 2953, br. 2422, 24 December 1941; VA, Nda, 1-2-19, 27 December 1941.
43 Aleksić, *Privreda Srbije*, 138, 140.
44 *Zbornik NOR-a*, I/1, 334.
45 *Obnova*, 18 July 1941, 3.
46 One analysis shows that in 1931, 87,167 civil servants and civil employees worked in Serbia (Isić, *Socijalna i agrarna struktura Srbije*, 28). Some recent research shows that in 1939/1940, 203,357 permanent and temporary civil servants were employed in the civil service of the Kingdom of Yugoslavia. There is no information on how many refer to Serbia. As in other parts of the country, it was probably a slightly larger number than 10 years earlier. The state was only able to reduce the number of daily, part-time and contractual civil servants; see Grgić, 'Uprava u Savskoj banovini', 342.
47 IAB, UgB, k. 2953, br. 2422, 24 December 1941.
48 For instance, in the case of married female civil servants the minimum of first-class subsistence, which only included Belgrade, was 2,500 dinars for a wife and spouse and 500 dinars for each child. There were some interesting cases in which the husband's salary was less than the subsistence minimum. Then the female civil servant was allowed to continue working, if she wanted to. She would not receive a salary, but the difference up to the prescribed minimum. The Ministry of Finance created very detailed instructions for all possible variants involving female civil servants and their spouses, with or without children or other family dependants, income level, price classes, etc. (Državni arhiv Srbije (State Archives of Serbia) DAS, Ministarstvo finansija (G-15), f. 1, 4 June 1941).
49 Zbirka fotografija, Narodni muzej Čačak (Collection of photographs, National Museum Čačak), I–1610.
50 *Službene novine*, 18 June 1941, 1.
51 *Službene novine*, 18 June 1941, 1.
52 Škodrić, *Ministarstvo prosvete i vera u Srbiji 1941–1944*, 116; Majdanac, *Pozorište u okupiranoj Srbiji*, 41–8.
53 *List uredaba vojnog zapovednika u Srbiji*, 31 May 1941; *Novo vreme*, 3 June 1941, 2.
54 Mraović, *Od surove stvarnosti do alternativne realnosti*, 168.
55 The measure did not include Slovenians and Germans; see VA, Nda, 74-9-2, K. I br. 1999, 28 September 1942.
56 VA, Nda, 1-2-1, str. pov. br. 3, 9 January 1941.
57 *Službene novine*, 6 August 1941, 1–2.
58 Škodrić, *Ministarstvo prosvete i vera u Srbiji 1941–1944*, 121. Under 'any' reasons (number 3), the lists of dismissed civil servants often mention, in addition to disciplinary violations ('neglect of duty' or 'leaving the place of duty' without the knowledge and approval of superiors, 'taking lightly the duties'), political orientation ('left-wing orientation') and behaviour in their private life (associating with 'suspicious persons'); see: IAB, UgB, SP IV-11, 192/91, k. 192, pov. br. II 62, 28 January 1942. Number 4 primarily referred to active or retired civil servants whose existence 'does not depend on whether they will be in service or not'. This meant they had other sources of income such as real estate or land; see VA, Nda, 72-1-2, I br. 2473, 30 October 1942.
59 *Službene novine*, 6 August 1941, 2.
60 Va, Nda, 20-5-43, br. 7130, 24 March 1942.
61 Škodrić, *Ministarstvo prosvete i vera u Srbiji 1941–1944*, 125.
62 VA, Nda, 72-6-71, 9 December 1941; VA, Nda, 21II-5-18, pov. br. 1175, 10 October 1942; Škodrić, 'Women and Wage Labor in Occupied Serbia 1941–1944', 2020, 82.
63 Škodrić, *Ministarstvo prosvete i vera u Srbiji 1941–1944*, 125. IAB, UgB, SP IV-11, 192/91, k. 192, pov. br. II 62, 28 January 1942.
64 Milićević, 'Činovnici u okupiranoj Srbiji 1941–1944', 2018, 76.
65 The decree elaborated on one provision of the law which referred to the fact that 'state authorities', whenever required by 'general interest', could decide to terminate the service of

civil servants. It was applied in parallel and had less legal force than the law, which allowed ministers to avoid it whenever they could, considering the occupation a temporary state.
66 Cvetković et al. (eds), *Kolaboracionisti pred sudom OZNE*, 436.
67 Miletić (ed.), *Aprilski rat 1941*, 694.
68 *Službene novine*, 18 June 1941, 1.
69 'Kriegswirtschaftsverordnung', *Deutsches Reichsgesetzblatt*, vol. 1939, part I, No. 163, 1609–13.
70 From June 1941, the Commissariat for Prices and Wages, which was under the direct supervision of the Germans, primarily the General Plenipotentiary for the Economy, Franz Neuhausen, dealt with this.
71 Milićević, 'Ishrana u okupiranom Beogradu 1941–1944', 2012, 87–8.
72 Milićević, 'Činovnici u okupiranoj Srbiji 1941–1944', 2018, 78–9. VA, Nda, k. 71-1-2, 30 October 1942.
73 For example, civil servants of salary grade VI, academically educated, married, with two children and with 10 years of service, had 4,344.28 dinars on 20 June 1943, while civil servant trainees of salary grade VIII, academically educated and unmarried, had 2,793.64 dinars DAS, Komesarijat za cene i nadnice (G-6), f. 234, Pregled kretanja cena, koštanja života i kupovne moći u Beogradu 1943).
74 *Zbornik NOR-a*, XII/3, 788.
75 Above all, this referred to civil servants who had a large number of children and lived in small towns (DAS, G-6, f. 185, br. 31455, 8 November 1943).
76 DAS, G-6, f. 268, br. 15 January 1943.
77 Milićević, 'Srpsko građanstvo u okupiranoj Srbiji 1941–1944', 174–6.
78 VA, Nda, 34-9-57, 8 March 1943.
79 For more on this, see Milićević, 'Činovnici u okupiranoj Srbiji 1941–1944', 2018, 82–3.
80 The president of the municipality in Leskovac was dismissed from this position, but he continued to enjoy the support and protection of the occupation authorities and even received new responsibilities; see Stojanović, 'Strahinja Janjić i Srpski Gestapo'.
81 Škodrić, *Ministarstvo prosvete i vera u Srbiji 1941–1944*, 283.
82 Mraović, *Od surove stvarnosti do alternativne realnosti*, 170.
83 VA, Nda, k-72-1-2, 6 June 1942.
84 Karapandžić, *Prikazi emigrantskih i otadžbinskih knjiga*, 173–5.
85 Mazower, *Hitler's Empire,* 435.
86 IAB, OGB, k-224, f-1-456/43, br. 26239, 5 December 1942; Milićević, 'Činovnici u okupiranoj Srbiji 1941–1944', 2018, 78.
87 VA, Nda, 20B-3-38, pov. br. 822, 21 July 1942.
88 *Službene novine*, 6 August 1941, 2.
89 Isić, 'Mihailo Avramović u Nedićevom aparatu vlasti', 1997. Mihailo Avramović was then almost 80 years old and retired. The collaborationist government put pressure on him, and even threatened him, to accept the position of president of the Privileged Agrarian Bank. As he later claimed, he understood this as an opportunity to choose between two options, the camp and the position.
90 Jews, and among them civil servants of Jewish origin, were, as everywhere in Europe, almost immediately included in mandatory labour in accordance with the racial policy of Nazi Germany. They cleared the ruins caused by the bombing of Belgrade, removed garbage, emptied public latrines and pulled corpses out from under the rubble.
91 *Kuluk* was also practised in interwar Yugoslavia, mostly in the countryside. During the occupation, *kuluk* was implemented in accordance with Articles 66–70 of the Law on Internal Administration and later also in accordance with Article 1 of the Decree amending and supplementing this law as of 19 August 1942. Those initially exempted were state officials, persons permanently employed by German authorities, German companies or companies that worked for the German authorities and the military force, coastal and transport workers with the identification of the new regime labour organisation, the Serbian Union of Work, and active service members of the National Service for the Renewal of Serbia; see *Obnova*, 26 September 1942, 5.
92 Janjetović, *'U skladu sa nastalom potrebom ...'*, 58–9.
93 Janjetović, *'U skladu sa nastalom potrebom ...'*, 56–7.
94 *Novo vreme*, 20 February 1943, 4.
95 *Novo vreme*, 6 June 1943, 3.

96 Privatna arhiva. Kolekcija fotografija Bratislava Stankovića (Private archive. Bratislav Stanković collection of photographs).
97 *Novo vreme*, 2 March 1943, 4; *Novo vreme*, 18 March 1943, 4.
98 Each employee, regardless of whether they were active or not (retired), received 7.5 kg of wheat flour per family, 15 kg of potatoes and 5 kg of beans; see IAB, OGB, k. 230, f. 1, II br. 17294, 16 September 1943.
99 This regulation, issued on 30 December 1941, prescribed that all citizens between the ages of 17 and 45, regardless of employment, might be called to mandatory work in certain plants and economic branches. On 4 August 1942, the measure was tightened by increasing the age limit to 55 years and converting the prison sentence into forced labour; see *Službene novine*, 30 December 1941, 1; *Službene novine*, 4 August 1942, 1.
100 *List uredaba za okupiranu srpsku teritoriju*, 26 March 1943; *Novo vreme*, 27 March 1943, 3.
101 Some civil servants also worked in mines, such as in Bor. Their families were to have special relief in terms of supplies; see *Novo vreme*, 20 February 1943, 3; *Novo vreme*, 26 March 1943, 4; Janjetović, 'U skladu sa nastalom potrebom …', 136–44. Mandatory work for certain groups of female civil servants such as doctors was introduced by the Decree on Mandatory Work of Doctors from September 1942. They were obligated to work in order to prevent epidemics; see *Službene novine*, 1 January 1942, 1.
102 *Novo vreme*, 5 August 1942, 3. Thus, for example, civil servants of the Labour Exchange released for money various persons who were forced to do 'mandatory work'. The average cost of release was about 40,000 dinars, which was slightly below the average annual salary of a civil servant in 1943. 109 persons were arrested and 82 persons were sentenced to prison and forced labour. They were publicly branded by being led through the streets of Belgrade under guard. They also carried banners with derogatory inscriptions; see *Obnova*, 18 March 1943, 5; Muzej grada Beograda (Belgrade city museum), I2/2-3651. Civil servants could also be sentenced to forced labour for other crimes, primarily in cases of helping the resistance movement; see Janjetović, 'U skladu sa nastalom potrebom …', 68.
103 Aleksić, 'Prinudni rad u Srbiji u Drugom svetskom ratu'.

Bibliography

Aleksić, Dragan. *Privreda Srbije u Drugom svetskom ratu*. Beograd: Institut za noviju istoriju Srbije, 2002. (Cyrillic)

Aleksić, Dragan. 'Prinudni rad u Srbiji u Drugom svetskom ratu'. In *Logori, zatvori i prisilni rad u Hrvatskoj/Jugoslaviji 1941–1945, 1945–1951. Zbornik radova*, edited by Vladimir Gajger et al., 133–50. Zagreb: Hrvatski institut za povjest, 2010.

Borković, Milan. *Kontrarevolucija u Srbiji. Kvislinška uprava 1941–1944*, 1–2. Beograd: 'Sloboda', 1979.

Božović, Branislav. *Beograd pod komesarskom upravom 1941 godine*. Beograd: Institut za savremenu istoriju, 1998. (Cyrillic)

Brkić, Staniša. *Ime i broj*. Beograd-Kragujevac: Muzej žrtava genocida, 2020. (Cyrillic)

Čalić, Mari-Žanin. *Socijalna istorija Srbije 1815–1941. Usporeni napredak u industrijalizaciji*. Beograd: Clio, 2004. (Cyrillic)

Connelly, John. 'Nazis and Slavs: From Racial Theory to Racist Practice', *Central European History* 32/1 (1999): 1–33.

Cvetković, Srđan, Ristanović, Rade and Stambolija, Nebojša (eds.). *Kolaboracionisti pred sudom. Saslušanja Milana Nedića, Dragomira Jovanovića, Tanasija Dinića i Koste Mušickog pred organima OZNE*. Beograd: Institut za savremenu istoriju, Društvo istoričara Srbije, 2018. (Cyrillic)

Dević, Nemanja. *Partizani u Srbiji 1941. Oslobodilački ili revolucionarni rat?* Beograd: Institut za savremenu istoriju, 2021. (Cyrillic)

Dimić, Ljubodrag. *Kulturna politika Kraljevine Jugoslavije 1918–1941*, III. Beograd: Stubovi kulture, 1996. (Cyrillic)

Grgić, Stpica. 'Uprava u Savskoj banovini (1929–1939). Između državnog centralizma i supsidijarnosti'. Doktorska disertacija. Sveučilište u Zagrebu, Odeljenje za hrvatske studije, Zagreb, 2014.

Grol, Milan. *Današnji razgovori o reformama koje predlažu ljudi 6-tog januara i u duhu 6-tog januara.* Kragujevac: [n. p.], 1940. (Cyrillic)

Isić, Momčilo. 'Mihailo Avramović u Nedićevom aparatu vlasti', *Tokovi istorije* 3–4 (1997): 230–40.

Isić, Momčilo. *Socijalna i agrarna struktura Srbije u Kraljevini Jugoslaviji.* Beograd: Institut za noviju istoriju Srbije, 1999. (Cyrillic)

Isić, Momčilo. *Pismenost u Srbiji između dva svetska rata.* Beograd: Institut za noviju istoriju Srbije, 2001. (Cyrillic)

Janićijević, Milosav. *Stvaralačka inteligencija međuratne Jugoslavije.* Beograd: Institut društvenih nauka – Centar za sociološka istraživanja, 1984.

Janjetović, Zoran. *'U skladu sa nastalom potrebom…'. Prinudni rad u okupiranoj Srbiji 1941–1944.* Beograd: Institut za noviju istoriju Srbije, 2012.

Janjetović, Zoran. 'Jugoslovenski Banat 1941'. In *Srbi i rat u Jugoslaviji 1941*, edited by Dragan Aleksić, 291–318. Beograd: Institut za noviju istoriju Srbije, 2014. (Cyrillic)

Janjetović, Zoran. *Collaboration and Fascism under the Nedić regime.* Belgrade: Institut za noviju istoriju Srbije, 2018.

Janjetović, Zoran. 'Dobrovoljni radnici iz Srbije u Nemačkoj 1941–1944', *Tokovi istorije* 2 (2019): 47–74.

Karapandžić, Borivoje. *Prikazi emigrantskih i otadžbinskih knjiga.* Beograd: Nova iskra, 1997. (Cyrillic)

Kerkez, Slobodan. *Društvo Srbije u Drugom svetskom ratu 1941–1945.* Niš: Centar za balkanske studije, 2004. (Cyrillic)

Koljanin, Milan. 'Srbija u nemačkom "novom poretku" 1941–1942', *Istorija 20. veka* 1 (2011): 65–86.

Kreso, Muharem. *Njemačka okupaciona uprava u Beogradu 1941–1942. Sa osvrtom na centralne okupacione komande i ustanove za Srbiju, Jugoslaviju i Balkan.* Beograd: Istorijski arhiv Beograda, 1979.

Lukač, Dušan. *Treći Rajh i zemlje Jugoistočne Evrope, 1933–1936*, I. Beograd: Vojnoizdavački zavod, 1982.

Majdanac, Boro. *Pozorište u okupiranoj Srbiji. Pozorišna politika u Srbiji 1941–1944.* Beograd: KIZ Altera i Udruženje dramskih umetnika Srbije, 2011. (Cyrillic)

Mazower, Mark. *Hitler's Empire: Nazi Rule in Occupied Europe.* London: Penguin Books, 2009.

Miletić, Antun (ed.). *Aprilski rat 1941. Zbornik dokumenata.* Beograd: Vojnoistorijski institut, 1987.

Milićević, Nataša. 'Ishrana u okupiranom Beogradu 1941–1944', *Tokovi istorije* 2 (2012): 77–91. (Cyrillic)

Milićević, Nataša. 'Srpsko građanstvo u okupiranoj Srbiji 1941–1944'. Doktorska disertacija. Univerzitet u Beogradu, Filozofski fakultet, Odeljenje za istoriju, 2016. (Cyrillic)

Milićević, Nataša. 'Činovnici u okupiranoj Srbiji 1941–1944', *Istorija 20. veka* 2 (2018): 69–86.

Milićević, Nataša and Nikodijević, Dušan (eds). *Svakodnevni život pod okupacijom 1941–1944. Iskustvo jednog Beograđanina.* Beograd: Institut za noviju istoriju Srbije, 2011. (Cyrillic)

Milošević, Slobodan D. *Izbeglice i preseljenici na teritoriji okupirane Jugoslavije 1941–1945. godine.* Beograd: Narodna knjiga, Institut za savremenu istoriju, 1981.

Moderna srpska država 1804–2004. Hronologija. Beograd: Istorijski arhiv Beograda, 2004. (Cyrillic)

Mraović, Marijana. *Od surove stvarnosti do alternativne realnosti. Propaganda vlade Milana Nedića 1941–1944.* Beograd: Medija centar 'Odbrana', 2019. (Cyrillic)

Pajić, Tomislav. *Prinudni rad i otpor u logorima Borskog rudnika 1941–1944.* Beograd: Institut za savremenu istoriju, 1991.

Pavlović, Stevan K. *Srbija. Istorija iza imena.* Beograd: Clio, 2004. (Cyrillic)

Pavlowitch, Stevan K. *Hitler's New Disorder: The Second World War in Yugoslavia.* New York: Oxford University Press, 2020.

Petranović, Branko. *Srbija u Drugom svetskom ratu 1939–1945.* Beograd: Vojnoizdavački i novinski centar, 1992.

Petranović, Branko and Žutić, Nikola (eds). *27. mart 1941. Tematska zbirka dokumenata.* Beograd: NICOM, 1990.

Ristović, Milan. *Nemački 'novi poredak' i Jugoistočna Evropa, 1940/41–1944/45: planovi o budućnosti i praksa.* Beograd: Vojnoizdavački i novinski centar, 1991.

Rutar, Sabina, 'Employment of Labour in Wartime Serbia: Social History and the Politics of Amnesia'. In *Serbia and Serbs in World War Two*, edited by Sabina Remet and Ola Listhaug, 44–69. New York: Palgrave Macmillan, 2011.

Schmid, Sanela and Pisari, Milovan (eds). *Prinudni rad u Srbiji: proizvođači, korisnici i posledice prinudnog rada 1941–1944*. Beograd: Centar za istraživanje i edukaciju o Holokaustu, 2018.

Shepherd, Ben. *Terror in the Balkans: German Armies and Partisan Warfare*. London: Harvard University Press, 2012.

Škodrić, Ljubinka. *Ministarstvo prosvete i vera u Srbiji 1941–1944. Sudbina institucije pod okupacijom*. Beograd: Arhiv Srbije, 2009. (Cyrillic)

Škodrić, Ljubinka. 'Women and Wage Labor in Occupied Serbia 1941–1944: Policy of Collaborationist Government and German Occupation Authorities', *Tokovi istorije* 3 (2020): 69–95.

Stojanović, Aleksandar. 'Strahinja Janjić i Srpski Gestapo'. In *80 godina od izbijanja Drugog svetskog rata na prostoru Jugoslavije i stradanja grada Kragujevca. Novi pomaci ili revizija istorije*, edited by Dmitar Tasić and Lela Vujošević, 261–87. Kragujevac: Centar za naučnostraživački rad Srpske akademije nauka i umetnosti i univerziteta; Beograd: Institut za noviju istoriju Srbije, 2021. (Cyrillic)

Trklja, Nikola (ed.). *Ratni dnevnik Lazara Trklje 1941–1944. Otkopana istina*. Beograd: Službeni glasnik, 2020. (Cyrillic)

Zbornik dokumenata i podataka o narodnooslobodilačkom ratu jugoslovenskih naroda, I/1. *Borbe u Srbiji 1941. godine*. Beograd: Vojnoistorijski institut, 1949. (*Zbornik NOR-a*) (Cyrillic)

Zbornik dokumenata i podataka o narodnooslobodilačkom ratu naroda Jugoslavije, XII/3. Beograd: Vojnoistorijski institut, 1978. (*Zbornik NOR-a*)

Zundhauzen, Holm. *Istorija Srbije od 19. do 21. veka*. Beograd: Clio, 2009. (Cyrillic)

5
Exploitation and care: public health aspirations and the construction of the working-class body in the Budapest Museum of Social Health, 1901–1945

Eszter Őze

This chapter examines how the working class was integrated into the system of capitalism through the exploitation and care of its bodies. I analyse the history, contexts and function of the Museum of Social Health[1] (1901–1945) in Budapest, Hungary, in integrating the working class into the world of wage labour. I will address how those in power saw and perceived the bodies of industrial wage labourers who moved into the cities during this period and how this representation became integrated into the exploitive logic of industrial capitalism.

Social and public health museums made claims and proposals concerning the bodies of the population and functioned as public institutions of the social and institutional system. The social museums that emerged around 1900 include, besides the one in Budapest (opened in 1901), those in Paris (Musée social, 1894), Charlottenburg (Reichsmuseum für Unfallverhütung und Gewerbehygiene, 1903), Frankfurt am Main (Soziales Museum, 1902), Harvard, Cambridge (Social Museum, 1907) and Vienna (Gesellschafts- und Wirtschaftsmuseum, 1924). They dealt with themes such as education, health, housing, leisure, eugenics and a range of other issues associated with the working class. To this end, a fine-tuned museal presentation system was developed, based on the new social reform plans, to make visible the aims, legislation and phenomena relating to the health of the working class. In most cases, the museums functioned not only as exhibition venues but also as libraries, archives and research centres, with a different target audience in each case, which fundamentally influenced their operation. The development of these museums provided space for the representation of the existing body culture, an awareness of diseases, public health and health policy.

I will discuss how early twentieth-century state care was connected to discipline, labour regulation and control over bodies. What was the ideological context of the museum in Budapest in representing the working-class bodies of industrial capitalism? Why was the institution of the museum considered a suitable instrument for the emancipation, integration and caring control of the working class? I argue that the reason for the museum's creation can be understood primarily through the workings of nineteenth-century cultural representation and political integration. Cultural representation is linked to the functioning and maintenance of the power of the day, and to this end I analyse the position of this institution in the relationship between power and knowledge.

The theoretical tradition that examines museums as institutional manifestations of power and knowledge relations[2] links the museum primarily to the history of the nineteenth-century bourgeois public sphere.[3] Within an art-historical interpretative framework inspired by Michel Foucault, the starting point for analysis is that museums were not institutions of confinement but of presentation. Thus, they also had complex disciplinary and educational functions. Museums presented objects and associated knowledge that had hitherto been confined to private spaces, only offering private contemplation. However, as museums were opened to the public during the nineteenth century, they became a means of propagating and legitimising power. It is, therefore, necessary to carefully examine what changes were needed to enable the Museum of Social Health to present fundamental elements of working-class life (the use of the body, housing, education) that were at odds with the bourgeois notion of intimacy and that were presented in museums in the form of ethnographic displays—if included at all.

While an important starting point for my analysis is the art-historical approach that examines exhibitions and museums as institutionalised relations of power and knowledge, I argue here that the museum as an institution should not be analysed as a new form of spectacle related to the civic public (like galleries or department stores). Instead, it is much more fruitful to consider it within the context of the institutionalisation of work by further expanding the analytical viewpoint to include Michel Foucault's notions of biopolitics and biopower.[4]

Biopolitics denotes a new type of mechanism from the late eighteenth and early nineteenth centuries concerning the practice of power, whereby the study of fundamental biological traits of the human species became a strategic tool. The object of power, both economically and politically, was no longer the individual but the collective body of the population, whose biology was scientifically studied and regulated.[5] This biopower was a prerequisite for the emergence of capitalism, as Foucault argued, since this system of production could only really 'take off' when the human body became part of this production mechanism, and economic processes were in harmony with the biology of the population.[6] Thus, a system of power procedures had to be developed that would both increase the workforce, thereby increasing coercion (and thus the efficiency of labour), and extend productive lifespan, without increasing (visible) domination.[7] Discipline emerged as a disguise of labour coercion, which had marked work relations much more visibly in the past.

In the case of the museum, we can see that the institution addressed social issues as part of the work sphere's integrating institutional system, and in this context, it also presented new administrative techniques and cultivated problem-solving proposals. As it was aimed at educating the urban labourer, we can utilise the Foucauldian notion of biopolitical thinking to examine how the bourgeoisie localised its regulations, primarily related to its own body, the body in general, its longevity, vitality and child-bearing aspect, in the living environment of the wage-earning urban labourer.[8]

I aim to show that the Budapest Museum of Social Health was a state institution that served to both represent power and integrate wage labour into the world it sought to construct. It was precisely for this dual function that the museum institution was chosen by the government. Specific museum practices and tools were deployed to construct a narrative of the progress of humanity in the spaces of the Museum of Social Health. The emphasis on the workforce and national unity sheds light on how the curators viewed the working classes and their place in the society they envisioned. Since the museum's collection was destroyed in the Second World War, I will examine the catalogues of the largest exhibitions: the International Exhibition of Occupational Safety and Labour Welfare (1907), the War and Public Health Exhibition (1915), the exhibition on Social Health (1932) and the Eugenics and Heredity Exhibition (1934).

Hungarian industrial wage labourers

From the mid-nineteenth century, an integrating institutional system of labour began to emerge: wages, fixed working hours, the contractual relationship between employer and employee, and labour relations became a structuring force in society. In Hungary, industrialisation emerged around 1860 in a process that was repeatedly halted and reinitiated until the beginning of the Second World War. The period was defined by the complex political, economic and infrastructural process of separation from the Austro-Hungarian Monarchy, the establishment and fall of the Socialist Federative Republic of Councils in Hungary between March and August of 1919 and the Horthy regime, which was established after the revolutions of 1918–1919 and which almost completely reduced the Left's ability to take any possibility of formal political action into account. When the museum opened its doors, Hungary was still part of the Austro-Hungarian Monarchy, while the years of territorial transformation, radical population reduction, wartime inflation and financial crisis that followed the First World War had a profound impact on the formation of the Hungarian working class, its social position, its living standards, its working hours and its wages.

Hungarian manufacturing industry started to develop in the second half of the 1860s. Although nineteenth-century Hungary was primarily an agrarian society, the proportion of the working population making a living from agriculture fell from 75 per cent in the 1850s to 62.4 per cent in 1910, partly because of the strengthening of manufacturing.[9] In addition, the number of small craftsmen declined radically, as they were absorbed into the unskilled working class alongside former agricultural labourers. In 1848 the census counted 23,400 Hungarian workers, but in 1888 there were ten times as many, while the overall population increased by a much smaller share. Despite the acceleration of the growth of this segment of workers around the turn of the century, it was not until the First World War that they reached a critical mass, and the numbers of day labourers and domestic servants correspondingly declined.[10] Alongside the industrial workforce, the most important stratum of the wage labour force was the group of workers specialising in transportation and infrastructure.

The Hungarian working class included skilled immigrant workers. They had a better financial status and had also received a better education. Unskilled and skilled workers – some of whom came from Austria and Germany or were Hungarians of other ethnicities – differed in terms of education and lifestyle. Educated workers attended lower and upper secondary industrial schools, and their wages were higher than those of the uneducated workers. They also played a prominent role in the formation of trade unions. Uneducated workers had no other choice than to work as unskilled or day labourers. They were excluded from trade unions for many years and were welcomed by political parties as the 'crowds of the people's assembly'.[11] Between 1900 and 1910, the number of industrial workers increased by 43 per cent. Two-thirds of the industrial workforce and 40 per cent of the factory workforce were skilled workers even as late as the 1910s. In addition to skilled workers, the other large stratum of factory workers, 35–40 per cent, was made up of miners, often working seasonal jobs, and workers in construction and sugar production.[12] In short, the working class in Hungary was divided by origin, nationality and education, by radical differences in wages and in living and housing conditions, and also by the possibility – or impossibility – of political organisation.

Until the significant inflation that followed the First World War, the average weekly wage of an industrial worker was around 15 to 20 crowns (a loaf of bread cost about 0.25 crowns in the early 1900s), while the average working time per day in manufacturing ranged from nine to eleven hours.[13] In the extended period this chapter is dealing with, economic and social conditions deteriorated seriously after the First World War: the real (value of the) wages did not reach prewar levels even after 1938.[14] The social situation of Budapest wage-earners in the late 1920s and 1930s is well illustrated by the development of their housing conditions. In 1925, for example, nearly 83 per cent of the approximately 65,000 workers' dwellings were kitchen–bedroom flats and only about 15 per cent had two full rooms, a proportion that declined even further as the 1930s approached. At the same time, there were improvements in other aspects: the proportion of workers' dwellings with bathrooms, for example, increased by 90 per cent between 1925 and 1935. In 1929, half of the working population lived in dwellings with electricity and two-fifths had running water, but about 58 per cent still lived in dwellings with little or no heating.[15]

Nearly 50 per cent of the country's population born between 1900 and 1910 were employed later as industrial wage labourers, while of those born between 1910 and 1930 only 33 per cent were so employed. This was because urbanisation in the country declined considerably, being essentially confined to Budapest, because of the territorial loss and radical population reduction after 1920. Despite the relative decline of the working population, in absolute terms the working class was rapidly growing, as the country counted 465,000 industrial wage workers in 1920, 660,000 in 1930 and 770,000 at the end of the 1930s.[16] During these decades, with the development of new industries such as electricity and communications, and with the training of apprentices in large factories, the educational and literacy levels of the working class were raised. However, the proportion of skilled workers did not exceed that of unskilled workers. Subsequently, these unskilled workers became the most populous segment of the wage-earning workforce in factories. An important reason for this was that the iron and mechanical engineering industry declined from the late 1920s, while the textile industry – which employed unskilled workers as its principal labour pool – grew stronger. This was linked to an increase in the proportion of women in the workforce, from 23 per cent in 1913 to 31 per cent in 1929 and 32 per cent in 1938.[17]

Labour became a political issue once the (male) workers gained the right to vote, with labour conflicts being increasingly regulated on the level of the nation-state. Trade unions and associations, social security and welfare institutions as well as the system of job allocation were all newly emerging institutions that made the institutionalisation of wage labour possible.[18] The institutions associated with wage labour became socially, economically and politically decisive, a process that also brought a new type of social integration and strengthened the nation-state.[19] The museum's space was one of the locations where these changes were brought to the forefront. This was a novelty, as the musealisation of the social question and the utilisation of the working class's bodies were practices quite alien to nineteenth-century museums. Museum representation thus became a sociopolitical issue, determining which subjects could be displayed in a state museum.

Representation of the 'social question'

Industrialisation came at the cost of mass impoverishment and other crises, which called for the social integration of the new wage workers. The extent of the problem turned it into a politicised issue, and different levels engaged in challenging what became known as the 'social question'. One of these levels was that of the social museums. As described by the historian Robert Castel,[20] the social question was an almost insoluble problem that involved the relations that structure society and therefore it was also linked to the question of solidarity, the problematic bond that ensures the interconnection of society's constituent parts. In the nineteenth century, the social question was understood as the complex set of problems that covered the difficulties of those who earned their living from their work and the problems arising from their lack of political rights. Thus, it was concerned with the social situation of workers, their living conditions, labour relations and political organisation. Therefore, according to nineteenth-century analysts to whom Castel refers, the social question was also the result of a dismantling of the order, which gave rise to a class of workers who were seeking political representation, lived on wages, had problems of subsistence and adapted their lives to their working hours.[21]

In other words, it was primarily the institutional system of the world of work that integrated the working class into society, and the emergence of the social question was an important element of this integration. As the social question was taken out of the competence of the Church and employers, it transformed into a political issue and became a state responsibility. In the context of a changing industrial society, moral weakness was no longer seen as the sole source of problems but was also linked to the factor of existential conditions. Living conditions such as housing, unemployment and poor health care were investigated and later identified as influential aspects. Consequently, poverty and pauperism, hitherto treated as individual failings, began to be analysed as a mass phenomenon.[22] The presentation of social and health problems was organised in museum spaces along the lines of nineteenth-century notions of scholarship and compassion,[23] revealing institutions not only as collections of facts and scientific data but also as archives of the ideological and moral convictions of the time, and as sites of the institutionalisation of a new science related to the analysis of society.

For Hungary, the period between the 1870s and the First World War was also a decisive antecedent for managing social issues and developing the political-economic system. The expansion of Budapest accelerated after the unification of Pest and Buda in 1873, and a sudden growth of the city's population justified the development of municipal public welfare institutions from the 1870s onwards. Budapest's population grew from 361,000 to 881,000 between 1881 and 1910, while in 1892 public welfare expenditure in Budapest accounted for 4.5 per cent of the city budget. From 1910 until the First World War, this figure fell to 2.9–3.5 per cent.[24] In the capital of agrarian Hungary, rapid industrialisation did not in effect promote wage labourers' economic and social (or sociopolitical) integration. The administrative institutions could not develop a network of organisations and reform provisions that would have counteracted the ongoing disintegration of society. The need for social integration was also reflected in the expansion of political integration. With a radical increase in the population of Budapest, the proportion of people entitled to vote was 5.58 per cent in 1899 and 8.68 per cent in 1910. The most important innovation was the establishment of state-level social security systems, as opposed to a decentralised system of poor relief. However, despite all the political will for reform, from the 1870s onwards one-off relief operations were carried out instead of the consistent development of the welfare system.[25]

The presentation of the social question became a central task of public museums, including the Budapest institution. This was fundamentally explored through two questions: who is worth caring for, and whose task is it to provide this care? In the process of enforcement of state and municipal regulations, there was a distinction between the group of people in need of care, namely wage workers, and the criminalised group of poor people without formal employment, for example those who lived from begging or illegal prostitution.[26] A person could claim state care if they were in work, that is, if they participated as a key figure in organised production processes. This was measured and evaluated in accordance with the categories of civic respectability (security, self-control and independence), in line with the social vision of the time.[27] In fact, with the emergence of industrial capitalism, formal work – with wage work as its poster child – became a moral category, and the institutional system of the work sphere became the primary means of social integration.[28]

The Budapest Museum of Social Health

The Budapest Museum of Social Health was a state-funded institution whose mission changed several times between 1901 and 1919, in line not only with current political events but also with the changing circle supporting the museum. The development of the museum's collection was initiated alongside the establishment of the institution. Its founding collection consisted of objects originating from the World's Fairs of Brussels in 1897 and Paris in 1900, mainly on the topics of workers' housing and industrial accidents. In the first few years following its foundation, the museum developed its library, which grew mainly between 1901 and 1903, covering the subjects of workers' housing, accident and health insurances and public welfare. The museum's acquisition strategy followed the transforming body of the institution's patrons and was closely aligned with the themes of the day. The first known major addition to the collection took place in 1908 when the Ministry of Commerce (led by Szetrényi József, who was also the leader of the International Association of the Workers' Insurance), which maintained the museum, issued a decree requiring industrial inspectors[29] to share with the director of the institution all the protective equipment, sanitary appliances, welfare institutions and any other material they had collected during their practice concerning occupational accidents and health hazards.

The museum organised exhibitions not only on workers' welfare and welfare measures but also on public health and hygiene: until the First World War, two strands competed in the presentation of industrial hygiene and social endeavour unfolding in the library and the exhibition space. At the time of its launch, the agricultural policy writer Menyhért Szántó (who later retired with the title of Deputy State Secretary) believed that the main aim of the institution's journal, *The Social Museum Bulletin*, was the emancipation of the working class through the presentation of social policy measures and the necessary 'tools' (welfare institutions for workers, work safety measures, improvements of health and hygiene).[30]

In 1912, the museum's existence was reaffirmed, but its aims changed. At the International Exhibition of Hygiene in Dresden in 1911, the Austro-Hungarian pavilion's exhibition material was partly supplied by the Social Museum. It became an 'institutional organ of public health education': in addition to accident prevention, workers' insurance and workers' welfare, it also began to focus on public diseases, sexually transmitted diseases and alcoholism.[31] From 1912, Dr Géza Marschan (1879–1917) – a lawyer and member of the League of General Secret Electoral Law, the Society of Social Sciences and the Martinovics Masonic Lodge – was appointed deputy director of the museum to improve the inadequate results of the institution.[32] From that year onwards, the name of the museum's journal was changed to *The Social Museum Review* and it was restructured: new permanent columns were launched, such as 'Social Conditions', 'Workers' Protection', 'Workers' Insurance', 'Employers', 'Workers' Organisations', 'Strikes and Exclusion', 'Conciliation', 'Arbitration', 'Labour Market', 'Unemployment', 'Housing and Construction', 'Social Health', 'Education and Training', 'Unions' and 'Welfare Institutions' – to name but a few. From 1901 onwards, the problem of tuberculosis, considered to be a widespread disease at the beginning of the century, was addressed, as well as social policy issues such as the urban housing programme. The discourse also included new forms of state-level assistance, the education of the working classes and, from 1914 onwards, social and health issues in the war hinterland.[33]

However, the articles' subject headings remained similar to those of the previous years. The diversity of the writers publishing editorials in the journal in the period before the First World War illustrates the complexity of the intellectual groups concerned with the issues of the social reform movements and sheds light on the continuous crossing of the left–right divide. In 1911, for example, the Roman Catholic priest, politician and university professor Ottokár Prohászka emphasised the institution of industrial supervision and wrote about the importance of personal service in charity.[34] In 1913, Ervin Szabó, a left-wing social scientist and library director, identified disseminating social thought as his primary goal.[35]

After its partial closing in 1919, the health museum was finally reopened in 1927, with the support of the United States-based Rockefeller Foundation, as the Social Health Institute and Museum.[36] György Gortvay, the new director, regarded the museum primarily as an organ of collective social education, which 'could make work more economical by disseminating knowledge'.[37] From then on, by ministerial order, it was no longer just a museum but also a specialised inspectorate for public health organisations and a propaganda institution for health policy.[38] From the point of view of exploitation and integration, it is striking that in his remark Gortvay connected the notions of social care and wage work. By advancing knowledge, both of workers and employers, the efficiency of work would be increased, a consideration which could take on many dimensions, ranging from the reduction of accidents to the right nutrition to the prevention of diseases. The obsession with the 'economical' became an important value, to which Gortvay linked education: he saw the education of the working class as a means to benefit capitalism, and their labour power as the most important element in establishing capitalism.

What becomes apparent is the immediate focus on the body. Previously, the worker's body had not been approached as something to be disciplined and subjected to calculations. What had changed? Foucault argued that the poor living and working conditions that severely damaged the bodies of nineteenth-century wage-earners illustrate the ignorance of the bourgeoisie in thinking about the life chances of others. The first step in the process of habituating the bodies of the working class to care and discipline was the utilisation of shared urban spaces. Living and moving together in a common space was associated with the spread of diseases. At the same time, the working conditions of industrial capitalism, especially with the development of heavy industry, demanded the permanent supply of a mobile and flexible workforce acting in high-risk conditions, which is why workers became a demographically measured and regulated category. Moreover, if the urban wage-earning workforce became an integral part of society, it was necessary to maintain its physical fitness and moral purity in a uniform manner.[39]

The study of the general character of the population included, in addition to demographic calculations and projections, two other important themes and tools that were worthy of museum representation: the 'degeneration' of the population, on the one hand, and the presentation of the labour protection and care institutions, on the other. That is to say, the perception of population as an economic and political problem also involves the question of how resource surveys operate statistics as a means of describing the state: once the warlike, the taxpayers, the productive and those counted as labourers had been analysed and calculated, the next aim was to ensure the physical strength and moral purity of society. To maintain this, therefore, two directives had to be adhered to: on the one hand, that the various deviations and disabilities should be weeded out, and on the other, that the physical strength of a society thus unified should be ensured through a system of caring institutions. To achieve this goal, governments came to focus on eliminating deviations from the desired norm and fostering a system of caring institutions that ensured the physical strength of a society thus united.[40]

Thus, the valorisation of the body and the emergence of body culture are closely linked to the construction of bourgeois hegemony. Since it was the bourgeoisie who occupied central positions in the making of the capitalist society, the biopolitical regulation of the working class should be considered in the triple relation of 1) the bourgeoisie, 2) workers from 'outside the borders' and 3) workers from 'inside the borders'. It is crucial to take these aspects into account because the Austro-Hungarian Monarchy and later Hungary did not have the access to cheap labour – the bodies – from 'outside the borders' that colonial empires such as Britain and France had. This implies that the bodies of the working class became objects of cultural representation in the Museum of Social Health and were presented as an antagonism staged in opposition to the bodies of the bourgeoisie: in their healthy state, the bodies of the working class were primarily cheap labour, the preservation of which could therefore become an economic interest of the nation.

It is important to note that the museum's management believed it could only exist as a state institution. According to this view, on the one hand, the modern state needed to take up an increasing number of 'social needs and social causes', as director Gortvay claimed, thereby mobilising the language of the social question. And, on the other hand, Gortvay continued, the modern state needed health propaganda to 'establish public understanding toward the functioning of its public health and social policy institutions and to teach people that maintaining health is a collective responsibility'.[41]

An informative comment on the state of the museum in 1927 is seen in the Budapest travelogue of Albert Thomas, a French politician, diplomat and then president of the International Labour Organization. Although Thomas wrote enthusiastically about the museum's existence and highlighted the fact that the museum had collections rather than being a mere research centre, he noted the 'deplorable' state of both the library and the collection as well as the general lack of development, support and maintenance. He also observed that, despite the poor conditions and the lack of heating, the institution had visitors. The collection, according to Thomas, consisted of posters, diagrams, images and models showcasing the importance of social and industrial hygiene, of protection against work accidents and of good childcare, and showing how the standards of housing could be raised. He considered the collection unit on the history of Hungarian medicine particularly impressive and well-maintained, and even outstanding in comparison with other international examples.[42]

The date and circumstances of the museum's reopening, as well as its inaugural exhibition, are indicative of the new health policy that the institution intended to represent. In September 1928, the Fifth International General Assembly of Industrial Accidents and Occupational Diseases met in Budapest to discuss the legitimacy of social hygiene as a discipline in its own right. The reopening of the museum in Budapest was timed to coincide with the meeting. Its opening exhibition was titled Quackery (Kuruzslás) and its exhibits later became a separate collection group and a part of the permanent exhibition. Until its reopening, the museum had mainly focused on the visualisation of data and on models of industrial machinery. The design of the new exhibition broke away from the previous interior design and created probably the most spectacular exhibition in the history of the institution, with waxworks of folk and colonial medicine figures and cures on display in the exhibition space acting as deterrent examples. The collection was continuously developed and in 1933 it was divided into 14 sections, mainly consisting of diagrams, models and photographs. The objects were exhibited in the following thematic areas: accident prevention and worker protection, industrial health, traffic safety, first aid, tuberculosis, alcoholism, sexual ethics, pornography, folk medicine, medical history, maternal and infant health, balneology, general hygiene and anatomy.

The attention given to public hygiene and health development in museums emerged due to industrial capitalism through the twentieth-century rhetoric of progress. Norms concerning the deployment of the body applied primarily to the bodies of the new class within the

Hungarian nation. As a result, two contradictory mechanisms of cultural representation were set in motion: the bodies associated with labour, which were not to be interpreted according to the norms of the bourgeois class, had to be isolated, seen differently, made part of and cared for by the new social unit based on labour.

Museum tools of integration

The emergence and development of the Museum of Social Health reflected the power dynamics of the time. Indeed, through its scientific course, it can be seen as an institutional manifestation of the relationship between power and knowledge.[43] Very obviously, it was the bourgeoisie who defined the values and imposed them on the working class in a universalising claim. Since they held the economic and political power in the late nineteenth century, they were in a suitable position to propagate this discourse.[44] Indeed, the notion of universalisation was the primary practice of the museum. When speaking of the practice of universalisation, I refer to the museum representation that defines civic norms, knowledge and practices as applicable to and desirable by all.

The space of the grand-scale World's Fairs (from 1851 onwards), which brought together various nations, was particularly well-suited to make this 'bourgeois universalism'[45] visible, especially by bringing together everything into one space, creating one big unified spectacle. The tension between the idea of glorious, unified humanity and this hierarchical ordering had a double result in terms of representation: it led to a visible separation of the qualities and achievements associated with 'civilised' and 'savage' nations and to the presentation of the superiority of the 'civilised' people in a system of interdependence.[46] An important rhetorical element of the exhibition space presentation was the presentation of the universal unity of humanity, which at the same time was essentially part of the hierarchy between different nation-states, races and classes.

The Museum of Social Health exhibitions followed a very similar logic. Yet, the issue was further complicated because the wellbeing and health of the population were at the heart of the exhibitions, and the representation of allegedly aspirational values was placed alongside the injured, diseased body of the industrial worker. The involvement of the urban workforce was crucial because it was the primary target group. The challenge was that the nation's development and its ideal of humanity as linear progress had to be reconciled with anomalies such as illness and high mortality rates. To tackle this challenge, the museum continuously tried to adapt the way in which it represented the workforce.

The International Exhibition of Occupational Safety and Labour Welfare was held in 1907 in the Industrial Hall of the museum. It was organised by the National Association of Mechanical Engineers, with the support of the Ministries of Commerce, of Agriculture and of Home Affairs.[47] The exhibition was launched at the instigation of the employers' representatives in response to the introduction of the 1907 Workers' Compensation Act and showcased the technical equipment and devices available to prevent accidents. The Act regulated insurance against accidents at work, an essential reform of the existing institution for health insurance. The 1907 law was expected to prevent the spread of social democratic ideas by making the working classes aware of the state's care and by integrating the labour movement, first and foremost through the trade unions.[48] The event was international; a number of Western nations represented group by group public or private institutions engaged in improving working conditions.[49] There were separate sections on safety and sanitary equipment for industrial and factory sites, protective equipment for machinery used in certain industries, equipment for testing industrial diseases and workers' welfare institutions, including workers' housing as well as schools and shelters for the disabled.[50]

The exhibited objects revolved around the bodies made sick by industry-level manufacturing. New inventions related to manufacturing were also shown, and they were often based on prior industrial accidents and diseases, which were to be curtailed, and on the emerging new health trend, 'industrial hygiene'. The factories that exhibited their developments were those at the forefront of industrial hygiene, that is, they claimed to be protecting workers' lives and used the museum space for showcasing this. This suggests that the exhibition was primarily intended to give a stage to the factories, to present a selection of products linked to industrial capitalism, rather than to advance workers' protection.[51] For these factories – which participated as private exhibitors – the exhibition provided a constant advertising platform for a month and a half, where they could present the institution itself and how they contributed to the latest developments in the field of improving working conditions.

Although the exhibition catalogue repeatedly stated that the target audience of the exhibition was factory workers, no exact figure on attendance is available. For this purpose, opening hours were extended and admission fees kept low. However, an anonymous contemporary reviewer, a physician, pointed out that workers could not afford to visit the exhibition because, in addition to the cost of entrance fees, it would reduce their working hours and, therefore, their wages.[52] Yet, there was a clear interest in bringing workers into the museum. Perhaps the best illustration of the needs and aims is that some factory managements came with their workers to see the exhibition – an initiative encouraged by the exhibition committee as the 'employers' organisation'. According to the introduction of the exhibition catalogue, recognising and considering the interests of the working class was a new and prominent task. The capital of the working class was its workforce, and the exhibition aimed to make the working class aware of the importance of preserving its workforce in its own interest, as it was put:

> Our domestic manufacturing industry, with the introduction of State accident insurance, does not yet see the great social tasks to be solved here as exhausted but seeks and recognises the real interests of the working class in the prevention of accidents and the systematic defence against them, and in this sense wishes to take care of the workers' only capital: the workforce and its preservation, and in this way seeks to make the workers aware of the indispensable necessity of protection against accidents, above all in the interests of the working class.[53]

The catalogue presented the state and industrialists as working hand in hand to advance the interests of the workers through the protection of their bodies. But it also left no doubt that the workers themselves carried a responsibility in this matter. By stating that the 'exemplary facilities which have been established in our newer factories to promote workers' health and general welfare have vividly demonstrated the dedication and progress of Hungarian industry in the field of workers' protection', employers gave the impression that their protective measures were the most modern and advanced, thereby implying that ongoing accidents could not be their fault but had to be attributed to workers who were not 'aware' and not sufficiently educated.[54] The working classes were, in theory, able to enter the exhibition space and admire the products of exemplary factories that were invested in protecting and shaping their bodies. They would then learn that the preservation of their health was essential for the company, the employer and, by extension, the state.

This dimension of care for the workers became entangled with the discourse surrounding the nation's unity and the integration of labour in the exhibition. This is well illustrated by the poster of the exhibition

(Figure 5.1), which shows an angel with a laurel wreath, holding out his blessing hands to the workers in the foreground, with the Industrial Hall (Iparcsarnok) building in the background. The poster is linked to two iconographic traditions: first, the figure raising its bare arms is a symbol

Figure 5.1 Poster of the International Exhibition of Occupational Safety and Labour Welfare of 1907. © National Széchenyi Library, Collection of Posters and Small Prints.

of inspiration, and the laurel-covered head represents victory and virtue. Second, and perhaps more importantly, the angel is also iconographically linked to the Patron Saint (the Virgin Mary – Patrona Hungariae) in the Hungarian pictorial tradition. So the visual network of meanings also contains a reference to the constitution, alluding to national unity. The poster symbolises that the working class can be integrated through the work they accomplish and that their physical strength must be protected because of the work they do, centring the museum as driver of this universally beneficial endeavour.

Alongside issues directly related to the work floor, the museum also targeted aspects of wage workers' daily lives. Alcoholism was a particular focus of several exhibitions, with pictures and statistical analysis highlighting the 'terrible destruction caused by alcohol among workers'.[55] Again drawing on scientific authority, they also exhibited anatomical preparations of internal organs damaged by alcohol consumption. Among the diseased organs and their photos, visitors could see posters of workers' insurance funds, which detailed the effects of alcohol consumption. Statistics on alcoholism and certain diseases and illnesses caused by poor hygiene were displayed in the exhibition area, separately from the bodies and habits presented as healthy. As a result, the workforce was confronted with bad habits damaging their health, juxtaposed with a coherent narrative of progress and new products from the factories highlighted as exemplary institutions. Designed in this way, the exhibition presented the worker's body as part of a unit, namely along with the products of the factories on the site of production. At the same time, the workforce itself was disconnected from that very same body and treated separately, along with the products of the factories, on the side of production. Just like production techniques and safety equipment, knowledge about the workers' bodies and health was also standardised. Both served to increase productivity and advance economic growth.

The paradox was that the intrusion into workers' private lives intensified at a time otherwise characterised as an emancipatory moment in Western history, with the strongest evidence being the extension of the suffrage. What is noteworthy here is that, although it is likely that not many workers visited the museum, the exhibition did aim to attract a working-class audience: the visitors, the urban wage-earners, could easily find themselves in the position of walking among the products of idealised factories worthy of displaying, and being confronted with negative tendencies linked to their own body, such as alcoholism, neglect of the body and illness.

Eight years later, the rhetoric of the 1915 War and Public Health Exhibition suggested that the preservation of the workforce became as important as health, with working capacity essentially becoming an accompaniment to health. Hungary, still part of the Austro-Hungarian Empire, was deeply involved in the First World War, and with millions of men drafted, the preservation of the working population became a major concern. The main message of the exhibition was 'Let us live and work to stay healthy and fit for work'.[56] Moreover, the emphasis on work and life had shifted, with the catalogue suggesting that work was a way of staying healthy: 'There is a misconception that work is bad for your health. On the contrary, idleness is bad for health, whereas work, a non-excessive form of it at least, is not only the most valuable source of income but also the maintainer of our physical health.'[57]

Two of the most devastating consequences of the war, infant mortality and poor child health, were also addressed in the exhibition:

> If a healthy and hard-working man is the treasure of his country, then the child – who is destined to succeed the preceding generation and continue the work that they have begun – is the country's future. The new generation should be more vigorous in body and spirit than the preceding to stand its ground in the struggle of aspiring nations and advance humanity.[58]

Since children were the guarantee of a future based on the toil of the current healthy, hard-working generation, it was crucial to protect their health. The idea that mental and physical improvement from generation to generation was necessary in order for the population as a whole to rise above and overcome other nations was a central argument of the eugenic thinking of this age.[59] In this fashion, the problem of alcoholism was no longer linked to industrial health, as the primary concern was not the risk of accidents to workers under the influence of alcohol but specific 'effects' that were genetically inherited, leading to 'degenerative changes over generations'.[60]

Compared to the 1907 exhibition, the catalogue authors in 1915 made much more concrete proposals concerning social policy:

> Protecting the health of the child starts with protecting the mother. Certain occupations are dangerous not only to the mother's health but also to the foetus (industrial poisons). Therefore, it is desirable that mothers, especially in the last stages of pregnancy, should be spared both the hard work and the harm of industrial occupations

in particular. … Another important thing to do is train mothers to care for their babies. … [I]t is necessary to give the child time to practise various sports and accustom them to the changing weather conditions. Only such a child will become a truly hard-working individual, able to stand up to the hardest rigours of life and duty.[61]

Besides conceptualising work as a duty, this discourse followed the fundamental premise that the next generation held the potential for development and improving on the previous generation. The next generation's upbringing was exclusively associated with women and the female body, which had a double implication. On the one hand, the female body became part of the issue of inheritance, as the children's health was linked to that of the mother. Reproduction and infant mortality were considered a priority issue because of the severe labour shortage during the war, so maternal health also emerged as a fundamental problem on the health agenda. On the other hand, the woman's body was associated with both her industrial and reproductive labour. Women's reproductive work was unsurprisingly not counted as work – they had no contractual employment relationship – and the four-week maternity allowance in the Workers' Compensation Act did not reward reproductive work but rather a return to the factory floor. At the same time, the exhibition conveners urged that women be given priority insurance while working during pregnancy because this could potentially protect the next generation. The representation shows that women and women's work were integrated into the narrative of shared purposeful development if they were represented as capable of child-bearing and performing reproductive work.

In 1928, the museum opened a new permanent exhibition that focused on industrial health, occupational safety and accident prevention in separate sections, indicating that these questions remained severe public health issues. From the late 1920s, the exhibitions' discourse on labour became increasingly intertwined with social Darwinist and eugenicist arguments that legitimised competition between nations and portrayed the common progress of humanity in a hierarchical but unitary order.[62]

Eugenics and work

The institutionalisation of the eugenics movement took place in several stages, first within academic and then within political circles.

Neither politically nor in terms of disciplinary affiliation can the eugenics groups in Hungary be considered unified. The museum served as a forum for this public debate and the institutionalisation of eugenics. The eugenic discourse was prominent throughout almost the entire existence of the Museum of Social Health, indicating that the public health paradigms of the late nineteenth and early twentieth centuries should be examined within the scientific-political narrative of the healthy national body. Also linked to the social question, eugenics offered the possibility of renewing the nation's collective body through its biologisation. Emphasising the scientific narrative of the era offered a space for imagining how to defend the glories of the past – the powerful Austro-Hungarian Empire – from an unsatisfactory present and create an imagined future.[63]

The critical question of the eugenic discourse was how to redefine the individual body as a collective body and how this collective body could, as a unit, cope with cultural and biological degeneration.[64] By approaching the working class, and its bodies and habits, collectively, representatives of eugenics formulated proposals to strengthen, improve and shape the community as a single organism. In this way, a political and cultural imaginary of the collective body would emerge through which it would become the object of scientific thought and of discipline. The guidelines, including appropriate biological, medical and statistical methods, developed by the representatives of science, had to be implemented by the state, which was capable of putting the interests of the community above those of the individual.[65]

Social Darwinism, which legitimised cultural and political competition between peoples and races, was in perfect harmony with the systematisation and hierarchy of the museum. This is why the Social Museum, which dealt with social issues, public health and hygiene, was able to fulfil the function of a complex institution called into life by biopolitical thinking, linked to the disciplining-caring concept of biopolitics. Changes in the direction of the eugenic discourse were strongly influenced by the political events of the time and their histories, and were related not only to race but also to class. In Hungary, however, class-based selection was more hidden. An example of class-based eugenic thinking was the question of internal migration between rural and urban areas and the formulation of population policy guidelines linked to this:

> With the turn of the twentieth century, eugenicists everywhere had become increasingly concerned with the social and biological implications of accelerated urbanization – served by large-scale internal

migrations from rural to urban areas – and industrialization, which resulted in a deteriorating standard of living and worsening hygienic conditions in working-class social environments. The nation's health was thus viewed and interpreted through the lens of eugenics. Within this context, the individual's alleged biological deterioration became conterminous with a perceived collective degeneration, an imbalance that had to be remedied through appropriate eugenic, social and medical interventions.[66]

A good indication of the 'hidden' nature of the class aspect of the eugenics issue in Hungary is the fact that in 1911 the Alliance of Smallholders (Kisgazdák Szövetsége) submitted a memorandum to the Minister of the Interior, which was forwarded to the National Council of Public Health (Országos Közegészségügyi Tanács) for consideration. The memorandum addressed three problems: early marriage practices, contraception (and child-bearing – the single-child system) and infant mortality. In the memorandum, the alliance wants the state to intervene to increase the number of families (i.e. the state should end the practice of families having only one child); secondly, it asks the state to pass a law to prevent the young population from marrying too early, and thirdly, to prevent the practice of abortion. As historian Marius Turda argues, the mixing of the issues of marriage, contraception and infant mortality in the memorandum was not accidental. Since agrarian proletarian families were generally smaller than urban ones, the preservation of the Hungarian peasant family became an act of nationalism. For the Alliance of Smallholders, the goal was to promote demographic growth, a goal with which the above demands were all in accord, including the natalist idea of presenting the larger family with more children as the ideal. But the establishment of such large families was not expected of landlords and aristocratic elites, thus protecting large family wealth from being fragmented by the birth of more children. So at the same time, all this demographic growth was not imposed on the aristocracy and the landed classes. As Turda points out, attempts to limit family size were less about racial protectionism and more about preserving class and social status, thus limiting fertility by discriminating on the basis of class. The memorandum was rejected by the National Council of Public Health in 1911, which declared it to be unjust discrimination in the eyes of the peasantry and the working classes.[67]

Although not legally implemented, this rhetoric of state-organised natalist politics surfaced again in the museum's leaflets. After 1919, the eugenicists, mainly Géza Hoffmann (Consul General for Race Health and

Population Policy), proposed the promotion of ruralisation, which the Institute of Social Health and the Museum tried to make the population aware of from the 1920s onwards, for example through leaflets with the slogan 'Don't emigrate to the cities, don't leave your home' (Figure 5.2). The propaganda for moving to the countryside and, even more so, for staying in the countryside was based on a population policy directive drawn up in the 1920s, which saw the peasantry as the key to fertility and to overcoming the demographic crisis.

Until the First World War, the museum dealt with the subject of eugenics primarily in its periodicals, and only in the late 1920s did it become a theme in exhibitions. After the museum was reopened in 1927, it held two exhibitions on public health and eugenics: the Social Health Exhibition in Budapest in 1932 and the Keszthely Exhibition, organised in Keszthely in collaboration with the Balaton Association. The main exhibition section of the latter, with the most extensive display of objects, was dedicated to Population Policy and Reproduction. In this space, the exhibition was concerned with birth and death rates, marriage and child-bearing. The spread of the eugenics discourse is also reflected in the exhortative text of the exhibition poster (Figure 5.3): 'Every human being is the bearer of an infinite past and responsible for an infinite

Figure 5.2 Leaflet of the Museum of Social Health used in propaganda against emigration from the villages after 1928: 'Don't emigrate to the cities, don't leave your home.' © Gortvay György. Népegészségügyi Múzeum Munkája. Budapest: Egyesült Kő-, Könyvnyomda, 1935.

Figure 5.3 Exhibition poster on the topic of social health protection of the year 1932. © Gortvay György. Népegészségügyi Múzeum Munkája. Budapest: Egyesült Kő-, Könyvnyomda, 1935.

future. Anyone who feels a responsibility towards the next generation should visit the exhibition on social health protection at the Museum of Public Health.'[68] The poster translated into consumable rhetoric the idea at the heart of the eugenics discourse that the fate of future generations is determined by the community living in the present through the transmission of different traits. The graphic elements of the brochure also illustrate this: the image of a man descending a flight of stairs, his figure emerging ever more sharply from the blur of the past.

The Eugenics and Heredity Exhibition of 1934 additionally aimed to 'clarify the more important questions concerning heredity'. The natalist idea of the 1920s leaflets is reflected in the infographics of this exhibition held in the Museum of Social Health, which depict village work and conditions: 'The reproduction of the Hungarian population is ensured by the Hungarian village. If the cradles are empty, the nation will age. Bp.'s [Budapest's] reproduction rate is 0.1 per cent. The reproduction rate of small communities is 12.7 per cent.' The exhibition for urban workers showed visitors that life and work in the villages was the source of the much sought-after population growth that helped the nation survive. As well as presenting the latest achievements of the science of eugenics, the exhibition dealt with the reproduction of the European population and, in particular, with the growth of the Hungarian population in terms of the stratification of society.[69]

Conclusion

The aim of this chapter was to show how we can better understand museum displays and the art world of the late nineteenth and early twentieth centuries by extending art-historical and museological concepts and questions to the history of work. Taking into account concepts of industrial labour and exploitation also allows us to understand the change that took place in the mid-nineteenth century with the emerging of a new visual order, which coincided with the institutionalisation of labour. As a result, the concept and sites of spectacle were transformed, including the way it was presented in museums.

In examining the Budapest Museum of Social Health, I started from Foucault's assertion that the history of industrial capitalism and the history of biopolitics are inseparable. Therefore, the museum must be understood as part of the institutional system integrating the world of labour as an element of the institutionalisation of labour. Observing that the emergence of body culture was closely linked to the construction of bourgeois hegemony, I argued that the commodification of enforced labour was the central concern of biopolitical thought.

As we have seen, social and biopolitical issues were very closely linked in the history of industrial capitalism. The museum's alleged primary audience was the urban working class, and its exhibits were related to social issues and public health legislation. At the same time, the cheap industrial workforce that emerged at the end of the nineteenth century marked a turn in the history of museums at least as significant as the emergence of museums in the public sphere: the lower classes were turned from spectators into exhibited 'objects'. Their bodies, health and reproductive work were presented alongside new inventions and products from companies and nation-states that competed with one another. Needless to say, the manufacturing of products was associated with the work of their inventors and not with the work of the people who created them.

I have shown that the Hungarian Museum of Social Health was primarily a site of public education, where the task became one of showing the anonymous, or rather the typical, as opposed to individual objects and memories. The urban working classes' poverty, ill health or sick bodies did not fit into any of the existing categories of the museums of the time. On the contrary, taking advantage of the public museum's role by the end of the nineteenth century, the museum conveners wanted to display knowledge that was bound up with the present and that would have been invisible in the museum's previous representational practices. Here, two contradictory elements of the notions associated with the museum institution were in tension. On the one hand, the nineteenth-century museum was the principal institution for representing the nation-state. On the other, it was the unquestioned arena of scholarship, presenting the entirety of the world's knowledge in the encyclopedic tradition to those admitted to its premises. The museum's task was to organise the accumulated knowledge into a specific system and thus establish and present an unquestionable hierarchy.[70] Thus, the body of labour and its living and working conditions became part of this hierarchy when they were placed in the exhibition space of social museums. Yet, presenting the social question in museums did not make the working class visible to the visitors. Instead, it was a matter of associating social problems with the working class and bringing the problems themselves into the space of representation.

Notably, it is still unclear today how many workers visited the museum or even how many visitors it had overall. If the working class was not the main target as visitors of the exhibitions, shall we consider the Museum of Social Health a think-tank where those with a stake in controlling the industrial workforce met? After all, it was the ruling class and leading capitalists who shaped and curated the exhibitions. During the transformation to industrial capitalism in Hungary, they required new strategies to make people work. Seen in this light, the propagated discipline of the new wage labourers emerges as a form of coercion, and the alleged care of their bodies represents a new form of control, both envisioned with the aim of increasing productivity and maintaining the workforce.

Notes

1. Henceforth I will use the official names of the museum, which have changed over time: Social Museum; Social, Health Education and Public Health Museum; Institute and Museum of Public Health; and Social Health Institute and Museum. If I refer to the museum in general, I will use the name Museum of Social Health, although it was never used in this way.
2. Crimp, 'On the Museum's Ruins'; Bennett, *The Birth of the Museum*; Bennett, 'Culture and Governmentality'; Hooper-Greenhill, *Museums and the Shaping of Knowledge*.
3. See Habermas, *Strukturwandel der Öffentlichkeit*; Bennett, 'Culture and Governmentality'.
4. Foucault, *The History of Sexuality*, 140–1.
5. Foucault, 'Society Must Be Defended', 241–7.
6. Foucault, *The History of Sexuality*, 141.
7. Closely linked to this new order of domination, in which concepts of discipline and care were formed around the body of the population, was the issue of sexuality. In the late eighteenth century, the 'technology of sex' became a state affair in the Western world, removed from the institution of the Church and mediated by pedagogy, medicine and economic sciences. This is particularly significant in our case as the Museum of Social Health was created precisely at the intersection of these three disciplines: it was an educational institution founded by the state in collaboration with the leading representatives of medicine and public administration; see Gortvay, *Népegészségügyi Múzeum Munkája*, 9–11; Foucault, *The History of Sexuality*, 116.
8. Foucault, *The History of Sexuality*, 122–5. The complex context is well illustrated by the ongoing debate on the Hungarian specificity and conceptual change of citizenship or civilisation, often in the light of comparisons with Western European countries; see Gyáni, 'A polgárosodás történelmi problémája', 98–119; Kocka, 'Bürgertum und bürgerliche Gesellschaft im 19. Jahrhundert'. The bibliography compiled by Károly Halmos contains almost 400 items on the subject: see Halmos, 'A polgárról, a polgáriról és a polgárosodásról szóló irodalom, 1988–1992', 131–47.
9. Kövér, 'Iparosodás agrárországban', 264.
10. Rézler, 'A magyar nagyipari munkásság kialakulása, 1867–1914', 358–62; Laczkó, 'A magyar munkásosztály fejlődésének fő vonásai a tőkés korszakban', 369.
11. Rézler, 'A magyar nagyipari munkásság kialakulása, 1867–1914', 363–4. All translations in the chapter are those of the author and Patrick Tyler, who assisted in the translation.
12. Laczkó, 'A magyar munkásosztály fejlődésének fő vonásai a tőkés korszakban', 372–3.
13. Kövér, 'Iparosodás agrárországban', 268.
14. Laczkó, 'A magyar munkásosztály fejlődésének fő vonásai a tőkés korszakban', 150.
15. Gyáni, 'Bérkaszárnya és nyomortelep – A Budapesti munkáslakás múltja', 418–19.
16. Laczkó, 'A magyar munkásosztály fejlődésének fő vonásai a tőkés korszakban', 148.
17. Laczkó, 'A magyar munkásosztály fejlődésének fő vonásai a tőkés korszakban', 149.
18. On the cultural aspect of this, see K. Horváth, 'A munkáskalokagathia pillanata', 47–75.
19. Bódy, *Az ipari munka társadalma*, 7.
20. Castel, *From Manual Workers to Wage Laborers: Transformation of the Social Question*, 17.
21. Bódy, *Az ipari munka társadalma*, 75.
22. Castel, *From Manual Workers to Wage Laborers: Transformation of the Social Question*, 217–33.
23. The philosopher and politician Gáspár Miklós Tamás argues that the mixture of Christian compassion, sympathy and pity for the suffering and exploitation of the subjugated classes became the starting point of liberal-inspired social improvement efforts; see Tamás, 'Eötvös: A nyugat-keleti liberális'.

24 Vörös and Spira, *Budapest története a márciusi forradalomtól az őszirózsás forradalomig*, 377–579; Thirring (ed.), *Budapest félszázados fejlődése 1873–1923*, 47.
25 Melinz and Zimmermann, 'Sozialpolitisierung der Fürsorge oder Sozialreform?', 85–6.
26 Gyáni, 'A regulázó gondoskodás', 17.
27 Gyáni, 'A regulázó gondoskodás', 11–28; Petrák, *A szervezett munkásság küzdelme a korszerű társadalombiztosításért*; Bódy, *Az ipari munka társadalma*; Zimmermann, *Divide, Provide and Rule*.
28 Bódy, *Az ipari munka társadalma*.
29 'Statutory protection for workers included the first Industrial Act of 1872 and the second Industrial Act of 1884, which stipulated that the employer was obliged to provide the necessary conditions for healthy and safe work in his factory, with the potential possibility of a fine if the requirements were not met. More state intervention was provided by Act XXVIII of 1893, which further defined the employer's duty to protect workers and ordered the establishment of an industrial inspectorate to supervise factories'; see Nyilas, 'Szociálpolitika', 254.
30 Szántó, 'Munkásjóléti intézmények', 1909.
31 Gortvay, *Népegészségügyi Múzeum Munkája*, 10.
32 'Szociálpolitika: A Társadalmi Múzeum', 24.
33 Őze, 'Társadalmi Múzeum', 9–14.
34 Prohászka, 'A személyes szolgálat a jótékonyságban', 1–4; for a similar contemporary perspective, see Marschan, 'Az iparfelügyelet jelentősége', 1–11.
35 Szabó, 'Cím nélkül', 1–3.
36 The Rockefeller Foundation provided the capital injection for the Social Health Institute and Museum in the late 1920s; see Gortvay, 'Népegészségügyi Múzeum', 153; Bán, 'Ersatz és történelem', 368–84. Although the comparison with the United States may seem remote, there are certain parallels, not only in the initial logic but also in the organisations behind the institutions. In the United States, for example, the 1900s–1920s saw the concentration of a vast social surplus in private foundations and the public sector, which became a significant source of social regulation. The availability of these resources helped expand public education and public health care, while the power of the law sanctioned the relevant measures. While all this was a response to social problems and an effort towards a solution, it was also a politically encouraged penetration into the life of working-class communities: schools imparted industrial discipline; charities and their in-house scientists spread their ideas of 'the proper way of living'. Moreover, public health officials began to oversee the ghettos of immigrants; see Ehrenreich and Ehrenreich, 'The Professional-Managerial Class', 16.
37 Gortvay, *Népegészségügyi Múzeum Munkája*, 3.
38 Gortvay, 'Népegészségügyi Múzeum', 154.
39 Foucault, *The History of Sexuality*, 126.
40 Foucault, 'Society Must Be Defended', 244–50.
41 Gortvay, *Népegészségügyi Múzeum Munkája*, 3.
42 Thomas and Bódy, 'Utazás Bécs–Budapest–Belgrád–Athén: Napi jegyzetek', 152–70.
43 Bennett, *The Birth of the Museum*; Crimp, 'On the Museum's Ruins', 45–52.
44 Wallerstein, *Historical Capitalism with Capitalist Civilization*, 85.
45 Marx and Engels, 'Manifesto of the Communist Party'.
46 As Paul Young, citing Immanuel Wallerstein, points out, in nineteenth-century exhibition spaces, universalism was not a 'free-floating' ideology but a propagated discourse of those who held economic and political power in the world economic system; see Wallerstein, *Historical Capitalism with Capitalist Civilization*, 85; Young, 'Mission Impossible: Globalization and the Great Exhibition', 20.
47 The exhibition did not belong exclusively to the Social Museum. However, the museum played a crucial role in its preparation, and the objects, photographs and other exhibits purchased by the Ministry of Trade were later added to the museum's collection; see Szántó, 'Balesetügyi, iparegészségügyi és munkásjóléti kiállítás Budapesten', 1907, 650.
48 Bódy, 'A "társadalom kora"', 19. The above logic is illustrated, for example, by an article on the exhibition in 1907: 'This exhibition will perhaps silence the unfounded attacks that accuse Hungarian society of carelessness and proclaim that no one cares about the workers in Hungary. Only the socialist agitators. Take a look at this exhibition, and you will see that we are keeping pace with foreign countries and trying to do everything in our power to protect

the workers from accidents, take care of their physical health and well-being and educate them intellectually'; 'Nemzetközi balesetügyi és munkásjóléti kiállítás'.
49   Balesetügyi Kiállítás, an entry from the Révai Nagy Lexikon, 'Balesetügyi kiállítás', 495.
50   Szántó, 'Balesetügyi, iparegészségügyi és munkásjóléti kiállítás Budapesten', 1907, 651–6.
51   Nemzetközi Balesetügyi és Munkásjóléti Kiállítás katalógus.
52   Bród, 'A nemzetközi balesetügyi kiállítás', 105.
53   Nemzetközi Balesetügyi és Munkásjóléti Kiállítás katalógus, 2.
54   Nemzetközi Balesetügyi és Munkásjóléti Kiállítás katalógus, 1.
55   Szántó, 'Balesetügyi, iparegészségügyi és munkásjóléti kiállítás Budapesten', 1907, 659.
56   Szántó and Tomor (eds), Budapesten az Országházban rendezett had- és népegészségügyi kiállítás katalógusa, 4.
57   Szántó and Tomor (eds), Budapesten az Országházban rendezett had- és népegészségügyi kiállítás katalógusa, 205.
58   Szántó and Tomor (eds), Budapesten az Országházban rendezett had- és népegészségügyi kiállítás katalógusa, 201.
59   On the development of the eugenics discourse in Hungary, see Turda, Eugenics and Nation in Early 20th Century Hungary, 185–7.
60   Szántó and Tomor (eds), Budapesten az Országházban rendezett had- és népegészségügyi kiállítás katalógusa, 213.
61   Szántó and Tomor (eds), Budapesten az Országházban rendezett had- és népegészségügyi kiállítás katalógusa, 202.
62   See Turda, Modernism and Eugenics; Turda, Eugenics and Nation in Early 20th Century Hungary.
63   Turda, Modernism and Eugenics, 6; Balibar-Wallerstein, Race, Nation, Class.
64   Turda, Modernism and Eugenics, 5.
65   Turda, Eugenics and Nation in Early 20th Century Hungary, 3; MacMaster, Racism in Europe 1870–2000, 31.
66   Turda, Eugenics and Nation in Early 20th Century Hungary, 7.
67   Turda, Eugenics and Nation in Early 20th Century Hungary, 101–2.
68   Gortvay, Népegészségügyi Múzeum Munkája, 101.
69   Gortvay, Népegészségügyi Múzeum Munkája, 105.
70   See Bennett, Pasts Beyond Memories, 27–33; György, Az eltörölt hely – a Múzeum, 40–4.

Bibliography

Balibar, Étienne and Wallerstein, Immanuel. Race, Nation, Class: Ambiguous Identities. London/New York: Verso, 1991.
Bán, Zsófia. 'Ersatz és történelem: Az amerikai eugenika-mozgalom rejtett narratívája a tárgyalótermi drámák tükrében'. In Bevésett nevek: Az Eötvös Loránd Tudományegyetem holokauszt- és második világháborús emlékművének felavatásához kapcsolódó konferencia, edited by Teri Szűcs, 376–84. Budapest: ELTE BTK, 2015.
Bennett, Tony. The Birth of the Museum: History, Theory, Politics. London/New York: Routledge, 1995.
Bennett, Tony. 'Culture and Governmentality'. In Foucault, Cultural Studies and Governmentality, edited by Jack Z. Bratich, Jeremy Packer and Cameron McCarthy, 47–66. New York: Suny Press, 2002.
Bennett, Tony. Pasts Beyond Memories: Evolution, Museums, Colonialism. London/New York: Routledge, 2004.
Bódy, Zsombor. 'A "társadalom kora": Munkásbiztosítás és munkaügy Magyarországon a 19. és a 20. század fordulóján', Aetas 19/1 (2004): 5–31.
Bódy, Zsombor. Az ipari munka társadalma: Szociális kihívások, liberális és korporatív válaszok Magyarországon a 19. század végétől a második világháborúig. Budapest: Argumentum, 2010.
Bród, Miksa. 'A nemzetközi balesetügyi kiállítás', Iparegészségügy 6/24 (1907): 105–6.
Castel, Robert. From Manual Workers to Wage Laborers: Transformation of the Social Question. New Brunswick/London: Transaction Publishers, [1995] 2002.
Conklin, Alice L. In the Museum of Man: Race, Anthropology, and Empire in France, 1850–1950. London: Ithaca, 2013.

Crimp, Douglas. 'On the Museum's Ruins'. In *The Anti Aesthetic: Essays on Postmodern Culture*, edited by Hal Foster, 45–52. Port Townsend, WA: Bay Press, 1985.
Ehrenreich, Barbara and Ehrenreich, John. 'The Professional-Managerial Class', *Radical America* 11/2 (1977): 7–31.
Farkas, Tamás. 'Fajbiológia, szociáldarwinizmus, eugenika: Turda, Marius: Eugenics and the Nation in Early 20th Century Hungary', *Socio.hu* 7/1 (2017): 61–9.
Foucault, Michel. *The History of Sexuality, Vol. 1: An Introduction*. New York: Pantheon, 1978.
Foucault, Michel. 'Society Must Be Defended'. In *Lectures at The Collège de France, 1975–76*, edited by Mauro Bertani and Alessandro Fontana, 236–65. New York: Picador, 2003.
Frazon, Zsófia. *A múzeum és kiállítás: Az újrarajzolás terei*. Budapest–Pécs: Gondolat, 2011.
Fülöp, Zsigmond. 'Az eugenetika követelései és korunk társadalmi viszonyai', *Huszadik Század* 12/23 (1911): 308–319.
Gortvay, György. *Népegészségügyi Múzeum Munkája*. Budapest: Egyesült Kő-, Könyvnyomda, 1935.
Gortvay, György. 'Népegészségügyi Múzeum', *Szociálpolitikai Értesítő* 8/1 (1990): 152–65.
Gyáni, Gábor. 'A regulázó gondoskodás'. In *'A tettetésnek minden mesterségeiben jártasok': Koldusok, csavargók, veszélyeztetett gyerekek a modernkori Magyarországon*, edited by Pál Léderer, Tamás Tenczer and László Ulicska, 11–28. Budapest: Új Mandátum, 1998.
Gyáni, Gábor. 'Bérkaszárnya és nyomortelep. A budapesti munkáslakás múltja'. In *Magyarország Társadalomtörténete II. 1920–1944*, edited by Gábor Gyáni, 417–33. Budapest: Nemzeti Tankönyvkiadó, 2000.
Gyáni, Gábor. 'A polgárosodás történelmi problémája'. In *Történészdiskurzusok*, 98–119. Budapest: L'Harmattan, 2002.
György, Péter. *Az eltörölt hely – a Múzeum: A múzeumok átváltozása a hálózati kultúra korában: New York, Természettörténeti Múzeum – egy példa*. Budapest: Magvető, 2003.
Habermas, Jürgen. *Strukturwandel der Öffentlichkeit: Untersuchungen zu einer Kategorie der bürgerlichen Gesellschaft*. Luchterhand: Neuwied am Rhein, 1962.
Halmos, Károly. 'A polgárról, a polgáriról és a polgárosodásról szóló irodalom, 1988–1992', *Aetas* 9/3 (1994): 131–47.
Hooper-Greenhill, Eilean. *Museums and the Shaping of Knowledge*. London: Routledge, 1992.
Horváth, Zsolt. K. 'A munkáskalokagathia pillanata: Költészet, társadalomkritika és a munkáskultúra egysége: Justus Pál és a Munka-kör'. In *'… fejünkből töröljük ki a regulákat': Kassák Lajos az író, a képzőművész, szerkesztő és közszereplő*, edited by Gábor Andrási, 47–75. Budapest: PIM–Kassák Alapítvány, 2010.
Kocka, Jürgen. 'Bürgertum und bürgerliche Gesellschaft im 19. Jahrhundert: Europäische Entwicklungen und deutsche Eigenarten'. In *Bürgertum im 19. Jahrhundert: Deutschland im europäischen Vergleich, vol. I*, edited by Jürgen Kocka, 11–78. Munich: Deutscher Taschenbuch Verlag, 1988.
Kövér, György. 'Iparosodás agrárországban'. In *Magyarország Társadalomtörténete I. A reformkortól az első világháborúig. 1. kötet*, edited by György Kövér, 264–87. Budapest: Nemzeti Tankönyvkiadó, 1997.
Krafft-Ebing, Richard von. *Psychopathia Sexualis: The Classic Study of Deviant Sex*. New York: Arcade, [1886] 2011.
Kreuder-Sonnen, Katharina and Renner, Andreas. 'Einleitung: Gesellschaft, Kultur und Hygiene in Osteuropa', *Jahrbücher für Geschichte Osteuropas* (Neue Folge) 61/4 (2013): 481–8.
Laczkó, Miklós, 'A magyar munkásosztály fejlődésének fő vonásai a tőkés korszakban'. In *Magyarország Társadalomtörténete I. A reformkortól az első világháborúig. 1. kötet*, edited by György Kövér, 367–76. Budapest: Nemzeti Tankönyvkiadó, 1997.
Laczkó, Miklós, 'A magyar munkásosztály fejlődésének fő vonásai a tőkés korszakban'. In *Magyarország Társadalomtörténete II. 1920–1944*, edited by Gábor Gyáni, 143–57. Budapest: Nemzeti Tankönyvkiadó, 2000.
MacMaster, Niel. *Racism in Europe 1870–2000*. Hampshire: Palgrave, 2001.
Marschan, Károly. 'Az iparfelügyelet jelentősége', *A Társadalmi Múzeum Szemléje* 1/4 (1914): 1–11.
Marx, Karl and Engels, Friedrich. 'Manifesto of the Communist Party'. In *Marx Engels Selected Works, vol. 1*, 98–138. Moscow: Progress Publishers, [1848] 1969.
Melinz, Gerhard and Susan Zimmermann. 'Sozialpolitisierung der Fürsorge oder Sozialreform? Kommunale Wohlfahrt in Budapest und Wien vor 1914', *Wiener Geschichtsblätter* 47 (1992): 84–101.

Nagy, Dániel. 'Séta A Kuruzslás Birodalmában – Babona és tudatlanság meglepő kinövései finom vitrinekben – Boszorkányok, csalók, szélhámosok visszaélései az egészség rovására', *Tolnai Világlapja* 23 (1936): 42–3.
Nemzetközi Balesetügyi és Munkásjóléti Kiállítás katalógus. Budapest: Kiadó, 1907a.
'Nemzetközi balesetügyi és munkásjóléti kiállítás', *Magyarország* 14 (1907b): 4.
Nyilas, Mihály. 'Szociálpolitika', In *Magyarország a XX. században, II. KÖTET Természeti környezet, népesség és társadalom, egyházak és felekezetek, gazdaság*, edited by Margit Balogh, István Bekény, Dezső Dányi, László Élesztős, László Mihály Hernádi, Iván Oros and Tibor Tiner. Szekszárd: Babits Kiadó, 1996–2000.
Őze, Eszter. 'Társadalmi Múzeum: A szociális és egészségügyi nevelés intézménye', *Korall – Társadalomtörténeti Folyóirat* 80 (2020): 5–29.
Palló, Gábor. 'Darwin utazása Magyarországon', *Magyar Tudomány* 170/6 (2009): 714–26.
Perecz, László. '"Fajegészségtan" balról jobbra: Az eugenika század eleji recepciójához: Madzsar és Pekár'. In *A totalitarizmus és a magyar filozófia: Tanulmányok*, edited by Tamás Valastyán, 200–15. Debrecen: Vulgo, 2005.
Petrák, Katalin. *A szervezett munkásság küzdelme a korszerű társadalombiztosításért*. Budapest: Táncsics, 1978.
Praznik, Katja. 'A Feminist Approach to the Disavowed Economy of Art'. In *Art Work: Invisible Labour and the Legacy of Yugoslav Socialism*, 35–46. Toronto: University of Toronto Press, 2021.
Prohászka, Ottokár. 'A személyes szolgálat a jótékonyságban', *A Társadalmi Múzeum Értesítője* 3 (1911): 1–4.
Révai Nagy Lexikon. 'Balesetügyi kiállítás'. In *Révai Nagy Lexikona 2. kötet*, 495–6. Budapest: Révai Testvérek Irodalmi Intézet RT, 1911.
Rézler, Gyula. 'A magyar nagyipari munkásság kialakulása, 1867–1914'. In *Magyarország Társadalomtörténete. I. A reformkortól az első világháborúig. 2 kötet*, edited by György Kövér, 357–67. Budapest: Nemzeti Tankönyvkiadó, 1997.
Stoler, Ann Laura. *Race and the Education of Desire: Foucault's History of Sexuality and the Colonial Order of Things*. Durham/London: Duke University Press, 1995.
Szabó, Ervin. 'Cím nélkül', *A Társadalmi Múzeum Szemléje* 1/4 (1913): 1–3.
Szántó, Menyhért. 'Balesetügyi, iparegészségügyi és munkásjóléti kiállítás Budapesten', *Közigazgatási Szemle* 38 (1907): 649–60.
Szántó, Menyhért. 'Munkásjóléti intézmények', *A Társadalmi Múzeum Értesítője*, 1 (1909): 3–16.
Szántó, Menyhért and Tomor, Ernő (eds.). *Budapesten az Országházban rendezett had- és népegészségügyi kiállítás katalógusa*. Budapest: Kiadó, 1915.
'Szociálpolitika: A Társadalmi Múzeum', *Szociálpolitikai Szemle* 2 (1912): 24.
Takács, Ádám. 'Biopolitika és nemzeti állapot: Egy foucault-i problematika rekonstrukciója'. In *Kötőerők: Az identitás történetének térbeli keretei*, edited by András Cieger, 15–28. Budapest: Atelier Francia–Magyar Társadalomtudományi Kutatóközpont, 2009.
Tamás, Gáspár Miklós. 'Eötvös: A nyugat-keleti liberális'. In *Törzsi fogalmak II*, 9–145. Budapest: Atlantisz, 1999.
Thirring, Gusztáv (ed.). *Budapest félszázados fejlődése 1873–1923*. (Statisztikai Közlemények 53). Budapest: Budapest Székesfőváros Statisztikai Hivatal, 1925.
Thomas, Albert and Bódy, Zsombor. 'Utazás Bécs–Budapest–Belgrád–Athén: Napi jegyzetek', *Aetas* 3 (2014): 152–70.
Turda, Marius. 'Faj és nemzet: A nemzeti felsőbbrendűség a 19. század végi Magyarországon', *Kétezer* 16/6 (2004): 57–67.
Turda, Marius. *Modernism and Eugenics*. Basingstoke: Palgrave, 2010.
Turda, Marius. *Eugenics and Nation in Early 20th Century Hungary*. Basingstoke: Palgrave, 2014.
Turda, Marius and Weindling, Paul (eds.). *Blood and Homeland: Eugenics and Racial Nationalism in Central and Southeast Europe, 1900–1940*. Budapest/New York: Central European University Press, 2007.
Vörös, Károly and Spira, György. *Budapest története a márciusi forradalomtól az őszirózsás forradalomig*. Budapest: Akadémiai, 1978.
Wallerstein, Immanuel. *Historical Capitalism with Capitalist Civilization*. London/New York: Verso, 1995.
Weber-Felber, Ulrike. 'Die Weltausstellungen des 19. Jahrhunderts: Medium bürgerlicher Weltsicht'. In *Kult und Kultur des Ausstellens: Beiträge zur Praxis, Theorie und Didaktik des*

Museums, edited by Margarete Erber-Groiß, Severin Heinisch, Hubert C. Ehalt and Helmut Konrad, 90–102. Vienna: WUV–Universitätsverlag, 1992.
Young, Paul. 'Mission Impossible: Globalization and the Great Exhibition'. In *Britain, the Empire, and the World at the Great Exhibition of 1851*, edited by Jeffrey A. Auerbach and Peter H. Hoffenberg, 3–27. London: Routledge, 2008.
Zimmermann, Susan. *Divide, Provide and Rule: An Integrative History of Poverty Policy, Social Policy, and Social Reform in Hungary under the Habsburg Monarchy*. Budapest: Central European University Press, 2011.

Part II
Confronting coercion

Digital drawings with watercolours © Dariia Kuzmych, 2021

6
Subdued wage workers: textile production in Western and Islamic sources (ninth to twelfth centuries)
Colin Arnaud

In *Yvain ou le Chevalier au Lion*, an Arthurian romance written by the French poet Chrétien de Troyes in 1177 or 1180, the knight Yvain must stay the night in a cursed place named the Castle of Ill Adventure. In this castle, he finds an enclosure with 300 captive maidens who weave silk and golden clothes. The damsels explain that their king was once captured by the lord of the castle and his champions, two horrible demons, and in exchange for his freedom, he sends 30 maidens from his kingdom to the demons every year. Surprisingly, the captive girls are presented as working for a wage. This striking combination of unfree and wage labour has been interpreted in diverse ways: did Chrétien de Troyes combine the setting of a *gyneceum*, a manorial women's textile workshop mostly evidenced for the European early Middle Ages, with the new monetised labour relations of his time?[1] Or did he describe an Oriental situation, according to his representations of what should resemble an Islamic or Byzantine state-run textile workshop, in a period in which silk fabrics from the Orient represented a luxurious import product?[2]

Marxist categories that dichotomise free wage labourers and unfree workers such as slaves and feudal bondspersons have long influenced social history. According to this opposition, only free labourers can commodify their manpower on their own; slaves are themselves a commodity and bondspersons are not remunerated – on the contrary, they give a tribute in labour and in kind to their lord in exchange for protection and arable land.[3] From this perspective, the paying of a wage to an unfree captive worker appears paradoxical, also because the advantage of using coercive labour is the non-necessity of remunerating the workers. Recent work on global labour history points out the forms of entanglement between remunerated labour and unfree labour.[4]

This approach has the potential to shed new light on a broad variety of different times and places throughout history. In fact, in the period between 800 and 1200, in the context of textile production, we find evidence of labour relations that are both forced and remunerated, in the European West as well as in the Islamic world.

For the general narrative of the history of capitalism, both areas play an important role: whereas Western Europe up to the late Middle Ages experienced the rise of a productive and commercial economy, accompanied by the emergence of wage labour markets and early capitalistic enterprises, the economy of the Islamic area, while staying at a high level, seems to have stagnated and been surpassed by the Western one.[5] The despotic power of Islamic rulers and an excessive control by the state of the economic sphere can be considered one reason for this evolution. The divergent development is exemplified in textile production. Whereas in the eleventh century, silk fabrics from the Orient were imported to the West, which did not have its own silk production, from the fourteenth century on, Western silks and textiles were exported to the Orient, indicating that the Western textile industry had partly overtaken the Oriental one.[6] Did labour relations play a role in this process? Did Western production involve a more efficient working process? The historiographical clichés seem to support this assumption: whereas in Islamic regions the production of fine fabrics occurred in public *ṭirāz* workshops, in Western Europe it was developed by merchant-entrepreneurs of free cities. The *ṭirāz* factories produced primarily (but not only) the signed embroidered robes of honour that the Islamic ruler bestowed on his officers. They are generally considered as state workshops supplying the court and eventually using tributary or forced workers,[7] while private European merchant-entrepreneurs produced for profit and employed free wage workers or subcontractors.[8] From this perspective, whereas the *ṭirāz* factory workers apparently experienced forced employment, either through an order of the state or as a form of tax or tribute, late medieval European workers were supposed to enter voluntarily into an agreement with the main entrepreneur, as petty entrepreneur (subcontractor) or directly as wage worker.

This chapter will try to move beyond these narratives by analysing, without apriorism, material, normative and narrative sources that describe labour relations. My focus is on the twelfth century, a period for which documents are available for both regions and that is considered to mark a transition to a market economy for the Latin West. I draw on architectural evidence to confirm the existence and spatial arrangement of production sites in both cases. Regarding the written documents,

I analyse administrative tractates that describe the operating mode of Egyptian *ṭirāz* workshops. For the Latin West, comparable documents on manorial textile workshops are only available for the earlier centuries of the Middle Ages. For the twelfth century, I will focus on narrative sources involving textile workers employed and paid by a lord. More than an opposition between East and West, the sources show that in both regions labour coercion and labour remuneration could be combined in diverse ways. Consistently considering gender roles, I examine here different types of coercion and their interplay with forms of remuneration: physical and spatial coercion on the one hand (spatial ordering of the workplace reducing mobility or not), and legal coercion on the other hand (legal status of workers, and contract or legal agreement between labourer and master/employer).

Archaeological evidence of unfree textile labour in the Western Middle Ages up to the twelfth century

In the early Middle Ages, textile workshops that belonged to manorial lords were called *genitium* (for *gyneceum*) in medieval Latin and employed female servants (*ancille*) to make clothes for the needs of the demesne.[9] The *genitium* workers were mostly bondmaids who belonged to the landlord. Several denominations were used: *ancilla*, *lida*, *mancipium* and *genitiaria*.[10] As serfs, they were bound to their demesne, had no right to leave it and could not be sold or donated separately from it.[11] The *capitulare de villis*, an ordinance of Charlemagne serving as guide to the governance of the royal real estates, composed around 800, contains some indications on how *genitia* should operate. The *genitia* of the king had to be supplied with certain material and tools, showing that several stages of production were completed there: not only weaving but also combing and dyeing.[12] The *genitium* was not a single large building but rather an area surrounded by fences (*sepes*) and well-closed doors, so that the women could work well (*qualiter opera nostra bene peragere valeant*). It contained huts (*case*), heated workshops (*pisles*) and canopies (*tegurie*).[13] The term *pisla* or *pensilis*, sometimes used as synonym for *genitium*,[14] referred to a heated room, that is, a room with a fireplace for dyeing and processing clothes in winter. The canopy seems to refer to a covered, semi-open space for work during the summertime.

Archaeological excavations of fortified manorial courts in Germany and England from between the ninth and the twelfth centuries have discovered domanial textile workshops. They correlate only partially with the normative spatial arrangements described in the *capitulare de villis*. In Germany, the courts and castles of Gebesee, Helfta, Mühlhausen and Tilleda included in their inner or outer baileys several pit houses that served as workshops, some of them with archaeological findings indicating textile production (loom weights, loom ditches).[15] Those textile pit houses were not particularly isolated from the other ones. However, in Tilleda, additionally to the pit houses, five bigger textile workshops have been excavated, the biggest one with a length of 29.60 m and a breadth of 6.20 m, where up to 24 persons could work. In the Frisian court 'alte Boomborg', in the Thuringian court Husen and in the domanial court Goltho (Lincolnshire, England), long textile workshops of similar size have also been found. They do not present particular signs of physical isolation within the court. For Goltho and Tilleda at least, the workshops were located at the edge of the bailey near the fortified wall, which enabled a partial seclusion of the area.[16] The bigger workshops could be used for larger textiles covering walls and furniture. However, a rather scattered distribution of smaller workshops seems to be more frequent in manorial courts, such as in the castle of Gebesee in Germany.[17]

We have scarce written evidence of *genitia* from the eleventh century onwards. For instance, the numerous charters concerning the Curtis Entzenweis near Passau mention a *genitium* until 1111. In 1220, a comparable charter mentions other edifices such as the mill, but the *genitium* has disappeared.[18] Over time, the term received a peculiar connotation. At the end of the twelfth century, Ugguccio of Pisa defined *genitium* as a 'brothel or weaving workshop (*textrinum*), where women gather for prostitution or for wool working'.[19] In 1183, when the bishop of Salzburg donated to the canons of the Church of St Rupert a bondgirl named Adelhaid, he specified that she was not to serve 'in the making woollens or in the *genitium*, but in the most honest offices'. Work on wool and in the *genitium* was thus not considered as an honest occupation, but a *genitium* apparently still existed.[20] However, the term *textrinum* became more recurrent up to the eleventh century. This word could be used as a synonym of *genitium*, but it came to have a broader acceptance. Whereas *genitia* referred to large, articulated spaces, a simple weaving cellar could be designated as *textrinum*. In a sermon against the heretical sect of the Cathars written after 1163 for the diocese of Cologne, Abbot Eckbert of Schönau explains that the Cathars are named weavers (*texerants*) in France, because they say that the real Christian faith is nowhere else but in their secret meetings (*conventiculis*) that take place in cellars and weaving workshops or in underground houses of this kind (*in cellariis et textrinis et hujusmodi subterraneis domibus*).[21] Probably, *textrinum* also meant a group of weaving pit houses of the kind that archaeology evidences at least from the ninth to the twelfth century in several manorial complexes.

Indeed, we have archaeological evidence of domanial textile production dating into the twelfth century. Weaving activity in the royal palace of Tilleda in Saxony has been verified for the period between the tenth and the twelfth centuries.[22] In the settlement of Klein Freden in Lower Saxony in North Germany, a series of weaving pit houses was abandoned at a time not before the end of the twelfth century.[23] The several unheated pit houses from the twelfth century that were found in Gebesee could not have been used as permanent dwellings:[24] they might have served as workshops for the serfs from the surrounding farms, but it is also possible that seasonal and occasional hired workers lived and worked there during the warmer months. Indeed, during the twelfth century, we can observe a trend of hiring remunerated workers in the domanial economy also for agriculture.[25] Other sources from the same period present weavers as mobile workers who moved from place to place to offer their services. In a hagiographic biography of Adalbero of Würzburg from the end of the twelfth century, we can read about a poor, homeless boy who wandered in search of work as a weaver.[26] In 1157 the council of Reims depicted the Cathars as weavers who went from place to place, changed their names and entrapped girls into sin.[27] The link between weaving and mobility appears to be new and suggests that textile workers were no longer merely immobilised bondspersons, but free hired workers. Moreover, while the terms used for textile workers of the early medieval *genitia* always had the feminine form and were not linked to any specialisation, evidence from the twelfth century refers to male workers and to their specialisation in weaving.

However, apart from entrepreneurs, the professionalisation and shift to remunerated labour does not automatically mean an immediate change from domanial textile production to market production. Indeed, archaeological evidence has shown that domanial production did not fade away before the end of the twelfth century. Thus, it is probable that the use of hired workers for textile labour began in the demesnes themselves. In the next section I will analyse in greater detail a source from the twelfth-century Low Countries on hired weavers working and living in a domanial context that confirms this assumption.

The hired weavers of Villa Inda

The Deeds of the Abbots of St Truiden in Limburg from 1135 relate a strange story about the hired weavers of Villa Inda:

> There is a type of hired persons (*hominum mercennariorum*) whose business (*officium*) is to weave cloth from linen and wool. They are generally regarded as more impudent and haughtier than other hired persons. To diminish their haughtiness and pride and to avenge a personal injury, a certain poor rustic from the villa named Inda thought up this diabolical trick.[28]

Villa Inda (Kornelimünster near Aachen) was the demesne of the Inda abbey and had a rural character. The 'poor rustic' was probably a bondsman of the demesne, whereas the hired weavers – apparently all men – were most probably employed by the demesne itself and lived there at least for a certain time, long enough to entertain conflictual relationships with peasants, which becomes apparent by the 'diabolical trick' that was played on them. The trick was quite original: with the help of the judges (*iudices*) and others, the peasant built a false ship with wheels. He obtained permission from the potentates of the villa (*potestates*) – who were most likely the de facto employers of the weavers – that the weavers had to pull it with rods from Villa Inda to Aachen. The procession over a distance of about 10 km, which must have been perceived as a ridiculous spectacle, received such acclamation beyond the people of Aachen that it moved on, reaching Maastricht, Tongeren, Borgloon and finally St Truiden on its way. Against the recommendations of their abbot, so the chronicle continues, the inhabitants (*oppidani*) of St Truiden finally brought the ship to their town. They commanded the weavers of their villa to keep watch by the ship day and night.

> Meanwhile, in a secret complaint coming from the bottom of their heart, the weavers invoked God, the fair and almighty judge, that they were humiliated with such ignominy, although they lived according to the right way of the ancient Christians and of the Apostles, who worked day and night with their own hands so that they might be fed and clothed and could provide for their children. They asked themselves and complained wailfully, why they were touched by this ignominy and opprobrious energy more than other hired men (*mercennarii*), since among Christians there were many offices more despicable than theirs, for they did nothing despicable,

no activity that implied a sin to Christians. It is better to be simply lowly and out-of-favour than to enter in contact with the impurity of sin. A rustic and poor weaver is better than an urban and noble judge, who robs orphans and despoils widows.[29]

The weavers of Villa Inda were specialised *mercennarii*, which means that they worked for in-kind payment or money.[30] According to the chronicle, they defined themselves as 'rustic', that is, they came from the countryside and worked there, probably in the domanial *textrinum*, for the monastery of Kornelimünster. The other hired men mentioned, called *mercennarii*, were probably also employed by the domanial administration itself for agricultural or artisanal activities, which testifies to the employment of hired workers in different occupations.

It is even likely that the weavers of Villa Inda belonged to the category of free itinerant weavers directly hired by the *judices* and *potestates* of the villa. They had the same bad reputation as the wandering heretics and defended themselves as not being impious, responding to implicit allegations of sinfulness that were attached to itinerant people in search for work. By contrast, in this episode, they appeared remarkably obedient for hired people who were said to be impudent, given that they followed the instruction to transport the false ship over a long distance, while surely knowing that this was unproductive work. Although the action of taking the ship to Aachen had nothing to do with their work as weavers, they did not reject the order of the authorities of Villa Inda. Apparently, the relation of dependency between the weavers and the local authorities was all-encompassing.

The fact that the hired weavers obeyed their employers and carried out tasks beyond textile production calls attention to the lack of conceptual separation between person and workforce. For the ancient Greeks, 'the wage laborer was regarded as a "hireling" who did not so much "hire out" … his labor power, but who placed himself temporarily with his whole person in a dependent position'.[31] There is also similar evidence of this idea in Roman texts.[32] It is altogether conceivable that hired workers in the medieval demesnes likewise saw themselves as temporary bondspersons who had to obey their employer in all aspects, not only for work. However, we do not necessarily need to refer to ancient examples to understand the subjection of the weavers in relation to the representatives of the lord: the *potestates* of the villa were the highest authority in the place; they administered public affairs and dispensed justice. Due to their political and legal position, the weavers had no possibility of appealing against their order. While the peasant who organised the joke with the ship seemed to have good relations with the authorities of the villa, the weavers were apparently not well integrated in the local community and had no notable supporters who could defend them. More than a mere fusion between person and workforce, the fact that the employer was the one who had the political power and who dispensed justice – a common scenario in twelfth-century demesnes – created a particular context of coercion far beyond the sphere of labour.

The female silk weavers of *Yvain*

The episode of *Yvain* mentioned at the beginning of the chapter seems to refer to a comparable situation, even if the constellation of factors is different. Chrétien de Troyes wrote the novel in 1177 or 1180, half a century after the episode of the weavers of Villa Inda. *Yvain* is fiction, but the episode of the weaving maidens is surprisingly rich in realistic details, in contrast to other episodes of the same novel that are marked by a more fantastic style.[33] While the location is completely fictitious and without direct reference to a real place, the details on labour relations – particularly on wage – seem to recall concrete issues debated among Chrétien's audience. The challenge is to understand which representations and discourses Chrétien de Troyes refers to through the depiction of the silk workers. As often happens in the novel, in one of the protagonist's numerous secondary adventures the Arthurian knight Yvain is on the road to the royal court as he needs to stay overnight at the Castle of Ill Adventure. The first description of the maidens alludes to their absolute poverty and their immobilisation in the castle. As Yvain arrives at the castle,

> [he] reached a vast room, very high and brand new. He found himself before a courtyard enclosed by large stakes, round and pointed. Between the stakes, he saw up to three hundred young girls harnessed to various works. They wove gold and silk threads, each as best as possible, but an absolute destitution prevented most from wearing a headdress or a belt. At the chest and elbow their coats were torn; their shirts were soiled in the back. Hunger and distress had thinned their necks and made their faces livid.[34]

The historian David Herlihy has made a connection between the fictive textile workshop of *Yvain* and the *gynecea* of the Carolingian period (751–911), whose history was introduced in the first section of this chapter.[35] Indeed, there are a number of physical similarities between early medieval *genitia* and the enclosed workshop described in *Yvain*. The *capitulare de villis* issued by Charlemagne around 800 mentions an enclosed working place for the workers of the *genitium* that resembles the enclosed outdoor workshop described in *Yvain*: the place where the 300 women worked was a courtyard (*prael clos*) in front of a high new hall, enclosed by a wall of great sharpened stakes.[36] *The illustration at the beginning of the chapter* enhances the aspect of spatial imprisonment through the depiction of pointed stakes that surround the working women. While the Arthurian maiden weavers are imprisoned in the castle, the fences of the courtyard do not technically imprison them, since the door is not closed (Yvain opens it), but the tall, pointed stakes symbolise their imprisonment. In the *capitulare de villis*, the well-closed doors and fences have an explicit disciplinary function: they reduce interactions with the entourage during labour and force the labourers to focus on work.

The illustration depicts the working women surrounded by a fence and by the clothes they weave and spin: the restrictions on their freedom are based not only on a spatial setting but also on their legal labour conditions. In both cases, the early medieval *genitium* and the workshop in *Yvain*, the workers are unfree women. However, as we have seen before, the spatial arrangement of early medieval *genitia* seems less repressive than in the court of *Yvain*. Moreover, the 300 girls in *Yvain* were no serfs but captive hostages. Finally, Carolingian *genitia* usually hosted around 20 workers, in any case no more than 40, according to the evidence.[37] The great number of women in the Arthurian romance can be interpreted as a mere fantasy of the author, a sensational hyperbole for the entertainment of the audience.

Some scholars have criticised the assumption that Chrétien would refer to Carolingian structures that had nearly disappeared in the twelfth century.[38] The architectural evidence, however, suggests that the domanial workshops had not disappeared after the Carolingian period. Rather, they were eventually called by other terms and subsequently did see a gradual decline during the twelfth century. After that, rather than the types of spatial settings for textile production, it was the types of workers that seemed to change in the central centuries of the Middle Ages. Chrétien de Troyes describes the labour conditions of the 300 fictive maidens through their own complaint:

> We will always weave silk clothes and are not better dressed. Always we shall be poor and naked, always we shall be hungry

and thirsty. We will never be able to procure more food. We have very little bread to eat, very little in the morning and in the evening even less. From the labour of her hands, each will obtain, in all and for all, only four pennies for the pound. With that, it is impossible to buy food and clothes, because the one who earns twenty shillings a week is far from being out of business. And rest assured that none of us brings in twenty shillings or more. That would be enough to enrich a duke! We are in poverty and the one for whom we struggle is enriched by our work. We stay awake for most of our nights and all day to bring in even more money because he [the lord and exploiter] threatens to mutilate us if we rest. That is why we dare not take rest.[39]

The maidens apparently receive a wage, but they complain that this wage does not cover the high cost of living. This deficit forces them to work even harder, day and night without rest, as they say. Through this paradoxical situation, Chrétien de Troyes seems to denounce the risks of wage labour in a context of power imbalance. The employer of the 300 weavers seems to have many advantages by paying his captive workers. The maidens are made to work by a combination of spatial and legal coercion and insufficient financial remuneration. The exploiter uses typical strategies of physical compulsion: he locks the maidens up in a court with fences for better control and threatens to brutalise them if they rest. Yet, according to the description of labour conditions in the text, the wage is the maidens' main incentive to work so hard.

However, their wage is surely not the result of a negotiation between a free worker and an employer in the labour market. Since the damsels, as hostages, lack legal rights and freedom of movement, the exploiter can determine all the conditions for the remuneration: not only the amount of payment, but also what he provides and what the workers have to pay for out of their wages. Additionally, the maidens cannot leave the castle, and the lord and his people probably even furnish the damsels with food and dress at the highest prices. That seems to be the situation that is implicitly described in the text: the damsels receive a correct piece rate in money, but in this castle, even a remuneration worthy of a duke would not suffice to buy enough food and dress. The lord provides them with a little bread in the morning and in the evening. At this point the maidens are constantly in need of money: they are forced to work more to survive. Wage becomes an efficient mechanism of coercion in the context of unfree labour. While the Arthurian romance describes a worst-case scenario, in reality this mechanism of coercion was probably used in a more subtle way. No need to be a cruel demon in a castle to profit from the coercive mechanism of financial remuneration and controlled consumption. An asymmetrical relation between employer and employee, a relationship of dependence, a situation of immobility or an imperfect labour market could create comparable conditions.

The workers of the Islamic *ṭirāz*

The combination of lord and employer is also to be found in the official textile workshops of the Islamic era, the so-called *ṭirāz* factories that might have been a source of inspiration for Chrétien de Troyes's tale about the 300 girls weaving and embroidering silk.[40] Representations of Islamic courts could have been transported to France through the Crusader states of Palestine[41] or through the Sicilian court of the Hauteville that itself operated some kind of palatial *ṭirāz*.[42] Indeed, silk clothes and embroideries were at that time a speciality of Islamic fabrics, particularly from Egypt, and they were also exported to Western Europe.[43] The *ṭirāz* factories of Fatimid Egypt (969–1171) were controlled by the caliphal administration and were 'considered one of the most important of administrative responsibilities in the government, along with oversight of the mints, the post, and the bureaus of taxation', as the historian Norman Stillman has claimed.[44]

The production and delivery of robes of honour (*khil'a*) – which the ruler gave to their officials every year in order to confirm their function and their allegiance – was a monopoly of the caliph. Every robe of honour was decorated with a *ṭirāz* border with inscriptions praising the caliph; thus they were a sign of the ruler's sovereignty,[45] just like the caliphal inscriptions on coins and the obligation to praise the caliph at every Friday sermon. While Carolingian *genitia* mostly had a supply function for the demesne, *ṭirāz* factories played an important role for the prestige of the state. They were, however, also linked to the market economy. Indeed, while some garments were only used by the court, other products were marketed to a broader population. The inscription of the *ṭirāz* borders specified the workshop of origin and differentiated workshops for the exclusive use of the court (*ṭirāz al-khassa*) and workshops for everyone who could afford to buy them (*ṭirāz al-'amma*).[46]

Ṭirāz 'factories' (*dār al-ṭirāz*) were seldom specialised buildings. According to the *Khiṭaṭ*, a book on the topography and history of Egypt written by al-Maqrīzī at the beginning of the fifteenth century, in Cairo, at the end of the Fatimid Caliphate (1171), 'the mansion (*dār*) of the vizier Yaʿqub ibn Killis which, today, includes the Ṣāḥibīya School, the *Darb al-Ḥarīrī* (Street of the Silk Worker) and the Saifīya School, was made into an institution (*dār*) where brocade and silk (*ḥarīr*) were woven for the requirement of the Fatimid Caliphs, and which became known as *Dār al-Dībadj*.[47] If a mansion could be transformed into a textile factory, the spatial configuration of such edifices was quite unspecific. The workshops were probably scattered in diverse rooms of the palace. This so-called *dār al-dībāj* (house of brocades) was located in the centre of Cairo between the Al-Azhar Mosque and the central south–north axis. A pleasure pavilion, the belvedere al-Ghazala, at the bank of the Nile, was the residence of the manager of the *ṭirāz* who was responsible for the supply of clothes to the court.[48] Moreover, there is topographical evidence of a *ṭirāz* in declining twelfth-century Baghdad. The Baghdadi Islamic erudite Ibn Ǧawzī mentions a *ṭirāz* in the quarter of Bāb al-Ṭāq, at the bank of the Tigris, near the great bridge. The mentioned *ṭirāz* was a part of the palace of Muʿizz al-Dawla, a Buyid ruler of the tenth century, and was named 'the wonderful window'. As in Cairo, the palace of a former ruler in the heart of the city was converted into a *ṭirāz* factory, emphasising the official aspect of the institution.[49]

Further increasing the geographical diversity, the Caliphate of Cordoba also introduced *ṭirāz* factories in Al-Andalus. The chronicles of Ibn Ḥayyāt narrate the visit of the Caliph al-Hakam II to the *dār al-ṭirāz* of Cordoba outside the walls in the northern periphery near the cemetery of the Bāb al-Yahūd (Gate of Jews) in 972. An unusually large building from the tenth century has been excavated in this area. While the archaeologists assumed they had found a suburban farm (*almunia*),[50] the Arabist Antonio Arjona Castro has interpreted it as the *dār al-ṭirāz*.[51] The historian of architecture Felix Arnold, who has studied the edifice, does not discuss the possibility that the building hosted a *ṭirāz* and believes that it was a palace complex.[52] However, as our other examples show, it was indeed common to find a *ṭirāz* factory as part of a palace, which would support Castro's theory.

The architecture and location of *ṭirāz* factories as part of former palaces in the city centre provide no explicit evidence of spatial coercion or segregation. What about the status of the workers and the working conditions? Maya Shatzmiller, a historian of labour in medieval Islam, claims that textile production in medieval cities featured a variety of workers, such as slaves, forced labour recruits and waged labourers. It is, however, difficult to know which types of worker worked at the *ṭirāz* workshops and which did not.[53] Some scholars emphasise the despotic state-run management of *ṭirāz* factories with excessive labour control and fiscal burdens.[54] In contrast to this, other scholars show that the state did not necessarily impede private investment, participation of free artisans and ṭirāz production for the market, all of which were in fact widespread.[55] Against the backdrop of these two opposite positions, it is useful to examine the ambiguous cases of labour relation between tributary and wage labour in the Islamic sources.

Maya Shatzmiller has analysed the division of labour in medieval Islam through an extensive list of occupations mentioned in a large range of sources. She concludes that the 'list did not reveal the existence of any manufacturing occupations specifically related to a state's factory. ... The same occupations, and sometimes the very same individuals, worked in both private and State production.' Moreover, ṭirāz production was not centralised under a single roof: putting out or buying in of spun threads was common. For that reason, and to better understand the broader picture of labour relations, we also need to search for workers working for, but not necessarily within, the *dār al-ṭirāz*.[56]

In 1047 the Persian traveller Nāṣir-i-Khusraw described the fabrics produced in Tinnis, an important city of the Nile Delta: 'The *Qaṣab* and *Buqalamūn* made for the sultan [the Fatimid Caliph] are paid for at their exact value; thus the workmen work willingly for him, as by contrast to the other countries where the government and the sovereign impose forced labour on the artisans.'[57] The author was probably thinking of places he had already travelled to, such as Iran and the Levant. According to this assumption, forced labour and hired labour were two possibilities for ṭirāz workers. The motivating function of wage labour in comparison to forced labour is assumed in this passage, also whether in this case forced labour is to be understood as occasional tributary labour requested by the government of free artisans.

During the visit of the Christian patriarch Dionysius to Tinnis in approximately 815 AD, that is before the Fatimid dominion in Egypt, Coptic weavers complained:

> Our town is encompassed by water. We can neither look forward to a harvest nor can we maintain a flock. Our drinking water comes from afar and costs us four dirhams a pitcher. Our work is in the manufacture of linen which our women spin and we weave. We get from the dealers half a dirham per day. Although our earning is not sufficient for the bread of our mouths we are taxed for tribute and pay five dinars a head in taxes. They beat us, imprison us, and compel us to give our sons and daughters as securities. For every dinar they have to work two years as slaves.[58]

In this case, the coercion in labour coincided with the monetisation of the economy, which is also alluded to in the case of *Yvain*'s female weavers. Wages were too low and the cost of living too high. No subsistence economy was possible and everything, even drinking water, had to be purchased. The tax tributes ordered by the government exacerbated the weavers' need for money, and tax debt was transformed into forced work performed by younger relatives. We must take from this that labour coercion appeared in the context of and, indeed, as the very consequence of monetisation.

Some administrators described how the *ṭirāz* office worked, giving some indication of labour relations. The Egyptian official Ibn Mammātī, in his book from the second half of the twelfth century that describes the administration of the Ayyubid Sultanate, explains the organisation of the *ṭirāz*:

> This service has an inspector, an overseer, a controller and two accountants. Now if any sort of article is required to be manufactured, a list is made out by the Office of the Wardrobe [*Dīwān al-Khizāna*] and sent to them [the *ṭirāz* officers] along with the required [or computed] money, and gold thread for their expenses. When the chests are brought back, they are compared with the chits which went with them, and checked.

We notice that the *ṭirāz* is not described as a factory but rather as an administration among others, a service, an office that coordinates the production for the court. The passage also contains a large amount of information about remuneration:

> If the value comes to more than has been spent on it, the excellent nature of the employees [or employers][59] is inferred from that, but they derive no benefit from it at all – that is to say the surplus. If the value is less than the expenditure, the extent of the deficiency is elucidated and the requisition is made from the *Dīwān*, and the employees [or employers] are required to pay it. The employees [or employers] take the responsibility of payment on themselves and extract it from the gold embroiderers. A series of happenings of this kind in what they bring, indicates the dishonesty of their characters.[60]

The *ṭirāz* office received the orders from the Office of the Wardrobe, which was responsible for the final quality control of the products.

Neither the Office of the Wardrobe nor the ṭirāz office seemed to be interested in the marketing of the products. The Office of the Wardrobe acted as a client, the ṭirāz office as a mere executor – it could not hope for any profit from, for example, increased product quality. The permanent staff of the ṭirāz office mentioned here was exclusively composed of overseers on different levels, rather than workers. The embroiderers who stitched ornaments on the fabrics were probably paid by piece and hired on request. If the quality was lower than expected, the ṭirāz officers had to pay the difference, a sum that they demanded from the gold embroiders in return. Although Ibn Mammātī considered this an iniquitous practice, it corresponds to the principle that a hired artisan was financially responsible for the result.[61] That means that the worker was seen as a free, independent and responsible actor, a business partner of the ṭirāz office, rather than a dependent wage worker. The text disappoints those who expect an army of forced workers in ṭirāz factories – as alluded to in *Yvain*.

Another Egyptian administration tractate, written by al-Makhzūmī just a few years after the one by Ibn Mammātī, provides further information on the control measures that were in place in textile production, apart from the negative financial incentives that overseers placed on embroiderers. The authorised expert of the ṭirāz office ('ārif) gave the embroiderers clear written instructions containing all the technical details of the commissioned embroidery. At the end of the production process, the expert exercised thorough control over the final product with different techniques. The text describes common faults of the embroiderers: a lower quality of gold, an insufficient amount of threads in the embroidered lines, or a lower quantity of gold on the gold thread. This account reveals the leeway that workers had, which testifies to a certain degree of autonomy, as it is unlikely that the embroiderers were closely supervised due to their outsourced work performance. If they had been under supervision from the beginning, such flaws would not have happened. We can infer from this that the control of the production occurred after, not during, the production process. Embroiderers apparently worked alone and with autonomy, probably outside the ṭirāz in their own workshops.[62]

Both texts denote an elaborated and hierarchised control system in the ṭirāz office, but also the relative autonomy of the workers, who were considered subcontractors and business partners rather than wage labourers. More than a place for enclosed production, the ṭirāz appears as a control hub for the finished production. The labour relation between embroiders and ṭirāz seems to have been closer to that of a European late-medieval putting-out system than to that of early medieval *genitia*. Furthermore, beyond this independent status, the embroiderers were disciplined in their production through their remuneration, more specifically through potential deductions on remuneration in case of unsatisfactory work.

Conclusion

The case studies presented in this chapter give insights into the labour relations of textile workers of the twelfth century in the West and in Islamic regions. Due to the scarcity of sources for this period, it is very difficult to make conclusions about representativeness. The available documents present possibilities, but they also enable us to glimpse some elements of the discourse on labour relations of the time. They show what was conceivable and in which categories the authors spoke about those labour relations.

In this regard, this study has revealed some important findings. First, it has unveiled a variety of combinations of legally unfree and wage labour in the Latin and in the Arabic worlds. Second, remunerated labour could lead to an increased level of coercion in labour, particularly if the employer had political influence on the worker. In all our examples, the remunerated labourers worked for a lord or for the state, and legal dependence interfered in labour relations. In around 1135, the hired male weavers of Villa Inda showed absolute obedience to their employer beyond their weaving task. The captive female weavers in *Yvain* were subjected to complete immobilisation in the castle, so that their remuneration and the costs of their basic consumption could be set arbitrarily by their employer, rather than by market mechanisms. The workers of the Islamic *ṭirāz* offices appeared to work largely as independent artisans, but they could be forced to work by debts or according to a tributary system, and the quality of their production was controlled at the end, eventually with the threat of holding back their remuneration. In almost all cases, monetisation of labour relations aggravated labour coercion instead of reducing it.

The cases presented here stem from different types of sources and regions, which are usually not considered together. It is, however, worthwhile to combine them as they can offer an alternative to the common narratives. For example, the twelfth-century Islamic *ṭirāz* workers seem to have had a more independent status than the hired weavers in the West – the contrary of what is suggested by the usual narrative of economic divergence between the two cultures.

With regard to *Yvain* and its potential as a historical source, it can be noted that, although the weaving maidens of *Yvain* work on silk fabrics, the setting of the Castle of Ill Adventure appears to be closer to early medieval domanial workshops than to *ṭirāz* palaces. If Chrétien de Troyes had Oriental models in mind, he probably had poor knowledge of *ṭirāz* palaces and transposed them into a European domanial setting. Moreover, the issue of monetisation and high living costs against the backdrop of insufficient salaries seems to come from direct observations, as the monetary mentions are very precise – even if other evidence has shown that such issues also occurred in Islamic societies. In *The illustration at the beginning of the chapter*, the clothes woven by the women form infinite ribbons linked to the fences of the enclosure and also to the bread and water on a table. This perhaps illustrates the interactions of spatial, juridical/political and economic parameters that we need to consider for the understanding of labour coercion in all the cases examined here.

Notes

1 Herlihy, *Opera Muliebria*, 88.
2 Burns, *Sea of Silk*, 37–69, particularly 43–4. See also Ciggaar, 'Chrétien de Troyes'.
3 Marx, 'Lohnarbeit und Kapital', 379.
4 Van der Linden, *Workers of the World*, 20–7. See also Brass, *Labour Regime Change in the Twenty-First Century*; Steinfeld and Engerman, 'Labor – Free or Coerced?'.
5 Maddison, *Contours of the World Economy 1–2030 AD*, 69–73, 381; Rubin, *Rulers, Religion, and Riches*; Kuran, *The Long Divergence*.
6 Jacoby, 'Silk economics'; Munro, 'Medieval woollens'.
7 Serjeant, *Islamic Textiles*; Serjeant, 'The *Ṭirāz* System'; Yedida K. Stillman et al., 'Ṭirāz'.
8 Munro, 'Medieval woollens'; Holbach, *Frühformen von Verlag*.
9 Garver, *Women and Aristocratic Culture*, 230; Obermeier, 'Ancilla', 217–29.
10 Herlihy, *Opera Muliebria*, 82–5; Obermeier, 'Ancilla', 225–7.
11 Vadey, 'Serfdom'. See also Bourin and Freedman, *Forms of Servitude*.
12 *Capitulare De Villis*, 59–60, chapter 43: 'Ad genitia nostra, sicut institutum est, opera ad tempus dare faciant, id est linum, lanam, waisdo, vermiculo, warentia, pectinos laninas, cardones, saponem, unctum, vascula vel reliqua minutia quae ibidem necessaria sunt'.
13 *Capitulare De Villis*, 60, chapter 49: 'Ut genitia nostra bene sint ordinata, id est de casis, pis[a]lis, teguriis id est screonis; et sepes bonas in circuitu habeant et portas firmas qualiter opera nostra bene peragere valeant.'
14 Andreolli, 'Tra podere e gineceo', 36.
15 Herdick, *Ökonomie der Eliten*, 75–80, 82–9.
16 Herdick, *Ökonomie der Eliten*, 81–2, 92–4; Zimmermann, 'Archäologische Befunde frühmittelalterlicher Webhäuser', 135–9.
17 Donat, *Gebesee*.
18 Herlihy, *Opera Muliebria*, 91–2.
19 Andreolli, 'Tra podere e gineceo', 36.
20 Herlihy, *Opera Muliebria*, 85.
21 Eckbert von Schönau, '*Sermones contra Catharos*', col. 14.
22 Dapper and Udolph, 'Tilleda'; Grimm and Leopold, *Tilleda*, 49–54, 92–3; Grimm, 'Tilleda'.
23 König and Geschwinde, 'Tuche und Pferde', 329–32; König et al., *– Lütken Freden wisk–*, 148.

24 Donat, *Gebesee*, 119.
25 During this period, the Cistercians established the so-called grange systems, using lay brothers and hired people instead of serfs for agricultural work: Schreiner, 'Brot der Mühsal', 148.
26 'Vita Adalberonis episcopi Wirziburgensis', 144.
27 *Sacrorum conciliorum*, 843.
28 *Gisleberti Trudonensis Gesta Abbatum Trudonensivm*, 77–8, chapter 11; translated by the author, following Herlihy, *Opera Muliebria*, 92–3.
29 *Gisleberti Trudonensis Gesta Abbatum Trudonensivm*, 78, chapter 12; translated by the author, following Herlihy, *Opera Muliebria*, 92–3.
30 Feller, 'Le vocabulaire de la rémunération', 162.
31 Van der Linden, *Workers of the World*, 40.
32 Möller, 'Die mercennarii in der römischen Arbeitswelt', 318.
33 Noble-Kooijman, 'La Pire Aventure d'Yvain'.
34 Chrétien de Troyes, *Le Chevalier au Lion*, v. 5184–5199; passage translated in Brouquet, 'Girls at Work in the Middle Ages', 19.
35 Herlihy, *Opera Muliebria*, 77–81.
36 Chrétien de Troyes, *Le Chevalier au Lion*, v. 5182–5191.
37 Herlihy, *Opera Muliebria*, 81–3, Andreolli, 'Tra podere e gineceo', 34–5; Obermeier, '*Ancilla*', 225; Herdick, *Ökonomie der Eliten*, 81–2.
38 Burns, *Sea of Silk*, 42; Sophie Cassagnes-Brouquet refuses the link with the *gynecea* and only retains the link with the new realities in the cities of Champagne and Flanders of his time: Cassagnes-Brouquet, 'The Worst of Adventures', 231; see also Noble-Kooijman, 'La Pire Aventure d'Yvain'.
39 Chrétien de Troyes, *Le Chevalier au Lion*, v. 5292–5319; passage translated in Brouquet, 'Girls at Work in the Middle Ages', 19–20.
40 Burns, *Sea of Silk*, 43–4, 181–3; Hall, 'The Silk Factory in Chrestien de Troyes' Yvain'.
41 Burns, *Sea of Silk*, 147–52; see also Cahen, *Orient et Occident*; Gaube, *Konfrontation der Kulturen?*
42 Burns, *Sea of Silk*, 56–9; see also Lipinsky, 'Tiraz = Ergasterium'; Seipel, *Nobiles officinae*.
43 On the denomination of oriental clothes like *panni alexandrini* (= cloth from Alexandria) in French literature, see Burns, *Sea of Silk*, 181–3. On the production of expensive Egyptian Fatimid cloths according to Arabic sources, see Serjeant, *Islamic Textiles*, 135–64.
44 Norman A. Stillman, *Arab Dress*.
45 Springberg-Hinsen, *Die Ḥila*, 60–129.
46 Jacoby, 'Silk economics', 215–6; Dolezalek, *Arabic Script on Christian Kings*, 80–1.
47 Maqrizi, Kḥiṭaṭ, quoted in Serjeant, *Islamic Textiles*, 151.
48 Serjeant, *Islamic Textiles*, 152.
49 Ibn Ǧawzī, manākib Baġdad, quoted in Serjeant, *Islamic Textiles*, 25.
50 Murillo Redondo et al., 'Informe-Memoria'.
51 Castro, 'Posible localización'.
52 Arnold, 'Eine Islamische Palastanlage'.
53 Shatzmiller, *Labour in the Medieval Islamic World*, 244–9, 352–9.
54 Combe, 'Une Institution de l'État Musulman'; Yedida K. Stillman et al., 'Ṭirāz'.
55 Ashtor, *A Social and Economic History*, 150–3; Frantz-Murphy, 'A New Interpretation'.
56 Shatzmiller, *Labour in the Medieval Islamic World*, 245–6.
57 Quoted in Serjeant, *Islamic Textiles*, 143.
58 Quoted in Serjeant, *Islamic Textiles*, 138. Dinar is gold and dirham is silver. Originally, 10 dirham equalled 1 dinar.
59 Because of the absence of vocals, we cannot determine if the Arabic word is *mustakhdimīn* or *mustakhdamīn*, that is, if it is a passive or active participle. In both cases, it is certain that the ṭirāz staff is meant here, who were employees of the office but also employers of the embroiderers and other textile workers.
60 Ibn Mammātī, 'Book of Diwans', quoted in Serjeant, *Islamic Textiles*, 151; original: Ibn Mammatī, *Kitab al-qawanīn al-dawanīn*, 330–1.
61 Burns, *Sea of Silk*, 57.
62 Cahen, 'Un texte inédit relatif au ṭirāz égyptien'.

Bibliography

Andreolli, Bruno. 'Tra podere e gineceo: Il lavoro delle donne nelle grandi aziende agrarie dell'alto medioevo'. In *Donne e lavoro nell'Italia medievale*, edited by Maria Giuseppina Muzzarelli, Paola Galetti and Bruno Andreolli, 29–40. Torino: Rosenberg & Sellier, 1991.

Arnold, Felix. 'Eine Islamische Palastanlage am Stadtrand von Córdoba', *Madrider Mitteilungen* 51 (2010): 419–54.

Ashtor, Eliyahu. *A Social and Economic History of the Near East in the Middle Ages*. Berkeley: University of California Press, 1976.

Bourin, Monique and Freedman, Paul (eds). *Forms of Servitude in Northern and Central Europe: Decline, Resistance and Expansion*. Turnhout: Brepols, 2005.

Brass, Tom. *Labour Regime Change in the Twenty-First Century: Unfreedom, Capitalism, and Primitive Accumulation*. Leiden/Boston: Brill, 2011.

Brouquet, Sophie. 'Girls at Work in the Middle Ages'. In *A History of the Girl: Formation, Education and Identity*, edited by Mary O'Dowd and June Purvis, 13–31. Cham: Springer International Publishing, 2018.

Burns, E. Jane. *Sea of Silk: A Textile Geography of Women's Work in Medieval French Literature*. Philadelphia: University of Pennsylvania Press, 2009.

Cahen, Claude. 'Un texte inédit relatif au ṭirāz égyptien', *Arts asiatiques* 11/1 (1965): 165–8.

Cahen, Claude. *Orient et Occident au Temps des Croisades*. Paris: Aubier Montaigne, 1983.

Capitulare De Villis: Cod. Guelf. 254 Helmst. der Herzog August Bibliothek Wolfenbüttel, edited by Carlrichard Brühl. Stuttgart: Müller und Schindler, 1971.

Cassagnes-Brouquet, Sophie. 'The Worst of Adventures: The Knight Yvain and the Silk Weavers (Late Twelfth Century)', *Clio* 38 (2014): 228–33. Accessed 9 June 2023. https://doi.org/10.4000/cliowgh.313

Castro, Antonio Arjona. 'Posible localización de los restos arqueológicos del Dar al-Tiraz (Casa de tiráz) en Córdoba musulmana', *Boletín de la Real Academia de Córdoba de Ciencias, Bellas Letras y Nobles Artes* 147 (2004): 137–46.

Chrétien de Troyes. *Le Chevalier au lion (Yvain)*, edited by Mario Roques. Paris: Garnier, 1960.

Ciggaar, Krijnie N. 'Chrétien de Troyes et la "matière byzantine": Les demoiselles du Château de Pesme Aventure', *Cahiers de Civilisation Médiévale* 32/128 (1989): 325–31.

Combe, Etienne. 'Une Institution de l'État Musulman: Le *Dâr al-Tirâz*, Atelier de Tissage', *Revue des Conférences Françaises en Orient* 11 (1947): 85–92.

Dapper, Michael M. C. and Udolph, Jürgen. 'Tilleda'. In *Reallexikon der Germanischen Altertumskunde*, second edition, vol. 35, 167–9. Berlin/New York: de Gruyter, 2007.

Dolezalek, Isabelle. *Arabic Script on Christian Kings: Textile Inscriptions on Royal Garments from Norman Sicily*. Berlin: De Gruyter, 2017.

Donat, Peter. *Gebesee: Klosterhof und königliche Reisestation des 10.-12. Jahrhunderts*. Stuttgart: Theiss, 1999.

Eckbert von Schönau. 'Sermones contra Catharos'. *Patrologiae Cursus Completus: Series Latina*, vol. 195, col. 11–102. Paris: Jean-Paul Migne, 1855.

Feller, Laurent. 'Le vocabulaire de la rémunération durant le haut Moyen Âge'. In *Rémunérer le Travail au Moyen Âge: Pour une histoire sociale du salariat*, edited by Patrice Beck, Philippe Bernardi and Laurent Feller, 154–64. Paris: Éditions Picard, 2014.

Frantz-Murphy, Gladys. 'A New Interpretation of the Economic History of Medieval Egypt: The Role of the Textile Industry 254–567/868–1171', *Journal of the Economic and Social History of the Orient* 24/3 (1981): 274–97.

Garver, Valerie L. *Women and Aristocratic Culture in the Carolingian World*. Ithaca, NY: Cornell University Press, 2009.

Gaube, Heinz (ed.). *Konfrontation der Kulturen? Saladin und die Kreuzfahrer*. Mainz: Philipp von Zabern, 2005.

Gisleberti Trudonensis Gesta Abbatum Trudonensivm VIII–XIII: liber IX opus intextum Rodvufi Trudonensis, edited by Paul Tombeur. Turnhout: Brepols, 2013.

Grimm, Paul. 'Tilleda: Beiträge zu Handwerk und Handel in der Vorburg der Pfalz Tilleda', *Zeitschrift für Archäologie* 6 (1972): 104–47.

Grimm, Paul and Leopold, Gerhard. *Tilleda: Eine Königspfalz am Kyffhäuser*, vol. 2: *Die Vorburg und Zusammenfassung*. Berlin: Akademie-Verlag, 1990.

Hall, Robert A. 'The Silk Factory in Chrestien de Troyes' Yvain', *Modern Language Notes* 56/6 (1941): 418–22.

Herdick, Michael. *Ökonomie der Eliten: Eine Studie zur Interpretation wirtschaftsarchäologischer Funde und Befunde von mittelalterlichen Herrschaftssitzen*. Mainz: Verlag des Römisch-Germanischen Zentralmuseums, 2015.

Herlihy, David. *Opera Muliebria: Women and Work in Medieval Europe*. Philadelphia: Temple University Press, 1990.

Holbach, Rudolf. *Frühformen von Verlag und Großbetrieb in der gewerblichen Produktion (13.-16. Jahrhundert)*. Stuttgart: Steiner, 1994.

Ibn Mammatī. *Kitab al-qawanīn al-dawanīn*, edited by Azīz Suriāl Atīya. Cairo: The Royal Agricultural Society, 1943.

Jacoby, David. 'Silk Economics and Cross-Cultural Artistic Interaction: Byzantium, the Muslim World, and the Christian West', *Dumbarton Oaks Papers* 58 (2004): 197–240.

König, Sonja and Geschwinde, Michael. 'Tuche und Pferde. Der hochmittelalterliche Wirtschaftshof Klein Freden bei Salzgitter'. In *Archäologie Land Niedersachsen: 400000 Jahre Geschichte*, edited by Mamoun Fansa and Frank Both, 329–32. Stuttgart: Theiss, 2004.

König, Sonja, Hanik, Susanne and Wolf, Gisela. – *Lütken Freden wisk–: Die mittelalterliche Siedlung Klein Freden bei Salzgitter vom 9.-13. Jahrhundert: Siedlung, Fronhof, Pferdehaltung*. Rahden in Westfalen: Verlag Marie Leidorf, 2007.

Kuchenbuch, Ludolf. *Bäuerliche Gesellschaft und Klosterherrschaft im 9. Jahrhundert: Studien zur Sozialstruktur der Familia der Abtei Prüm*. Wiesbaden: Steiner, 1978.

Kuran, Timur. *The Long Divergence: How Islamic Law Held Back the Middle East*. Princeton/Oxford: Princeton University Press, 2011.

Lipinsky, Angelo. 'Tiraz = Ergasterium: Le officine d'arte nel Palazzo Reale di Palermo', *Archivio Storico Siracusano* 10 (1964): 5–24.

Maddison, Angus. *Contours of the World Economy 1–2030 AD: Essays in Macro-Economic History*. Oxford: Oxford University Press, 2007.

Marx, Karl. 'Lohnarbeit und Kapital'. In *Kapital und Politik*, 367–97. Frankfurt am Main: Zweitausendeins, 2008.

Möller, Cosima. 'Die mercennarii in der römischen Arbeitswelt', *Zeitschrift der Savigny-Stiftung für Rechtsgeschichte: Romanistische Abteilung* 110 (1993): 296–330.

Munro, John H. A. 'Medieval Woollens: The Western European Woollen Industries and their Struggles for International Markets, c. 1000–1500', in *The Cambridge History of Western Textiles*, vol. 1, edited by David Jenkins, 228–324. Cambridge: Cambridge University Press, 2003.

Murillo Redondo, Juan F. et al. 'Informe-Memoria de la Intervencíon arquelógica de urgencia en el aparcamiento bajo el Vial Norte de Plan Parical Renfe (segunda fase)', *Anuario Arqueológico de Andalucia* 3/1 (2000): 356–69.

Noble-Kooijman, Jacques-Kees. 'La Pire Aventure d'Yvain: Aventure, conjointure, manufacture dans Le Chevalier au Lion', *Anastasis: Research in Medieval Culture and Art* 6/2 (2019): 67–84. Accessed 9 June 2023. https://doi.org/10.35218/armca.2019.2.04.

Obermeier, Monika. *'Ancilla': Beiträge zur Geschichte der unfreien Frauen im Frühmittelalter*. Pfaffenweiler: Centaurus, 1996.

Rubin, Jared T. *Rulers, Religion, and Riches: Why the West Got Rich and the Middle East Did Not*. Cambridge/New York: Cambridge University Press, 2017.

Sacrorum conciliorum nova et amplissima collectio, vol. 21, edited by Gian Domenico Mansi. Venice: Antonius Zatta, 1776.

Schreiner, Klaus. 'Brot der Mühsal: Körperliche Arbeit im Mönchtum des hohen und späten Mittelalters. Theologisch motivierte Einstellungen, regelgebundene Normen, geschichtliche Praxis'. In *Arbeit im Mittelalter. Vorstellungen und Wirklichkeiten*, edited by Verena Postel, 133–70. Berlin: Akademie Verlag, 2006.

Seipel, Wilfried (ed.). *Nobiles Officinae: Die königlichen Hofwerkstätten zu Palermo zur Zeit der Normannen und Staufer im 12. und 13. Jahrhundert*. Wien: Kunsthistorisches Museum, 2004.

Serjeant, Robert Bertram. *Islamic Textiles*. Beirut: Librairie du Liban, 1972.

Serjeant, Robert Bertram. 'The Tirāz System'. In *Patterns of Everyday Life*, edited by David Waines, 137–76. Aldershot: Ashgate, 2002.

Shatzmiller, Maya. *Labour in the Medieval Islamic World*. Leiden/Boston: Brill, 1994.

Springberg-Hinsen, Monika. *Die Ḥila. Studien zur Geschichte des geschenkten Gewandes im islamischen Kulturkreis*. Würzburg: Ergon, 2000.

Steinfeld, Robert and Engerman, Stanley. 'Labor – Free or Coerced? A Historical Reassessment of Differences and Similarities'. In *Free and Unfree Labour: The Debate Continues*, edited by Marcel van der Linden and Tom Brass, 107–26. Bern: Peter Lang, 1997.

Stillman, Norman A. *Arab Dress: A Short History from the Dawn of Islam to Modern Times*. Leiden/Boston: Brill, 2003.

Stillman, Yedida K., Sanders, Paula and Rabbat, Nasser, 'Ṭirāz'. In: *Encyclopaedia of Islam*, second edition, Leiden/Boston: Brill, 2012. Accessed 9 June 2023. http://dx.doi.org/10.1163/1573-3912_islam_COM_1228

Vadey, Liana. 'Serfdom: Western Europe'. In *Encyclopedia of European Social History: From 1352–2000*, vol. 2, ed. by Peter N. Stearns, 369–78. Detroit: Scribner, 2001.

Van der Linden, Marcel. *Workers of the World: Essays toward a Global Labor History*. Leiden/Boston: Brill, 2008.

'Vita Adalberonis episcopi Wirziburgensis'. In *Monumenta Germaniae Historica: Scriptores*, vol. 12, edited by Wilhelm Wattenbach: 127–47. Hannover: Hahnsche Buchhandlung, 1856.

Zimmermann, Wolf Haio. 'Archäologische Befunde frühmittelalterlicher Webhäuser: Ein Beitrag zum Gewichtswebstuhl', *Jahrbuch der Männer vom Morgenstern* 61 (1982): 111–44.

'ONE GETS RICH, ONE HUNDRED MORE WORK FOR NOTHING'

7
'One gets rich, one hundred more work for nothing': German miners in Medici Tuscany

Gabriele Marcon

Cristof Tegler came from too far away to give up. He had travelled from Nuremberg to the Medici silver mines of Pietrasanta (Versilia, Tuscany) in search of underground treasures. Until he arrived on an autumn day in 1545, hopes and fears had driven his actions during his one-month trip to Tuscany. Now, roaming across the Tuscan landscape and surveying all the promising spots for setting up new mines, Tegler felt the perils of this quest in his own body. He entered galleries and tunnels that were in a state where they could collapse at any time. He kneeled on the ground and followed the signs left by the ores in water streams, rocks and vegetation. The search for precious metals and the hazards it entailed eventually led to rewarding discoveries. Yet it also exacted a physical toll on his body. Bowing over in cramped shafts and galleries earned him the name of *il Gobbo* ('the hunchback'), a word that fellow miners used to address the physical deformation caused by his work.

Mining is not an easy task, and early modern people were well aware of its risks. Yet underground treasures such as gold and silver generated what the historian of science Tina Asmussen describes as 'an affective dimension' in people's response, a driving force that attracted men and women to the mines through the promise of economic and social remuneration.[1] As a miner and metalworker born in Nuremberg and trained in one of Europe's most technologically advanced mining regions – the Erzgebirge (Ore Mountains), currently situated at the border between Germany and the Czech Republic – Tegler possessed the necessary expertise to turn this dangerous work into economic profit.[2] His contemporaries referred to him as a *Bergverständiger* – literally a knower of the mountain, a mining expert who drew place-based knowledge of metals from everyday interaction with nature. In the silver mines of Pietrasanta,

Tegler discovered new deposits of silver-bearing ores as early as 1545, the same year he arrived, which he described as a promising field where he 'found ores in many places'.[3] Being an experienced metalworker, he was also prepared to win silver from the ores through the adoption of metallurgical and alchemical processes. He was, in a way, a treasure hunter of his time.

The arrival of German experts was paramount to the development of the mining economy of sixteenth-century Tuscany. Between the 1540s and the 1560s, approximately 130 German male and female miners worked in the silver, copper, lead and alum mines scattered across the territories controlled by the Medici family, whose members were the rulers of Florence and future Grand Dukes of Tuscany.[4] It was a multifaceted labour migration. Germans arrived with their families or alone, usually in crews of 2 to 12 miners. They came from various parts of Central Europe: some arrived from Sankt Joachimsthal a year after Tegler's first surveys; others came from the Tyrolean mines of Schwaz, Persen and Bolzano.[5] Their migration was the result of the decision taken by the Medici in the early 1540s to reopen ancient silver, lead and alum mines in their dominion. This initiative was part of a larger political programme aimed at restoring the economic and commercial power of the family over the Tuscan territories. Following the arrival of German experts, the Medici traded these precious metals through commodity networks meeting foreign and domestic demand.[6] In this context, German miners were the pioneers who paved the way for the emergence of mining economies in one of the leading states of the Italian Renaissance.

This chapter draws upon sources housed in the Florentine archives and written by German miners that reveal much of the ambiguity of mining migrations. In the early modern period, the allure of underground treasures promised monetary returns, yet women and men who decided to embark on this endeavour gambled with their own lives every day.[7] What is especially remarkable, the allocation and remuneration of labour activities, which miners performed underground or on the surface, were not static, and could change over time, even within a short period of time.[8] Even though the legal and customary administration of the mines provided miners and officials with some guidelines and guarantees, employers' needs could change miners' working conditions at any time, introducing, for example, longer working hours at short notice when the mining of ores had to be accelerated due to production demands. This chapter aims to offer a bottom-up account of the impacts of employers' shifting decisions on miners' everyday activities. More generally, it seeks to discover what it meant to be a miner in sixteenth-century Tuscany.

German male and female miners who worked in the Medici mines offer an illuminating perspective on this human experience. Leaving highly productive mines behind in their places of departure, they arrived in newly reopened mining districts with little knowledge of the future outcomes of this migration.[9] While existing scholarship has focused on the role of German experts in boosting mining production in early modern Italy, this chapter centres on the uncertainties of mining migrations.[10] It first examines the promises and anxieties that underpinned mineral discoveries by focusing on the early activities of German miners in the Medici silver mines. German miners could rely on skills developed in high-yielding mining regions in Central Europe. Their expertise fuelled expectations of finding new mineral deposits in uncharted territories and allowed them to receive higher wages than locals. Yet, as is subsequently shown, they also came under the dominion of the Duke, which made them vulnerable to changes in their status as workers and modes of payment that were imposed on them top-down.

The chapter further examines these labour relations by drawing on the illustration of a miner extracting precious metals from the ground (p. 165) to provide an account of the experience of labour, coercion and remuneration. More specifically, the aquarelle by Dariia Kuzmych serves as an opportunity to reflect on the human efforts and economic concerns that revolved around mining from the perspective of those who performed it.[11] The man in the image is sunburned; the sun sheet barely covers him. He is leaning forward and carries a heavy backpack with rocks. He is searching for mineral deposits on his own, pointing at the self-employed work German miners were allowed to perform in the mines. Yet, as will be shown, the promises of monetary remuneration and decision-making entailed in self-employment did not play out in everyday practice as expected. The autonomy legally granted to German miners did not prevent them from coming under severe coercion exerted by their employers, which made them susceptible to forced relocation and increased the physical toll that mining took on their bodies.

Between promises and anxieties

In the early modern period, the underground world, and the treasures it concealed, created hopes and promises of quick enrichment. The discovery of mineral resources evoked material desires that fostered movement to the mines and transformed remote mountain areas into places of economic, social and cultural dynamism. Between the late fifteenth and early sixteenth centuries, the allure of metals was responsible for rapid demographic growth and the creation of mining towns in Saxony, Bohemia, Hungary and Tyrol.[12] News about mineral deposits circulated quickly across Europe and shaped the ways in which people thought about mining. In the territories of the Holy Roman Empire, women and men of any rank and with no connections with the mines could invest in mining activities through the purchase of financial and speculative instruments (called *Kuxe*) that guaranteed profits on shares of the mining production in exchange for contribution costs.[13] Mining also engendered new labour opportunities and attracted female and male labourers to the mines.[14] As legal owners of underground resources, rulers subcontracted mining activities to miners and shareholders, while holding pre-emptive rights on mined ores.[15] At the same time, mineral discoveries encouraged territorial rulers to grant privileges to anyone willing to embark on this quest. These ranged from fiscal exemption to autonomous jurisdiction, and facilitated the purchase of food and raw materials for the needs of the mines.[16]

As has been rightly pointed out, not all this dynamism can be explained through the lens of economic and labour history.[17] Spiritual, divine and magical forces were felt to shroud the underground world and this had a significant impact on shaping the sociocultural aspects of mining. Legends and folklore depicted miners' adventures in the subterranean world by narrating their encounters with spirits, goblins and other creatures that affected the real and imaginary humans' interaction with mining.[18] Folklore and legends articulated the rhythm of new discoveries and portrayed early modern mines as rewarding places for achieving material desires.

Despite its attractiveness, the discovery of precious metals came with a price. Most of the stories narrating the finding of new deposits show desperate miners on the edge of financial bankruptcy, their destiny hanging on the unpredictable will of the goddess Fortuna.[19] In a late fifteenth-century Latin text depicting the relationship between nature and mining in Central European mines, the impotence of miners vis-à-vis the underground world emerges clearly.[20] Two friends debate the opportunities of investing in the mines. One of them, Florian, warns his companion that 'you'd better roll the dice, and suddenly you can earn more – or lose everything you have'. Surprised, his friend Arnolph replies: 'So mining is not that one true and fair thing for which nobody is penalised?' 'What do you think?' asks Florian. 'You can see [that] if one gets rich, one hundred more work for nothing; they plunge in for gold and silver, yet dig out dirt and rocks.'[21] The uncertainty and promises of rich discoveries and material returns defined for contemporaries what historians described as 'an area of ambiguity: on the one hand, mining was a divine gift and a gateway to untold wealth, on the other a sure path to the unforeseen and life-threatening'.[22]

These ambiguities characterised the Medici mining initiative in the sixteenth century. In 1542, the soon-to-become Grand Duke of Tuscany Cosimo I de' Medici reopened silver and lead mines in the north- and south-western territories of the duchy. The mines had been previously worked by the Etruscans in ancient times, and after the short-lived activities of a mining partnership in the mid-fifteenth century, they had fallen into disuse. Cosimo I reorganised the mining activities in the years 1542 to 1546 under the supervision of local functionaries. However, the Medici officials' expertise lay in tax farming rather than mining and metallurgical operations, and soon the difficulties they encountered in refining silver-bearing ores necessitated the recruitment of experts from abroad.[23] The Italians had heard about the success and reputation of German miners beyond the Alps, and so, men and women from Saxony, Tyrol, Carinthia, Slovakia and Hungary with administrative, organisational and practical skills in the most relevant and essential activities of mining – finding mineral veins, digging deep shafts, refining ores and allocating labour – were drawn to the Medici mines.[24] In the 20 years to follow, Medici intermediaries in Saxony and Tyrol recruited around 40 workers – including married couples – who came to work as miners, overseers, silver assayers and skilled labourers. They were followed by at least 100 more who moved autonomously to Tuscany.[25]

Before travelling southwards, Germans knew all too well that mining was a risky business. In the mining industry, nobody could foresee how deep ores would run into the mountains, and what kind of investment and labour costs would have to be met before profits could be yielded.[26] Initial mineral discoveries often revolved around easy-to-reach surface deposits. However, these generated short-lived profits and were usually soon abandoned. Mineral ores that ran deeper underground were richer, but required substantial capital to solve flooding and ventilation issues created by the excavation of low-depth shafts.[27] The historian Sebastian Felten has recently argued that 'the proof of these imaginary veins were the diggings [and that] acting on this kind of knowledge was a leap of faith'.[28]

These uncertainties exposed German miners in Medici Tuscany to financial risks and existential anxieties. On the one hand, those who moved individually across mines – mostly middle-aged men – based their decisions on speculative information and word of mouth that depicted the Tuscan mines as a promising labour opportunity.[29] On the other hand, those crews of miners who were directly recruited by the Medici intermediaries were given more guarantees by the mining administration, such as advance payments that covered travel costs for them and their families.[30] However, once they arrived in Tuscany, these debts had to be paid off, and miners' economic returns depended on whether they struck it lucky or not. Payments made in advance generated forms of coercion that transformed the labour relationship between German miners and the Duke into a debtor–creditor relationship.

Even though moving to Tuscany inevitably meant facing the uncertainties of mining, German miners could rely on some advantages. Timing and skills were particularly on their side. Being the first experienced miners to work in uncharted mining fields could prove a determinant factor, and thus the Tuscan mines were a promising economic opportunity in the eyes of German miners.[31] They were experienced in finding mineral ores underground, an expertise that allowed them to establish new mines before others, find rich and unexploited veins, and request mining rights in the most profitable spots. These skills elevated German miners above their Italian counterparts. Cristof Tegler, for example, proved his skills by processing silver-bearing ores extracted in Pietrasanta. This operation yielded better outcomes than the ones Medici officials had been able to produce before, and attests to the technical superiority of German experts over local practitioners.

Timing also translated into miners' remuneration. As first discoverers of new veins, German miners requested mining investitures that allowed them to operate new mines as self-employers – a right they had also enjoyed in their areas of origin. Because the Medici Duke – like other territorial rulers in continental Europe – exerted legal ownership over underground resources, miners could ask for permission to operate their own mines and sell the extracted minerals to the Medici enterprise. Between 1547 and 1551, German miners obtained mining rights as first discoverers on 6 out of the 12 new mines established in the Pietrasanta district.[32] In so doing, miners sold the extracted ores to the Duke and added these earnings to the weekly wages they already received as employees of the Medici enterprise. Tegler explained this mechanism in a letter written to the Duke in 1545. By adding the profits German miners could make through self-employment, he argued that 'the poor labourer could benefit' from selling ores to the Duke.[33]

Skills were another important factor enabling German miners to gain economic profits through migrating. In the period from the 1540s to the 1560s, two German experts – Cristof Tegler and Hans Glöggl, a factor from Tyrol – were appointed mine managers in Pietrasanta and came to decide on the allocation and remuneration of labourers in the mines. Consequently, wages in the Medici mines were set at higher rates for Germans than for local workers. Because Germans were more skilled than Italians in the eyes of the mine managers, highly remunerated tasks such as overseeing, silver assaying and smelting were allocated to Germans. The wage gap emerged also in cases where Germans and Italians performed the same labour tasks. German male hewers, who made up a large proportion of the miners, earned 6 lire while Italians earned 5, and this double standard continued until the mines' shutdown in 1592. The wage gap also characterised women's work, which was pivotal in mining activities, particularly for the economic strategies of families.[34] German women worked in the smelting furnaces alongside their husbands, and performed ore washing activities that prepared the minerals for the smelting phase. In the Medici mines, German managers allocated to German women better remunerated and longer-term tasks vis-à-vis local female labourers, who mostly performed auxiliary work such as hauling and charcoal making.[35]

Despite the uncertainties that characterised mining activities, hopes trumped doubts, and German miners moved southwards in search of underground riches. Germans with authority over the organisation of labour in the Tuscan mines sought to meet their expectations by increasing remuneration. However, skills did not protect them from a variety of issues, such as coercion and risky working conditions.

Mining for the Duke

Despite the looming risks, the endeavours of the German miners started off well. However, they would soon take a turn for the worse. While Tegler found 'good and rich veins' when he first arrived in 1545, the silver yield of the Medici mines never reflected the high expectations generated by the Germans' new discoveries.[36] This also held true in the following years, even though promising signs of underground deposits were also found in Campiglia (Maremma), where in 1556 two miners from Saxony surveyed the mines and stated that 'in Germany [we] have never seen something as beautiful as in this mountain'.[37] Apparently, a lot of veins and ores initially appeared to have potential, but silver outputs did not reach the vertiginous peaks of the mines in the German-speaking countries. In 1549, the Pietrasanta mines produced 397 pounds of silver, which was half of the amount yielded eight years before by the Schneeberg district, one of the most productive mining fields in Saxony.[38] Even though Tegler's metallurgical experiments had come to yield better results than when he had just arrived four years earlier, his mineral processing method produced debased silver. Indeed, the fact that silver extracted in Pietrasanta was not sent to the Florentine mint and transformed into coins confirms its impurity.[39] This suggests that German mining knowledge, even though it was of the highest standards, could not straightforwardly and easily be transplanted to a different ecological system; the *Bergverständiger* was confronted with the limitations of his skills. The rate of new discoveries remained high, yet many of the mines shut down shortly after their opening. Things looked bleak for the indebted Germans and their high expectations. To cap it all, local officials, who had no authority over the technical aspects of the industry, secretly reported on the Germans' activities to the Duke and often questioned their expertise and criticised their slower-than-expected advancement.[40]

Low productivity in the mines prompted the Duke to reinforce his economic position in the late 1540s. While the silver was not used in the state's mint, it was handed over to the Medici's workshops and crafted by the silversmiths, alchemists and artisans working for the court.[41] Lead extracted in Campiglia was processed in the arsenal in Livorno. Here it was used to manufacture cannon balls that were successively distributed to the galleys of the ducal fleet and to coastal fortifications.[42] Because the supply of alum was pivotal for the dyeing process of Florentine textile manufacturing, where it was used as a mordant, the Medici sought mining initiatives in Val di Cecina to free themselves from their dependence on the Papal State production.[43] The centralised administration of the Medici mines sought to protect the territorial rulers' economic interests in natural resources. The Duke did not allow any merchant entrepreneurs to operate the mines, and was the ultimate recipient of every single ounce of silver extracted from his territory. Miners with wages and self-employed miners with mining rights alike were bound to obey these orders.

Decreased expectations for metal production motivated Cosimo to acquire any source of revenue across the district to increase his profits. Between 1548 and 1551, Germans held shares on the mines they had discovered, but the Duke progressively bought out these shares. Cosimo owned several mines in the district, and partnered up with Germans in those mines where they had (until then) worked as self-employed. In August 1548, the factor of one of these formerly self-employed enterprises – the one that operated the Santo Spirito or Heiliger Geist mine – was bought out with 36 lire and 18 soldi when 'his Excellency raised by seven shares his participation in the mine, from 25 to 32 shares'. In October, Cosimo acquired another 12 shares of the same mine, owned by 'Tomaso Farsetter todesco', apparently also a German, for 1 lira per share.[44] Cosimo's invasion into new mines continued in the following years. This shift did not relocate miners to other sites of employment, but rather turned them from self-employed into waged labourers as they continued their work in the same mines.

The end of self-employment and the transformation into a wage labour relation represented a form of coercion that generated a loss of revenues for German miners. They had been promised autonomy but then quickly learned the lesson that sovereigns like Cosimo could change the rules of the game as they pleased. The dependent work relation that German miners had with the Duke also emerged from the relocation of the former according to the needs of the mines. In the summer of 1558, German miners were sent to Campiglia to boost extractive activities. The fact that they could be deployed across different mines was a widespread feature characterising their labour relations in Tuscany. Germans' skills in mining and metallurgical operations were in demand in several copper, lead and alum mines across the Medici territory, and the managers demanded to deploy the workers at their will.[45] The authority of the mine managers was almost ubiquitous as it was conveyed directly from the Duke. In the mines, they ranked higher than local officials, and miners were bound to their will by an oath they swore to them and to the mining enterprise as soon as they arrived in Tuscany. As a result, German miners, once in Tuscany, were not the agents of their own mobility.

Being bought out of their shares, and being largely powerless against forced relocation, German miners came to work the Duke's mines as time-wage labourers and could only rely on the earnings made as employees of Cosimo's enterprise. Their wages were calculated in shifts of 10 hours per day and amounted to a weekly salary of 6 lire. Even though they were entitled to higher wages than the Italians, the Germans argued that it was not enough in a country where 'everything is more expensive than in Germany'. Their complaints about low incomes addressed the difficulties in paying the prices for bread and meat, which were extraordinarily high in Tuscany, while in Germany 'we could find everything for a fair price'.[46] These grievances turned into several protests, and in 1558 German miners threatened to return to their countries if wages were not increased.

The new mine manager Hans Glöggl from Tyrol, who replaced the deceased Tegler in 1558, obtained ducal permission to increase German hewers' wages from 6 to 7 lire.[47] Despite this raise, poor working conditions and environmental circumstances continued to challenge Germans' remuneration in Medici Tuscany.

The perils of mining

People in early modern times believed that nature and humans were entangled in a complex relationship. In mining, for example, both were equally affected by the technological advancements that allowed miners to dig deeper shafts. This activity transformed the environmental landscapes around the mines, yet the increasing manipulation of the Earth through labour was not seen as a form of domination of humankind over nature. Indeed, while people extracted minerals from the Earth with the aim of thriving above the ground, the Earth would take her revenge underground.[48] Tegler's physical deformation was one of the ways in which nature exerted her toll. Bowing over in cramped shafts, hammering and hauling off rocks, smelting metals in ovens and furnaces – these were necessary to the advancement of mining. But they also exposed its practitioners to severe health issues. These ranged from diseases that altered the strength and flexibility of the bones to respiratory illness caused by the inhalation of dusts and other poisonous fumes. These were illnesses which slowly ate up the body, but miners also understood the mine as a workplace where instant death could manifest at any moment.[49]

Alongside these 'common' perils, German miners in Medici Tuscany had to deal with additional threats. For instance, the miners in the lead mines of Campiglia faced extremely precarious living and working conditions. These mines were located in a sparsely populated area which was heavily plagued by malaria over the sixteenth century. Water supply was scarce because the mines lay far away from water sources and mules transporting water buckets needed days to reach the district. Before the creation of a big lodge to house miners in 1558, which eventually improved their living conditions, miners inhabited small makeshift shelters made of wooden planks that were located in the immediate vicinity of the pits' entrances.[50] The precarious situation experienced by miners shows that the Medici administration did not dispense the structural and material means to provide miners with the necessary resources against hazardous labour activities.

The inadequate efforts to supply food to the mines further reflected the perilous condition of this workplace. Because the pollution caused by mining and metalworking activities in the surrounding territories prevented miners from growing crops and breeding cattle, mining districts needed a constant supply of food and other primary goods. Some levels of trade and consumption of wheat and meat in the mines of Central Europe were so impressive that rulers and merchants were forced to find exceptional logistic solutions to food supply.[51] However, food in the Medici mines was not supplied as smoothly as Germans had expected, which was another disappointment of their expectations about working in Tuscany. In 1558, after 13 years of activity, Hans Glöggl felt the need to remind the Duke that 'His Excellency has to guarantee fiscal privileges to those merchants who supply the mines with every good'.[52] Speaking on behalf of his countrymen, the German mine manager also lobbied for the purchase of certain nourishment that would better feed 'such rough and big people [the Germans]'.[53] Indeed, Glöggl argued that without oxen and buttered dark-rye bread, 'these workers cannot get the usual strength to work'.[54] Despite these attempts, the mines continued to receive local products, such as white bread and young calf beef, which Medici officials often sold to miners at higher than market prices.

Climatic conditions also put severe constraints on the work of German miners. Mine workers in Tuscany were exposed to temperatures far different from those in cooler Central Europe. This played out in two ways. First, in the southern parts of Tuscany, miners worked in open-pit mines. This decision was connected to the geological conformation of the territory. In the mines surrounding the medieval castle of Rocca San Silvestro in Campiglia, silver-bearing ores were richer on the surface, and, contrary to the Pietrasanta mines, where shafts and tunnels were built to reach in-depth ores, the digging was carried out through the removal of overburden from a large area at low depth. Second, this method, which was also used in the iron mines of the nearby island of Elba, required miners all year round. In the summer, Germans turned over rocks and quarried large residuals of earth under the scorching temperatures of the Tuscan summer.[55]

The relocation of around 20 German miners from Pietrasanta to Campiglia in 1558 revealed the toll of working in the open sun. In August, usually the hottest month of the year, Medici officials reported that out of the roughly 20 German miners sent to Campiglia in that year, at least eight to ten got sick. Their conditions worsened very quickly, and four men and a woman died in the following weeks. The Medici officials attributed the wave of diseases to the lack of drinking water and the poor housing conditions in the mines. At the end of the summer, of the entire crew sent to Campiglia, seven had died, while six had refused to work and openly expressed the intention to go back to Germany. As soon as the mine manager Hans Glöggl – who apparently got sick too in the same period – received the news of the protests, he imprisoned the disobedient miners, and after one week, transferred them back to Pietrasanta.[56]

Conclusion

The combination of the textual information retrieved from archival sources and the multidimensional setting of the image brings us closer to the complementary layers that characterised work in early modern mines but are often lost in the documentary evidence about the past. Searching for metals in a rocky landscape, male and female miners were experiencing in their bodies and minds the ambiguities of work with an unforeseen outcome. The allure of precious metals generated by the uncharted mining fields of early modern Tuscany shaped their expectations about the products of their labour. Observing the landscapes, they recognised promising spots, pictured in their minds the possible infrastructures, and imagined the variety of ores still concealed underground. Miners possessed knowledge about the natural world and deployed embodied skills that allowed them to recognise the signs left on the surface by ores running underground. This expertise gave them a degree of confidence, and lowered the pressure of travelling a long way to test their luck.

Working in new territories generated hopes, but also anxieties. Miners invested everything they had in the Tuscan mines. They were already indebted to the Duke at the time of their arrival, as the Medici had paid for their journey to Tuscany. Wages were slightly higher than those paid to local miners, but they were mostly intended to attract them to work for the Duke, and to justify the employer's control over their mobility across Tuscany. Searching for minerals individually became more difficult, as the Germans soon found out that the Duke was a partner with a heavy hand. Indeed, they had to work in the mines owned by the Duke, who was eager to profit from their skills. Working for the Duke meant moving to different sites of extraction that exposed them to more hazardous labour conditions. The burden of labour was heavier in the Medici mines of Campiglia, where food was expensive, water was not drinkable and the heat scorched the miners' bodies as they toiled.

The search for precious metals engendered a vortex of contrasting directions that pulled German miners towards hopes and fears, richness and poverty, life and death. Work in the Medici mines exacted a high toll on them. Coercive mechanisms of labour and migration left them with no choice but to continue digging until they found something. However, success in mining was uncertain: skills did not always protect workers from the unpredictability of work. Higher wages entailed migration control and speculative food prices set by local officials, only two elements that reveal the uncertain nature of monetary remuneration. High degrees of coercion and disappointing revenues led to most of the Germans leaving Tuscany by 1560, just 15 years after Tegler's arrival. The Medici mines eventually shut down in 1592, concluding a brief period of Tuscan mining during which a few made extraordinary riches while most ended up 'working for nothing'.

Notes

1. Asmussen, 'Wild Men in Braunschweig – Economies of Hope and Fear in Early Modern Mining', 2020, 43.
2. On the social, cultural and economic aspects of mining production in the Ore Mountains, see Schattkowsky and Albrecht (eds), *Das Erzgebirge im 16. Jahrhundert. Gestaltwandel einer Kulturlandschaft im Reformationszeitalter*; and the contributions therein. For a material history approach to the technology and knowledge of early modern metalworkers, see Smith, 'Vermillion, Mercury, Blood, and Lizards: Matter and Meaning in Metalworking'.
3. '[…] nella quale ho trovato in più luoghi della miniera'. One of the most important footprints of Tegler's passage in the Medici mines is a letter sent to Duke Cosimo de' Medici on 21 December 1545 and translated from the German into Italian. The letter is transcribed in Morelli, 'Argento Americano e Argento Toscano. Due Soluzioni Alla Crisi Mineraria Del Cinquecento', 1984, 195–201. In this chapter, I cite the Italian transcription. All translations from the Italian and any resulting errors are my own.
4. Morelli, 'The Medici Silver Mines (1542–1592)', 1976.
5. For a general overview of the presence of German miners in Medici Tuscany, see Fabretti and Guidarelli, 'Ricerche sulle iniziative dei Medici in campo minerario da Cosimo I a Ferdinando I', 143–50.
6. Morelli, 'The Medici Silver Mines (1542–1592)', 135–39.
7. Asmussen, 'Glück Auf! Fortuna und Risiko im Frühneuzeitlichen Bergbau', 2016, 31–5.
8. On shifts in labour relations in the mining industry, see Barragán Romano, 'Dynamics of Continuity and Change', 2016.
9. For an analysis of mining migrations in early modern Europe, see Stöger, 'Die Migration europäischer Bergleute während der Frühen Neuzeit', 2006.
10. On German miners in early modern Italy, see Ludwig and Vergani, 'Mobilità e Migrazioni Dei Minatori (XIII–XVII Sec.)'.
11. Hereby I refer to the work of Tina Asmussen on the Harz mountains. See Asmussen, 'Glück Auf! Fortuna und Risiko im frühneuzeitlichen Bergbau', 2016; Asmussen, 'Wild Men in Braunschweig – Economies of Hope and Fear in Early Modern Mining', 2020.
12. For a comprehensive account of mining in early modern Europe, see Bartels and Rainer, *Der Alteuropäische Bergbau. Von den Anfängen bis zur Mitte des 18. Jahrhunderts*.
13. Asmussen, 'The Kux as a Site of Mediation: Economic Practices and Material Desires in the Early Modern German Mining Industry'.
14. On women's work in the mines, see Karant-Nunn, 'The Women of the Saxon Silver Mines'.

15 Neumann, 'Imagined Investors: Markets, Agents, and the Saxon Mining Administration'.
16 Ingenhaeff and Bair (eds), *Bergbau und Berggeschrey. Zu den Ursprüngen europäischer Bergwerke*. 8. Internationaler Montanhistorischer Kongress Schwaz in Tirol/Sterzing in Südtirol 2009. Tagungsband.
17 Asmussen and Long, 'Introduction', 2020. For new research trajectories on early modern mining, see the special issue of *Renaissance Studies* edited by Tina Asmussen and Pamela O. Long (34/1, 2020).
18 Dym, 'Mineral Fumes and Mining Spirits', 2006.
19 Asmussen, 'The Kux as a Site of Mediation', 170–3.
20 Niavis; Krenkel, *Iudicium Iovis*, 39. Cited in Asmussen, 'Glück Auf! Fortuna und Risiko im Frühneuzeitlichen Bergbau', 2016, 34. All translations from the German and any resulting errors are my own.
21 'Florian: Hole lieber die Würfel und im Handumdrehen wirst du noch mehr dazu gewinnen. Arnolph: So ist es nicht mit den Erzbergwerken, das ist eine ehrliche und gerechte Sache, ohne dass jemand benachteiligt wird. Florina: Was sagst Du? Du siehst doch, wie viele in höchste Not geraten sind, und wenn einer reich wird, so arbeiten hundert umsonst; sie stecken Gold und Silber hinein und bekommen Dreck und Steine heraus.' Cited in Asmussen, 'Glück Auf! Fortuna und Risiko im Frühneuzeitlichen Bergbau', 2016, 33–4.
22 Asmussen, 'Wild Men in Braunschweig', 2020, 39.
23 For the early stages of the Medici mining initiative, see Fabretti and Guidarelli, 'Ricerche sulle iniziative dei Medici', 143–62.
24 For these and more skills developed in Central European mines, see Bartels, 'The Production of Silver, Copper, and Lead in the Harz Mountains from Late Medieval to the Onset of Industrialization'.
25 Marcon, 'Duchi, Mercanti, Passaporti e Minatori. La Logistica Delle Migrazioni Di Mestiere Nell'Europa Del Cinquecento', 2020.
26 Asmussen, 'Glück Auf! Fortuna und Risiko im Frühneuzeitlichen Bergbau', 2016, 35–6.
27 On the relationship between financial capital and mining, see Safley, 'Mercury Mining and Miners'.
28 Felten, 'The History of Science and the History of Bureaucratic Knowledge', 2018, 410–11.
29 Tegler anticipated these outcomes in his letter. See Morelli, 'Argento Americano e Argento Toscano. Due Soluzioni Alla Crisi Mineraria Del Cinquecento', 1984, 197.
30 Marcon, 'Duchi, Mercanti, Passaporti e Minatori', 2020, 81–4.
31 On the importance of being the first in the mining business, see Felten, 'The History of Science and the History of Bureaucratic Knowledge', 2018, 409–12.
32 On the mechanisms regulating mining rights in Medici Tuscany, see Farinelli, 'Dall'Erzgebirge alla Toscana di Cosimo I Medici. Il Lavoro Minerario e Metallurgico secondo "Le ordine et statuti […] sopra le cave et meneri" del 1548', 86–90.
33 '… e che el povero [minatore] potesi avere qualche utile'. Cited in Morelli, 'Argento Americano e Argento Toscano', 1984, 197.
34 See Marcon, 'Wages Unpacked: Remuneration, Negotiation, and Coercion in the Medici Silver Mines', 2022. For a detailed account of the multifaceted labour activities performed by early modern women in the mines, see Murillo, 'Laboring Above Ground', 2013.
35 Marcon, 'Wages Unpacked', 2022, 69–71.
36 '… bella e potente vena che viene alla luce'. Cited in Morelli, 'Argento Americano e Argento Toscano', 1984, 197.
37 '… dicano non aver mai visto sì bella cosa nella Magnia come in questo monte'. Cited in Farinelli, *Le miniere di Rocca San Silvestro nella prima età moderna. Organizzazione produttiva, cultura materiale, tecniche estrattive e metallurgiche nell'impresa di Cosimo I*, 219.
38 Data retrieved from Morelli, 'The Medici Silver Mines', 1976, 134, and Laube, *Studien über den Erzgebirgischen Silberbergbau von 1470 bis 1546*, 79–81.
39 See Morelli, 'The Medici Silver Mines', 1976, 138–9.
40 Among sceptical Medici officials, Giovanni Battista Donati, superintendent of the Campiglia lead mines, was concerned with the metallurgical methods proposed by the Germans. See Farinelli, *Le miniere di Rocca San Silvestro*, 184–6.
41 Morelli, 'The Medici Silver Mines', 1976, 138.
42 Morelli, 'The Medici Silver Mines', 1976, 138.
43 Farinelli, 'L'avvio delle iniziative granducali per la coltivazione dell'allume a Massa Marittima', 2009.

44 Marcon, 'Wages Unpacked', 2022, 62–67.
45 Marcon, 'Wages Unpacked', 2022, 66.
46 Marcon, 'Wages Unpacked', 2022, 69–70.
47 See Fabretti and Guidarelli, 'Ricerche sulle iniziative', 144.
48 These aspects are thoughtfully elaborated in Asmussen, 'Spirited Metals and the Oeconomy of Resources in Early Modern European Mining', 2020.
49 The fall of rocks and the collapse of mines were the principal causes of instant death. For a sixteenth-century account of miners' diseases, see Theophrastus (Paracelsus) von Hohenheim, 'On the Miners' Sickness and Other Miners' Diseases'.
50 Farinelli, *Le miniere di Rocca San Silvestro*, 245.
51 For food consumption and trade in Central European mines, see Schirmer, 'Ernährung im Erzgebirge im 15. und 16. Jahrhundert. Produktion, Handel und Verbrauch'.
52 'è di bisogno che vostra illustrissima Eccellenza concede libertà e francija a tutte le persone dello stato Suo che possino liberamente venire et vendere … ogni sorta di mercanzia necessaria all'uso humano'. Cited in Farinelli, *Le miniere di Rocca San Silvestro*, 240.
53 'persone rotze et grosse'. Cited in Farinelli, *Le miniere di Rocca San Silvestro*, 239.
54 'non trovano la forza solita per lavorare'. Cited in Farinelli, *Le miniere di Rocca San Silvestro*, 240.
55 For additional information on these aspects, see Farinelli, *Le miniere di Rocca San Silvestro*, 111–16.
56 Farinelli, *Le miniere di Rocca San Silvestro*, 61 and 244.

Bibliography

Asmussen, Tina. 'Glück Auf! Fortuna und Risiko im Frühneuzeitlichen Bergbau', *FKW//Zeitschrift für Geschlechterforschung und Visuelle Kultur* 7/3 (2016): 302–5.

Asmussen, Tina. 'The Kux as a Site of Mediation: Economic Practices and Material Desires in the Early Modern German Mining Industry'. In *Sites of Mediation*, edited by Susanna Burghartz, Lucas Burkart and Christine Göttler, 159–82. Leiden: Brill, 2016.

Asmussen, Tina. 'Spirited Metals and the Oeconomy of Resources in Early Modern European Mining', *Earth Sciences History*, 39/2 (2020), 371–88.

Asmussen, Tina. 'Wild Men in Braunschweig – Economies of Hope and Fear in Early Modern Mining', *Renaissance Studies* 34/1 (2020): 31–56.

Asmussen, Tina and Long, Pamela O. 'Introduction: The Cultural and Material Worlds of Mining in Early Modern Europe', *Renaissance Studies* 34/1 (2020): 8–30.

Barragán Romano, Rossana. 'Dynamics of Continuity and Change: Shifts in Labour Relations in the Potosí Mines (1680–1812)', *International Review of Social History* 61 (2016): 93–114.

Bartels, Christoph. 'The Production of Silver, Copper, and Lead in the Harz Mountains from Late Medieval to the Onset of Industrialization'. In *Materials and Expertise in Early Modern Europe: Between Market and Laboratory*, edited by Ursula Klein and E. C. Spary, 71–100. Chicago: University of Chicago Press, 2010.

Bartels, Christoph and Rainer, Slotta (eds). *Der Alteuropäische Bergbau. Von den Anfängen bis zur Mitte des 18. Jahrhunderts*. Geschichte des Deutschen Bergbaus 1. Münster: Aschendorff, 2012.

Dym, Warren. 'Mineral Fumes and Mining Spirits: Popular Beliefs in the Sarepta of Johann Mathesius (1504–1565)', *Reformation & Renaissance Review* 8/2 (2006): 161–85.

Fabretti, Magda and Guidarelli, Anna. 'Ricerche sulle iniziative dei Medici in campo minerario da Cosimo I a Ferdinando I'. In *La Toscana in età moderna (secoli XVI–XVIII): politica, istituzioni, società.*, edited by Mario Ascheri and Alessandra Contini, 139–217. Firenze: Olschki, 2005.

Farinelli, Roberto. 'L'avvio delle iniziative granducali per la coltivazione dell'allume a Massa Marittima', *Mélanges de l'Ecole française de Rome. Moyen-Age* 121/1 (2009): 69–82.

Farinelli, Roberto. 'Dall'Erzgebirge alla Toscana di Cosimo I Medici. Il Lavoro Minerario e Metallurgico secondo "Le ordine et statuti […] sopra le cave et meneri" del 1548.' In *I codici minerari nell'Europa preindustriale: archeologia e storia*, edited by Roberto Farinelli and Giovanna Santinucci, 83–112. Sesto Fiorentino: All'insegna del giglio, 2014.

Farinelli, Roberto. *Le miniere di Rocca San Silvestro nella prima età moderna. Organizzazione produttiva, cultura materiale, tecniche estrattive e metallurgiche nell'impresa di Cosimo I*. Siena: Nuova Immagine, 2018.
Felten, Sebastian. 'The History of Science and the History of Bureaucratic Knowledge: Saxon Mining, circa 1770', *History of Science* 56/4 (2018): 403–31.
Ingenhaeff, Wolfgang and Bair, Johann (eds). *Bergbau und Berggeschrey. Zu den Ursprüngen europäischer Bergwerke*. 8. Internationaler Montanhistorischer Kongress Schwaz in Tirol/Sterzing in Südtirol 2009. Tagungsband. Innsbruck: Berenkamp, 2010.
Karant-Nunn, Susan. 'The Women of the Saxon Silver Mines'. In *Women in Reformation and Counter-Reformation Europe: Public and Private Worlds*, edited by Sherrin Marshall, 29–46. Bloomington: Indiana University Press, 1991.
Krenkel, Paul (transl.). 'Paulus Niavis: Zwei Gespräche aus dem Thesaurus Eloquentiae des Niavis'. In *Iudicium Iovis oder das Gericht der Götter über den Bergbau: Ein literarisches Dokument aus der Frühzeit des Deutschen Bergbaus*, edited by Paul Krenkel, 39–40. Berlin: Akademie Verlag, 1953.
Laube, Adolf. *Studien über den Erzgebirgischen Silberbergbau von 1470 bis 1546*. Berlin: Akademie Verlag Berlin, 1974.
Ludwig, Karl-Heinz and Vergani, Raffaello. 'Mobilità e Migrazioni Dei Minatori (XIII–XVII Sec.)'. In *Le Migrazioni in Europa Secc. XIII–XVIII. Atti delle 'Settimane di Studio e Convegli' dell'Istituto di Storia Economica 'Francesco Datini'*, edited by Simonetta Cavaciocchi, Serie II, 25, 593–622. Firenze: Le Monnier, 1994.
Marcon, Gabriele. 'Duchi, Mercanti, Passaporti e Minatori. La Logistica Delle Migrazioni Di Mestiere Nell'Europa Del Cinquecento', *Quaderni Di Scienza e Politica* 11 (2020), 75–94.
Marcon, Gabriele. 'Wages Unpacked: Remuneration, Negotiation, and Coercion in the Medici Silver Mines', *Comparativ. Zeitschrift für Globalgeschichte und Vergleichende Gesellschaftsforschung* 32/1 (2022): 55–74.
Morelli, Roberta. 'The Medici Silver Mines (1542–1592)', *Journal of European Economic History* 5/1 (1976): 121–39.
Morelli, Roberta. 'Argento Americano e Argento Toscano. Due Soluzioni Alla Crisi Mineraria Del Cinquecento', *Ricerche Storiche* 1 (1984): 163–201.
Murillo, Dana Velasco. 'Laboring Above Ground: Indigenous Women in New Spain's Silver Mining District, Zacatecas, Mexico, 1620–1770', *Hispanic American Historical Review* 93/1 (2013): 3–32.
Neumann, Franziska. 'Imagined Investors: Markets, Agents, and the Saxon Mining Administration'. In *Markets and their Actors in the late Middle Ages*, edited by T. Skambraks, J. Bruch and U. Kipta, 71–100. Berlin: De Gruyter, 2020.
Safley, Thomas Max. 'Mercury Mining and Miners: The Transition from Boutique Metal to Strategic Commodity in the 16th Century'. In *Labor Before the Industrial Revolution: Work, Technology and their Ecologies in an Age of Early Capitalism*, edited by Thomas Max Safley, 198–231. London/New York: Routledge, 2018.
Schattkowsky, Martina and Albrecht, Helmuth. *Das Erzgebirge im 16. Jahrhundert. Gestaltwandel einer Kulturlandschaft im Reformationszeitalter*. Vol. 44. Schriften zur Sächsischen Geschichte und Volkskunde. Leipzig: Leipziger Universitätsverlag, 2013.
Schirmer, Uwe. 'Ernährung im Erzgebirge im 15. und 16. Jahrhundert. Produktion, Handel und Verbrauch'. In *Landesgeschichte in Sachsen. Tradition und Innovation*, edited by Rainer Aurig, Steffen Herzog and Simone Lässig, 129–44. Bielefeld: Verlag für Regionalgeschichte, 1997.
Smith, Pamela H. 'Vermillion, Mercury, Blood, and Lizards: Matter and Meaning in Metalworking'. In *Materials and Expertise in Early Modern Europe: Between Market and Laboratory*, edited by Ursula Klein and E. C. Spary, 29–49. Chicago: University of Chicago Press, 2010.
Stöger, Georg. 'Die Migration europäischer Bergleute während der Frühen Neuzeit'. *Der Anschnitt. Zeitschrift Für Kunst und Kultur im Bergbau* 58/4–5 (2006): 170–86.
Von Hohenheim, Theophrastus (Paracelsus). 'On the Miners' Sickness and Other Miners' Diseases'. In *Four Treatises of Theophrastus von Hohenheim called Paracelsus*, edited by Henry E. Sigerist, translated by George Rosen. Baltimore: Johns Hopkins University Press, 1941.

ENTANGLED DEPENDENCIES

8
Entangled dependencies: the case of the runaway domestic worker Emine in late Ottoman Istanbul, 1910

Müge Özbek

Up to the mid-nineteenth century, slavery remained a common source of domestic labour in elite households of the Ottoman Empire.[1] The first anti-slavery efforts started with the restrictions on the slave trade in the mid-nineteenth century. After a slow and gradual process of decline, domestic slavery had almost disappeared by the early 1900s, becoming restricted to a small number of primarily elite households. Finally, after the revolution of 1908, a law mandating a complete abolishment of slavery was issued to purge the empire of slavery.[2] Hence, the great majority of women and girls who performed domestic work in early twentieth-century Istanbul were legally free people. However, the legal abolishment of slavery did not lead to the immediate replacement of slave labour with so-called 'free' wage labour. Ehud Toledano, for instance, contends that 'the gradual, yet resistant, decline of the established practice of domestic slavery did not easily bring about wage-labor arrangements for servants and frequently beslemes (feedlings) took their place'.[3]

Beslemes (feedlings) or *evlatlıks* (adoptees) were two common terms applied to girls and young women hired out mainly from impoverished rural communities to well-off households as live-in domestic workers – both terms presenting an exploitative and often abusive labour process as benevolence. For many poor parents or relatives, hiring out the young females of the family as domestic labourers was acceptable and even became customary in some areas of Anatolia. Sending out girls for domestic work reduced the number of mouths to feed and provided some money for the subsistence of remaining family members. Additionally, domestic work in well-off households was believed to be training for marriage and housewifery. Orphaned children and widowed women were also commonly sent out as domestic servants to relieve the burden that other kin or community members might have otherwise assumed for their care.[4]

The historians Yahya Araz and Irfan Kökdaş demonstrate that the actual transaction of children could be realised through slightly varying modalities. A common practice was that brokers would visit villages and towns from time to time and take several children with them to be placed in urban households, mainly in Istanbul. In exchange, they would give the girls' family members a price.[5] From the 1880s on, as a part of increased government concern over the movements of people in the empire, the brokers were compelled to register these transactions in local courts. Alternatively, family members of the girls would take them to Istanbul and place them into service via a broker they contacted in Istanbul. Thirdly, governmental officials posted to different parts of the empire would recruit girls and women in the places they travelled to and bring them to Istanbul when they moved back.[6]

We may assume that most of these transactions were realised through oral contracts. Yet written agreements kept by the Şeria Courts also became common, particularly after the 1880s, as shown by Araz and Kökdaş. In these contracts, the transaction was officially referred to as *icâr-ı sagir/e* (hiring out of boys/girls). These contracts defined the relationship between the two parties – who could be a family member and the employer or a broker, depending on the situation – and contained details such as the child's age, the amount of the wage and how the wages would be paid.[7]

Most studies of late Ottoman domestic labour highlight that the exploitation of vulnerabilities of late Ottoman domestic servants was informed by and comparable to that of enslaved people in households. According to the sociologist Ferhunde Özbay, 'slavery as an institution' disappeared in the domestic context, but it transformed to other practices such as adoption, in which, according to Özbay, the master–slave relation was emulated.[8] Following a similar approach, the historian Nazan Maksudyan, in her work on the recruiting of orphaned children into domestic service, claims that the exploitation and abuse of children in the recruiting households were hidden under the guise of charity.[9] The historian Madeline Zilfi, on the other hand, points out that female domestic work in the Ottoman Middle East was characterised by the blurred boundaries between domestic work and service, female servant and female kin. According to Zilfi, the continuation of domestic slavery until the turn of the twentieth century had also been crucial for defining the nature of late Ottoman domestic practices.[10]

Drawing on the individual case of Emine, this essay aims to go beyond the dichotomy of slavery versus 'free' (wage) labour and provide an insight into the lived reality and experience of a late Ottoman domestic worker who suffered severe forms of labour exploitation and coercive labour conditions as well as poor remuneration. It also opens a gateway to understanding coercive dynamics in late Ottoman domestic work and uncovering the more general power dynamics and hierarchies embedded in the mobility, work and remuneration patterns of the period and the intimately related entangled dependencies that emerge from these patterns.

To go beyond the standard dichotomy of 'free' and 'unfree' labour, the global historian Marcel van der Linden suggests focusing on 'diverse empirical cases' and identifying and analysing specific forms of bonded/coerced labour. For this, he pinpoints 'three moments of coercion' consisting of entry into, period of and exit from work, which can be further subdivided into a plethora of mutant forms.[11] In this chapter, I employ van der Linden's approach to understand the power relations and coercive dynamics in Emine's work experience during different phases of her formally remunerated labour relation. Through Emine's individual case, the essay will trace novel forms of social and governmental scrutiny that targeted women's lives, bodies and labour (poorly paid or unpaid), as well as the severely exploitative working conditions they were forced to endure and the intertwining restrictions on their freedom and mobility.

Finally, I argue that the routine manner in which women's im/mobility was controlled, and how the borders of countries, cities, neighbourhoods, working places and houses were made more or less porous for them, were among the primary means by which solitary poor and working women's lives, bodies and labour were made readily exploitable – a fact too often ignored and dismissed in traditional histories of the city, as it was in their times. The gendered forms embedded in the remuneration of female labour, observable in the case of Emine, are also related to the dynamics of severe exploitation and coercion of girls and women. Emine's case provides an opportunity to learn about her peculiar individual story, as it sheds light not only on the entangled power dynamics that shaped lower-class women's experiences but also on the nature of domestic work and its remuneration in late Ottoman Istanbul.

Through a close reading of the documents in the police file that concern Emine's case, I will answer the following questions: from where, for which reasons and how did she come to Istanbul? Why did she decide to move? Was she assisted, manipulated or coerced to do so? How was she commodified and delegated to the place she ultimately served? Could she leave this place and job quickly? Where could she go? Where could she not go? Could she move in public spaces with ease? Was she able to/permitted to find another job or another place to live in?

In Dariia Kuzmych's beautiful watercolour (p. 185), a young woman is depicted on the border between domestic and urban space. On the one hand, she is tightly bound to the domestic space through the hems of her dress, a detail that tacitly reminds us of the gender dynamics behind this bond. On the other hand, Kuzmych refrains from depicting her as a victim and makes us sense her power as she holds on to her desire to live freely through courage and resistance. The artist leads us beyond the limits of historical knowledge, which is often incomplete, and makes us consider how it must have felt to be a domestic worker in late Ottoman Istanbul – bound to your employer's household by your hems and yet having the will and courage to live your own life in the city.

The case file

Emine's file is located in the Ottoman Archives section of the Turkish Republic Presidential State Archives in Istanbul. The catalogue code is DH.EUM.THR 28/65. The Ottoman archival catalogues are assembled in a top-down, three-shaped format that conforms to the structural hierarchy of Ottoman bureaucracy in that period. In this case file, 'DH' stands for Dahiliye Nezareti (Ministry of Interior), 'EUM' stands for Emniyet-i Umumiye Müdüriyeti (Department of Public Security), and finally 'THR' stands for *tahrir defterleri* (record books). The numerals 28 and 65 stand for the number of the book and number of the file, respectively.

The file is composed of four single-paged documents. The first document is the petition (*istida*) that Emine herself submitted to the Department of Public Security in Istanbul. The second document contains temporary orders and notes from various police officers involved in the investigation process. The third document is a statement by Emine's employer, Ishak Cevdet Paşa, which he had to provide to the local police station in response to Emine's petition. Fortunately, Ishak Cevdet Paşa also submitted Emine's employment contract alongside his statement. The agreement is copied at the top of the page, preceding Ishak Cevdet Paşa's statement. The fourth page is blank.

Emine's life course as a domestic worker: entry, extraction, exit – three phases of labour coercion

The documents in this file are inevitably marked by omissions, erasures, fabrications and possibly lies. Still, they document the sequence of events that defined the course of Emine's life as a domestic worker: her entry into domestic work; her stay in Ishak Cevdet Paşa's household in Istanbul as a live-in domestic worker for 12 years; her attempts to escape her work; and finally, the likely remand of custody back to her father. In these documents, it is also possible to discern the elements of coercion that define Emine's experience as a young female remunerated domestic worker.

Emine's entry into domestic work

Emine moved from her hometown Ereğli to Istanbul to be employed as a domestic worker in Ishak Cevdet Paşa's house in 1899 when she was 12 years old. Her recruitment was conducted on the grounds of a hiring-out contract authorised by the Sharia court in Ereğli. In the petition she submitted to the police, Emine recounts her entry into domestic work: '1 or 2 years ago, I was given out to the house of the retired (*mütekaidden*) Ishak Cevdet Paşa in Akarçeşme in the Gedikpaşa neighbourhood by my father to serve.'[12] In the court record, her father, Hasan Ağa, employs the wording, 'I order the renting-out and dispatching and submission of my twelve-year-old daughter Emine, as her father and custodian, because I am not able to provide for her, as is the custom to serve, starting from the date of the document for an indefinite period in Istanbul in the house of esteemed Ishak Cevdet Paşa.' Ishak Cevdet Paşa, on the other hand, states that 'Hasan Ağa from Ereğli left the above-mentioned Emine, his twelve-year-old daughter, in our service.' The choice of words in these three different accounts indicates that Emine's move to Istanbul and her employment were the results not of her own will, but of her father's – although 'will' is a complicated concept in this case. The account by Emine's father illustrates both his economic desperation and his patriarchal power over his daughter's life, mobility and labour.

Emine's father, Hasan Ağa, was a porter in the Port of Ereğli, a midsize town on the Black Sea coast. In the nineteenth century, port cities on the Black Sea coast flourished due to the commercialisation and commodification processes related to the further integration of the Ottoman Empire into global capitalist networks. This general trend brought about rapid impoverishment among port workers and increased labour struggles in various regions, including the Black Sea ports.[13]

Given this context, we might infer that Emine came from a poverty-stricken, working-class background characteristic of a midsize port city on the Black Sea coast. Emine's employer Ishak Cevdet Paşa was a retired soldier. During his career, he was among the most senior military advisers to Sultan Abdulhamid II and a member of the High Committee of Military Inspection, which was involved in strategic military planning and policy-making at that time. His military title was *ferik* in Ottoman Turkish, equivalent to a major-general in today's terms. This makes clear that Ishak Cevdet Paşa was among the military elite of the time, with access to Sultan Abdulhamid II's inner circle of power. The socioeconomic inequality between the two families, the poverty which compelled Emine's father to send his daughter to serve, and the wealth and power of Ishak Cevdet Paşa's urban household were the basis of their agreement.

From the available documents, we cannot know for sure whether or not Emine was willing to move to Istanbul as a live-in domestic worker. For her, accepting this arrangement might have been the obvious choice, given her family's poverty and inability to provide for her. She may or may not have had the power to object to her father's decision. What we know for sure is that her father's decision to rent her out was socially accepted, and so her consent was not required to establish the legal authority of the contract.

Emine's escape attempts from Ishak Cevdet Paşa's house

We understand that Emine lived in Ishak Cevdet Paşa's house for about 12 years. However, we cannot learn much about the circumstances of her everyday life in her employer's house. The case file only reveals that Emine did not always accept her living and working situation: she made three consecutive attempts to escape Ishak Cevdet Paşa's household but was forced to return after her first two attempts. In the petition she finally submitted to the police, Emine states: 'Recently, I had to leave because my comfort was spoiled.' This wording implies mistreatment or at least discomfort of some kind, but details are lacking. What Emine may be trying to do here is justify why she abandoned the service in her employer's home, thereby preventing a third enforced return, without making outright accusations against her employer. It is also highly likely that the phrasing of her petition was mediated and distorted by the scribe she would have had to employ.

Upon the submission of Emine's petition, Ishak Cevdet Paşa was invited to the local police station in his neighbourhood and asked about the situation. While responding to Emine's implication of mistreatment and discomfort in her petition, Ishak Cevdet Paşa states that 'she escaped from the house without any reason'. He claims she was 'undutiful', 'not subservient at all' and also 'of slightly lower intelligence'. He also asserts that Emine's father, who was called to take back his daughter after her earlier attempts to escape, 'pleaded for Emine to stay with them', and consequently, 'out of pity we agreed to employ her until now reluctantly'. In his statement, Ishak Cevdet Paşa not only refutes Emine's implication of mistreatment but also accuses her of being an undutiful woman and portrays his recruitment of Emine as a form of charity.

Emine's submission to her father

In his statement, Ishak Cevdet Paşa also declared that this time he was no longer willing to employ Emine and that her father had already been notified to come and take back his daughter. This procedure apparently had also been followed in the previous escape attempts. We do not know what happened to Emine after this point. It is most probable that she was remanded to her father. Then, she might have been placed in another well-off household as a domestic worker or taken back to her hometown by her father.

The involvement of the police

In the late Ottoman context, it was not defined as a crime in and of itself if a female domestic worker abandoned service. However, such an act was perceived as an indication of deviance, moral laxity or aversion to work, and was often associated with an inclination towards prostitution. Even without the official definition of crime, this could be grounds for the arrest and confinement of workers who escaped service. This may be related to concerns or anxieties general to the middle class, and administrative concerns connected with the rapid urbanisation of Istanbul in the nineteenth century and the increased surveillance and organised policing of urban populations that these anxieties entailed.

In the mid-nineteenth century, with the acceleration of urbanisation, governmental treatment of the urban poor in the Ottoman Empire entered a decisive stage. A new interpretation of work as opposed to idleness was emerging – work with productive and disciplinary qualifications. In the 1890s the Ottoman government issued two consecutive vagrancy acts as part of the efforts to control the urban poor. Darülaceze, the first modern poorhouse of the empire, opened its doors in 1896, a few months after the introduction of the second vagrancy act. These acts defined differentiation between the deserving and undeserving poor. Those unable to work, the disabled, the aged and the very young were defined as the deserving poor. Through these acts, able-bodied, unemployed and unskilled male immigrants to Istanbul were assumed to be idle and therefore susceptible to the charge of vagrancy.[14]

Curiously, women were not subject to vagrancy acts. Yet, this did not mean they were allowed to move in the urban space freely. In the late Ottoman Empire, the image of single, poor women visible in the metropolitan area without a male attendant was already defined as a problem. The image of solitary, poor women oscillated between persons in need of protection and a feared pathology, a danger to public health and a threat to middle-class morality and family life. The issue was frequently discussed in the press, and administrative authorities tried to find ways to return such women to domestic settings.[15]

When a female domestic worker left the house where she worked, the word used to define her act was 'escape'. In most cases, following the employer's complaint, the police started an investigation to find the runaway domestic worker. If she was found, she was kept in police custody until she was returned to her employer or her family.[16] It is most probable that the police arrested Emine after each of her three attempts to abandon her work and that she submitted her petition while in police custody. Although the involvement of the police is not explicit in the documents, it was most probably not hidden deliberately. Instead, it was not accounted for because it was common practice, understood as such by all parties involved.

Remuneration and contract

In the original employment contract between Ishak Cevdet Paşa and Emine's father, the monthly payment for Emine's work was set as follows: 'a 20 *kuruş* monthly salary – 15 *kuruş* of the amount mentioned above will be charged and used for the subsistence, clothing and basic needs of the aforementioned minor, whereas the remaining five *kuruş* will be kept on her behalf'. In 1897, a few years before Emine was hired, the daily wage for an unqualified male worker was 8.5 *kuruş*, and the salary for a qualified worker was 18 *kuruş*. Compared to these wages, the monthly salary agreed for Emine is abysmally low. The documents also indicate that she did not receive these payments herself. In her petition, Emine states, 'they refrain from giving me my belongings and paying my allowances that accumulated during this period. I request that you order to establish justice on this matter.' On the other hand, Ishak Cevdet Paşa states that

Emine's father, who came to Istanbul occasionally during Emine's period of employment, 'collected the accumulated earnings of his daughter'. Ishak Cevdet Paşa also highlights that if there were any remaining money that he had to pay, he would pay it to Emine's father, Hasan Ağa, when he arrived in Istanbul to retrieve his daughter. This means that Emine's control over the money paid for her work was clearly restricted.

This is also related to the fact that domestic work was primarily considered a form of charity, as implied by Ishak Cevdet Paşa above. Or instead, there was ambiguity about whether it was charity or work, which shaped the reality and experiences of domestic workers. They were legally free. Yet, they were bound to the households for which they worked through a discourse of paternal protection that the women were supposed to need and enjoy. Hiring a domestic employee was often portrayed as a benevolent act through which the employers provided shelter and subsistence to a needy woman and child. Paying them for this was unimaginable, but small amounts might be delivered to their families, as in Emine's case.

While writing about orphaned children employed as domestic workers, the historian Nazan Maksudyan argues that

> employment was regarded as a form of charity: They performed household chores, and the employers, in return, pledged to supply the child's basic needs – shelter, food, and clothing. The employers paid no wage relying on the assumption that taking custody of a child was a benevolent act that did not result in an employer-employee relationship.[17]

At best, the work of these young women in other people's households was regarded as an apprenticeship for married life and a chance for social mobility in the form of a better marriage. When they were leaving, the ideal way of doing this was getting married; they were not paid their wages but gifted dowries. Nezahat Hanim, who lived in an upper-class household in Istanbul before the First World War, recalls that 'there was a continuous circulation; they were trained, made their dowries, grew up and then left. They were replaced by newcomers.'[18]

Interpreting coercion in a remunerated labour relation

Emine's case provides essential insight into how girls and young women from impoverished provincial backgrounds were commodified in their capacity to work as live-in domestic workers in well-off Istanbul households. It sheds light on the role of gendered power relations in shaping patterns and dynamics of severe labour exploitation and coercive labour in domestic work. This case also provides a way to interrogate the crucial links between patriarchy, the control of mobility and labour coercion in a more general sense.

In legal terms, Emine was a free individual and a contracted wage worker. However, in an adult-dominated, patriarchal and class-based reality, she was situated in a network of relationships and obligations, which tied her into a practically unpaid labour relationship with a bond that was extremely hard for her to disavow. First of all, her father possessed the customary and legal power to decide to send his minor daughter off to Istanbul to be employed as a domestic worker without need for her consent. Once in Istanbul, she was immobilised behind the walls of her employer's house for 12 years by a gendered form of social bondage. Even when she grew into adulthood, she was not permitted to abandon her employer's household of her own will because she was deemed a household dependant rather than a free worker or a free person, due to her gender and her single status. In her multiple attempts to escape her employer's house and her job, she was arrested by the police and forced to return either to her employer or, presumably, to her father.

I identify three strongly interrelated fundamental mechanisms that locked Emine into a coercive labour relationship. The first one is the traditional and legal setting that enabled the senior adults of households to move children and younger women back and forth between households without needing their consent. The second one is the patriarchal collaboration of family members and employers in their unified effort to keep female domestic workers bound to typical traditional households. Negotiations between family members and employers were marked by the context of stark socioeconomic disparity between the two parties. Both parties co-perpetuated a circuit of female labour coercion, mainly by classifying and keeping women and girls as household dependants and low-paid or unpaid workers, a situation from which both families and employers benefited. Third, the over-policing of lower-class women in urban settings robbed female domestic workers of the ability to abandon their employers' households and live on their own in Istanbul, further securing and solidifying their dependent status.

Overall, Emine's case provides us with yet another example that destabilises the static conceptualisations of 'free' and 'unfree' labour, 'waged' and 'unwaged' work, and 'voluntary' and 'forced' movement as discrete and easily isolated categories, shedding light, through the entangled dependencies that shaped Emine's experience, on the nature of female labour and work. It also offers us a fresh perspective for investigating more general questions, such as: what makes women particularly vulnerable to severe labour exploitation and coercive labour in so-called feminised industries, such as domestic service, caregiving and sex work? How and why did patriarchal relations create and maintain coerced labour? Finally, this case is a reminder that the way in which severe labour exploitation, very low-paid or underpaid work, and coercive labour relations were established was also, and crucially, a matter of governing the mobility – and immobility – of the workers themselves.

Notes

1. This chapter relies on a shorter data-based story published online within the framework of the COST Action 'Worlds of Related Coercions in Work'; see https://dkan.worck.digital-history.uni-bielefeld.de/?q=story/entangled-dependencies-case-runaway-domestic-worker-emine-late-ottoman-istanbul-1910.
2. Şen, *Osmanlıda Köle Olmak*, 45–7; Erdem, *Slavery in the Ottoman Empire and its Demise*, 27–8.
3. Toledano, *As if Silent and Absent*, 73.
4. For studies on Ottoman female domestic work, see Özbay, *Turkish Female Child Labor in Domestic Work*; Araz, *Osmanlı Istanbul'unda Çocuk Emeği*; Maksudyan, 'Foster-Daughter or Servant, Charity or Abuse', 2008.
5. Araz and Kökdaş, 'In Between Market and Charity', 2020.
6. Araz and Kökdaş, 'Istanbul'da Ev Içi Hizmetlerinde Istahdam Edilen Kuzeybatı Anadolulu Kız Çoçuklarının Göç Ağları Üzerine bir Değerlendirme', 2018, 45–7.
7. Araz and Kökdaş, 'Istanbul'da Ev Içi Hizmetlerinde Istahdam Edilen Kuzeybatı Anadolulu Kız Çoçuklarının Göç Ağları Üzerine bir Değerlendirme', 2018, 42, 44.
8. Özbay, *Turkish Female Child Labor in Domestic Work*.
9. Maksudyan, 'Foster-Daughter or Servant, Charity or Abuse', 2008.
10. Zilfi, *Women and Slavery in the Late Ottoman Empire*.
11. van der Linden, 'Dissecting Coerced Labour', 297.
12. The translations of the original texts from Turkish to English are the author's own.
13. Nacar, 'Free Trade or an Alternative Path', 2016.
14. Özbek, '"Beggars" and "Vagrants" in State Policy and Public Discourse During the Late Ottoman Empire', 2009.
15. Balsoy, 'Bir Kadın Hastenesi Olarak Haseki Hastenesi ve 19. Yüzyıl Istanbul'unda Bikes ve Bimesken bir Kadın Olmak', 2015. Özbek, '"Disorderly Women" and the Politics of Urban Space in Early Twentieth-Century Istanbul'.
16. For exemplary archival cases of runway domestic workers, see BOA, ZB, 422/157, 1323. Teşrinisani.27 (10 December 1907), BOA, ZB, 429/26, 1322.Şubat.20 (5 March 1907), BOA, ZB, 437/60, 1320.Teşrinievvel.09 (22 October 1904), BOA, ZB, 437/96, 1320.Şubat.13 (26 February 1905), BOA, DH.EUM.THR, 34/70, 1326.Mayıs.15 (28 May 1910), BOA, DH.EUM.THR, 96/7, 1328.R.07 (18 April 1910).
17. Maksudyan, 'Foster-Daughter or Servant, Charity or Abuse', 2008, 489.
18. Duben and Behar, *Istanbul Households*, 142–4.

Bibliography

Araz, Yahya. *Osmanlı Istanbul'unda Çocuk Emeği: Ev İçi Hizmetlerde Istihdam Edilen Çocuklar (1750–1920)*. Istanbul: Kitap Yayınevi, 2019.

Araz, Yahya and Kökdaş, Irfan. 'Istanbul'da Ev İçi Hizmetlerinde Istahdam Edilen Kuzeybatı Anadolulu Kız Çoçuklarının Göç Ağları Üzerine bir Değerlendirme', *Tarih Incelemeleri Dergisi* 33 (2018): 41–68.

Araz, Yahya and Kökdaş, Irfan. 'In Between Market and Charity: Child Domestic Work and Changing Labor Relations in Nineteenth-Century Ottoman Istanbul', *International Labor and Working-Class History* 97 (2020): 81–108.

Balsoy, Gülhan. 'Bir Kadın Hastenesi Olarak Haseki Hastenesi ve 19. Yüzyıl Istanbul'unda Bikes ve Bimesken bir Kadın Olmak', *Toplumsal Tarih* 257 (2015): 80–4.

Başaran, Betül. *Selim III, Social Control, and Policing in Istanbul at the End of the Eighteenth Century*. Leiden: Brill, 2014.

BOA (Ottoman Archives of the President's Office), ZB, 422/157, 1323.Teşrinisani.27 (10 December 1907).

BOA, ZB, 429/26, 1322.Şubat.20 (5 March 1907).

BOA, ZB, 437/60, 1320.Teşrinievvel.09 (22 October 1904).

BOA, ZB, 437/96, 1320.Şubat.13 (26 February 1905).

BOA, DH.EUM.THR, 34/70, 1326.Mayıs.15 (28 May 1910).

BOA, DH.EUM.THR, 96/7, 1328.R.07 (18 April 1910).

Duben, Alan and Behar, Cem. *Istanbul Households: Marriage, Family and Fertility, 1880–1940*. Cambridge: Cambridge University Press, 2002.

Erdem, Hakan. *Slavery in the Ottoman Empire and its Demise 1800–1909*. London: Palgrave Macmillan, 1996.

Hamadeh, Shirine. 'Mean Streets: Space and Moral Order in Early Modern Istanbul', *Turcica* 44 (2013): 249–77.

Karpat, Kemal H. 'Ottoman Population Records and the Census of 1881/82–1893', *International Journal of Middle East Studies* 9 (1978): 237–74.

Karpat, Kemal H. *Ottoman Population, 1830–1914: Demographic and Social Characteristics*. Wisconsin: The University of Wisconsin Press, 1985.

Lévy-Aksu, Noémi. *Osmanlı Istanbulu'nda Asayiş 1879–1909*. Translated by Serra Akyüz Gönen. Istanbul: Iletişim Yayınları, 2017.

Maksudyan, Nazan. 'Foster-Daughter or Servant, Charity or Abuse: Beslemes in the Late Ottoman Empire', *Journal of Historical Sociology* 21 (2008): 488–512.

Nacar, Can. 'Free Trade or an Alternative Path: The Queue System and Struggle over the Conditions of Work in Ottoman Ports, 1900–1910', *Middle Eastern Studies* 52 (2016): 772–86.

Özbay, Ferhunde. *Turkish Female Child Labor in Domestic Work: Past and Present*. Istanbul: ILO/IPEC, 1999.

Özbek, Müge. '"Disorderly Women" and the Politics of Urban Space in Early Twentieth-Century Istanbul, 1900–1914'. In *Crime, Poverty, and Survival in the Middle East and North Africa: The "Dangerous Classes" since 1800*, edited by Stephanie Cronin, 51–64. London: I. B. Tauris, 2019.

Özbek, Nadir. '"Beggars" and "Vagrants" in State Policy and Public Discourse During the Late Ottoman Empire: 1876–1914', *Middle Eastern Studies* 45 (2009), 783–801.

Şen, Ömer. *Osmanlıda Köle Olmak*. Istanbul: Kapı Yayınları, 2007.

Toledano, Ehud R. *As if Silent and Absent: Bonds of Enslavement in the Islamic Middle East*. New Haven: Yale University Press, 2007.

van der Linden, Marcel. 'Dissecting Coerced Labor'. In On *Coerced Labor: Work and Compulsion after Chattel Slavery*, edited by Marcel van der Linden and Rodríguez García, 293–322. Leiden: Brill, 2016.

Zilfi, Madeline. *Women and Slavery in the Late Ottoman Empire: The Design of Difference*. New York: Cambridge University Press, 2010.

THE DILEMMA OF BEING A 'GOOD WORKER'

9
The dilemma of being a 'good worker': cultural discourse, coercion and resistance in Bangladesh's garment factories
Mohammad Tareq Hasan

In November 2012, a factory fire killed about 117 ready-made garment (RMG) workers in Tazreen Fashions in Dhaka. Soon after, in April 2013, the collapse of the Rana Plaza killed 1,134 workers.[1] These two tragic events resulted in national protests and raised international awareness of the working conditions in Bangladeshi garment factories.[2] A decade later, however, millions of workers still suffer from low salaries, irregular or delayed payments, long overtime, tight work schedules, curtailed leave and benefits, the sudden closure of factories without payment of due wages and few collective bargaining opportunities.[3] The situation of these garment factories is depicted in the illustration by Dariia Kuzmych (p. 201). The image clearly consists of two parts, separated by a collapsing column: the lower part reflects workers' protests and tragic events in which workers were killed, while the upper part shows textile production in the closed space of a factory – diligent workers under supervision on the production floor of a factory. The image contrasts the production of clothing and the situation of workers with the destruction and exploitation caused by the RMG industries.

As the illustration shows, there have been many incidents of labour protest in Dhaka and all over Bangladesh in the recent past. Led by left-wing political parties and labour unions, workers have demonstrated for and demanded wage increases and better work conditions throughout the country.[4] Following a large-scale protest on 29 July 2010, factory owners and the government agreed on a new wage structure. The entry-level minimum wage was set at BDT (Bangladeshi taka) 3,000 per month (USD 42), allegedly to maintain competitive pricing of the product in the global market. This was 60 per cent of what the workers sought at the time. Still, some factory owners choose not to adopt it.[5] In later changes, the minimum wage was raised to BDT 5,300 (USD 66) per month in 2013 and BDT 8,000 (USD 95) per month in 2018.

In this context, I have investigated through ethnographic fieldwork how workers of different ages, rural backgrounds and geographic mobility engage in spontaneous or collective resistance on the production floor – without the involvement of trade unions, which are an uncommon feature in Bangladeshi RMG factories.[6] To contextualise resistance and understand workers' general attitude towards their work, this study explores their perception of coercive practices, their actions and reactions in the face of coercion of different magnitudes, and the role of cultural discourses in the perception and practice of coercion and resistance. These aspects of coercion, resistance and cultural discourse are crucial because the rapidly developing garment industry in urban areas since the 1980s has increased rural–urban migration of young women in Bangladesh – women workers constitute roughly 70 per cent of the workforce in the RMG sector.[7] Furthermore, a new dimension of social mobility has emerged as the result of women's (and also men's) access to the formal labour market, that is, remunerated work, and as the consequence of their (women's) opportunity to move from the private sphere to the public sphere and from the agricultural sector to the industrial sector. Consequently, garment workers (especially women) are praised for their contributions to the family, the factory and the nation – and the notion of the 'good worker' has become central.[8]

With its social status, the promise of upward mobility and the feeling of gratitude towards one's employer, salaried work prompted efforts to be a good worker. One could claim that the discourse of the good worker facilitated exploitation and made people accept their situation.[9] On the other hand, trying to be a good worker – reinforced by the understanding of one's 'worth' as a formal employee and being part of the workers' solidarity group – pulled these people in the opposite direction: to contest coercion and aim to improve working conditions. Thus, as this chapter will show, many workers felt a dilemma stemming from the impossibility of reconciling both sides of being a good worker. Based on my ethnographic findings, I argue that 'cultural discourses' enabled workers to build solidarity groups – in the form of a sisterhood/brotherhood – to resist unjust conditions such as low wages, long working hours or delayed payment of wages in the factories. Conversely, these discourses also created ambivalences in collective resistance and facilitated coercion. The inherent paradoxes of cultural discourses became evident when workers faced dilemmas during the collective resistance or even on ordinary days of factory work. For instance, should they continuously work to achieve production targets? Should they help co-workers who were facing harsh supervision? Should they consider the factory owner's benefit as he provided them with work or join a demonstration demanding wage increases? In other words, workers must choose between adhering to the cultural construction of gratitude towards the job provider and acting in solidarity with co-workers. Therefore, while aiming to become good workers, they faced dilemmas about their rights and responsibilities towards co-workers, supervisors and factory owners. I thus argue that individual (mundane) and (organised) collective resistances in the garment factory were often conflicted, internally contradictory and ambivalent.[10]

In the factory, I found a mutual fashioning of human beings – the production of material objects coincided with the constitution of people, social relations and cultural discourses.[11] One should also note that we could find parallels of the notion of the good worker in our economic paradigm of the idea of the 'good consumer' – someone ready to pay a higher price for products sourced from factories with better working conditions. Or a 'good employer/factory owner' who, from the workers' perspective, pays out salaries on time.[12] This shows that the idea of the good worker is contextual and mutually constitutive. While the ethnographic focus of this chapter is a particular factory, the 'rhythm of work', 'chain of coercion' and 'commodity supply chain' also have global dimensions.

This research is based on 15 months of ethnographic fieldwork in 2015–2016, with additional visits in 2017 and 2018, among the garment industry workers in a factory in Gazipur, Dhaka. I spent my time inside the garment factory and in the garment workers' homes. I participated in informal gatherings and talked with managers, supervisors, workers and helpers/assistant operators. During the fieldwork, I was a participant observer. In fact, attentive listening to everyday perspectives and concerns and participating in people's routine or daily activities is conducting participant observation; the outcome is the systematic, detailed, nonjudgmental and accurate description of events, behaviours and artefacts in the social setting.[13]

The following sections first introduce the power structure of the factory, where the idea of a good worker was constructed around the production process. Second, they explore the establishment of informal solidarity groups and 'fictitious kinship networks' that workers used to help each other and find relief from the intense work pressure.

Third, collective action, which developed primarily from disputes regarding wages, is highlighted to detect strategies of resistance and their connection to discourses of obligation between employer and workers. Overall, the chapter demonstrates that the labour-management strategies involved disciplinary schemes institutionalised by local cultural discourses and practices, claiming that, alongside formal authority, several additional mechanisms and practices worked in punitive and coercive ways.

Production processes and power structures

I conducted the fieldwork in a knitting garment factory that produced sweaters. There were approximately 2,000 workers (50 per cent of whom were women). The first step of the production process was to collect the yarn in hank or spool form, which was later wound into cones in the 'winding section'. The knitting operators collected the wound cones from the 'knitting distribution' section. Once the operators had knitted different pieces of the sweaters, they delivered those to the 'quality control section'. Upon approval for measurements and design, the sweater panels were distributed in the 'linking section'. After different knitted panels were linked, loose yarns from the knitted parts were trimmed in the 'trimming section'. Then the sweaters were checked for faults by the 'light checking machine'. If required, minor knitting faults were fixed in the 'mending section'. Next, button attaching and holing were completed in the 'sewing section', only after the knitted sweaters were approved by the light checking. Afterwards, sweaters were washed and ironed. Finally, after rechecking everything in the 'finishing section', the knitted sweaters were folded and packed for shipment.

Usually, workers began at 8 a.m. and worked until 1 p.m., when they had a one-hour lunch break. They went back to work at 2 p.m. and often worked until 7 p.m., including two hours of overtime. During the peak season (May–October),[14] workers were expected to stay until 9 p.m., with the possibility of working until midnight. If they worked beyond 7 p.m., they were granted a 15-minute break and were offered factory refreshments. The government had set a minimum wage for the garment industries: in the latest announced wage structure of 2018, a worker would get a basic salary, an additional 50 per cent of the basic salary as house rent allowance, a fixed medical allowance, and conveyance and food expenditure.[15] As per the appointment letters, they were expected to work 208 hours (8 hours a day for 26 days) per month.

If they worked more than 8 hours a day, they would get their basic hourly income for each hour (the overtime rate is a relative share of the basic income). However, appointment letters did not contain information about the production target they would be expected to achieve.

Workers handed in their identity cards and timesheets at the factory gate at the beginning of the working day, and received their cards back when the day's work was over. The administration noted the length of their shift on the card for that day in the interim. Employees received an attendance bonus of BDT 400 (USD 4.5) every month. However, if they were more than 10 minutes late for three or more days or missed a day of work for any reason, they did not get the incentive. The factory also gave a 'production bonus' for those who worked at a 'piece rate'[16] rather than a fixed salary. In the factory, those directly involved in producing clothes (such as the sewing or crochet operators) usually worked for a piece rate. Piece rates were typically announced during the first week of the month. The fees differed depending on the complexity and whether the production was on the factory's contract or was subcontracted from another factory. The finance department finalised the salary considering the piece rates, which the production floor manager distributed to the supervisors. The salary was then paid in cash by the supervisors. Regarding the monthly payday, workers were unsure when their money would be distributed.

To boost productivity and efficiency, garment factory management differentiated and split jobs; for the production section, they recruited helpers (assistant operators), operators, senior operators, supervisors, floor managers and production managers. Additional employees were involved in the factory's quality control, packing, administration, business expansion and marketing. However, I will focus on the factory floor, where each designation has distinct duties and authority in relation to the others. Helpers – recruits with no prior expertise in the clothing industry – became operators as they gathered experience and could work independently. Some advanced to senior operators as they gained more expertise and knowledge of the machinery. The supervisors were given more distinct tasks than the operators. They were in charge of reaching production quotas in their respective sections. Supervisors connected the operators and floor managers, allocated work among the operators, monitored their production targets, repaired minor machine issues, described the designs to the operators and demonstrated the work process (if needed) and periodically checked the quality of the products. Supervisors collaborated with the floor manager, who collaborated with the production manager to develop a production schedule. The floor manager calculated the amount of yarn required through trial manufacturing and ordered accordingly. He bore a more significant share of the responsibility for timely output than the supervisors. Once production began, the floor manager (with the supervisors) reviewed the goods regularly to ensure that the production standard in design and quality was met. Floor managers were responsible for both production planning and management.

A 'good worker' always meets the production target

On the factory floor, I saw several situations where supervisors demanded that operators work more or faster. The operators, by contrast, desired longer intervals between tasks. Because the supervisors monitored the work of the operators to meet production targets, they constantly sought to compel the operators to work without taking breaks. Furthermore, new operators who were slower than experienced ones were subjected to tighter supervision. 'New operators are supervised and forced to work continually,' one of my interlocutors revealed.[17] In response to my question 'What characteristics distinguish a good operator?', one of the supervisors replied, 'A good operator is loyal to the task and exhibits excellent behaviour.' Supervisors wanted operators to cooperate when they urged them to fulfil the production quota on time, to build the notion of a good worker in adhering to the supervisor's standards and demonstrating dedication to achieving the production target.

One could argue that supervisors aimed to create and maintain good operators on the production floors while having only a few tools at their disposal to achieve production targets or compel workers to work continually. They exerted control over the workers by exercising their authority over the 'recommendation for leave'. Any type of leave of absence required the approval of a supervisor. Furthermore, supervisors oversaw the manufacturing line and determined who would work on which pattern. If a supervisor instructed an operator to work on new designs every three or four days, the operator's income would be substantially reduced for those being paid by the piece, or the production bonus would be forfeited. This was because each new pattern required the operator to understand the design, which impeded the workflow. When machines broke down and needed repairing, or when needles had to be changed, operators relied on supervisors to get tools and extra needle supplies from the stock department. Workers also depended on supervisors to ensure they were gauging the products correctly and to remedy minor measurement issues by tweaking the machines.

The supervisors' authority was also apparent in how they managed the workplace and made decisions about overtime for the workers. Operator Jesmin claimed that supervisors reprimanded and penalised employees who failed to fulfil production targets on time. Supervisors occasionally falsely marked their cards as punishment, noting that they had left the factory at 5 p.m. instead of 7, thereby causing them to forfeit two hours of extra pay. While working too slowly was held against operators, working faster did not lead to relief. As Jesmin explained, 'Everyone is occupied when there is work. If I go too far behind, the operator behind me may be able to assist me if she completes her duties before I do. Senior management may occasionally request assistance from other operators.' Jesmin noted:

> An operator's capacity is known to supervisors. They do not, however, account for potential breaks required by an individual. For example, we occasionally need to get a sip of water or use the restroom. The time required is not included in the production target by supervisors. We cannot use the bathroom or take breaks if we must make 120 pieces per hour. When we do take breaks, the supervisors reprimand us.

Jesmin further commented:

> I have to put in 2 hours of extra work on paper, for which we are paid. However, we frequently must put in an additional 30 minutes of labour without being paid; occasionally, it even goes up to an hour. In addition, the overtime rate is low in relation to our salary. … We have an additional 30 minutes of work per day. On occasions, the employees disobey. When that occurs, they [supervisors] do not fill out the attendance card for two to three days. Employees do not receive their attendance incentive if they miss even one day of work.

For the good worker that the supervisors aimed to create in the factory, the most evident requirement was meeting the production deadline. The demand to meet the production target became coercive for the operators because their income depended on its fulfilment. Overall, the production target worked as a 'motor' for payment of wages, the amount of wage, the work hours and hence workers' experience and perception of coercion in the factory.

From my conversations with the garment workers, I learnt that out of concern about not reaching the production target, managers frequently verbally harassed male employees and occasionally physically assaulted them, albeit only rarely. However, managers harassed female employees only verbally. Most of the time, workers could not publicly assist one another – the supervisor would reprimand anyone who offered to help fellow workers. Nobody attempted to challenge the supervisors' actions because they did not want to be identified as someone who undermined their authority on the production floor, risking a pay drop or making routine factory days challenging. When operators attempted to stand up for co-workers, I saw managers tell them not to meddle in others' personal affairs. Workers usually comforted those suffering by stating: 'If you want work, you must ignore and forget all such small incidents.' When I asked Asma, 'Why do workers not reach out to the general manager [GM] or production manager [PM] to reveal or complain about the supervisors' behaviour?', she said, 'The GM and PM never do anything. … The production target is the reason for this. They raise the target we must achieve by claiming that the government has raised pay. So how will they pay us more if we do not increase productivity?' Regarding the question of why fellow workers did not resist the supervisors' harsh behaviour by supporting workers who suffered abuse, she said:

> Everyone is experiencing the same thing. Thus no one can assist anybody else. Our relationships with superiors might sometimes become strained because they make us work harder. However, we get along well with the administration. When we complain about inappropriate behaviour or physical assaults, they act politely and talk nicely but never do the right things. The PM and GM never misbehave. However, supervisors or floor managers carry out this behaviour and, in a sense, the PM and GM support it.

Asma also emphasised that, in contrast, workers could work hard or efficiently manage time and thus avoid the supervisors' abuse. In the same vein, regarding garment work and their production targets, Rahima said:

> Supervisors assign us a production target. If we do not meet the target, the production shipment will be delayed. So, if production targets are not fulfilled, supervisors [and managers] must pressure employees to do better. We are eager to achieve the deadline and manufacture enough for shipment. As a result, we must work a little harder.

Similarly, Jesmin emphasised the workers' responsibility towards the factory so that problems regarding supervisors' harsh behaviour might not arise. 'If we work well, then this bad behaviour will not happen. However, the supervisors must also consider that the jobs might occasionally be difficult.' These complex statements reflect the workers' dilemma regarding harsh supervision and work pressure. The workers tended to seek a balance between meeting the production target, thus becoming a 'good worker', and the expectation that the supervisors would note their hardship.

Regarding complaints about bad behaviour by the supervisors, Firoz, a supervisor in the factory, said that some supervisors once in a while acted harshly but that the factory never endorsed such actions; instead, the factory management always urged the supervisors to focus on getting the job done without using harsh or abusive measures. He commented:

> We have meetings twice a week. We are trained not to misbehave with workers. We are taught that if we approach them in an egalitarian way, it persuades the workers to work harder. When we talk amicably and request something by saying, 'Brother/Sister, do it for the factory', they work enthusiastically, but if we use harsh words, then they are aggrieved and do not work well.

In the same vein as seeing the factory staff as a 'family', Firoz also emphasised the workers' (including his own) obligation towards the factory: 'Working sincerely and following the factory's rules, we all can move forward together. We must work for the improvement of the factory, and it, in turn, will surely improve our future.'

The factory structure constituted the workers as moral subjects through its supervision mechanisms. Workers also constituted themselves in the dynamic interactions with co-workers and others – including supervisors (and floor managers, production managers, general managers and factory owners). The categories of persons who worked at the factories, such as good operators (that is, those loyal to their responsibilities), initiated new subjectivities among the workers. This also allowed for the establishment of specific rules of conduct, such as fulfilling work targets or not interfering with others' matters. These included connotations of religious and familial ethics and loyalty.

Fictitious kinship networks and strategies of protest

Workers from the same locality – *desh* – within the factory formed solidarity groups and 'fictitious kinship networks' (sisterhood/brotherhood) to help one another. This can be treated as an ideology of relatedness beyond consanguinity and affinity – a network of relations that directly influenced workers' daily interactions and their perception of rights and obligations.[18] Several layers of this grouping also went beyond the original layer of *desh*, which illustrates the fluidity and adaptability of this idea. Workers from the same department tend to form solidarity, and all factory workers as a whole also develop a sense of belonging, including managers, supervisors and the owner. Despite many subdivisions, occasionally they all come together to meet the production target, the reasoning goes.

Rahima, a 20-year-old female operator, said:

> When I started working, the operators assisted me. I strived to learn from them. I noticed what they were doing and asked them how to use the equipment. One of the operators treated and coached me as if she were my elder sister [*sashon korse boro apa'r moto*]. She used to show me all she knew.

Besides learning to use the machines, operators devised ways to lessen the strain and have breaks from work, and holidays permitted by the supervisor. They would sometimes hide certain types of yarn, needles or other tiny repair kits they already had access to. Thus, they could take a short break to eat something or talk over the phone with family members while the supervisors searched the factory's stock for the needed item.[19] If workers took breaks, they would have to work longer hours afterwards to reach their production targets. Otherwise, they persuaded and pushed their bosses to give them short getaways. One day, I observed an operator asking for early leave after the lunch break, but the supervisor said, 'If you do not meet the production quota, I will not let you take a leave of absence. Yesterday, you left early.' The operator kept complaining and requesting time off. He began to converse with other operators, which upset their workflow. The manager then instructed him to obtain a slip for an early exit. When the operator left, the supervisor explained, 'He would have impeded the work of five other operators if I had not granted him the leave.'

Similarly, some operators kept pestering floor managers and supervisors for early salary payments or expressed discontent. I saw a scenario where the quality control rejected certain knitted goods and sent them back to the knitting area. After advising the operators of the issue, the supervisor inquired who had submitted their products. An operator replied, 'You will receive things according to the salary. We have not yet got last month's salary, even though it is practically the middle of the month.' The supervisor declared, 'The factory management told all the supervisors that they should not request any worker to continue working in the factory, anyone could leave if they are not happy with the "system" here.' Even though workers could not control when they would receive their salaries, they expressed their concerns. They indicated to the supervisors that if wages were not paid on time, it would be reflected in the quality of the products. As the factory needed products of a certain quality, the workers could use that as leverage in their favour, urging the management to disburse salary soon.

The garment industry managers often offered lower piece rates during the off-season. Because work was scarce in all factories across the country, and workers could not easily switch jobs, they had to accept lower wages. Supervisors did not usually force operators to work faster at such times when there was no chance of overtime. However, hourly productivity targets were the same. In contrast, during the peak season for knitting factories, the demand for operators in factories was high, and the piece rate consequently increased. One of the operators said, 'During peak season, we are the boss in the knitting sector.'

Besides such individual and sporadic protests, workers sometimes formed large demonstrations. In such cases, the primary point of contention was delay in wage payment – especially before the holidays for religious festivals following Ramadan (Eid-ul-Fite) and the Hajj pilgrimage (Eid-ul-Adha). Usually, the factory disbursed the salary not too soon before the beginning of the holiday as many workers might want to go on a holiday early; furthermore, it did not pay the full salary at once but withheld a portion to be paid later, so as to bring the workers back on time after the holiday.

Collective protests developed as workers perceived the factory owner to be exceptionally unfair. They would stop working and gather to discuss the factory's unjust policies about remuneration, leave and forced overtime. When such grievances developed, a few workers walked to different sections of the factory to ask other workers to stop working and support their protest. If someone did not join voluntarily, groups of workers forced them to stop, stating: 'Your protest will benefit all.' This also indicated a dilemma for the workers – they could be 'good workers', individually continuing production as expected by the supervisors, or they could join the collective protesting for their salaries.

Selina, a senior operator, described her experience of collective protests for increasing salary. She said the garment management had previously declared their wages would be raised at the start of 2016. However, when they received the payment in January 2016, they noticed their salary was not increased. When she confronted the managers, they replied that they had done 'as the factory owner instructed them'. This triggered the workers to lay down their work and exit the production area. A few supervisors and the production manager urged the workers not to stop working and said they would relay their message to the factory owner and general manager. However, the workers, now united across several production floors, insisted on speaking with the owner. Ultimately, the factory owner arrived to listen to their grievances. He asked: 'What made you stop working? I was unable to raise your pay because my father is unwell, and I have a financial problem.' Then one operator asked: 'How much money did you need for your father's treatment?' At this point, the owner said, 'I cared for you and always fulfilled your needs, but you did not consider my crisis and stopped production. Okay, I will increase your salary.' Saying this, he went off. As the owner referred to his habitual care for the workers before announcing a salary increase, the announcement also added to his list of displays of caring attitudes towards the workers. This gesture implied that workers would have to return the favour in the future, working long hours to meet the production deadlines – a form of the unspoken promise of 'give and take'. Criticising the lack of transparency in the communication, Selina remarked:

> If the factory management had mentioned the wage could not be increased starting in January for any reason, the workers might not have been so irate. It would not have happened if they had brought up this matter with the more experienced employees. The factory managers had previously discussed potential salary payment delays with us [senior operators and people who have worked there for a long time and know many people personally] and asked that we discuss with others [out of respect for the workers' devotion and sacrifice to the owner and as members of the fictitious family of the factory]; as a result, no issue arose.

Later, however, the pay of individuals who started and led the protest was not raised. Instead, the factory owner warned them that if they did it again, he would hand them over to the police for provoking a demonstration and unlawfully interfering with factory work. Indeed, a factory owner can bring legal action against any protesting employees. I learned about this strategy when I went out for tea with a supervisor. While returning, as I passed the factory gate, I noticed a list of names with photos of people and questioned him, 'What is this list for?' He said, 'The factory filed criminal cases against these workers [for unlawful stoppage of work and causing disruption/chaos].' Inquiring further, I asked why the company would file cases against the employees. He responded that they had organised a demonstration calling for an increase in the piece rate. Did women take part in mass protests? I asked, referring to a woman worker on the list who was charged along with seven males. He responded: 'They did, and she snatched the attendance cards of a few co-workers who did not want to stop working, preventing them from turning the cards in to the factory's time division and stopping them from working.' Workers needed the attendance card to get into the factory, and the factory administration used these cards to track their work. While this situation could be read as some workers coercing others to join the protest, it also indicates the dilemma that workers face during a protest; if they join the protest, their covenant with the factory is breached, and if they do not join, their covenant with their fellow workers is not met.

Overall, for workers, besides salary disbursement and increment, the other issues of dissatisfaction with the factory management concerned the Eid (Festival) bonus, leave encashment, holidays, piece rates, production targets and the overtime rate. Workers frequently admitted that they were unaware of their basic salary and overtime rates. One of the workers disclosed:

> My basic income is BDT 4,500, but my overtime is calculated at BDT 33 per hour. How much I am paid for overtime is a mystery to me. My basic salary should be BDT 5,000, in which case my overtime pay would be BDT 50 per hour. I have attempted to discuss this with the GM and PM, but they avoid my inquiries by claiming that 'We [GM and PM] do not understand the calculations.'

Another worker reported that 'employees in the apparel industry do not grasp how salaries are calculated. The worker's housing allowance is increased to raise the wage; management does not raise the basic salary since it would increase overtime pay.' Regarding these issues, Jesmin once said: 'The owner promises to increase wages in the future while threatening that those who want to work can do so and that if they are unhappy, they may quit the factory.' But as many workers continued working for eight to ten years, the factory became like a family; otherwise, they claimed, they would have quit. Being aware of the asymmetrical power relations, another operator said that, because of the deprivations, 'nobody at the factory has the factory owner's best interests in mind. Everybody curses the owner. On the Day of Judgment, the owner must make good on his debt to us. We merely work here to get by.' Here we see that while workers felt like kin to one another, some also believed the owner to be depriving them. This indicated an ambivalence in the workers' understanding of their relationship with the owner: while the workers felt gratitude towards the factory owner, they also felt exploited. Hence, workers constantly faced a dilemma about their situations and the ways forward.

Cultural discourse and coercion: dilemmas in resistance

I made an effort to understand the garment workers' feelings of sadness and anguish throughout our discussions and to comprehend the thinking behind their actions – or lack of actions – in reaction to coercion in the factory. Conversations with the garment workers revealed why they endured the coercive working conditions and occasionally engaged in collective protests. I asked one of the interlocutors why she took on so much pressure. 'Why do you not try and set an achievable production target by discussing it with the factory supervisor?' She replied:

> Pressure builds up gradually as it moves towards us from the top. Because of this, the manager occasionally misbehaves, employs slang and sometimes – although rarely – slaps or otherwise physically harasses employees. How can we help fellow workers? The factory will lose the contract if we cannot fulfil the shipping target, and if the factory loses the contract, we will not get paid. We work in the factory because we lack education and cannot obtain a regular job; as a result, we are forced to make a living by working in a garment factory. We must thus tolerate the managers' harsh behaviour. If we want to work in garments, we must endure all of this. … The factory depends on our labour. We must produce quality products and meet the deadline. If the goods are subpar, the buyer will reject the order and refuse to pay. If the factory does well, it is because of us; if it fails, we are to blame.

We might infer from this statement that factory workers had internalised and accepted the tough working conditions. They believed they had to endure harsh words because they could not find work outside the garment industry. They also thought that once the factory accepted an order, it was their responsibility to fulfil it, even if it required them to labour nonstop for a prolonged period of time. This shows that the factory management had successfully shifted responsibility to the workers. The wellbeing of the factory required the workers to make sacrifices and endure physical pain. One worker mentioned that 'we must praise those who provide for our food [and seek their betterment]', which resonates with the famous Bangla saying *nun khai jar, gun gai tar*.[20] Thus, it was appropriate for the workers to respect and appreciate the factory management to whom they felt indebted rather than rebel against them. Cultural discourses relating to their perceived obligation to the factory owner contributed to the coercive power of the factory management.

We could find historical traces of similar cultural discourses across the country. Since the 1980s, Bangladesh's economic landscape has transformed from a predominant focus on agriculture-based subsistence to a focus on remunerated industrial work. Despite this transition, cultural discourses fundamental to the traditional patron–client relations remained crucial. Prior to the widespread mechanisation of agriculture and the development of microcredit, the poorer segments of society felt entitled to a share in the wealth of the rich since they were in a patron–client relationship.[21] In times of adversity, the poor might forage on the lands and ponds of the wealthy for subsistence. In return, the rural affluent occasionally demanded unpaid labour and support from the poor. Similar obligations among hierarchically related people were found as far back as in the Mughal era (1526–1857). In Mughal political culture, everyone from the emperor down to the lowest servant was bound together by mutual obligations articulated through the ideology of 'salt' (*nemok*). Salt was used to convey a mundane but metaphorical meaning: patrons protected clients, who in turn gave loyalty to patrons.[22] Two aspects were fundamental to this patron–client relationship, namely expressions of gratitude and an avoidance of treacherousness. In the garment industries, I found another feature: the feeling of guilt (if the unspoken promise of helping each other could not be upheld) was widespread. The sense of guilt became dominant due to equating the factory's success with the workers' success.

Furthermore, because factory management placed the burden of producing quality products and fulfilling deadlines (which were often impossible) on the workers, they exploited their guilt to force them to work longer overtime hours and occasionally at weekends. As a result, the workers exploited themselves to meet the additional production targets and improve their factories. The cultural discourses inhibited spontaneous collective protests from forming, being sustained and bringing much change as some workers sided with the factory management (reflecting workers' dilemmas). One of the operators explained:

> Every time a demonstration occurs, the management learns who started it via its 'spy workers' among staff and employees. They compile a list and hand it to the entrance gate so these workers can never re-enter the factory. They are instructed to leave and return later to collect their remaining pay. When someone is dismissed, the other employees can only express their sympathy after the initial outcry. Before being turned over to the police, those named before the Eid holiday [religious festival] had their salaries withheld from them and were asked to go to the administrative office.

I inquired who these spy workers were and why they did this. He continued:

> A few individuals offer the factory owner information. Some are from the same district [region], and some were hired based on a recommendation. They constantly give the factory owner or the production manager information about the factory. These persons – acquainted with the owner or the management or with someone close to them – always put the *Malik's* [owner's] interests first.

By conversing with the workers, I learned that, even in the absence of a mass demonstration, factory management had information about 'who talks with whom and about what'. As a result, when management or a supervisor determined that a person might become a threat to their authority, this individual was put under pressure and compelled to quit the job. Furthermore, the recruiting approach offered factory owners an advantage in better regulating labour discontent. I discovered that, in general, the factory management displayed posters in the surrounding regions, disseminated information through public announcements and even issued notices on the production floor when labourers were needed. As a result, many workers could notify their friends, relatives or neighbours. This procedure of hiring workers created a hierarchy of relationships in the factory, and layers of obligation were formed – as noted earlier, those who helped someone to make a living must be paid back, if not in material terms, then at least with gratitude. As a result, the workers in the factory entered a patron–client relationship at various levels – involving co-workers, supervisors, managers or owners.

For instance, one operator described his initial experience of working in a garment factory as follows: 'When I first joined, my brother introduced me to my supervisor. My brother instructed me never to act improperly around him. He also suggested requesting my supervisor for help if ever I face any issues. Since then, I have always listened to what my supervisor says.' The statement indicated that these workers always faced a dilemma in choosing between their rights and their responsibilities towards co-workers, supervisors and factory owners. In addition, harming the person who helped one to make a living in any way was regarded as *nemok harami* (treacherousness). Hence, if someone wanted to join a different factory for a slight salary increase or did not want to work long hours before shipment deadlines, they were similarly perceived as someone who committed something immoral. Of course, workers did not always face real-life consequences. Nevertheless, the understanding of an unwritten pact influenced how the workers acted and reacted to perceived moments of coercion in the factory.

Conclusion

My research indicates that labour management tactics incorporated many disciplinary schemes that were institutionalised by local cultural discourses and practices rather than being purely authoritarian or paternalistic. In large part due to internal complexities of discourse, the ways in which workers responded to labour processes and large-scale resistance movements were frequently ambivalent and internally contradictory.[23] This case reveals how certain discourses mutually shape people's actions, and how the production of social relations is part of the production of material objects and vice versa.[24] Larger socioeconomic forces markedly shaped the workers' subjectivities.[25] In the factory, expressions such as 'loyalty to work', 'work target', 'individual responsibility', 'not interfering in others' matters' and 'efficient time management' created new subjectivities that motivated the workers to manage themselves to become 'good workers'. Still, these new subjectivities required intense supervision as the whole process revolved around production targets and wages. Becoming a 'good worker' was a contradictory process: since it was widely believed that the factory benefited the employees by giving them a job and the chance to earn a paycheque, they had to do every possible thing in the owner's or factory's interest; yet the idea of brotherhood/sisterhood promoted loyalty to fellow workers and denoted 'each worker is prepared to sacrifice for the other'.

As a result, affiliations among employees that are voluntarily formed respond to circumstances that are seen as coercive and are rooted in the cultural discourses and prevalent value systems that influence everyday lives in Bangladeshi society. In the power dynamics, the dominant factory management or owner frequently gave material and social favours to maintain control of the workers. The subordinate operators thus had grounds for ambivalence about resisting the relationship. Therefore, there was tension between different discourses, so that workers faced dilemmas about their rights and responsibilities, and notions of loyalty and treacherousness led to the fluidity of solidarity among the workers. Collective resistance cannot be sustained and remains in flux. The findings suggest that even though incidents of collective resistance pose little challenge to the broader power relations of the factories, it is essential to note that these forms of contestation and resistance led to diverse outcomes, including effects on working conditions in favour of the workers.[26] Finally, the interplay between physical control, the threat of legal punishment and cultural discourses conditioned the perception and practices of labour coercion in salaried work of the RMG industries in twenty-first-century Bangladesh.

Acknowledgements

This chapter emerged from the PhD project 'Industry, Work, and Capitalism in Bangladesh: An Ethnography of Neoliberalism in the Asian Tiger Economy' (Hasan 2018), Dept of Social Anthropology, University of Bergen (UiB). The PhD project was part of the ERC Advanced Grant project 'Egalitarianism: Forms, Processes, Comparisons' (project code 340673), running from 2014 to 2019 and led by Bruce Kapferer. The project also received financial support from The Meltzer Research Fund and the Fredrik Barth – Sutasoma/University of Bergen Fellowship in Social Anthropology. This chapter was finalised during a fellowship at the International Institute for Asian Studies (IIAS), the Netherlands. The library resources at Leiden University and the research facilities of IIAS were instrumental in the writing process. Furthermore, the article immensely benefited from the comments and suggestions from my supervisors at UiB, Professor Knut Mikjel Rio and Professor Bjørn

Enge Bertelsen, and co-fellows at IIAS, Dr Aditya Kiran Kakati, Dr Benjamin Linder and Dr Hedwig Waters. Finally, thanks to the book editors for their feedback and for enabling this academic exercise.

Notes

1. Ahmed, 'At Least 117 Killed in Fire at Bangladeshi Clothing Factory'; ILO, 'The Rana Plaza Disaster Ten Years On: What Has Changed?'; Clean Clothes Campaign, 'Rana Plaza'.
2. The garment sector in Bangladesh has created a massive amount of employment over the last 30 years. It employs more than 4 million people of a working population of 76 million in about 5,000 garment factories (national and multinational) throughout the country.
3. Muhammad, 'Wealth and Deprivation', 2011, 23; Hasan, 'What do Recent Layoffs in RMG Factories Entail?'; Hasan, 'Will the Future be Better for RMG?'; Hasan, 'Whose Sustainability is it anyway?'.
4. See Mirdha, 'Garment Sector Saw Highest Industrial Disputes in 2017'; Ahmed, Raihan and Islam, 'Labour Unrest in the Ready-Made Garment Industry of Bangladesh', 2013, 70; Hossan, Sarkar and Afroze, 'Recent Unrest in the RMG Sector of Bangladesh', 2012, 208–9; Muhammad, 'Wealth and Deprivation', 2011, 25; Islam and Ahmad, 'Contemplating Sustainable Solutions to Garments Sector Unrest'; Alam, 'Recent Unrest in Garment Sector in Bangladesh'.
5. Muhammad, 'Wealth and Deprivation', 2011, 26.
6. See Human Rights Watch, *Whoever Raises their Head Suffers the Most*, 4.
7. Bhuiyan, 'Present Status of Garment Workers in Bangladesh', 2012, 38.
8. See Hasan, 'Industry, Work, and Capitalism in Bangladesh'; Hasan, *Everyday Life of Ready-made Garment Kormi in Bangladesh*.
9. Edwards, 'Individual Traits and Organisational Incentives', 1976, 57–9.
10. Scott, *Domination and the Arts of Resistance*.
11. Graeber, 'Turning Mode of Production Inside Out', 2006, 69–71.
12. These constructions all depend on the buyer's perspective on a 'good factory', with supplies being shipped on time, and a 'good retailer', who takes the initiative to source from factories with better working conditions paying higher prices.
13. Marshall and Rossman, *Designing Qualitative Research*, 281.
14. For knitting factories that supply winter clothes to retail brands, the peak of production usually lasts from early to late summer.
15. However, as mentioned earlier, the demand for increased wages previously led to violent protests. The importance of income from garment work becomes apparent from the following comment of a worker (in 2017): 'I began with a salary of BDT 5,300 that has already increased to BDT 6,200. However, when I work 2 hours extra every week, I make roughly BDT 7,000 per month. The most I can make with overtime benefit is around BDT 8,000. After paying rent and food, I send the remainder to my parents. I am confident that they will not misappropriate my earnings. They keep it safe for me. The savings from my earnings go into a bank. I occasionally buy clothing for my daughter. When I receive my salary, I set aside BDT 4,000 for food and rent, which costs roughly BDT 3,200. I attempt to save roughly BDT 3,000 every month.' Hence, garment work is incredibly significant for most of the workers.
16. In the garment factory, workers were paid by two methods: either a fixed monthly salary or piece wages.
17. All the quotations are the author's translations.
18. See Hasan, *Everyday Life of Ready-made Garment Kormi in Bangladesh*, 149–87.
19. See Ong, *Spirits of Resistance and Capitalist Discipline*, 210–12.
20. See also, for discussion of this from a moral economy perspective, Hasan, 'Moral Economy of Female Garment Workers', 2018, 146–51.
21. See Rudra, 'Local Power and Farm-level Decision-making', 250–2; Rahman and Wahid, 'The Grameen Bank and the Changing Patron–Client Relationship in Bangladesh', 1992, 318–9; Breman, 'Labour and Landlessness in South and South-East Asia', 231–2; Datta, *Land and Labour Relations in South-West Bangladesh*, 83–9; Islam, 'The Informal Institutional Framework in Rural Bangladesh', 99; Mannan, 'Rural Power Structures and Evolving Market

Forces in Bangladesh', 292; Makita, 'Changing Patron-Client Relations Favourable to New Opportunities for Landless Labourers in Rural Bangladesh', 2007, 255–6.
22 Eaton, *The Rise of Islam and the Bengal Frontier, 1204–1760*, 164.
23 See Stoler, 'Plantation Politics and Protest on Sumatra's East Coast', 1986, 125; Cooper, *The Dialectics of Decolonisation*, 9–15; Cross, 'Neoliberalism as Unexceptional: Economic Zones and the Everyday Precariousness of Working Life in South India', 2010, 358–62.
24 Graeber, 'Turning Mode of Production Inside Out', 2006, 69–71.
25 See Hardt, 'The Global Society of Control', 1998, 148.
26 For a similar argument, see Scott, 'Everyday Forms of Peasant Resistance', 1989, 37–48.

Bibliography

Ahmed, Farid. 'At Least 117 Killed in Fire at Bangladeshi Clothing Factory', *CNN*, 25 November 2012. Accessed 16 August 2022. https://edition.cnn.com/2012/11/25/world/asia/bangladesh-factory-fire/index.html.

Ahmed, Shaheen, Raihan, Mohammad Zahir and Islam, Nazrul. 'Labour Unrest in the Ready-Made Garment Industry of Bangladesh', *International Journal of Business and Management* 8/15 (2013): 68–80.

Alam, Korshed. 'Recent Unrest in Garment Sector in Bangladesh', *MediaWatch*, 21 July 2010. Accessed 8 August 2014. http://epo-mediawatch.blogspot.com/2010/07/recent-unrest-in-garment-sector-in.html.

Bhuiyan, Md Zafar Alam. 'Present Status of Garment Workers in Bangladesh: An Analysis', *IOSR Journal of Business and Management* 3 (2012): 38–44.

Breman, Jan. 'Labour and Landlessness in South and South-East Asia'. In *Disappearing Peasantries?: Rural Labour in Africa, Asia and Latin America*, edited by Deborah Fahy Bryceson, Cristobal Kay and Jos E. Mooij, 231–46. London: ITDG Publishing, 2000.

Clean Clothes Campaign. 'Rana Plaza'. Clean Clothes Campaign (n.d.). Accessed 6 June 2023. https://cleanclothes.org/campaigns/past/rana-plaza.

Cooper, Frederick. *The Dialectics of Decolonisation: Nationalism and Labour Movements in Post-war Africa*. Paper prepared for the Power Conference, Program in the Comparative Study of Social Transformations. Ann Arbor: University of Michigan, 1992.

Cross, Jamie. 'Neoliberalism as Unexceptional: Economic Zones and the Everyday Precariousness of Working Life in South India', *Critique of Anthropology* 30 (2010): 355–73.

Datta, Anjan Kumar. *Land and Labour Relations in South-West Bangladesh: Resources, Power and Conflict*. New York: St Martin's Press, 1998.

Eaton, Richard Maxwell. *The Rise of Islam and the Bengal Frontier, 1204–1760*. Berkeley: University of California Press, [1978] 1993.

Edwards, Richard C. 'Individual Traits and Organisational Incentives: What Makes a "Good" Worker?', *The Journal of Human Resources* 11 (1976): 51–68.

Graeber, David. 'Turning Mode of Production Inside Out: Or, Why Capitalism is a Transformation of Slavery', *Critique of Anthropology* 26 (2006): 61–85.

Hardt, Michael. 'The Global Society of Control', *Discourse* 20 (1998): 139–52.

Hasan, Mohammad Tareq. 'Industry, Work, and Capitalism in Bangladesh: An Ethnography of Neoliberalism in the Asian Tiger Economy'. PhD thesis, University of Bergen, 2018.

Hasan, Mohammad Tareq. 'Moral Economy of Female Garment Workers: The Relevance of The History of Inequalities of Class and Gender in Rural East Bengal/Bangladesh from 1947 to the Present', *Social Science Review [The Dhaka University Studies, Part-D]* 35 (2018): 135–55.

Hasan, Mohammad Tareq. 'What do Recent Layoffs in RMG Factories Entail?', *The Daily Star*, 22 September 2019. Accessed 7 June 2021. https://www.thedailystar.net/opinion/news/what-do-recent-layoffs-rmg-factories-entail-1803214.

Hasan, Mohammad Tareq. 'Will the Future be Better for RMG?', *Dhaka Tribune*, 13 June 2020. Accessed 7 June 2021. https://www.dhakatribune.com/opinion/op-ed/2020/06/13/op-ed-will-the-future-be-better-for-rmg.

Hasan, Mohammad Tareq. 'Whose Sustainability is it Anyway?', *Dhaka Tribune*, 12 January 2021. Accessed 7 June 2021. https://www.dhakatribune.com/opinion/op-ed/2021/01/12/op-ed-whose-sustainability-is-it-anyway.

Hasan, Mohammad Tareq. *Everyday Life of Ready-made Garment Kormi in Bangladesh: An Ethnography of Neoliberalism*. Cham: Palgrave Macmillan, 2022.

Hossan, Chowdhury Golam, Sarker, Md. Atiqur Rahman and Afroze, Rumana. 'Recent Unrest in the RMG Sector of Bangladesh: Is this an Outcome of Poor Labour Practices?', *International Journal of Business and Management* 7 (2012): 206–18.

Human Rights Watch (HRW). '*Whoever Raises their Head Suffers the Most': Workers' Rights in Bangladesh's Garment Factories*. USA: Human Rights Watch, 2015. Accessed 04 June 2023. https://www.hrw.org/report/2015/04/22/whoever-raises-their-head-suffers-most/workers-rights-bangladeshs-garment.

ILO (International Labour Organization). 'The Rana Plaza Disaster Ten Years On: What Has Changed?', International Labour Organization (April 2023). Accessed 6 June 2023. https://www.ilo.org/infostories/en-GB/Stories/Country-Focus/rana-plaza.

Islam, Mohammad Sirajul and Sonia Ahmad. 'Contemplating Sustainable Solutions to Garments Sector Unrest', *The Daily Star*, 10 July 2010. Accessed 10 August 2014. http://archive.thedailystar.net/newDesign/news-details.php?nid=146098.

Islam, S. Aminul. 'The Informal Institutional Framework in Rural Bangladesh'. In *Hands Not Land: An Overview of How Livelihoods are Changing in Rural Bangladesh*, edited by Kazi A. Toufique and Cate Turton, 97–104. Dhaka: Bangladesh Institute of Development Studies, 2002.

Makita, Rie. 'Changing Patron-Client Relations Favourable to New Opportunities for Landless Labourers in Rural Bangladesh', *Journal of South Asian Development* 2 (2007): 255–77.

Mannan, Manzurul. 'Rural Power Structures and Evolving Market Forces in Bangladesh'. In *Civil Society and the Market Question*, edited by Krishna B. Ghimire, 271–98. Hampshire: Palgrave Macmillan, 2005.

Marshall, Catherine and Rossman, Gretchen B. *Designing Qualitative Research*. London: Sage, 2016.

Mirdha, Refayet Ullah. 'Garment Sector Saw Highest Industrial Disputes in 2017', *The Daily Star*, 1 May 2018. Accessed 1 May 2018. https://www.thedailystar.net/business/garment-sector-saw-highest-industrial-disputes-2017-1570120.

Muhammad, Anu. 'Wealth and Deprivation: Ready-Made Garments Industry in Bangladesh', *Economic & Political Weekly* 15 (2011): 23–7.

Ong, Aihwa. *Spirits of Resistance and Capitalist Discipline: Factory Women in Malaysia*. Albany: State University of New York Press, 1987.

Rahman, Atiur and Wahid, Abu N. M. 'The Grameen Bank and the changing patron-client relationship in Bangladesh', *Journal of Contemporary Asia* 22 (1992): 303–21.

Rudra, Ashok. 'Local Power and Farm-level Decision-Making'. In *Agrarian Power and Agricultural Productivity*, edited by Desai Meghnad, Susanne Hoeber Rudolph and Ashok Rudra, 250–80. Delhi: Oxford University Press, 1984.

Scott, James. 'Everyday Forms of Peasant Resistance', *The Copenhagen Journal of Asian Studies* 4 (1989): 33–62.

Scott, James. *Domination and the Arts of Resistance: Hidden Transcripts*. New Haven: Yale University Press, 1990.

Stoler, Ann. 'Plantation Politics and Protest on Sumatra's East Coast', *The Journal of Peasant Studies* 13 (1986): 124–43.

10
Border plants: globalisation as shown to us by the women living at its leading edge

Eva Kuhn

'My name is Carmen Durán.' The film *Maquilápolis: City of Factories* (2006) begins with a pan inside a factory that lands on the face of the person both speaking and holding the camera.[1] Carmen Durán tells us that she works in a 'maquiladora', an assembly factory in the Tijuana free trade zone located on the US–Mexican border. This factory is owned by the multinational corporation Panasonic. Durán says that she has previously worked in eight other assembly plants, that she has three children and is a single mother, like the majority of the maquiladora workers. Later, when we get to know her daily routine, it becomes clear that Carmen Durán (shown in Figure 10.1) has to fit 12 hours of paid factory work and 24 hours of unpaid care work into one day.

The gendered division of modern labour does not hold once a heterosexual marriage breaks up, or when a woman with a child decides to get along without a man.[2] Durán leaves work at 7.00 a.m. She picks up her kids at her ex-father-in-law's house and they go home to their house. She heats up the soup of the day before, washes the kids and gets them ready for school. After she takes them to school, she cooks, washes clothes and dishes and picks the kids up again at 4.00 p.m., then spends some time with them. After that she prepares for work. 'Maybe I get to sleep for an hour or two. Or sometimes I don't sleep and just go off to work.' Furthermore, we learn that the money she earns is not enough to cover the basic needs of her family: she earns US$11 a day and works six days a week. 'To buy a jug of water, you have to work about an hour, to buy a gallon of milk you work a little over two hours.'[3]

Maquilápolis is a documentary film by Vicky Funari and Sergio De La Torre, filmed in Tijuana in the Mexican state of Baja California from 2000 to 2006. The film was made in close collaboration with the subjects

Figure 10.1 Factory worker Carmen Durán in the film *Maquilápolis: City of Factories*, directed by Vicky Funari and Sergio De La Torre, 2006. © David Maung.

it focuses on: women who work in the assembly plants. With those who live and work in the hidden realms of globalised capitalism taking the lead in talking to the viewers and showing them around, the film sheds a sharp light on what Nancy Fraser called capitalism's 'dirty secret': the fact that the accumulation of capital goes hand in hand with severe exploitation by not compensating 'a portion of workers' labour time'.[4] Furthermore, the film uncovers the background conditions of this exploitation, which Fraser calls the 'even dirtier secret' of capitalism: the fact that its functioning depends on unwaged social reproduction, on treating nature as disposable and on policies compliant with its demands.[5] Through the voices and images of the film's subjects, coerced by the promise of a better life or of a living at all, we learn about the disastrous ecological consequences of this industry central to – yet at the margins of – the functioning of the globally dominant system. And we witness the women workers' double and triple burden through poorly paid productive and unpaid reproductive labour, complicated by a devastated environment and a national policy that has been corrupted in its values by the pressure of the multinational corporations.

Remarkably, the film suggests that it is precisely the relation between unwaged reproductive work and the loving concerns for their children, friends and neighbourhood that empowers the employees to work for a change, to contest the dreadful working conditions and thus

Figure 10.2 Factory workers in the film *Maquilápolis: City of Factories*, directed by Vicky Funari and Sergio De La Torre, 2006. © David Maung.

fight against the capitalist mechanisms of exploitation of human beings and the environment. In this way, the film reveals the revolutionary potential of these women (shown in Figure 10.2), these (unpaid) reproductive and (poorly paid) productive workers, who form the indispensable basis of the neoliberal system. Carmen is not only a maquiladora worker and a homeworker but also a *promotora*, and thus an activist who works to ensure that her colleagues can inform themselves about their rights, support each other in care, and advocate for better working conditions.[6] The initial filmic gesture implies this self-empowerment in the symbolism of its production, because it is Carmen herself who holds the camera and sets the scene.[7] Lourdes Luján, the other protagonist of this film and friend of Carmen, explains that *promotoras* are women who have worked in the factories and have learned by doing and through their own investigations about their rights as women and as workers:

As a *promotora* you promote the law. What little you know you pass on. [As a *promotora*] I can't stay quiet anymore. I have to defend whatever right is being violated. You sow the seeds of what you have learned. You are a student, and gradually you become a teacher.[8]

The self-empowerment of the first shot is continued in the collaborative production of *Maquilápolis*, with Carmen and Lourdes among those involved. According to the production statement, the factory workers who appear in the film 'have been involved in every stage of production, from planning to shooting, from scripting to outreach'.[9] These conditions of production are reflected in the aesthetic form of the film. The workers are not portrayed from the privileged position of artists working in the cultural field, nor are they represented as only victims of the system. Instead, the protagonists present themselves by taking their own pictures or staging themselves in collectively developed images (as in Figure 10.3). The film features video diaries of their daily lives and activities, and the women appear in front of and behind the camera, always referring to the audiovisual means – to camera and microphone – that create the speaking and sounding images of themselves and of their situation. In different ways they appropriate the privilege of having the *point of view* by guiding the camera themselves: the colours of the vests of the workers make their rank in the factory instantly recognisable to their bosses. The person in red is a group leader, the one in yellow a supervisor and the one in blue an operator. This is what we learn from the two protagonists who lead us camouflaged in a car across the site.

Thus, the film is seemingly a collectively made manifesto of (feminist) solidarity and collective resistance by those who are unrestrainedly exploited by the global system. Through the collaborative method of this film, the systematically exploited workers emerge as the highly competent multitasking survivors that they in reality are, as

Figure 10.3 Teresa Loyola and other factory workers display the components they assemble, in *Maquilápolis: City of Factories*, directed by Vicky Funari and Sergio De La Torre, 2006. © David Maung.

well as life-loving and gentle resistance fighters capable of confronting a violent and globally dominating regime from within. The film-makers Funari and De La Torre made this collective movie possible. They set the concept, gave the platform and provided the protagonists with equipment, techniques and skills they could use to work on their common film – as a way to amplify their own voices and to enter into another public sphere that a film might open up through its reception at worldwide film festivals and on YouTube. This method seems to reflect the theory and practice of 'Deep Listening' developed by Pauline Oliveros, who is credited with the original score for this film. She worked on methods to make existing spaces such as caves produce sound, or to give a physical setting to the perception of the sonorities of these places.[10]

'We first heard the word *maquiladora* in the 1960s.' Naty Guizar's voice is accompanied by an aerial shot that follows an abstract line reinforced by corrugated metal walls and other devices that enhance the effect of division into two parts. This is how the film continues. 'The *maquiladora* changed everything, because they paid better wages than in the rest of Mexico. That is what we migrants came looking for.'[11] Like Ciudad Juárez and the other cities on the US–Mexican border, Tijuana was involved in a political programme that the Mexican government pushed with the United States in the mid-1960s to mitigate the high unemployment caused by the downfall of the Bracero Program, a policy lasting from 1942 to 1964 that mobilised Mexican farm workers to seasonally work on US farms.[12] The measure can be interpreted as a reaction to an international labour and accumulation crisis that the philosopher and activist Silvia Federici linked to the observation that 'everyone was on the move in the late '60s. Students, industrial workers, women, Native Americans.'[13] Federici described how by then it had become clear that the framework of the capitalist organisation of labour was under threat, as the gender and international division of labour on which capitalist accumulation had been based was being questioned in many corners of the world and undermined, not only by strikes. This was followed by a period of 'capitalist experiments', as Federici puts it: a search for new models that would allow the companies and the states to re-establish command over labour.[14]

A maquiladora is a factory close to the border, in which single components or materials imported from abroad are assembled into semi-finished or finished products and then exported for consumers in the US and other countries. This special legal construct allowed foreign, majority-American companies to produce tax-free and employ cheap labour without respecting any domestic laws on environmental and worker protection. In 1994, with the North American Free Trade Agreement (NAFTA), Tijuana became even more fertile soil for sowing factories.[15] By the end of the 1990s, there were nearly 4,000 plants on the border, owned by Panasonic, Sanyo, Samsung, Nellcor Puritan, La Estrella, Tocabi, Deltech, Sohnen, IFSA, Santomi, Nypro, Optica Sola, Kelmex, Rectificadores Internacionales, Powerware and others. Among them are many companies that produce the technology on which our mobile, digital and obsessively visual society is based. Carmen Durán directs the sharp eye of her little camera at a factory on the hill: 'There is Sony', and she moves the camera down and shows a little boy laughing at it: 'And this is my son.' The topographical situation reflects the power relations in place: 'The industrial city is up on the mesa [flat-topped hill], and we are down below.'[16] Yet, by participating in the production of this film, Durán fights the exploiters with their own weapons, or rather with the products that are manufactured by her and her peers.

Making women work

A gigantic transnational zone has emerged out of the seeds of these international agreements, powered by the labour of migrants and women. In this borderland, globalisation has transformed Mexico's rural life into a high-tech slum for millions of people. The flourishing of the maquiladora industry was accompanied by the destruction of local economies. The removal of import barriers for foreign companies, for example, has meant that a large number of Mexican farmers have lost their livelihoods.[17] Where Carmen came from, at the age of 13, and why and from what she fled, the film does not tell us. Carmen tells us only that most of the women come to Tijuana 'eager to work, work, work'.[18] Some of these women introduce themselves to the viewers through their voices a sequence exemplary for the chorus structure developed for this film and the multi-vocal narration that is part of it. 'I am from the state of Michoacán, there are no jobs there like we have here.' 'I am from Guadalajara, Jalisco!' 'I am from Sola de Vega. Oaxaca.' 'I am from Mazatlán.' 'I was born in Sinaloa.' These women came to Tijuana because the father lost his job, because there was violence in the family, because their family broke apart or simply because they had the wish to earn their own money and become independent women. A lot of the maquiladora workers seek to make a living for their families beyond the traditional family arrangement, which is the standard model in Mexico.[19] In this arrangement, the man works for money in the public space while the woman stays at home to do the unwaged domestic work, in a realm that is considered private, even though in reality it provides the basic condition for the functioning of the public sphere.[20] And so, these women moved from a structure oppressive under the pretext of tradition to one oppressive under the pretext of progress.

In the film we see signboards on which multinational companies advertise for female workers: 'Panasonic URGE ensambladoras', for example. And on the poster, we see a woman working behind a computer. Carmen tells us that she likes her job because she's learning to operate digital tools. But there's a problem with lead contamination: 'You breathe lead every day.' She explains that the companies for which she has worked have never informed her of the risks from toxic chemicals in the factory. 'I've started to get spots and sores on my body and these spots arise from contact with the paste we use. And my doctor says I'm at risk for leukaemia.' Durán also has to be careful not to bring her unhealthy work conditions home: 'Also, you can't wash your clothes with your children's or get close to your kids after you leave work because it affects them too.'[21] Towards the end of the film, we learn that it is this very illness for which she eventually gets dismissed from Panasonic from one day to the next. And if somebody gets pregnant and is not regarded as fit for work, she will also be fired on the spot. As the maquiladora worker and *promotora* Magdalena Cerda sums it up: 'Along with [the companies'] capital comes their impact on the environment and on people's health.'[22] By means of the social situation in which these women find themselves through their intersecting roles as industry workers and mothers, the double and triple exploitative mechanisms of a globalised system that blindly follows the accumulation of capital become evident. Carmen and her peers not only do the social reproductive work, but also provide their lives for the continuous running of production. And this production, in turn, produces effects, which consume not only their labour time and lifetime but also their own bodies.[23] As if to mock this downward spiral, another signboard shows a blond man with the title 'thinking about expansion ...'.

When we look into the courtyards of the factories through the workers' cameras, we see primarily women. Diana Arias tells us that when the maquiladora industry began, the women represented 80 per cent of the industry's labour force. 'They said we would make a good work force. Because we had agile hands and would be cheap and docile.'[24] This circumstance requires a 'move to history', as Nancy Fraser called it.[25] Here, it is exploited that women have been raised to be disciplined and diligent mothers as well as docile housewives who have been accustomed to not being paid for their work. By naturalising their labour as a 'labour of love', the fact is obscured that for the capitalist system their labour means the continuous supply of the workforce.[26] Women must work largely unwaged because economically unaffordable labour is the basis of a capitalist society.[27] Yet, their skills and abilities are not only used for the tacit reproduction of workers but also for an optimised production that consciously employs workers perceived as submissive and obedient.[28] Delfina Rodriguez stresses this clearly: 'Most of us, when we came from the South, we arrive completely ignorant. We were very young and didn't know what awaits us, what we'll be exposed to.'[29] Until the 1990s, the legal minimum age of 14 years in the maquiladoras was often undercut.[30]

Beyond visibility

The term 'maquiladora' derives from the word *maquilar*, which originally referred to the process of grinding wheat into flour in medieval Spain, and *maquila*, the grain retained by the miller as payment. Since then, the word has evolved to represent today's meaning: a manufacturing operation that processes imported raw materials or components into final or intermediate products to be sold in countries other than where they were manufactured. The factories in which these operations take place act as suppliers to large multinational corporations or are owned directly by them.[31] The foreign companies benefit primarily from cheap labour done by 'busy bodies', as Carmen calls herself and her colleagues.[32] 'Busy bodies' are the workers who ensure industrial production. At least theoretically, they occupy a very powerful position. If they collectively went on strike and stopped doing the work of production and reproduction, everything would stand still.[33] Yet, in practice, this is not the case.

'In Tijuana there is no way to draw anything from the soil, because there is no water, no way to draw anything from your environment. Here you have to make.'[34] The capitalist system has declared the idea of unlimited growth of capital to be absolute, and subordinates all social, ecological and creative processes to this interest.[35] The devastating destruction and poisoning of the borderland made visible in this film, as well as the excessive exploitation of the lifetimes and bodies of the maquiladora workers, point to the extent to which unregulated capital accumulation neglects the finite nature of natural resources. The penalty-free 'opportunity' to do this results in the accelerated concentration of companies in this free-trade area. It is as if one had to go to the border to be shown the aberration of this system in its clearest features.

Lourdes Luján realised, while showing us where she works, that she has never looked at the other side of the border. Subsequently, she films with her camera through a hole in the wall, a gesture that reinforces the impact of the border and its separation of two worlds: the Global North is the seat of the rich industrial nations and former colonisers, and the Global South is home to low-income people and former colonies. The latter is urged to keep costs down so that the former can maintain its privileged status – to put it as simply as the concept of the border suggests. The abstract line that is established at the beginning of the film separates not only two countries but also two realities whose binary contrast is maintained by the globalised world economy. The border must be constantly consolidated in order to create and re-create the difference that secures the power relations in place.[36] For those privileged by the system, these dichotomies also come with a question of visibility: outsourcing production logically entails its spatial distancing, a move into the invisible that becomes tantamount to the unconscious. And this invisibility, in turn, fits neatly with the commodified nature of the product, by which everything is measured in the capitalist system.[37] The product appears independent of its production conditions, detached. The receiver's attention is only drawn to production when the product does not work.

Against the logic of the product

Through its collaborative form of filmic production, *Maquilápolis* breaks with a common documentary practice of dropping into a location, shooting film and leaving with the product. By passing the cameras and microphones to the protagonists in the tradition of *cinéma-vérité* and by letting them tell their own stories and articulate their own concerns (as in Figure 10.4), by letting them perform the body movements and gestures they know by heart and have developed in common, the film-makers ensure that the film's voice is truly that of its subjects.[38] The physical authentication of what is being depicted in the film is particularly important because the film considers that these women working in the maquiladora industry are one of the most important sources of knowledge about globalised capitalism. They argue against its interpretation as a so-called 'cognitive capitalism', a term suggesting that digitisation has replaced most physical labour.[39]

The informatisation of work through the internet, and digitalisation in general, as well as the financialisation of the economy, have

Figure 10.4 Lupita Castañeda films a video diary as part of the film *Maquilápolis: City of Factories*, directed by Vicky Funari and Sergio De La Torre, 2006. © Darcy McKinnon.

by no means led to an 'end of work', as sociologist Jeremy Rifkin and Marxists such as Carlo Vercellone, Antonio Negri and Michael Hardt have claimed.[40] Rather, since the 1970s, a new industry has emerged, characterised by the diffusion and informalisation of production.[41] Durán, Luján and the other women speak to us from the abysses of a globalised world economy which is dominated by the logic of the product. This logic, however, obscures production – the actual process that turns raw material into end product. Carmen and her colleagues provide us with physically based insights into the repressed and unseen spaces of (re)production that they experience day and night. With the embodied knowledge of these women, the film argues against the tendency to forget about the physical processes of production, a tendency that stems from outsourcing and the product's detachment from its history. After all, the sparkling brand-new television set or video projector glitters from the shelves of the media market without saying anything about the way it is being produced.

What is true for the product is also true for the commercial use of media. There, too, considerable effort is made not to distract the viewer from the content of the image. In order to guarantee the undisturbed immersion of the viewer in a fictitious world, any confrontation with the conditions of production of the image is avoided. Who would ever consider a flyback converter when watching television, or think of the workers in the maquiladoras who assemble the pieces of the device? 'I assemble flybacks,' says Carmen Durán[42] after we are shown a sign in a shot from the highway that states: 'Tijuana la Capital Mundial de la Televisión'. Accompanied by Carmen's voice, a spinning television set appears against a red background and opens an experimental interlude. Gradually the electronic inner workings of the television set are made visible through post-production. Then Durán herself follows the object: mechanically driven, she rotates on her own axis, carefully holding the flyback she assembled in her hands. In addition to the flyback, she also presents herself, dolled and made up. Like Judy in Hitchcock's *Vertigo*, she stages her own object status as a woman in a patriarchally dominated world. Later, other women follow an identical pattern and advertise their activities and products in the same ironic way. They assemble filters, electrical components, oxygen masks, rings in machines, urinary bags, telephones, lenses, pantyhose, toys, intravenous tubes, batteries ... and the list could be continued.

Resistance

Before working for Panasonic, Carmen was employed by the major television manufacturer Sanyo for more than six years. She tells us that she liked the work and her colleagues, but not the way she was treated by the supervisors, who harassed and pressured her. Furthermore, she was exposed to toxic chemicals, her nose bled constantly, and she began to suffer from kidney troubles because she was not allowed to drink water. From one day to the next, she and all her colleagues were laid off because production had been moved from Mexico to Indonesia: labour was cheaper there.[43] The severance that the company should have paid to the employees in the case of its departure was never provided.[44] Consequently, Carmen filed a lawsuit. As this action had no effect, she started her own research. This process features in the film as one of two examples of self-empowered, and ultimately collective, resistance against prevailing injustice.

Carmen found out that the Mexican government, which is supposed to provide the workers with legal counsel, rarely collaborates with engaged lawyers who actually act on behalf of the workers. Together with her colleagues, she discovered that many unions exist only on paper. As *promotora*, Lupita Castañeda confirms for her workplace: 'We realised it was a union in name only ... because we went to see the union representative and there wasn't one.'[45] Finally, they came across Jaime Cota, an independent lawyer from the area who was willing to fight for the interests of the workers. He confirms the conclusion of the *promotoras*: 'In the maquiladora industry most unions are ghost unions – they protect the employer.' Cota explains that Sanyo was trying to drag out the payment of the severance: 'To irritate you, so you'll all give up.'[46] But they did not give up and set a precedent in opposition. With Jaime Cota, Carmen Durán settled the case in favour of the workers. They won against a huge, powerful company: like David against Goliath. And after 10 years of struggle, Sanyo paid much higher settlements than in the past, although still not the full amount that was required under the labour law.

The international agreements have gradually made Mexico very dependent on others, and corruption has become a universal phenomenon. Jaime Cota explains, for instance, that Mexico's federal labour law is actually favourable for workers. But the authorities do not uphold the law. Since the 1970s, the International Monetary Fund and the World Bank have made a series of loans to the Mexican government and these loans come with conditions. For example, the Mexican government has signed a letter of intention not to raise salaries. So, as Jaime Cota puts it: 'These institutions force Mexico to break its own laws.' Then he refers to the Mexican poet Sor Juana Inés de la Cruz and her question about whose sin is worse: the one who sins for pay, or the one who pays to sin?[47] 'Who is more to blame for violating our labour law: the government which is corrupted by the multinationals, or the multinationals which pay Mexico to break the law?'[48]

The discovery of the ghost unions by the *promotoras*, revealing the aim of preventing a union of workers at any price, confirms a point made by Silvia Federici in her critique of globalised capitalism.[49] Since 1989 the labour-intensive branches of Western industrial production have been outsourced to the former socialist countries of Eastern Europe and to parts of the 'Third World': to Mexico or the Philippines. There, production has been organised on the basis of so-called 'free production zones', where the adjective 'free' refers to the ability of employers to ignore the concerns and rights of the workers. This concerns, first of all, their right to organise.[50] Federici speaks of the construction of a 'global assembly line' that has allowed companies to move from one country to another to avoid labour struggles. Furthermore, they can move where production conditions are cheapest, while workers are forced to compete globally.[51] This meets with the experience of another *promotora* in the film, Vianey Mijangos: 'At my job they fire everyone who tries to start a union. They won't let you speak. They recently fired twenty people, and the

Labour Board did nothing.'[52] Due to the impossibility of being organised in unions, the workers organise themselves in alternative ways: by working as *promotoras*, by exchanging knowledge and by acting collectively in groups like Mujer Grupo Factor X, Chilpancingo Collective for Environmental Justice and Women's Rights Advocates.

The example of self-empowered resistance is linked to Lourdes Luján's observation on the surroundings of the working women's homes, especially by the river, which is very polluted. Lourdes has always lived in this neighbourhood, Chilpancingo, and when she was a child, the river was clean and they used to bathe there. 'When I got a little older and started working in the factories, I saw that the water was changing colours. Now sometimes it's black, green, red and foamy.'[53] Her children cannot play there anymore. Due to the topology, with the factory above and the village below, the chemicals of the factories end up in the neighbourhood of the workers. In the pictures we see children walking over self-made bridges to avoid contact with the liquids pouring down from the hill. 'People here have got sores on their legs and feet'; they get strange skin diseases: 'my daughter's spots are brown and always itchy. And my son too, he gets hives all over his body.'[54] Lourdes tells us that she started as *promotora* because of a sign inviting 10 women to participate in a health survey for the San Diego Environmental Health Coalition. When she started the survey, she noticed the following problems: 'Kids born without fingernails, skin allergies like this one on my face. I learned about cases of hydrocephalus where they have to put a shunt in the brain. I saw cases of anencephaly when babies are born without a brain and die at birth.'[55] The birth defects are caused by pollution, especially the waste left by an abandoned factory called Metales y Derivados (Figure 10.5), with about 6,000 tons of lead slag left exposed to the elements.[56]

Ironically, the company Metales y Derivados pursued a recycling mission. They transported cast-off car batteries to Mexico to retrieve the lead they contained. But the company did not adhere to environmental guidelines and was badly managed, so it was shut down in 1994 by the Office of Environmental Protection. Since then, the electronic waste has been soaking into the site and is making an impact on the environment and on people's health.[57] The owner of the factory, Jose Kahn, has an outstanding arrest warrant in Mexico but they cannot arrest him because he is currently in the US. He had fled when the government shut the factory, an event that was covered in the local newspapers. Now he owns the parent company in San Diego and reports a million dollars of profit each year. The film depicts the persistent demand of Lourdes and her allies, united under the name Chilpancingo Collective, to bring

Figure 10.5 The toxic waste site left behind by Metales y Derivados, a battery recycling factory; from the film *Maquilápolis: City of Factories*, directed by Vicky Funari and Sergio De La Torre, 2006. © Vicky Funari.

about a proper clean-up of the factory grounds. The film shows the women conferring in a highly motivated and vivacious manner, first in kitchens at their homes, and later in a self-built office, with the camera moving from hand to hand. Like a reporter, Luján summarises for the emerging film: 'We are advancing, *poco a poco* [little by little]. You can see positive changes.'[58] She announces a demonstration outside the Federal Environmental Protection Agency, to demand a visit by the environmental official: 'the big hotshot in charge of environmental health. We'll demonstrate day and night until he comes.'[59] Eventually, he came out and stated to the women that he could see the urgency, but that his hands were tied. He referred them to President Fox, whose answer was that Chilpancingo was not affected by pollution because the factory was so well covered.

'Our reality is very different from their vision.'[60] The women show us with their cameras that the factory is not well covered at all because the tarpaulins are torn up. The barrels where they dumped the slag are filled with holes and eaten away. We learn that a few years ago they dug a hole 30 feet deep and they found lead. 'Wind and rain bring lead down through our streets. Workers pass by and get lead on their shoes. They bring it into their workplace and homes.'[61] Again and again, it becomes clear that those who are privileged by the system abstract from the realities of those who are endangered and whose lives are made precarious by it. On a border tour organised by the Chilpancingo Collective, they meet Manuel Garcia Lepe, who holds a high position at the Baja California Office of Economic Development. He receives them in his office and is asked what kind of infrastructure, such as housing, water and electricity, they are providing for the workers. At first, he makes a sort of confession by saying that it is not easy to cope with the situation because the population develops faster than the services. Later, asked whether he thinks that the workers are living good lives and are being paid enough, he answers that there are a lot of stores in Tijuana and there are always people shopping, which means that the workers are well paid. 'You don't see people begging on the streets of Tijuana ... they have money in their pockets. They eat well, they have electricity in some way. People are in good condition in Baja California. They have all the standards of a city.'[62] And when Carmen Durán asks him if he goes around to see how the maquiladora workers live, he answers that this is a matter of course, that he would know his city very well, and that he knows people everywhere and knows that they are in good shape. Instead of looking at the workers at the table asking him questions, he affirms his own statements by nodding his head.

Against this background, it becomes apparent what this film achieves in particular and what the medium of film is capable of achieving in general. A camera can look away, but it can also look and listen and show the physicality and life realities of those who pay the price for the prosperity of others. Carmen and her colleagues built the shacks they live in on their own, often out of garage doors brought from the US that were thrown away. The houses have no foundation and the chemicals from the environment are washed directly under their feet. It is the first thing that Carmen allows herself after the payment of the settlement owed by Sanyo: to have a floor under her and her kids' feet. As we can see in the film, there is no running water and a lack of sewage lines. Puddles are sources of infection. Furthermore, people do not have proper electricity. The officially secured electronic lines supply the factories where saleable products are produced, but not the neighbourhoods where their workers live. While the workers in the factory connect electronic units so that the end devices are safe in any circumstance, at home they hang wires from the big lines manually, to have light in the evening and to listen to the radio. This is very dangerous: when the wires touch each other, they short-circuit and burn. Some children playing in the neighbourhood have already been electrocuted. 'Do you hear how the wires sizzle when they touch water?',[63] Carmen asks the camerawoman holding the microphone. And we listen, and we hear it. It is a sound expressing the constant tension, stress and anxiety of mothers or fathers who know what it means where their children are playing.

Human subjects

Going back to the beginning of the movie, we see 10 female workers in their blue work uniforms during the opening credits. They are lined up in front of an ochre desert background, giving a perfectly choreographed performance around which the camera circles. Synchronised and completely absorbed, they execute the same hand and arm movements in the air, rhythmically, with the utmost precision and care. These must be the gestures they perform every day in the factories. This image is highly ambivalent and forms a metaphor. On the one hand, we see the women acting as single elements of a perfectly working machine and, due to their position in the line and their uniforms, they seem infinitely interchangeable and replaceable at will. This is what they are from the perspective of the abstracting capitalist system. As the women of the neighbourhood and maquiladoras are working for change, the world changes too. In 2001, the global economic crises and the availability of cheaper labour in Asia began to pull the factories away from Tijuana. Carmen, Lourdes and their colleagues lost their jobs. 'Within globalisation, a woman factory worker is like a commodity ... and if that commodity is not productive, if she is not attractive for globalisation because she starts to defend her rights, then they look for that commodity elsewhere.'[64]

On the other hand, despite the seeming homogenisation, the cinematic performance metaphor depicts each woman in her particularity and absolute uniqueness. We will get to know these women better, thanks to the film, which listens to and spends time with them. Each of the several times that this opening image returns, we recognise the individual women better and we recognise the crowd as a group of friends and activists. We know about their daily struggles to ensure their very survival and that of their children and about their common political fight. We know about their lives and families, about the way they speak and listen, the way they laugh and are joyful and proud of their lives and achievements. Through its collaborative manner of production and the way it curates attention, *Maquilápolis* works in every single shot against the object status of its subjects. We hear Vianey Mijangos' voice: 'My work area is called the *clean room*. What I do is: I push the material into the round machine. With one hand I push, with the other

I remove. And I push and remove …' At the same time, she is wondering how everyone is doing at home: 'Did my son get home? How is he? Has he eaten? How are my little girls? Are they outside? Did they do their homework? Are they fighting? And I push, remove, push, remove …'[65] The workers who are treated as numbers by the system are shown as the fully complex characters they are. And by working against the objectification of the women workers, this film also works against the informatisation of media which is due to the same system that commodifies everything by means of abstraction.

Lourdes Luján and the Chilpancingo Collective have finally won their case. 'We took many strong actions and they never responded. Then we started getting international media coverage and they started to worry.'[66] In January 2004, the Mexican government and the US Environmental Protection Agency told them they would provide US$85,000 to begin the clean-up of Metales y Derivados. 'They see that we are strong. So, they are complying with all of our demands. It's like they are afraid of us.' On 24 June, after 10 years of struggle, Governor Eugenio Elorduy, Jerry Clifford, the secretary of the US Environmental Protection Agency, and Lourdes Luján and Marta Cervantes as representatives of the Chilpancingo Collective signed the accord that established the clean-up process from start to finish. As Lourdes Luján reflects: 'I'm struggling to give my kids a healthier, cleaner future. We did win the clean-up of Metales y Derivados but there are hundreds of factories still polluting.'[67]

Due to the finite nature of resources like human bodies, time and the environment, the capitalist plan based on an infinite exploitation of resources has no future. Yet, the collectively organised resistance of the women against their working conditions and against the environmental pollution caused by the factories presents a promising perspective. After their successful fight against their employers, the protagonists literally turn their backs on the exploitative industry, thereby concluding the film. An empty factory becomes a cinematographic metaphor for a new beginning. Sunlight from the outside penetrates the perforated walls of the provisional-looking factory and transforms the interior into a magical chamber. Carmen Durán says in the voice-over:

> Tijuana today has many faces. It is the Tijuana of injustice, of hunger, of insecurity, and of the maquiladora. But it is also the Tijuana of dreams. In the future I'd like to be a lawyer. But that is expensive. I have three kids to support. And I have to work and study.[68]

The initial image of the 10 women in the desert returns, and then we see the women as portraits in close-ups montaged one behind the other, looking directly into the camera. And one by one they turn their backs and step out of the past production line, dismissing or freeing themselves after being fired by the global players.

Notes

1 *Maquilápolis*, directed by Vicky Funari and Sergio de la Torre, Mexico, US, 2006. 68 min. See also the website of the film: http://www.maquilapolis.com (accessed 15 September 2022).
2 See Silvia Federici on the 'gender deal': 'Die Reproduktion der Arbeitskraft im globalen Kapitalismus und die unvollendete feministische Revolution', in: dies.: *Aufstand aus der Küche, Band 1 in der Reihe Kitchen Politics – Queerfeministische Interventionen*, München: Edition Assemblage, 2015, 21–86, 31.
3 Lourdes Luján in *Maquilápolis*.
4 Fraser, 'Behind Marx's Hidden Abode: For an Expanded Conception of Capitalism', 147.
5 Fraser, 'Behind Marx's Hidden Abode: For an Expanded Conception of Capitalism', 147.
6 On the concept and the history of the *promotoras* as activists, see Fernández et al., 'Muxeres en Acción: The Power of Community Cultural Wealth'; Cooke, 'Neoliberal Failures and Everyday Resistance in the Twenty-First Century'; Huesca, 'They are the Experts: A Worker's Agenda for Social Change in Mexico's Maquiladoras'; see also the website of the Maquiladora Health and Safety Support Network, http://mhssn.igc.org (accessed 15 September 2022).
7 The film-makers held a six-week workshop for the women *promotoras*, training them in how to film a documentary and how to use digital video cameras, which they then lent to the women.
8 Lourdes Luján in *Maquilápolis*.
9 Vicky Funari and Sergio de la Torre, 'Production Statement', http://www.maquilapolis.com/project_eng.htm (accessed 15 September 2022).
10 On the concept and practice of 'Deep Listening', see Oliveros, 'Quantum Listening: From Practice to Theory (To Practice Practice)'.
11 Carmen Durán in *Maquilápolis*.
12 See Snodgrass, 'The Bracero Program, 1942–1964'; Berndt, 'Maquiladora', 4, 185–91; Goodman, *The Deportation Machine: America's Long History of Expelling Immigrants*, reviewed by Goodfriend on the NACLA site: https://nacla.org/deportation-machine-review (accessed 15 September 2022).
13 See Federici, 'Women, Globalization and the International Women's Movement', 86; on the accumulation crisis, see Caffentzis, 'The Work/Energy Crisis and the Apocalypse'.
14 See Federici, Introduction to *Revolution at Point Zero*, 9.
15 See Carmen Durán in *Maquilápolis*; Berndt, 'Maquiladora', 185–191; 'Mexican Workers Since NAFTA'.
16 Carmen Durán in *Maquilápolis*.
17 See Morici, 'Free Trade with Mexico', 101; 'Mexican Workers Since NAFTA', 25.
18 Carmen Durán in *Maquilápolis*.
19 See Esteinou, 'The Emergence of the Nuclear Family in Mexico'; Germain, 'Women at Mexico: Beyond Family Planning Acceptors'.
20 See Federici, 'Wages against Housework'; Fraser, 'Behind Marx's Hidden Abode: For an Expanded Conception of Capitalism', 147.
21 Carmen Durán in *Maquilápolis*.
22 Magdalena Cerda in *Maquilápolis*.
23 See Taylor, 'The Abject Bodies of the Maquiladora Female Workers on a Globalized Border'.
24 Magdalena Cerda in *Maquilápolis*.
25 Fraser, 'Behind Marx's Hidden Abode: For an Expanded Conception of Capitalism', 147.
26 Federici, 'The Restructuring of Housework and Reproduction in the United States in the 1970s', 42.

27 See Federici, 'The Restructuring of Housework and Reproduction in the United States in the 1970s', 42; Bock and Duden, 'Work for Love, Love as Work: The Emergence of Housework in Capitalism'; Mariarosa Dalla Costa, 'Reproduzione e emigrazione' Reproduction and Emigration.
28 See Salzinger, *Genders in Production: Making Workers in Mexico's Global Factories*; Livingston, 'Murder in Juárez: Gender, Sexual Violence, and the Global Assembly Line'; Wright, 'From Protests to Politics: Sex Work, Women's Worth, and Ciudad Juárez Modernity'.
29 Delfina Rodriguez in *Maquilápolis*.
30 See Biemann, 'Transnationalität begreifbar machen, Performing the Border', 25.
31 See Berndt, 'Wirtschaftsgeografie. Das Fliessband und die Gewalt'.
32 Carmen Durán in *Maquilápolis*.
33 See Dalla Costa, 'A General Strike'.
34 Sonja Auguiano in *Performing the Border*, directed by Ursula Biemann, CH 1999, 43 min.
35 See Federici, 'Counterplanning from the Kitchen'.
36 See Biemann, 'An die Grenze gehen', 14.
37 See, for example, Piero Sraffa, *Production of Commodities by Means of Commodities*. Cambridge: University Press, 1960.
38 On *cinéma-vérité*, see Rouch. 'Die Kamera und der Mensch'; Hohenberger, *Die Wirklichkeit des Films. Dokumentarfilm. Ethnografischer Film. Jean Rouch*; Fregoso, 'Maquilapolis: An Interview with Vicky Funari and Sergio de la Torre'.
39 Leimbacher, 'Documentary Film and the "Body" of Knowledge'.
40 For a critical discussion of Hardt and Negri's theory of 'Immaterial Labor' and the concept of 'cognitive capitalism', see Federici, 'On affective labor'.
41 See Federici, 'The Reproduction of Labor Power in The Global Economy and The Unfinished Feminist Revolution', 101; on the concept of the 'fabbrica diffusa', see Lazzarato, 'Immaterielle Arbeit. Gesellschaftliche Tätigkeit unter den Bedingungen des Postfordismus', 45; Marchart, *Die Prekarisierungsgesellschaft. Prekäre Proteste. Politik und Ökonomie im Zeichen der Prekarisierung*, 51, 117.
42 Carmen Durán in *Maquilápolis*.
43 See Thanh Bui, 'Glorientalization: Specters of Asia and Feminized Cyborg Workers in the US–Mexico Borderlands'.
44 See the links to 'Mexico-related law and government resources' on the website of the Maquiladora Health and Safety Support Network, http://mhssn.igc.org (accessed 15 September 2022).
45 Lupita Castañeda in *Maquilápolis*.
46 Jaime Cota in *Maquilápolis*.
47 See Sor Juana Inés de la Cruz (1651–1695) in her poem 'You Foolish Men'. The official English translation is: 'Who is more to blame, though either should do wrong? She who sins for pay or he who pays to sin?' https://sorjuanadatabase.wordpress.com/2019/04/29/you-foolish-men (accessed 15 September 2022).
48 Jaime Cota in *Maquilápolis*.
49 See Federici, 'The Reproduction of Labor Power in The Global Economy and The Unfinished Feminist Revolution'.
50 See Federici, 'The Reproduction of Labor Power in The Global Economy and The Unfinished Feminist Revolution'.
51 See Federici, 'The Reproduction of Labor Power in The Global Economy and The Unfinished Feminist Revolution'.
52 Vianey Mijangos in *Maquilápolis*.
53 Lourdes Luján in *Maquilápolis*.
54 Lourdes Luján in *Maquilápolis*.
55 Lourdes Luján in *Maquilápolis*.
56 See 'Metales y Derivados Final Factual Record', NAELP, North American Environmental Law and Policy, Commission for Environmental Cooperation of North America, 2002, http://www.cec.org/publications/metales-y-derivados-factual-record/ (accessed 15 September 2022).
57 See Magdalena Cerda in *Maquilápolis*.
58 Lourdes Luján in *Maquilápolis*.
59 Lourdes Luján in *Maquilápolis*.
60 Lourdes Luján in *Maquilápolis*.

61　Lourdes Luján in *Maquilápolis*.
62　Manuel Garcia Lepe in *Maquilápolis*.
63　Carmen Durán in *Maquilápolis*.
64　Lupita Castañeda in *Maquilápolis*.
65　Vianey Mijangos in *Maquilápolis*.
66　Lourdes Luján in *Maquilápolis*.
67　Lourdes Luján in *Maquilápolis*.
68　Carmen Durán in *Maquilápolis*.

Bibliography

Berndt, Christian. 'Wirtschaftsgeografie. Das Fliessband und die Gewalt', *WOZ. Die Wochenzeitung*, 28 (11 Juli 2013).

Berndt, Christian. 'Maquiladora'. In: *Ortsregister. Ein Glossar zu Räumen der Gegenwart*, edited by Nadine Marquardt and Verena Schreiber, 185–91. Bielefeld: transcript, 2012.

Biemann, Ursula. 'An die Grenze gehen: Ein essayistisches Projekt'. In *Mission Reports. Künstlerische Praxis im Feld*, 9–15. Nürnberg: Verlag für Moderne Kunst, 2012.

Biemann, Ursula. 'Transnationalität begreifbar machen, Performing the Border'. In *Mission Reports. Künstlerische Praxis im Feld*, 17–32. Nürnberg: Verlag für Moderne Kunst, 2012.

Bock, Gisela and Duden, Barbara. 'Arbeit aus Liebe – Liebe als Arbeit: Zur Entstehung der Hausarbeit im Kapitalismus' [Work for Love – Love as Work: The Emergence of Housework in Capitalism], in *Frauen und Wissenschaft*, edited by Gruppe Berliner Dozentinnen, 118–199. Berlin: Courage Verlag, 1977.

Caffentzis, George C. 'The Work/Energy Crisis and the apocalypse'. In: Midnight Notes Collective (Hg.), *Midnight Notes Journal*, 3 (1979), 1–29.

Cooke, Erik. 2008. 'Neoliberal Failures and Everyday Resistance in the Twenty-first Century', *New Political Science* 30/2: 245–50.

Dalla Costa, Mariarosa. 'Reproduzione e emigrazione' [Reproduction and Emigration]. In *L'operaio multinazionale in Europa* [The Multinational Worker in Europe], edited by Alessandro Serafini, 67–96. Milan: Feltrinelli, 1974.

Dalla Costa, Mariarosa. 'A General Strike'. In *The Essential Feminist Reader*, edited by Estelle B. Freedman, 300–3. New York: The Modern Library, 2007.

Esteinou, Rosario. 'The Emergence of the Nuclear Family in Mexico', *International Journal of Sociology of the Family*, 31/1 (Spring 2005), 1–18.

Federici, Silvia. 'On Affective Labor'. In *Cognitive Capitalism, Education and Digital Labor*, edited by Michael A. Peters and Eergin Blut, 57–74. New York: Peter Lang, 2011.

Federici, Silvia. 'Counterplanning from the Kitchen' (1975). In Federici, Silvia. *Revolution at Point Zero: Housework, Reproduction, and Feminist Struggle*, 28–40. Oakland: PM Press, 2012.

Federici, Silvia. 'The Reproduction of Labor Power in The Global Economy and The Unfinished Feminist Revolution' (2008). In Federici, Silvia. *Revolution at Point Zero: Housework, Reproduction, and Feminist Struggle*, 91–111. Oakland: PM Press, 2012.

Federici, Silvia. 'The Restructuring of Housework and Reproduction in the United States in the 1970s' (1980). In Federici, Silvia. *Revolution at Point Zero: Housework, Reproduction, and Feminist Struggle*, 41–53. Oakland: PM Press, 2012.

Federici, Silvia. *Revolution at Point Zero: Housework, Reproduction, and Feminist Struggle*. Oakland: PM Press, 2012.

Federici, Silvia. 'Wages against Housework' (1975). In Federici, Silvia. *Revolution at Point Zero: Housework, Reproduction, and Feminist Struggle*, 15–22. Oakland: PM Press, 2012.

Federici, Silvia. 'Women, Globalization and the International Women's Movement', *Canadian Journal of Development Studies / Revue canadienne d'études du développement* 22 (2001), 1025–1036.

Fernández, J. S., Guzmán, B. L., Bernal, I. and Flores, Y. G. 'Muxeres en Acción: The Power of Community Cultural Wealth in Latinas Organizing for Health Equity', *American Journal of Community Psychology* 66 (2020): 314–24.

Fraser, Nancy. 'Behind Marx's Hidden Abode: For an Expanded Conception of Capitalism'. In *Critical Theory in Critical Times: Transforming the Global Political and Economic Order*, edited by Penelope Deutscher und Christina Lafont, 141–59. New York: Columbia University Press, 2017.

Fregoso, Rosa-Linda. 'Maquilapolis: An Interview with Vicky Funari and Sergio de la Torre', *Camera Obscura* 74 (2010): 173–81.
Germain, Adrienne. 'Women at Mexico: Beyond Family Planning Acceptors', *Family Planning Perspectives* 7/5 (1975), 235–8.
Goodman, Adam. *The Deportation Machine: America's Long History of Expelling Immigrants.* Princeton, NJ: Princeton University Press, 2020. Reviewed by Goodfriend on the NACLA site: https://nacla.org/deportation-machine-review (accessed 15 September 2022).
Hohenberger, Eva. *Die Wirklichkeit des Films. Dokumentarfilm. Ethnografischer Film. Jean Rouch,* Hildesheim: Georg Olms Verlag, 1988.
Huesca, Robert. 'They are the Experts: A Worker's Agenda for Social Change in Mexico's Maquiladoras', *Canadian Journal of Latin American and Caribbean Studies*, 31 (2006), 131–165.
Lazzarato, Maurizio. 'Immaterielle Arbeit. Gesellschaftliche Tätigkeit unter den Bedingungen des Postfordismus'. In *Umherschweifende Produzenten. Immaterielle Arbeit und Subversion*, edited by Toni Negri, Maurizio Lazzarato and Paolo Virno, 39–52. Berlin: ID Verlag, 1998.
Leimbacher, Irina. 'Documentary Film and the "Body" of Knowledge', *Critica Sociologica* 166 (2008), 26–38.
Livingston, Jessica. 'Murder in Juárez: Gender, Sexual Violence, and the Global Assembly Line', *Frontiers: A Journal of Women Studies*, 25/1 (2004), 59–76.
Marchart, Oliver. *Die Prekarisierungsgesellschaft. Prekäre Proteste. Politik und Ökonomie im Zeichen der Prekarisierung*. Bielefeld: Transcript, 2013.
'Mexican Workers Since NAFTA', *NACLA Report on the Americas* 39/1 (2005), 15.
Morici, Peter. 'Free Trade with Mexico', *Foreign Policy* 87 (1992), 88–104.
Oliveros, Pauline. 'Quantum Listening: From Practice to Theory (To Practice Practice)', December 1999. Accessed 5 September 2022. https://www.deeplistening.rpi.edu/deep-listening/.
Rouch, Jean. 'Die Kamera und der Mensch', *Kinemathek* 56 (1978), 2–22.
Salzinger, Leslie. *Genders in Production: Making Workers in Mexico's Global Factories.* Berkeley: University of California Press, 2003.
Snodgrass, Michael. 'The Bracero Program, 1942–1964'. In *Beyond the Border: The History of Mexican-U.S. Migration*, edited by Mark Overmyer-Velásquez, 79–102. New York: Oxford University Press, 2011.
Taylor, Guadalupe: 'The Abject Bodies of the Maquiladora Female Workers on a Globalized Border', *Race, Gender & Class*, 17/3 (2010), 349–63.
Thanh Bui, Long. 'Glorientalization: Specters of Asia and Feminized Cyborg Workers in the US–Mexico Borderlands', *Meridians*, 13/1 (2015), 129–56.
Wright, Melissa W. 'From Protests to Politics: Sex Work, Women's Worth, and Ciudad Juárez', *Modernity Annals of the Association of American Geographers*, 94/2 (2004), 369–86.

Part III
Manipulating labour relations

Graphic novel © Monika Lang, 2021–2022

NEGOTIATING THE TERMS OF WAGE(LESS) LABOUR

11
Negotiating the terms of wage(less) labour: free and freed workers as contractual parties in nineteenth-century Rio de Janeiro

Marjorie Carvalho de Souza

Artistic expeditions that traversed Brazil from north to south during the nineteenth century, driven by scientific interests or naturalistic curiosities, produced an enormous volume of pictorial records and travel accounts whose representations nourished for a long time the imagery and imagination around the world of the largest slaveholding society in the Americas.[1] Besides recording with wonder and astonishment aspects of the exuberant Brazilian fauna and flora, foreign designers, lithographers, printmakers and painters also portrayed the daily life of cities and towns. In these scenarios, the heterogeneous and conspicuous presence of workers with different nativities, ethnicities, legal status and professions did not go unnoticed.

Even if the nuances of the social and legal conditions of the people living in the urban space were difficult to perceive for these portrayers,[2] many of them nonetheless tried to depict the coexistence of workers with different legal statuses in the exercise of the same tasks and jobs. This is the case, for example, in the lithograph *Encaissage et pesage du sucre* (Figure 11.1),[3] made in 1861 by the French engraver Philippe Benoist, based on a photograph by Jean-Victor Frond. In this image, both freed and enslaved black labourers weigh and pack sugar, but they are distinguished by their clothing and footwear: the former are portrayed wearing shoes (an emblem of social ascension), while the latter go barefoot. Sometimes not distinguishable by any visible marker, enslaved, free and freed labourers worked alongside one another throughout the streets of Rio de Janeiro.

In recent years, a growing scholarship that combines visual and written sources has been devoted precisely to demonstrating that,

Figure 11.1 Philippe Benoist and Jean-Victor Frond, *Encaissage et pesage du sucre*, 1861. Lithograph on paper, 63.5 × 47.9 cm. Frond's photograph engraved by Benoist portrays slave and freed workers weighing and boxing sugar in the streets of Rio de Janeiro, distinguished by the use or lack of shoes, an iconographic sign of social distinction. Public domain, reproduced courtesy of Biblioteca Nacional Digital of Brazil.

until the eve of abolition, this combination of legal statuses was the most characteristic picture both in the rural enterprises of the plantations and in the manufacturing sites and emerging factories in the urban centres of Brazil.[4] The workforce included African- or Brazilian-born enslaved people, freedpeople (who had formerly been enslaved) and legally free White nationals and European immigrants. Beyond the different civil and political rights that people who were classified as 'enslaved', 'freed' and 'free' had by virtue of constitutional law,[5] the first legislative measures enacted after independence from Portugal in 1822 to regulate work also insisted on distinguishing workers by their nativity and ethnicity. This led to the creation of special contractual labour regimes with particular coercive elements for foreign immigrants, and to the exclusion of African-born people from the scope of the new legislation.

While legal historians have for a long time followed closely these official clear-cut categories to explore the access and non-access of workers to state-regulated contracts, this chapter departs from a puzzling empirical observation: the public notary offices of Rio de Janeiro, where hundreds of labour agreements were registered, were frequented by labourers of all kinds of legal statuses, places of origins and occupations. Even more striking, these people used the same legal language and appeared on the pages of the very same notarial books. Did they have more in common than the law intended? Judging from the diversity of remuneration and working conditions captured in these deeds, did working men and women of different backgrounds have the possibility to contest restrictions and exploitation? Were some of them, against all odds, able to use work contracts to negotiate wages and working conditions?

Drawing on the notarial books of the First Notary Office of Rio de Janeiro that I have accessed in the National Archive, this source-led study explores labour contracts as tools of coercion and of opportunity between 1830, when the first Brazilian law on labour contracts was enacted, and 1888, when slavery was abolished.[6] In the first part, I focus on eight labour contracts (which involved 18 workers) from a total documental set of 129 deeds found, the only ones among the sources consulted to correspond exactly to the targets par excellence of the new national labour legislation: unskilled European workers – so-called 'colonists'[7] – brought in to substitute for the enslaved workforce. In the second part, I examine labour contracts of freedmen, which they entered into in order to pay off the debts for purchasing their freedom. These represent the overwhelming majority (96 out of 129) of the labour contracts found in that public office. Through a closer look at this polychromatic and variegated collection, fixed patterns or ideal legal types of 'free' and 'unfree' work contracts disappear, unearthing indebtment backed up by law as a powerful tool to continue existing coercive relations as well as to create new ones.

Wage(less) freedom

On 13 January 1842, nine boys from the islands of Faial and São Miguel in the Azores, aged 12 to 16, appeared before the clerk of the First Notary Office of Rio de Janeiro to jointly register their work arrangements with the assistance of the Curator of Colonists (*Curador dos Colonos*), Francisco Thomas de Figueiredo Neves. In their deed of rental of services, they stated that they had arrived in the Empire's capital with the Brazilian ship *Saudade*, owing their fares to the ship's captain, and having no money with which to pay him. Having previously agreed with Luiz Correa de Azevedo, owner of the farm União in a rural village in the east-central area of the State of Rio de Janeiro, that he would pay for their fares, all the boys committed to offset their debts by providing the creditor with 'all their farming and cultivation services for three years'. During that period, no additional monetary remuneration was stipulated for them, with the lessee providing only 'the clothing and covering necessary to preserve them from cold', 'healthy and sufficient food for their nourishment' and 'treatment in their sicknesses with charity and zeal'.[8]

The public office where the young workers presented themselves was the first Notary Office created in Brazil,[9] and their contract of 1842 was the first deed recorded by foreign workers in its notarial books. Seven other contracts of Portuguese immigrants were registered by the same notary in the following decade. Despite Brazilian immigration politics, in view of the illegalisation of the transatlantic slave trade,[10] aimed to attract legally free workers from the entire European continent, labourers from Portugal and its impoverished islands formed the largest portion of colonists arriving in Rio de Janeiro, even decades after Independence. It is estimated that between 1851 and 1854, when about 33,000 migrants arrived in the Brazilian capital, 79.7 per cent of them (over 26,000 workers) came from Portugal.[11] The contracts of colonists found in the First Notary Office, such as the one of the nine boys from the Azores, attest to the 'chains of debt and coercion'[12] that structured the lives of many of the immigrant workers who went to Brazil. Trapped in debts incurred by the ship passage, they were obliged to provide 'services' for the employer-creditors who had advanced the travel expenses for the passage, often for years with no, or almost no, monetary remuneration.

Like the nine boys, João Tavares, a 10-year-old native also of São Miguel, committed himself in the same year, 1842, 'to every service compatible with his strength and age'.[13] Antonio Simões, 18 years old, born in the Third Island,[14] and José Antonio Amaro, 15 or 16 years old, from the Faial Island,[15] obliged themselves in 1843 to 'serve' their identical employer, who simultaneously was their creditor. In the same year, João Pedro D'Aguiar[16] accepted the obligation to render 'his services' in return for his passage from São Miguel Island, and João Pereira,[17] 18 years old, coming from the same place and arriving at Rio only a few weeks later, declared that 'his services were mortgaged' for the same purpose. Jozé dos Santos from Island Gracioza committed himself to compensate his passage with 'his services as a Creole' – a possible allusion to the service performed by Black enslaved people[18] – an obligation he assumed, according to the paper he signed, 'of his own free and spontaneous will'[19] in 1845. Remarkable in these formulations are the vague and general descriptions of the work awaiting the young migrants, which left it to the employer's discretion what type and amount of service was compatible with, or within the limits of, the worker's strength.

All colonists declared themselves to have entered their work arrangements to pay off the costs of their travels. These expenses were paid upon their arrival by their new employers and contractors directly to the ship captains; and the amount ended up structuring the duration of the upcoming work relation. For most of them, such as the nine boys from the islands of Faial and São Miguel, those arrangements meant receiving no remuneration beyond food, clothing and health care for the entire duration of the contract. The duration was determined based on a fictitious monthly salary that would, over time, pay off the entirety of the debt. In a few cases, only half the monthly salary would be used to amortise debt, while the other half was paid out to the worker 'for private expenses'. This monthly available sum often corresponded to the average amount received for a mere single day's work by a skilled manual labourer in Rio de Janeiro in the mid-century.[20] That this amount was too low is evidenced in one of the contracts, which predicted that the worker in question would likely require more money to live. If the case occurred that the lessee lent him additional money, this would likewise be added to the overall debt, further extending the period of (almost) wageless labour to which he would be subjected.[21]

Existing legislation, with its harsh penalties for breach of contract and severe mechanisms of contract enforcement, made it almost impossible for immigrant workers to get out of their bonds with their employer-creditors. In 1830, only eight years after Independence, Brazil enacted its first national law on labour contracts, applicable in principle to both Brazilian and foreign workers. It was intended to establish and regulate a labour force consisting of legally free people, including native, but especially White immigrant workers. In this regard, the law adopted quite a liberal contractual language. Yet, it also contained an exclusion of one category of workers from its ambit of application: the last article explicitly rejected *africanos bárbaros*, Black people born in Africa.[22] This made the 1830 statute not only a matter of workforce supply, but also a racial choice about how the envisioned 'transition to free labour' should look like If the arrival of Black enslaved workers was no longer allowed, neither were they welcome as free workers, as one of the deputies discussing the bill clearly stated: 'Black people are considered harmful to Brazil, not because they are slaves, but because they are Black.'[23]

That labour became one of the focal points of state reforms in postcolonial Brazil is not surprising in the context of the Atlantic pressures of the beginning of the century.[24] The rising prominence of Britain's crusade against the African slave trade led to important legal reforms in labour policies all over the continent. While many other countries, however, came to abolish slavery between the 1820s and the 1860s, it took Brazil until 1888 to end this institution. After all, it was a period of trial and error, as several laws did not prove to have the intended effect and had to be amended and reissued. In the case of the law of 1830, politicians and investors involved with migration policies soon came to see it as inadequate to regulate the written contracts with the colonists. And so, a second legislation on labour contracts was enacted only seven years after the first one. Under the initiative of the Sociedade Promotora da Colonisação do Rio de Janeiro, a private company founded in the capital of the Empire in 1836,[25] law no. 108 was approved on 11 October 1837, this time containing various measures on the provision of services exclusively involving colonists.[26] All contracts with foreign workers were henceforth tied to this particular law to regulate their labour relations.

The first statute of 1830 already contained unprecedented contract enforcement mechanisms. The most notable was that prison sentences, which were applied for interrupting the contract before the end of the fixed term, could be levied not only on workers but also on employers if they failed to pay the due amount to the workers. This amount included that due for services rendered plus half of the contracted remuneration and was predicted to prevent either party from breaching its reciprocal obligations established by the contract. At the same time, it left several important aspects of work relationships unregulated, including working hours or a possible termination of the employment relation.

The second labour legislation of 1837 was thus meant to expand and refine several legal means of control to the disadvantage of White immigrants. On the one hand, provision for sanctioning employers completely disappeared from the new regulation. For the worker-lessor, on the other hand, the penalties for breach of contract became noticeably more severe. The worker was now obliged to indemnify the employer not only when fired for a misconduct[27] but also in the case of quitting without what was phrased as 'just cause',[28] a concept that did not exist in the previous regulation. In the latter case, of justified dismissal by the employer, the worker was obliged to pay whatever was owed immediately, under the penalty of being arrested and sentenced to labour in the public works or to imprisonment with work (article 8). If the worker resisted, they would be arrested by the justice of peace wherever they were found and would remain in jail until they paid the lessee everything *in double* or served him without any financial remuneration for the entire time remaining to complete the contract (article 9). Despite the strictness of the 1837 law, which might have discouraged many from entering such a repressive employment relation, many young Portuguese workers, especially from the islands,[29] had no choice but to accept these conditions as their only ticket to a life on the new continent.

From the perspective of the Brazilian employers and legislators, the new regulation targeted the mobility of White immigrants for the time stipulated in the labour contract, and presented a clear restriction of migrants' mobility once landed in Brazil. The threat of imprisonment coupled with the doubling of debts ended up creating almost insurmountable obstacles to the termination of the contract, depriving the workers of the possibility of seeking alternative occupations or employers. Apart from running away, the only option left for the colonists to change their position was finding someone willing to assume their outstanding debt and become their new employer, which also included the function of a new creditor. This was likewise only possible with the consent of the former one. Indeed, one of the contracts in the notary book was registered by a colonist who resorted to a third party to negotiate an employment switch. Thomaz Jozé de Castro, creditor of Antonio Simões due to his travelling to Rio, had given him permission to look for a new contract with someone else. Joaquim Rodrigues da Costa showed himself willing to advance the payment still owed and accepted Antonio Simões to serve him for two years 'in any service that is compatible with his strength'. Simões, in return, obliged himself to serve his new lessee, subjecting himself, as all the other colonists mentioned, 'in everything and for everything to the provisions of the Law of 11 October 1837', of which he declared himself to be 'already aware because it was read to him'.[30]

Despite the small spaces of autonomy that individuals like Simões were able to craft, labour legislation in the 1830s clearly assured employers that immigrant White workers for whose arrival in Brazil they had made advance payments did not enter the 'free' labour market but remained bound for a significant length of time. As the involvement of the private Sociedade Promotora da Colonisação emphasises, these measures were designed to safeguard private investments in foreign labour migration, and the 'law of colonists' was the most blatant manifestation of this political agenda. However, while it expressly targeted colonists, notarial records from around the country[31] show that it came also to be applied to Black people, who experienced and even benefited from those same legal mechanisms from a quite different – but not completely opposite – legal and social position.

Freedom indebted

Neither Jean-Victor Frond nor the other travellers who visited Rio de Janeiro overlooked the fact that enslaved people performed the most diverse activities in the city, to the point of making it the scene of the richest extant pictorial record of slavery in Latin America.[32] Black enslaved women and men were key actors in the city's operations, being engaged in the production, collection and transportation of foodstuffs and goods, as well as the transportation of people; acting as factory workers and skilled craftsmen and artisans; being employed as 'printers, lithographers, painters, sculptors, orchestral musicians, nurses, midwives, barber-surgeons, seamstresses and tailors, goldworkers, gemcutters, butchers, bakers, sailors, ships' pilots, coachmen, stevedores, fishermen, hunters, naturalists and gardeners',[33] to name but a few of the extraordinarily varied functions they performed.

The strong presence of enslaved people began in the colonial period. Rio de Janeiro became the seat of colonial power in 1763 and later was transformed into the Court of the Lusitanian Empire (1808), becoming the first and only colonial city to host an overseas empire. This political visibility of the city was accompanied by intensified economic networks, making Rio de Janeiro one of the main destination ports of the transatlantic slave trade.[34] But it was not only a port of arrival. Especially after the transfer of the Portuguese royal family, the city remarkably intensified its reliance on the labour of enslaved people to implement a series of urban reforms.[35] While the majority of enslaved Africans did not remain in the city, enough were kept there to make Rio de Janeiro the main slave city of the Americas. At mid-nineteenth century, the number of enslaved people reached 80,000 and represented 40 per cent of Rio de Janeiro's population.[36]

In terms of both the diversified roles they played and also their numerical presence, the intensive employment of enslaved people impacted the landscape and functioning of the city.[37] For urban slaves, there were greater possibilities of hiring out their labour and being afforded different scopes of action and degrees of mobility compared to their counterparts on the plantations.[38] It was not uncommon in the cities and town centres of Brazil for enslaved people to have access to cash and market credit, act as commercial producers and consumers, own property, realise contracts and perform juridical acts in their everyday life. Many of these legal acts were in principle incompatible with their legal status as slaves but were daily practised, even in the context of financial or administrative institutions.[39]

One of the possibilities for legal action taken by enslaved workers was the registration of labour contracts in notary offices in the context of a manumission agreement. Having received loans from third parties for the purchase of their freedom, or sometimes contracting directly with their former masters or mistresses, these individuals signed labour contracts to compensate in services the purchase price of their manumission. By advancing this amount, they immediately received a certificate of unconditional freedom, and once 'in the enjoyment of freedom', by virtue and under the conditions of a separate legal act – the contract – they would compensate with services for the price of the self-purchased manumission. Among the 129 deeds in the notary book of the First Notary Office, which only registered a portion of all formalised transactions in the city, 96 were contracted by freed workers and, out of these, 93 were expressly associated with a manumission debt.

The two features highlighted in the contracts of Portuguese immigrants – the generality of the services rendered and the almost complete absorption of any monetary remuneration by debt – appear again as relevant aspects when turning to freed workers' contracts. Yet, this absence of money payment was not an absolute condition, even though it was an essential part of 81 out of 96 deeds. That 15 of the 96 freedpeople deeds provided for monetary wages shows how the negotiation around salary was nevertheless an open field of dispute.[40] The Black tinsmith Januario, hired on 30 October 1876, was to compensate the loan with which he bought his freedom with services, but he would still be paid 12,000 *réis* per month, having free 'the holydays, death celebrations or evenings'.[41] Belisia, committing to render 'the services the grantee needs' on 28 April 1869, was to pay in this way the price of her manumission, but would also receive 14,000 *réis* in Brazilian currency or seven pesos of Spanish currency at the end of each month.[42] That Januario was a skilled labourer and Belisia a domestic worker shows that the ability to bargain for one's own wage was not strictly or exclusively associated with professional specialisation. Other factors, such as personal relationships with one's employer, could also increase the worker's bargaining capacity. Perhaps this explains why, besides the salary, Belisia was additionally provided with lodging, food and medical care by her employer. Januario instead would only receive his work clothes.

Even among deeds in which no monetary retribution was foreseen, it was not rare to find it expressed or implied that the freedwomen and men could earn income in another way. Lucas owed the amount of 1,000,000 *réis* to João Maria Collação de Magalhães, who 'did him the favour of lending him in advance so he could obtain, as he obtained, his freedom from his master Francisco de Freitas'. Lucas committed himself on 6 October 1842 to work as a carpenter's officer at the lessee's property, with his services evaluated at 800 *réis* per day, until the effective payment of his debt. In this agreement, he was able to keep the salary of his Sunday and holiday labour. He could not, however, work on those holy days in other works than those of the lessee or his order.[43] Many others were incentivised to work in whatever jobs they could find, having 'the right to redeem this debt with money as soon as you have it, discounting the time you have served', as another deed reads.[44] It was 'understood that if it is possible for [the freedworker] to increase the monthly instalments, this increase will be taken into account',[45] expressly suggesting that freed labourers were able to accumulate extra income, even if formally 'all their services' were foreseen as being for the benefit of the employer-creditor. While we have to consider the limitations of freedwomen and -men in negotiating for wages, disposing of their own time and registering their preferences in a labour contract, the ability of workers who were just emerging from the world of slavery to influence their working conditions should not be underestimated, as the case of Belisia most clearly shows.

While it is true that in most of the freedpeople's contracts, a wageless life continued to be the norm, each of these contracts presupposed unique negotiations which were translated in unique ways. This becomes obvious when observing how very similar work could be valued at very different prices, decisively impacting the number of years for which the labourer would be compelled to provide services. While Dionizio José Elias, who had to pay the price of 400,000 *réis* for his manumission, obliged himself in 1861 to serve the Reverend Friar Francisco do Amor Divino, a Carmelite religious, for no less than nine years,[46] on the same day, in the same notary office, the freed Leopoldina rented 'her services' – described in an equally generic way, which suggests that both were unskilled workers – to pay for a manumission valued at a price almost five times higher, 1,900,000 *réis*, for the much shorter period of only five years, three months and ten days.[47]

Moreover, when no wages were stipulated beyond the compensation of debt, many other aspects of the working relationship were subject to negotiation and varied greatly from one deed to another. Most of the freedmen's deeds (61 out of 96) mentioned the provision of some or all of the basic necessities of survival (clothing, food, housing and treatment for illness), advantages that were sometimes stated in the most typical logic of paternalism, as obligations 'of a good master to his servants'[48] or of treatment 'as a member of the family',[49] and sometimes as a treatment of 'humanity appropriate to his condition of a free man'.[50] Even from unequal bargaining positions, these workers discussed and negotiated the terms and conditions of their work as active parties in their freedom deals, pressing for time, housing, food and health care. This shows that these agreements were the product of bilateral – although unbalanced – negotiations and mutual calculus of opportuneness, aimed at guaranteeing, even temporarily, a non-conflictual stability over the reception and provision of services.

This becomes apparent when reading one of these deeds more carefully, the 'Escriptura de contracto de locação de serviços', signed between the *parda*[51] Carolina and Caetano José de Paiva on 30 October 1871. Caetano and Carolina, once master and slave shortly before they became lessee and lessor before a notary public, also faced each other as appellant and defendant in the courts of Rio de Janeiro. Caetano, who had acquired Carolina from her former mistress, Anna Rosa de Jesus, was appealing against a sentence enacted by the municipal judge of the city in favour of a freedom suit brought by Carolina against Anna Rosa. Carolina alleged that her former owner, instead of assigning her to domestic service, 'had subjected her to an illicit life'. Caetano, who was now Carolina's master, filed an appeal against the decision with the intention of keeping her as a slave. Carolina then asked him to drop the suit in exchange for the promise that she would provide him with all domestic services for four years as compensation for the amount she had cost. The contract that Carolina and Caetano signed subsequently states that she 'thought it more reasonable and convenient for her interests to appeal to the lessee's generosity', considering 'that the appeal filed by the lessee against the sentence could not fail to have the effect of revoking it'.[52] The decision in her favour was thus doubtful,[53] and the uncertainty as to the success of the claim made negotiation a safer alternative: she would indemnify her price by negotiating her services, 'now that she is in full enjoyment of her freedom', and would do it 'in the form of the law of 11 October 1837, to whose conditions, penalties and jurisdiction she is subject'.

This concrete embedment of the law of 1837 was anything but casual. The expressed linkage with the law's 'penalties' and 'jurisdictions' recalled the specific coercive framework it constructed around colonists – a framework, as we saw, which was clearly aimed at protecting the employer's position and preventing the worker from evading the contract, and which it was in the employer's interest to extend over freedmen to ensure that they would have the same control mechanisms over them that they enjoyed over free migrant workers. Nonetheless, Carolina, and many freedwomen and -men like her, also found some 'convenience for their interests' in invoking it, as it opened up an alternative legal path to freedom for them.

It was the way in which they were to obtain a loan that paid their complete price of manumission, giving them an immediate and unconditional certificate of freedom. The provision of services to compensate this debt would be negotiated through a second act, a labour contract, and possible disputes over noncompliance with this contract would be subject to the rules and penalties provided for legally free workers. While conditionally manumitted slaves remained potential victims of re-enslavement during the whole century, an unconditionally manumitted slave who signed a labour contract could not have his or her freedom revoked just because of a breach of contract. That is why this path to freedom was so attractive: by separating into two different acts (a) the manumission (bought *una tantum* by the former slave through a loan) and (b) the contract which reimbursed the debt, the freedwoman or -man could be compelled to comply with the pact under the punitive mechanisms of the 1837 law (even with prison), but could not be re-enslaved anymore. Making manumission and the provision of services two separated acts meant that slave men and women like Carolina could finally be exempted from the re-enslavement threat. Thus the enforcement mechanisms of the law of colonists, initially conceived as a tool of coercion against free immigrant workers, ended up serving as a new path to freedom.

Conclusion

The notarial version of the contract, mediated by the notary's legal ventriloquism, is only the formal and initial record of a commitment, often expressed in the succinct form of an unbalanced bargain, and not necessarily the faithful portrayal of a continued experience. Nonetheless it offers testimony to concrete negotiations and the possibilities of legal action available to both parties. Notarial records provide proof that people of different legal statuses used the same legal instrument to register their work arrangements. A strict opposition between 'free' and 'unfree' labour, especially one based on the formal status a worker enjoyed under the law, misleads about the realities of both. The analysis of labour contracts has shown that not only their social but also their legal experiences were much closer to one another than legal historiography has hitherto assumed.

This chapter has shown that financial compensation was not uncommon for enslaved people, just as the absence of remuneration was not infrequent for free-born workers. As much as a legally free status could be associated with debt bondage, such as in the case of foreign immigrants (colonists), slavery practices accommodated wages and private property, and on this basis allowed many enslaved workers to acquire manumission by contracting their labour for a fixed period of time. In these written records, the frequent invocation by freed workers of legislative references from which they were expressly excluded underlines the constructedness of historiographical binaries based on legal distinctions of status and statutes and, ultimately, of the broader opposition between the law and social practice.[54]

Notes

1. On the abundant artistic and literary productions of travellers in nineteenth-century Brazil, see Barreiros, *Imaginário e viajantes no Brasil do século XIX*, especially the chapter on work and production ('trabalho e produção'), 137–78.
2. For some of the criticisms around the aesthetic stereotypes which marked this artistic production, see Rodrigues, 'Aspectos da escravidão brasileira', 2018.
3. Benoist and Frond, *Encaissage et pesage du sacre*, 54.
4. For a few crucial readings, see Espada Lima, 'Enslaved and Free Workers and the Growth of the Working Class in Brazil', 13; Mattos, *Laborers and Enslaved Workers*; Vitorino, 'Operários livres e cativos nas manufaturas: Rio de Janeiro, segunda metade do século XIX', 7.
5. The Constitution of the Independent Nation of 1824, while pointing to a liberal renewal of the legal system, also tried to reinforce distinctions of 'status' in the most typical logic of the *Ancien Régime*. While foreign and enslaved people were completely excluded from the nation's social body, freed people born in Brazil could vote only in primary and local elections, being excluded from the national elections to the Deputy and Senate Chambers and being completely ineligible to work as public servants. For the freed people born in Africa, there was no legal provision for becoming citizens after manumission, and some historians affirm that they were neither foreigners nor citizens, but instead were kept in the condition of statelessness; see Mamigonian, 'Os direitos dos libertos africanos no Brasil oitocentista: entre razões de direito e considerações políticas', 2015.
6. All of them have been scanned by the Brazilian National Archives and are available online on the *National Archives' Information System (SIAN)*, catalogued as BR RJANRIO 5D.0.LNO, notarial books n. 234 to 395, http://sian.an.gov.br.
7. European migrants brought in to work mainly in agricultural activities in the nineteenth century are referred to by both Brazilian legislation and historiography as 'colonos' in Portuguese. Throughout this chapter, I refer to them with the English translation of 'colonists'.

8 'Escriptura de locação de serviços que fazem Jozé Pereira e outros colonnos por seu Curador auctorisados à Luiz Corrêa de Azevedo', Livro 249 do 1o Ofício de Notas do Rio de Janeiro, tabelião: João Gomes Guimarães d'Aguiar, 13/01/1842, fls. 50r–50v.

9 This public office, created in the same act as the city foundation, was founded in 1565, under the initiative of the colonial government. Between 1830 and 1874 (when four new notary offices were founded in Rio de Janeiro), the city counted only three other notary offices. For the purposes of this research and aiming to cover a timeframe of almost six decades, I decided to focus on the first and oldest notary's office. For the history of Rio de Janeiro's colonial notary offices, see Macedo, *Tabeliães do Rio de Janeiro do 1º ao 4º Ofício de Notas: 1565–1822*.

10 In 1826 Brazil had signed a bilateral anti-trafficking treaty with the British government stipulating the year 1830 as the deadline for the abolition of the transatlantic trade of enslaved Africans. This measure – that would prove to be less effective than it promised – put at imminent risk the then most important source of workforce for Brazilian plantations, still profoundly reliant on slavery, and created great anxieties among planters about the alternatives to slave labour. Government initiatives to attract White European workers were a much older practice in Brazil, but it was only in those times that it became the 'panacea for all national problems'; see Meléndez, 'Reconsidering Colonization Policy in Imperial Brazil: The Regency Years and the World Beyond', 2014.

11 The estimations are from Luiz Felipe de Alencastro, based on documents preserved in the National Archives of the Torre do Tombo, in Portugal, in the fund 'Consulate of Portugal in Rio de Janeiro'; see Alencastro, 'Proletários e escravos. Imigrantes portugueses e cativos africanos no Rio de Janeiro, 1850–1872', 1988, 38. For the time period between 1842 (when the first contract of this study was registered) and 1856 (when the last one was recorded), Alencastro estimates that about 73,000 Portuguese arrived in Rio de Janeiro; see Alencastro, 'Proletários e escravos. Imigrantes portugueses e cativos africanos no Rio de Janeiro, 1850–1872', 52. See also Nunes, 'Portuguese Migration to Rio de Janeiro', 2000, 37–61.

12 The expression is borrowed from historian Joseli Nunes Mendonça, with reference to the extensive and complex chain of investments involved in the process of labour migration, including authorities of the country of origin, European and Brazilian shippers, and – as the final link in the chain – plantation owners; see Mendonça, 'On Chains and Coercion: Labor Experiences in South-Central Brazil in the Nineteenth Century', 2012.

13 'Escriptura de locação de serviços que faz João Tavares por seu curador ao Doutor Jozé Pereira Rego', Livro 249 do *1º Ofício de Notas do Rio de Janeiro,* tabelião: João Gomes Guimarães d'Aguiar, 07/10/1842, fls. 247r–247v.

14 'Escriptura de locação de serviços que faz Antonio Simões authorizado pelo Dr. Curador Geral dos Órfãos por ser menor de vinte hum annos á Joaquim Rodrigues da Costa', Livro 251 do *1º Ofício de Notas do Rio de Janeiro,* tabelião: Francisco Antonio Machado no impedimento de João Gomes Guerra de Aguiar, 28/07/1843, fls. 1r–1v.

15 'Escriptura de locação de serviços que faz José Antonio Amaro pelo tempo de três anos a Joaquim Rodrigues da Costa', Livro n. 251, do *1º Ofício de Notas do Rio de Janeiro,* tabelião: João Gomes Guimarães d'Aguiar, 15/09/1843, fls. 30r–30v.

16 'Escriptura de locação de serviços que faz João Pedro d'Aguiar a José Moutinho dos Reis', Livro 250 do *1º Ofício de Notas do Rio de Janeiro,* tabelião: João Gomes Guimarães d'Aguiar, 04/02/1843, fls. 89v–90r.

17 'Escriptura de locação de serviços que faz o colono João Pereira a Luiz Antonio Amaral', Livro 250 do *1º Ofício de Notas do Rio de Janeiro,* tabelião: João Gomes Guimarães d'Aguiar, 14/03/1843, fls. 127r–127v.

18 In nineteenth-century Brazil, the term *crioulo* generally applied to Black enslaved freed people born in Brazil, in contrast to those born in Africa, usually called *boçal* (when recently arrived) or *bárbaro* ('barbarous'). On the designations of enslaved and freed people of colour in Brazil, see Karasch, *Slave Life in Rio de Janeiro, 1808–1850*, 4–8; Macedo, *Tabeliães do Rio de Janeiro do 1º ao 4º Ofício de Notas: 1565–1822*.

19 'Escriptura de locação de serviços que faz o colono Joze dos Santos ao Dr. Jozé Coelho d'Almeida', Livro 254 do *1º Ofício de Notas do Rio de Janeiro,* tabelião: Francisco Antonio Azevedo no impedimento de João Gomes Guimarães d'Aguiar, 23/01/1845, fls. 25–25v.

20 Nineteenth-century Brazilian currency was *mil réis*, or a thousand *réis* (1$000). Historians estimate that by mid-century two units of *réis* were the average day's pay for a skilled manual labourer; see Espada Lima, '"Until the Day of His Death": Aging, Slavery and Dependency in

Nineteenth-Century Brazil', 2021, 72. In the contracts mentioned here, the average salary remaining after the monthly deduction of the debt instalment varied from two to a maximum of eight thousand *réis* per month, which was often presented as sufficient for 'private expenses'.
21 'Escriptura de locação de serviços que faz João Pedro d'Aguiar a José Moutinho dos Reis', 1843, fl. 89v.
22 The original sentence reads: 'Art. 7o. O contracto mantido pela presente Lei não poderá celebrar-se, debaixo de qualquer pretexto que seja, com os africanos barbaros, á excepção daquelles, que actualmente existem no Brazil'. Law of 13 September 1830, *Colecção das Leis do Império do Brasil* – 1830, 32–3.
23 In the session on 25 August 1830, Deputy Paulino de Albuquerque declared: 'Estou persuadido que a raça do Brazil venha a ser algum dia a unica e fazer desapparecer esta raça de homens pardos; pois que elles não são nocivos ao Brazil na qualidade de escravos, mas sim na qualidade de pardos'. *Annaes do Parlamento Brazileiro – Cammara dos Srs. Deputados, v. 2* (Rio de Janeiro, 1878), 426.
24 On the pivotal role of the labour question in the changing legal context of early nineteenth-century Brazil, see Dantas and Costa, 'O "pomposo nome de liberdade do cidadão": tentativas de arregimentação e coerção da mão-de-obra livre no Império do Brasil', 2016; Espada Lima, 'Trabalho e lei para os libertos na ilha de Santa Catarina no século XIX: arranjos e contratos entre autonomia e a domesticidade', 2006.
25 The company was officially created in January 1836, on the initiative of the Sociedade Auxiliadora da Indústria Nacional (SAIN), an intellectual association focused on the modernisation of productive activities in the Empire of Brazil, just six months before the bill was submitted to the Chamber of Deputies; see Meléndez, 'The Business of Peopling', 274.
26 The title of the original law declared this target: 'Dando varias providencias sobre os Contractos de locação de serviços dos Colonos'. See Law n. 108 of 11 October 1837, *Colecção das Leis do Império do Brasil* – 1837, 77.
27 Based on the law's article 7, the employer could fairly terminate the contract if: (a) the worker got sick, in such a way that he was unable to continue to work; (b) the worker was condemned to prison or to any penalty that prevented him from working; (c) the worker was habitually drunk; (d) the worker did an injury to the employer's safety, honour, property, wife, children or family; (e) the worker was revealed to be incapable of performing the service.
28 Based on the law's article 10, the employee could fairly terminate the contract if: (a) the employer did not comply with his contractual duties; (b) the employer did an injury to the worker, his honour, wife, children or family; (c) requested a service not predicted by the contract.
29 At the beginning of the nineteenth century, the Portuguese economy, already troubled by an archaic system of agriculture and an undeveloped manufacturing sector, deeply felt the loss of the trade monopoly with Brazil in 1808 and the complete loss of its most profitable colony in 1822. To increasing unemployment and poverty, which followed in the former metropolis, there was added a scattered and intensive military recruitment in the years of the Portuguese Civil War (1828–1834), which led many poor Portuguese, and the Azorean islanders in particular, to seek better living conditions through emigration. For a few but essential readings on this context, see Silva, 'Emigração legal e clandestina nos Açores de oitocentos (da década de 30 a meados da centúria)', 2009; Alves, 'Emigração portuguesa: o exemplo do Porto nos meados do século XIX', 1989; Leite, 'Portugal and Emigration: 1855–1914'.
30 'Escriptura de locação de serviços que faz Antonio Simões authorizado pelo Dr. Curador Geral dos Órfãos por ser menor de vinte hum annos á Joaquim Rodrigues da Costa', 1843, fls. 1r–1v.
31 Two other studies undertook systematic research in notary offices on labour contracts for the same timeframe as this paper, and they also indicate the prevalence of freed workers' contracts among the surviving notarial documents. For Florianópolis, see Espada Lima, 'Freedom, Precariousness, and the Law: Freed Persons Contracting out their Labour in 19th-Century Brazil', 2009; and for Campinas and São Paulo, see Ariza, *O ofício da liberdade: trabalhadores libertandos em São Paulo e Campinas (1830–1888)*.
32 Karasch, *Slave Life in Rio de Janeiro*, XVII.
33 Karasch, *Slave Life in Rio de Janeiro*, 205.
34 Between 1791 and 1807, nearly 160,000 enslaved Africans arrived in Rio de Janeiro, almost one third of all enslaved persons trafficked to Portuguese America. This is evidence, as Ynaê Santos suggests, of the new Atlantic connections that elites in the city and captaincy of Rio de

Janeiro established during the final decades of the eighteenth century; see Santos, 'Global Because a Slaveholding Order: An Analysis of the Urban Dynamics of Rio de Janeiro between 1790 and 1815', 2020.
35 Santos, 'Tornar-se corte. Trabalho escravo e espaço urbano no Rio de Janeiro (1808, 1815)', 2013.
36 New Orleans, for example, in 1860 counted 14,484 'bondspeople', which made Rio de Janeiro by far the city with the most important contingent of enslaved people of the Americas; see Karasch, *Slave Life in Rio de Janeiro*, XXI.
37 Santos, 'Global Because a Slaveholding Order: An Analysis of The Urban Dynamics of Rio de Janeiro between 1790 and 1815', 2020.
38 Dantas, 'Urban Slavery'.
39 Grinberg, 'A poupança: alternativas para a compra da alforria no Brasil (2ª. metade do século XIX)', 2011; Dias Paes, *Escravidão e direito: o estatuto jurídico dos escravos no Brasil oitocentista (1860–1888)*.
40 As John French points out, at the basis of the long persistence of 'false dichotomies' in historiography were, among other beliefs, the overly rigid understandings that (1) slavery was a legal status of civil 'non-freedom' as opposed to being 'free' in legal terms, even if dependent; and that (2) 'non-free' labour coincided with unpaid labour, as distinguished from free and paid labour; see French, 'As dicotomias entre escravidão e liberdade: continuidades e rupturas na formação política e social do Brasil moderno', 76.
41 'Escriptura de contracto de obrigação de serviços que fazem entre si Januario libertado por meio de pecúlio com Francisco Manoel Martins', Livro 345 do *1º Ofício de Notas do Rio de Janeiro*, tabelião Mathias Teixeira da Cunha, 30/10/1876, fls. 47v–48r.
42 'Escriptura de locação de serviços que faz a liberta Belisia a Dom Estanislau Camino digo a Antonio Pino', Livro 308 do *1º Ofício de Notas do Rio de Janeiro*, tabelião: Carlos Augusto da Silveira Lobo, 22/4/1869, fl. 41.
43 'Escriptura de locação de serviços que faz o pardo Lucas com João Maria Collação de Magalhães e obrigação', Livro 249 do *1º Ofício de Notas do Rio de Janeiro*, tabelião: João Gomes Guimarães Azevedo, 6/10/1842, fls. 243r–243v.
44 'Escriptura de contracto de locação de serviços que faz a preta liberta de nome Miguelina a João Antonio', Livro 345 do *1º Ofício de Notas do Rio de Janeiro*, tabelião: Mathias Teixeira da Cunha, 13/9/1876, fls. 9r–9v.
45 'Escriptura de locação de serviços que faz João preto e africano liberto a José Maria de Lima', Livro 359 do *1º Ofício de Notas do Rio de Janeiro*, tabelião: Mathias Teixeira da Cunha, 7/2/1879, fl. 92.
46 'Escriptura de locação de serviços que faz Dionizio José Elias ao Reverendo Frei Francisco Ruivo do Amor Divino na forma abaixo', Livro 282 do *1º Ofício de Notas do Rio de Janeiro*, 1861, fl. 90.
47 'Escriptura de locação de serviços que faz a preta liberta Leopoldina de Nação Mina a Antonio José da Silva Pinto', Livro 282 do *1º Ofício de Notas do Rio de Janeiro*, 1861, fl. 93v.
48 'Escriptura de locação de serviços que faz José Francisco Ribeiro na qualidade de Tutor do menor Anastacio Guilherme de Roquette', Livro 308 do *1º Ofício de Notas do Rio de Janeiro*, tabelião: Carlos Augusto da Silveira Lobo, 23/6/1869, fls. 174v–175r.
49 'Escriptura de locação de serviços que faz a liberta Belisia a Dom Estanislau Camino digo a Antonio Pino', 1869, fl. 41.
50 'Escriptura de locação de serviços que faz Marcos crioulo a José Maria Maciel Pinto', Livro 284 do *1º Ofício de Notas do Rio de Janeiro*, tabelião interino: Francisco de Paula Fernandes São Thiago, 6/1/1861, fls. 124r–124v. In this same deed, it was also foreseen that if the worker's services were sublet, his conditions could not be worsened and he should be well treated in the house where he had to go, continuing to be always under the responsibility of the first lessee, receiving the provisioning of clothing and health care, besides being given for his expenses the monthly remuneration of 6,000 *réis*.
51 Like the term *crioulo*, *pardo* also referred to Black people born in Brazil, usually of mixed ascendency, which is frequently translated to English as 'mulatto'; see Karasch, *Slave Life in Rio de Janeiro*, 4.
52 'Escriptura de contracto de locação de serviços que faz a parda Carolina a Caetano José de Paiva', Livro 317 do 1º Ofício de Notas do Rio de Janeiro, tabelião: Mathias Teixeira da Cunha, 20/10/1871, fls. 122–22v.

53 'Escriptura de contracto de locação de serviços que faz a parda Carolina a Caetano José de Paiva', 1871, fl. 122v.
54 Mariana Dias Paes has stressed the limited usefulness of common dichotomies in the historiography of law and slavery that usually oppose 'law' and 'reality', or 'law' and 'social practice'. She states that 'these distinctions turn out to be unproductive, insofar as they obscure the complex interactions that guide the everyday, non-slavery production of law. Legal categories and institutes do not have a meaning per se (although they are presented as if they did). Their concrete meaning is the result of shared understandings, customary practices, and everyday reiteration of forms.' Dias Paes, 'Direito e escravidão no Brasil Império: quais caminhos podemos seguir', 194.

Bibliography

Alencastro, Luiz Felipe de. 'Proletários e escravos. Imigrantes portugueses e cativos africanos no Rio de Janeiro, 1850–1872', *Novos Estudos* 21 (1988): 30–56.
Alves, Jorge. 'Emigração portuguesa: o exemplo do Porto nos meados do século XIX', *História: Revista da Faculdade de Letras da Universidade do Porto* 9 (1989): 267–89.
Annaes do Parlamento Brazileiro – Cammara dos Srs. Deputados, v. 2. Rio de Janeiro: Typographia Nacional, 1878.
Ariza, Marília Bueno de Araújo. *O ofício da liberdade: trabalhadores libertandos em São Paulo e Campinas (1830–1888)*. São Paulo: Alameda, 2014.
Barreiros, José Carlos. *Imaginário e viajantes no Brasil do século XIX: cultura e cotidiano, tradição e resistência*. São Paulo: UNESP, 2002.
Benoist, Philippe and Frond, Jean-Victor. Encaissage et pesage du sacre. In *Brazil pitoresco, álbum de visitas, panoramas, monumentos, costumes, etc., com retratos de Sua Majestade Imperador Dom Pedro II et Família Imperial*, edited by Charles Ribeyrolles. Paris: Lemercier, Imprimeur-Lithographe, 1861. Accessed 19 September 2022. https://bdlb.bn.gov.br/acervo/handle/20.500.12156.3/20584.
Dantas, Mariana. 'Urban Slavery', Atlantic History, *Oxford Bibliographies*, 28 April 2016.
Dantas, Monica Duarte and Costa, Vivian C. 'O "pomposo nome de liberdade do cidadão": tentativas de arregimentação e coerção da mão-de-obra livre no Império do Brasil', *Estudos Avançados* 30/87 (2016): 29–48.
Dias Paes, Mariana Armond. *Escravidão e direito: o estatuto jurídico dos escravos no Brasil oitocentista (1860–1888)*. São Paulo: Alameda, 2019.
Dias Paes, Mariana Armond. 'Direito e escravidão no Brasil Império: quais caminhos podemos seguir?' In *Constituição de poderes, constituição de sujeitos: caminhos da história do direito no Brasil (1750–1930)*, edited by Monica Duarte Dantas and Samuel Barbosa, 182–203. São Paulo: Cadernos do IEB, 2021.
'Escriptura de contracto de locação de serviços que faz a parda Carolina a Caetano José de Paiva', Livro 317 do 1º Ofício de Notas do Rio de Janeiro, tabelião: Mathias Teixeira da Cunha, 20/10/1871, fls. 122–22v.
'Escriptura de contracto de locação de serviços que faz a preta liberta de nome Miguelina a João Antonio', Livro 345 do *1º Ofício de Notas do Rio de Janeiro*, tabelião: Mathias Teixeira da Cunha, 13/9/1876, fls. 9r–9v.
'Escriptura de locação de serviços que faz a liberta Belisia a Dom Estanislau Camino digo a Antonio Pino', Livro 308 do *1º Ofício de Notas do Rio de Janeiro*, tabelião: Carlos Augusto da Silveira Lobo, 22/4/1869, fl. 41.
'Escriptura de locação de serviços que faz a preta liberta Leopoldina de Nação Mina a Antonio José da Silva Pinto', Livro 282 do *1º Ofício de Notas do Rio de Janeiro*, 1861, fl. 93v.
'Escriptura de locação de serviços que faz Antonio Simões authorizado pelo Dr. Curador Geral dos Órfãos por ser menor de vinte hum annos á Joaquim Rodrigues da Costa', Livro 251 do *1º Ofício de Notas do Rio de Janeiro*, tabelião: Francisco Antonio Machado no impedimento de João Gomes Guerra de Aguiar, 28/07/1843, fls. 1r–1v.
'Escriptura de locação de serviços que faz Dionizio José Elias ao Reverendo Frei Francisco Ruivo do Amor Divino na forma abaixo', Livro 282 do *1º Ofício de Notas do Rio de Janeiro*, 1861, fl. 90.

'Escriptura de locação de serviços que faz João Pedro d'Aguiar a José Moutinho dos Reis', Livro 250 do *1º Ofício de Notas do Rio de Janeiro,* tabelião: João Gomes Guimarães d'Aguiar, 04/02/1843, fls. 89v–90r.

'Escriptura de locação de serviços que faz João preto e africano liberto a José Maria de Lima', Livro 359 do *1º Ofício de Notas do Rio de Janeiro,* tabelião: Mathias Teixeira da Cunha, 7/2/1879, fl. 92.

'Escriptura de locação de serviços que faz João Tavares por seu curador ao Doutor Jozé Pereira Rego', Livro 249 do *1º Ofício de Notas do Rio de Janeiro,* tabelião: João Gomes Guimarães d'Aguiar, 07/10/1842, fls. 247r–247v.

'Escriptura de locação de serviços que faz José Antonio Amaro pelo tempo de três anos a Joaquim Rodrigues da Costa', Livro n. 251, do *1º Ofício de Notas do Rio de Janeiro,* tabelião: João Gomes Guimarães d'Aguiar, 15/09/1843, fls. 30r–30v.

'Escriptura de locação de serviços que faz José Francisco Ribeiro na qualidade de Tutor do menor Anastacio Guilherme de Roquette', Livro 308 do *1º Ofício de Notas do Rio de Janeiro,* tabelião: Carlos Augusto da Silveira Lobo, 23/6/1869, fls. 174v–175r.

'Escriptura de locação de serviços que faz Marcos crioulo a José Maria Maciel Pinto', Livro 284 do *1º Ofício de Notas do Rio de Janeiro,* tabelião interino: Francisco de Paula Fernandes São Thiago, 6/1/1861, fls. 124r–124v.

'Escriptura de locação de serviços que faz o colono João Pereira a Luiz Antonio Amaral', Livro 250 do *1º Ofício de Notas do Rio de Janeiro,* tabelião: João Gomes Guimarães d'Aguiar, 14/03/1843, fls. 127r–127v.

'Escriptura de locação de serviços que faz o colono Joze dos Santos ao Dr. Jozé Coelho d'Almeida', Livro 254 do *1º Ofício de Notas do Rio de Janeiro,* tabelião: Francisco Antonio Azevedo no impedimento de João Gomes Guimarães d'Aguiar, 23/01/1845, fls. 25-25v.

'Escriptura de locação de serviços que faz o pardo Lucas com João Maria Collação de Magalhães e obrigação', Livro 249 do *1º Ofício de Notas do Rio de Janeiro,* tabelião: João Gomes Guimarães Azevedo, 6/10/1842, fls. 243r–243v.

'Escriptura de locação de serviços que fazem Jozé Pereira e outros colonnos por seu Curador auctorisados à Luiz Corrêa de Azevedo', Livro 249 do 1o Ofício de Notas do Rio de Janeiro, tabelião: João Gomes Guimarães d'Aguiar, 13/01/1842, fls. 50r–50v.

Espada Lima, Henrique. 'Trabalho e lei para os libertos na ilha de Santa Catarina no século XIX: arranjos e contratos entre autonomia e a domesticidade', *Cad. AEL* 14/26 (2006): 137–75.

Espada Lima, Henrique. 'Freedom, Precariousness, and the Law: Freed Persons Contracting out their Labour in 19th-Century Brazil', *International Review of Social History* 54 (2009): 391–416.

Espada Lima, Henrique. 'Enslaved and Free Workers and the Growth of the Working Class in Brazil', *Oxford Research Encyclopedia of Latin American History* (2021): 1–28.

Espada Lima, Henrique. '"Until the Day of His Death": Aging, Slavery and Dependency in Nineteenth-Century Brazil', *Radical History Review* 139 (2021): 52–74.

French, John. 'As dicotomias entre escravidão e liberdade: continuidades e rupturas na formação política e social do Brasil moderno'. In *Trabalho Escravo: Brasil e Europa, Séculos XVII e XIX,* edited by Dou Libby and Junia Ferreira Furtado, 75–96. São Paulo: Anablume, 2009.

Grinberg, Keila, 'A poupança: alternativas para a compra da alforria no Brasil (2a. metade do século XIX)', *Revista de Indias* 71/251 (2011): 137–58.

Karasch, Mary C. *Slave Life in Rio de Janeiro, 1808–1850.* Princeton: Princeton University Press, 1987.

Leite, Joaquim da Costa. 'Portugal and Emigration: 1855–1914'. PhD dissertation, Columbia University, 1994.

Macedo, Deoclécio Leite de. *Tabeliães do Rio de Janeiro do 1º ao 4º Ofício de Notas: 1565–1822.* Rio de Janeiro: Arquivo Nacional, 2007.

Mamigonian, Beatriz. 'Os direitos dos libertos africanos no Brasil oitocentista: entre razões de direito e considerações politicas', *História* 34/2 (2015): 181–205.

Mattos, Marcelo Badaró. *Laborers and Enslaved Workers: Experiences in Common in the Making of Rio de Janeiro's Working Class, 1850–1920.* New York: Berghahn Books, 2017.

Meléndez, José Juan Pérez. 'Reconsidering Colonization Policy in Imperial Brazil: The Regency Years and the World Beyond', *Revista Brasileira de História* 34/68 (2014): 35–60.

Meléndez, José Juan Pérez. 'The Business of Peopling: Colonization and Politics in Imperial Brazil, 1822–1860'. PhD dissertation, University of Chicago, 2016.

Mendonça, Joseli Nunes Maria. 'On Chains and Coercion: Labor Experiences in South-Central Brazil in the Nineteenth Century', *Revista Brasileira de História* 32/64 (2012): 33–47.

Nunes, Rosana Barbosa. 'Portuguese Migration to Rio de Janeiro', *The Americas* 57/1 (2000): 37–61.

Rodrigues, Jaime. 'Aspectos da escravidão brasileira pelo olhar dos artistas estrangeiros', Brasiliana Iconográfica, 10 May 2018. Accessed 19 September 2022. https://www.brasilianaiconografica.art.br/artigos/20188/aspectos-da-escravidao-brasileira-pelo-olhar-dos-artistas-estrangeiros

Santos, Ynaê L. dos. 'Tornar-se corte. Trabalho escravo e espaço urbano no Rio de Janeiro (1808, 1815)', *Revista de História Comparada* 7/1 (2013): 262–92.

Santos, Ynaê L. dos. 'Global Because a Slaveholding Order: An Analysis of the Urban Dynamics of Rio de Janeiro between 1790 and 1815', *Almanack, Guarulhos*, no. 24 (2020): 1–31.

Silva, Susana Serpa. 'Emigração legal e clandestina nos Açores de oitocentos (da década de 30 a meados da centúria)'. In *Nas duas margens: os portugueses no Brasil*, edited by Ismênia Martins, Izilda Matos and Fernando de Sousa, 381–400. Porto: Edições Afrontamento & CEPESE, 2009.

Vitorino, Artur José Renda. 'Operários livres e cativos nas manufaturas: Rio de Janeiro, segunda metade do século XIX'. Paper presented at Jornadas de História do Trabalho, Pelotas, November 2002.

CONSTRUCTING DEBT

12
Constructing debt: discursive and material strategies of labour coercion in the US South, 1903–1964

Nico Pizzolato

In this chapter based on archival sources and contemporary accounts drawn from government files, political and civil rights association archives, newspaper articles and memoirs, I discuss how labour coercion was imbricated with conceptual notions and social practices of debt during the twentieth century. I will explore how planters and growers in the US South used debt to attempt to immobilise workers for the length of time that their labour was needed in the fields and to pay them cheaply, or not at all. As we will see, employers used monetary remuneration itself, often assumed to be one of the hallmarks of free labour, to entangle workers in coercive labour practices. The way this happened evolved along the chronology covered by this study, which spans from the first court cases of 'peonage' (being compelled to work to pay a debt) in 1903 to the end, in 1964, of the Programa Bracero, which brought to the US heavily indebted workers from Mexico.

The architecture of my inquiry into this nexus between debt, coercion and labour stands on the shoulders of at least two strands of historiography of labour of the southern United States. First, there is the work on the labour regimes in the South after Emancipation, from the classic studies of Eric Foner, Jonathan Wiener, Gavin Wright, and Ira Berlin's 'Freedmen and Southern Society Project' to the more recent work of Steve Hahn, Bruce Baker, Brian Kelly, Susan O'Donovan and John C. Rodrigue. In different ways, these scholars have contributed to my understanding of the transition from slavery to regimes of labour in the post-Reconstruction period, when sharecropping and tenancy transformed African-Americans into a class of wage workers and heads of household, but also kept them cash-strapped and dependent on the whims of landowners.[1] Secondly, I build on the studies that focus on the unfree aspects of those regimes, such as the classic *Shadow of Slavery* by Pete Daniel, Nan Woodruff's *American Congo*, Douglas A. Blackmon's *Slavery by Another Name* and the work of Risa Goluboff.[2] I also draw on a close analysis of the few contemporary sociological studies of landlord–tenant relations in the American South, mostly published in the 1930s, to examine the critique of racial and class relations that, in those texts, is often hidden between the lines. I accompany the historiographical account with a reflexive positioning of my work as historian who (re)constructs a narrative of the past within the limits of my world view and in dialogue not only with current debate about debt in contemporary capitalism, but also with the interpretative artwork created by illustrator Monika Lang through the collaboration with Anamarija Batista, Viola Müller and Corinna Peres, who all together established the dramaturgy of the illustration. I conclude my reflections by pointing to the constant change over time of that nexus between debt, labour and coercion that characterised the political economy of the rural South.

> Questioning the production of archival documents has always been a fundamental aspect of historical research. This was of particular relevance as I gained interest in what lies behind the social practice defined as 'peonage' in documents that I found first at the Archives of Labor and Urban Affairs in Detroit, then in the Department of Special Collections in Stanford and eventually in numerous other libraries and archives in the US and Europe. I was haunted by one of the first such documents that I encountered, an exposé by the Workers Defense League (WDL) – a socialist organisation that between the 1930s and the 1940s put the improvement of farm workers' conditions high on its agenda. 'DO YOU KNOW that SLAVERY still exists on American soil in this year of 1940?' shouted the document to its contemporary readers.[3] I did not know, and it was 2008. The 58-page pamphlet went on to describe an excruciating case of what the organisation described as 'slavery for debt', producing excerpts of first-person testimonies, which were actually oral accounts from 'debt slaves' turned into searing prose by the WDL activists. The document raised questions about where the 'voice' of the social actors lay about the agenda of the political campaign that denounced peonage and labelled it as 'slavery', about the origin of the term 'peonage', about the way in which protagonists actually made sense of what happened to them, and about the other institutions and actors involved in the 'production' of this social practice named 'peonage'.
>
> This led me to inquire further. The WDL archive was in dialogue with another archive no less involved in the 'conceptualisation' of such practice,

the one of the Department of Justice (DOJ), which had been organised by historian Pete Daniel in the course of the research later published in his book *The Shadow of Slavery* (1972). In the DOJ archive, the testimonies of sharecroppers of African descent were usually reported through the eyes of FBI investigators who reluctantly travelled to remote country plantations in the 'Black Belt', the region of cotton-producing counties across the American South, to check on the claims of activists, reporters and philanthropists who called attention to the plight of plantation workers. But the DOJ archives also contained original letters from the family members of the workers themselves, often women, who pleaded for the liberation of husbands, brothers or sons; or from sharecroppers who denounced the unfair deals that kept them tied to the land year after year. It was a stirring moment to come across those hand-written, barely decipherable stories; it also provided a fresh perspective on what I was accustomed to understand when I read the text of the Thirteenth Amendment to the US Constitution. Those letters provided a counterpoint to the narrow interpretation that the juridical and political institutions made of the amendment by evoking 'slavery' in its symbolic and metaphorical significance, which did not align with what the jurisprudence mandated.

A new slavery?

Indeed, many of those letters and testimonies talk about 'slavery' or being 'enslaved'. Was it the case? The Thirteenth Amendment (1865) had carried a 'dangerous' potential by stipulating that 'Neither slavery nor involuntary servitude … shall exist within the United States'.[4] The catch was in the phrase incidentally placed in the middle of the amendment's text, 'except as a punishment for a crime whereof the party shall have been duly convicted'.[5] The definition of crime varies from society to society. For African-Americans in the twentieth-century US South, loitering, vagrancy, being a *disorderly person*, a drunkard or a *tramp*, or simply leaving a job, could carry criminal consequences. Within a racialised system of law enforcement, common behaviours could also be socially constructed as crimes. In other cases, misdemeanours, such as stealing a farm animal (which in other states would carry a short sentence), were treated as felonies and carried harsher penalties than elsewhere. White Americans usually escaped punishment for these crimes, because these laws, in their actual application, were meant to control the labour and the bodies of African-Americans, not of White people. In reality, being charged for vagrancy meant only to be unemployed or just 'out of place', that is, out of the White man's labour control.[6]

With different nuances, these first-hand testimonies were all telling a similar story, and, when they were placed side by side, a common pattern emerged, even if it was one that evolved over time. At times landlords and authorities were inflating or just making up farmhands' debts and forcing Black people to work to repay them. While usually ignored by the law enforcement institutions, this was obvious to the contemporary observer. 'At the end of the season the sharecropper [is shown] that he is really in debt for seed, supplies and keep advanced during the year and he is forced … to remain for another year.'[7] At other times Black people were simply 'taken'. This was the case of African-American Floyd Thompson, arrested on his way to his sister's wedding, charged with a petty crime and forced to pay off the legal fee on a cotton field. The trial for such an offence was very swift. 'I was not allowed to have an attorney to represent me nor was I allowed to call witnesses to testify on my behalf. I was charged with interfering with labour,' said Thompson.[8] He *interfered with labour* because he did not want to pick cotton. The political economic regime treated such insubordination like a crime, but the coercion was interlinked with the mechanisms of production of a debt through the system of law.

The evolving mechanisms of coercion

At the turn of the twentieth century, the social organisation of labour in the rural South was still very much in the grips of the aftershocks of the emancipation of slaves. Its political economy, rooted in coercive labour practice and disrupted by emancipation, had evolved towards a new system. For instance, in the cotton plantations, this meant the change from work gangs supervised by an overseer, to single family plots under a share or tenancy cropping arrangement. As an ample historiography has discussed, this was the result of the political struggle over the configuration of rural work after 1865.[9]

In different ways, two strong undercurrents traversed the post-bellum plantation with consequences that had an impact well into the turn of the century. One current was the way African-Americans used their newly found freedom to seek autonomy and force concessions from the planter class who used to own them. The rise, during Reconstruction (the period that followed the Civil War), of decentralised sharecropping (working the land for a share of the crop) and tenancy contracts (renting the land by paying in goods or cash)[10] in the Cotton Belt testifies to that agency, and so do the cash wages and shorter working hours that African-Americans won where work remained organised in work gangs.[11] It is to be noted that in a sharecropping agreement, the landlord owns the crop, with which the debt will be repaid; in tenancy, the crop technically belongs to the tenant, but the landlord has a lien on it, because it will be used to repay the debt owed to them. (A third, even more precarious, category of plantation workers comprised workers paid in (low) wages and hired for a given period of time. Their precarity made them more susceptible to coerced labour conditions.) The other undercurrent swayed African-Americans towards forms of debt peonage, of convict labour, of domestic servitude, which testified to the enduring presence of coercion in shaping labour relations.[12] However, the mechanics of coercion that we can observe in the first half of the twentieth century were not only a legacy of the ante-bellum political economy and race relations; they were made anew, through the ways in which employers and workers renegotiated labour relations by contracting, manipulating, escaping debt, remuneration and punishment.

Social scientists and the 'plight of the sharecropper'

We could hardly interpret the testimonies in the archives without the context provided by the first social scientists who became interested in the social, cultural and economic organisation of the rural South, in counter-tendency to the rest of their profession. These researchers penetrated into a world that previously had been hidden from the view of any outsider. In fact, in the first half of the twentieth century, organised professional sociology was scarcely aware of rural African-Americans, or for that matter of African-Americans *tout court*, unless research corroborated predominant racist theorems about Black immorality and inferiority.[13] In the 1930s, however, as liberals gained more voice in Washington DC and as the Left – represented by organisations like the Workers Defense League or the International Labor Defense – agitated the newly found cause of the 'plight of the sharecropper',[14] there were some notable exceptions, which followed in the footsteps of the pioneering ethnographic and lyrical description of the Black Belt by W. E. B. Du Bois in *The Souls of Black Folk* (1903). In particular, Charles B. Johnson's *The Shadow of the Plantation* (1934) and Arthur F. Raper's *Preface to Peasantry* (1936) (respectively by an African-American and a White Southern liberal) considered how economics and culture interlinked in the rural South, where the decline in productivity of the plantation had not yet, in the eyes of these observers, ushered in a modern society. Their investigation reveals a society where debt percolates through the whole economic fabric, but they left understated the deeper significance of this debt.

Raper's *Preface to Peasantry* opens with an image of a cart carrying bales of cotton, and a question: 'To whom does this cotton belong: to the tenant farmer who grew it, to the landlord who furnished the tenant, or to the banker who financed the landlord?'[15] This 'Black Belt's riddle' refers to the consideration well known to contemporaries that the whole cotton economy was based on a chain of financial dependencies through which planters financed their operations – a system that had been established in the ante-bellum period where it inextricably linked cotton, slavery and finance. However, in the post-bellum South, when cotton fetched tendentially lower prices (within frequent fluctuations), this system jeopardised the ability of planters to repay the money they had borrowed from creditors.[16] Tenants and sharecroppers, in turn unable to recoup what the landlords had loaned them for seeds, implements and all the essentials of life, fell ever more into debt, entering what Charles Otken, a vehement early critic of the system, called 'debt peonage'.[17] Charles Johnson summarised the 'system' of debt formation in the cotton economy as follows:

> To the Negro tenant, the white landlord is the system; to the white landlord, the capital of the banks is the system. The landlord needs credit by which to advance credit to the tenants ... Because cotton lends itself best to this arrangement, cotton is overproduced and debts descend to obscure still another year of labor ... The demands of the system determine the social and economic relations, the weight of which falls heaviest upon those lowest down.[18]

This general criticism of the system of financing cotton obscured, however, fundamental differences in the way in which debt worked to constrain choices across class and racial divides. For instance, the debt between the planter and the bank put at risk the planter's property (which the planter used as collateral to borrow and therefore was at risk of losing), but the debt between the worker and the planter provided the latter with a nearly indisputable position of power that dominated the entire labour and social relation between the two. While the relationship of the planter with the creditor was a financial transaction that informed the planter's choices but remained distant from daily life in the fields, the debt contracted by the farm worker with the landlord allowed the latter to exercise extensive, unchecked power within the labour relation and, in sum, over the daily life of the labourer. This power was underpinned by the fact that, due to lack of literacy and the unfavourable relations of power, Black workers could not challenge the accounts and the figures established by the planter at the end of the crop lifecycle. Debt underpinned practices of labour coercion beyond being a financial transaction to characterise how landlords, usually White Americans, maintained and exercised their power over Black people.

By and large, Black mobility represented a threat to planters in the rural South because it created a competition among employers for workers that raised the cost of labour. In every situation where the planter stood to gain from workers' immobility, debt was the most frequent instrument that made such immobility possible.[19] Johnson's study of Macon County, Alabama, in a single year of the 1930s, provides a snapshot of the hold of debt on mobility (both social and geographical) of the population of African-American croppers and tenants: out of 237 families, the total population, 61.7 per cent 'broke even', meaning that they did not increase nor decrease what they owed to the landlords; 26 per cent went further into debt; and only 9.4 per cent made a profit (that is, decreased their debt or became debt-free) in comparison to the previous year.[20] It was widely known, as corroborated by both the literature and oral histories, that the end-of-the-year settlements between landlord and workers were tinged by irregularities and threats. Or, as Johnson put it in an understatement, 'It is, of course, impossible to determine the extent of exploitation of these Negro farmers, so long as books are kept by the landlord, the sale price of cotton known only by him, and the cost and interest on rations advanced in his hands.' Or, as a worker declared, 'We haven't paid out to Mr ------ in twelve years. Been in debt that long. See, when a fella's got a gun in your face you gonna take low or die.'[21]

In a way, therefore, being in debt was not about paying back money at all. Writing in the 1940s, Black historian Carter Woodson noted dryly, 'families of Negroes [were] bound to white landlords for debts they were never permitted to pay'.[22] The debts were in principle unredeemable because to settle them meant to be able to walk away free and to establish formal equality between the employer and the worker, which would have reduced the asymmetry in their relationship. Landlords used indebtedness as a tool of legal and spatial labour coercion and therefore had a vested interest in the perpetuation of such indebtedness; the main function of debts was to keep Blacks in the inferior position of those who owe. African-Americans' debt was 'unpayable' because in the eyes of Whites they should never ascend to the position of equality that is afforded to two economic actors who owe nothing to each other.

> The collaboration with illustrator Monika Lang and the editors of the volume challenged me in making intelligible a world of social practices that the historical protagonists navigated with a tacit knowledge – a vision of the world accustomed to the everyday entanglement of remuneration, debt, labour, race and power to coerce, which did not always correspond to the figures of speech that contemporaries used to describe it. Monika Lang's illustration (p. 272) captures this contradiction between the apparent manifestation of a practice and the tacit understanding of it through the device of the 'shadow' (a metaphor used also by some scholars foundational to this essay, as in Pete Daniel's 'shadow of slavery' or Charles Johnson's 'shadow of the plantation'). Her illustration foregrounds a White man, who looks like a well-tailored planter or merchant, handing a bag of cash to a Black worker. On the wall of a farmhouse we can see that this act, apparently akin to a contractual transaction among free agents, in reality projects a shadow of bondage. This is a stark visual representation of the mechanism of what was captured by the jurisprudence about peonage – legally defined in 1903 as being 'compelled to labor in liquidation of some debt or obligation, either real or pretended, against his will'.[23]
>
> The practice with which this jurisprudence was concerned revolved around the binding consequences of workers receiving an advance in cash or, more often, in kind, for work in the fields to be performed in the future and whether the worker should be compelled to labour against her or his will to pay this off (often, in practice, for an indefinite length of time). Although there were other entry points into 'peonage', such as the convict surety system (leasing a convict to a private employer for a fee) or downright physical threats, monetary remuneration proved a sticky one – one which Supreme Court sentences like *Bailey vs Alabama* (1911) tried, unsuccessfully, to eradicate. Advances in cash or kind were crucial for sharecroppers and tenants (and their families) in enabling them to pay for the costs of production (seed, tools and implements) and reproduction (food, clothes and medicines) during the lifecycle of the crop, but this remuneration subtly translated into a binding tool.
>
> It was an important line of inquiry for me to take seriously what the court referred to as 'pretended' debt as the source of bonded labour. The fictionality of the debt derived from the fact that it reflected a sum that did not match the actual money disbursed by the creditor. In this chapter I look at the different ways in which the 'pretension' could have

real consequences. We can therefore see debt in this specific context beyond its veneer of financial instrument to appreciate also its core as one of the discursive practices that enabled coercion in labour relations (as we will see below), that means as a disciplinary and normative tool that relied on the construction of a discourse of indebtedness that might or might not have had a financial basis. As explored by sociologist Tomáš Samec in the context of financing in the neoliberal housing market, the mechanical and structural features of the 'system' (a different one from Raper's, but enmeshed in indebtedness) alone do not explain how people's subjectivity (that of both the creditors and the debtors) is transformed by the process of fabricating indebtedness.[24] Thus, the discourse of indebtedness – a system of representation in which social actors engage in allegedly free and autonomous financial transactions that result in the debt of one party – was used to normalise an economic and social reality that was based on relations of power shaped outside of the market.

Debt and workers' subjectivity

As we are reminded by the case of the anonymous worker, quoted earlier, who did not receive any wages in 12 years, the horizon of time is always prominent whenever debt – a sum of money to be paid back in the future – exists. Debt shapes the subjective perception of time and the way it is categorised. Drawing on the work of the sociologist and philosopher Maurizio Lazzarato, it follows that debt allows capitalism, through the actions of the landlord in this case, to stake a claim on the future behaviour of the indebted and therefore, through notions of guilt and responsibility sustained by societal norms, has the power to shape subjectivity.[25]

Raper describes one way in which debt shaped the subjectivity of Black workers: 'There is a tacit agreement that the tenant will work for the landlord at a certain price at any time he needs him […] the landlord always reserving the right to request the tenant to take care of his own crop.'[26] In this case, the debt enabled the landlords to dispose of the time of the workers as they saw fit. It is remarkable that here Raper sees, correctly, a *tacit* understanding: the social practice has shaped the subjectivity so deeply that it is legitimised as an unspoken norm. The freedom of the workers to hire themselves out to another employer for casual work for wages existed only outside of this time marked by debt.

For the sharecropper, the horizon of temporality inflected towards the yearly 'settlement time', when debt could be lightened, upheld or increased. Escaping debt's hold on the lived experience of one's own temporality might require literally planning one's own escape from a plantation to which one is held 'captive' by debt. The spatial and temporal dimensions of immobility were connected in this case. Both the de jure and de facto practices constrained the right of Black rural workers to change employers, and the alleged debt (which stakes a claim on the debtor's future) to the planter was the device most commonly used to enforce this: a former landlord could claim back the indebted person and their family from the new landlord – a practice backed by the law enforcement agencies – or ask for their arrest if found in a town. Furthermore, violence was always at hand to monitor the workings of the labour market. Raper describes this process as follows: 'Thus robbed of his normal right to move, the propertyless farm worker can escape his lot only by fleeing the community, which involves considerable risk. Threats of flogging, murder follow and sometimes overtake the "debtor" who "slips off like a thief."'[27] Defiant, African-Americans tried to escape anyway, and when the escape was successful, they started afresh somewhere else. By moving across space, the individual might be able to reset the horizon of time.

The discursive construction of indebtedness

The question of discursive construction draws on another, related, aspect of debt: its symbolic power through which the moral hierarchies of the South were shaped. In his psychological account of the origin of morality, Friedrich Nietzsche investigated the primordial connection between debt and guilt in human history. The two words have a common root in many languages and an overlapping meaning, which led him to notice how an unpaid debt could be balanced by cruel acts of the creditor that harmed the debtor, at the same time extinguishing the latter's guilt – an intriguing suggestion to consider in the context of the US South, where Black rural workers, a class of debtors, were susceptible to various forms of violence from the White planters and employers, a class of creditors.[28]

The scholar Saidiya Hartman has studied perceptively the propositions in relation to debt of a number of self-help manuals for African-Americans published after the passing of the Thirteenth Amendment.[29] Published by White people, these manuals advised the newly emancipated slaves that the real meaning of their freedom was the responsibility to be self-disciplined and to pay their dues to society, of which they were now full members. They could do so through work and contentedness with their place in society. Work contracts between allegedly free and equal individuals now placed on African-Americans obligations that could not be left unattended. The rationale (and, it was implied, a precondition) for freedom was the disposition to work dutifully and to be thrifty, as planters decried tenants' indebtedness on their 'foolish expenditures' and games of dice.[30] This type of discourse thus framed 'freedom' in terms of what the individual owed to society, and an unwillingness to attend to those duties, such as fulfilling a contract with a planter, no matter the working conditions or remuneration, as 'guilt' that justified subjugation.

The notion of debt was racially tinged. When it concerned White Americans, defaulting or escaping debt was merely an individual failure to regulate one's own behaviour. However, in the case of Black rural workers, it concerned a vast class of workers and created the presumption that any such worker was at fault. (Indeed, the 'false pretence' law, which *Baley vs Alabama* (1911) tried to eradicate, stipulated literally that when a worker had received advanced remuneration from an employer, breaking the contract would create a presumption of guilt for the worker – a provision that was uniquely applied to rural African-Americans.) Debt justified the subordinate position of rural African-Americans as a class and race of labourers, whether or not they actually owed money at any particular point. In fact, while researching the visual representation of Black Southern farm workers, I can hardly distinguish the photo of a (financially) indebted Black worker from one who was not. In the photo that Carter Woodson captions in his book as a 'peon', the individual does not bear any special mark of his condition; she or he is virtually indistinguishable from any other poor Black labourer of the Black Belt.[31]

Credit, conversely, is linked to moral worth and standing in the community. According to Karl Marx, 'Credit is the *economic* judgement on the *morality* of a man.'[32] In this case the low moral status of the Black worker is confirmed by his scarce ability to gain 'real' financial credit (unless a White man would act as a guarantor of it); he is indebted for sums that have often been fabricated and discursively legitimised (through the idea that Black workers, collectively, 'owed' to the White society). The actual financial debts concerned only the advances on seed and food that the sharecropper received at the beginning of the year and that could be considered the planter's minimum investment for the productive and reproductive work necessary to grow the crops, from which he stood to gain most, if not all, of the profits. Ironically, it was the occasional ability of some Black workers to get 'actually' indebted to different actors that improved their chances of receiving a fair settlement at harvest time. This responded to the simple logic of playing out two actors against each other:

> Further than the stamp of personal worth which a loan implies, there is the fact that the tenant who is in debt to two or more influential people has secured for himself the protection against exorbitant claims ... for the merchant's interest in the tenant's crop may regulate the demands of the landlord.[33]

In other words, when a Black worker did manage to get indebted to someone else in addition to the planter, the scrutiny of another White figure over the returns of the crop (something that the Black worker was not in a position to undertake) would have deterred the planter from taking all the profits of the sales and make him agree to a fairer remuneration of the work, one that would allow the worker to also pay the other creditor.

Debt, guilt and peonage

The condition of perpetual susceptibility to indebtedness chimed with the presumption of guilt that impaired African-Americans who were prosecuted of any crime against Whites. All in all, Marx, Nietzsche and Hartman encourage us to consider the place of the discourse of debt and guilt in the moral hierarchy that underpinned the political economy of the South. This link is particularly evident in the way law enforcement and courts produced guilt, and therefore debt. But how did the production of guilt generate debt, which in turn coerced people to work in the same location for an extensive period of time?

The advantage of debt as a measure of guilt was that, in its facet as a financial predicament, it was expressed in a tangible sum of money owed to a landlord or to the county (in the case of a court fee); even though it was often fabricated or fictive, it was recorded in numbers on a ledger. We could take as an illustrative point any of the cases known of using such practices. For instance, the Supreme Court case *United States vs Reynolds* (1914) established that a man called Ed Rivers had been convicted by a state court in Monroe, Alabama, of petit larceny – a crime as trivial as stealing an apple. He was fined $15, with an added $43.75 in court expenses, three times the original fine. Reynolds, one of the local men who 'bought n*****s' (that is, implied in the language of the sentence, paid Black men's fines to obtain their labour afterwards), secured the services of Rivers until the latter repaid the full expenses incurred to be released. Rivers was now in debt to Reynolds. It is to be noted that while, in theory, had Reynolds not appeared, Rivers would have languished in prison until the day the Court decided otherwise, in practice, such judgements rested on the widespread awareness that men like Reynolds would come to 'buy' Black defendants. When a month later Rivers attempted to escape, the court imposed a further $87.05 on his debt, and another man, Broughton, took over the debt so now the sum was owed to him, as he had paid the whole amount to the State and to Reynolds. In this process, as the credit moved from employer to employer, so did the worker, even as he attempted to escape several times.

In the first decade of the twentieth century, the coercive aspects of labour came to be seen through the lens of debt when a sparse cohort of judges, reformers and activists constructed it as a form of 'peonage', by drawing a parallel with the Mexican peons indebted to hacienda landowners, the agrarian capitalists who controlled rural labour in many Latin American countries.[34] This practice had been banned by a federal law in 1867 after the US, in 1848, incorporated the northern part of Mexico into its territory. However, the law was only enforced at the turn of the century to address the problem of labour extracted from African-Americans in conditions of perpetual indebtedness. 'What is peonage?' asked a federal judge in *Clyatt vs United States* (1905), the first of such cases to reach the Supreme Court. 'It may be defined as a status or condition of compulsory service, based upon the indebtedness of the peon to the master. The basal fact is indebtedness.'[35]

Reformers' indignation against peonage (which stirred the federal judiciary into action) had to do with the fraud, malice or violence with which Black women and men were induced into debts as well as the deplorable living conditions that accompanied their predicament. Denouncing some of the entry points into coercive labour that I have outlined above, Mary Church Terrell, the civil rights and suffrage advocate, decried (quoting the progressive judge Emory Speer) the plight of the hundreds

> who are not even charged with a crime, but are accused of some petty offence, such as walking on the grass, expectorating upon the sidewalk, going to sleep in a depot, loitering on the streets, or other similar misdemeanours which could not by a stretch of the imagination be called a crime.[36]

Even more outrageous was the common practice of arresting Black people at harvest time with the trumped-up charge of being indebted to a landowner: 'the captured men are worked during the cotton-planting season, are then released with empty pockets and allowed to return to their homes'.[37] In the way the criminal justice system at county level was deployed to provide coerced labour, the boundary between legality and illegality of such practices was blurred. Few Black workers knew their rights or could access legal counsel to contest the kind of destiny that had befallen them.

Du Bois, Johnson and Raper assumed that these abuses were the pernicious effect of how the political economy of the Black Belt had transformed in the wake of slavery and in the shadow of the plantation. However, the culture of racialised labour management was so embedded that it stretched beyond the cotton plantations of Georgia or Arkansas, and persisted beyond the decline of the tenancy and sharecropping that followed Black migration outside of the South, agricultural mechanisation and the Second World War,[38] and beyond the flurry of federal and judicial activity that between 1939 and 1944 made less palatable and feasible the use of 'peonage' as an instrument to immobilise African-American labour.[39] The practices of racialised labour management continued by adapting to the vulnerabilities of another group of farm workers.

Mexican migrants: change and continuity

In the 1940s, officers of the Department of Justice detected how a new group of farm workers were being increasingly entangled in similar entrapments to African-Americans.[40] During the 1920s and 1930s, first in Texas and then in other border states, growers found ways of drawing Mexican migrants into coercive labour practices that had long been inflicted on African-Americans. This was starkly visible in the case of sharecropping in the cotton fields of South Texan counties, where, in those years, planters attempted to coerce Mexican farmers through debt dependency. A Texan planter candidly declared, '[The Mexicans] are generally always in debt, mine are always in debt. We pay them out when we take them over from somebody else to get them free. I paid $250 debt to get one Mexican.'[41] While a perspective of 'the shadow of the plantation' suggests that social practices of coercion persisted in the same locale across time because they were a cultural legacy of plantation slavery, looking to a different population of workers suggests that it spread across space too, adapting to new forms of rationalisation of production and different (more impersonal) contractual arrangements: the key continuity was the centrality of the construction of debt within a racialised labour management of agricultural production.[42]

Thus, between the 1920 and the 1940s, Texan growers anchored Mexican women and men to the land (for instance through the same form of sharecropping that is described above) when it was convenient to them, while at other times they secured workers for the limited period of the harvest but without the intention to provide for them for the rest of the year. In this latter case, immobilisation of the workers had to be timed to what the market dictated was the optimal harvest moment, in relation to the price that crop would fetch at a given moment. On the other hand, harvesting was also more susceptible to any delay or disruption caused by recruitment of workers or the performance of labour. As time progressed, growers sought Mexican agricultural workers mainly for intensive seasonal work, during which growers needed to keep them tied to the fields.

In effect, by the end of the 1940s, as African-Americans moved northward in ever growing numbers to escape racial oppression, poverty and violence, the rural labour force was rapidly transforming to one of Mexican nationality or Mexican origin. Workers came also from other parts of the American continent and from further afield, such as from the Caribbean, the Philippines or Japan, but Mexicans were predominant. Between 1942 and 1964, Programa Bracero was the system that provided growers with a Mexican workforce bound by short-term contracts to a single employer and subject to deportation. The programme was governed by bilateral agreements regulating recruitment, remuneration and mobility. Undocumented migrants also reached the fields of the South-West, whenever they could not find admission to the Programa, which attracted far more applicants than it could admit.[43] What was appealing in the use of these workers was widely understood and candidly expressed: 'The Braceros are in a situation where docility is enforceable. Moreover, they can be had generally on schedule when needed and can be easily got rid of when the job is done,' commented a priest, sympathetic to the workers, who regularly visited the fields in California (together with Texas, the main destination for Mexican immigrants).[44] If African-Americans had been treated as second-class citizens, Mexican labourers, technically, were not citizens at all. The 'docility' of Mexican migrants was often commented upon as an inherent feature of their allegedly inferior race; however, it took on a different significance when interpreted within the relation of power with the employers. In fact, as the quote suggests, docility was not inborn, but 'enforced', and debt played an important role in this.[45]

Migrants' debt as enabler of coercion

Mexican migrants arriving in the US, whether as contract workers like the *braceros* or as undocumented workers, arrived already in debt. They often used their little property at home as collateral to secure a small loan (usually from moneylenders) or borrowed from friends and family the sum necessary to travel to recruitment centres or to the border. In the long waits before being assessed by recruitment centres, applicants incurred additional expenses for food and shelter. In the process of migration, they often encountered the need to pay *la mordida*, a bribe to officials to get ahead in the recruitment process. For instance, *bracero* aspirant José Esequiel Adame (who would go on to become a cotton picker in Big Spring, Texas) remembered how he waited many days at a recruitment centre in Chihuahua before entering the list of the selected ones thanks to a bribe of 700 pesos. (In the same years, the late 1940s, the weekly wage for mine workers was 50 pesos.[46]) Others, such as Barnabé Álvarez Díaz, had to pay the bribe twice, having been cheated out of the money by a swindler the first time.[47]

Growers were keenly aware of the costs, both legal and illegal, that the migration process entailed. In fact, they sometimes arranged to pay the bribes themselves, through proxy agents, and then deducted what was owed from the workers' paycheques.[48] As we have seen, in the Black Belt it was common to fabricate debts that African-Americans did not really owe or that they had already paid out; in the case of temporary contract workers from Mexico, growers concentrated their efforts on making existing workers' debts as difficult to pay as possible, so as to raise the stakes for those who wished to leave before the end of the contract or who rebelled against the pace and conditions of work imposed. In both cases, debt functioned as a means for employers to obtain labour and to secure it according to their needs. In other words, the existence of a debt underpinned the coercion within the relationship.

One way to foster workers' debt was to turn them into 'captive consumers'. In their narratives, many of which are collected in the Braceros History Archive, workers often complained about the food they were served, which they had to pay for with the maximum price allowed by the contract, with deductions from wages. While the amount, quality and variety of food for *braceros* was established by the bilateral agreements between the US and Mexican government to which growers subscribed when requesting workers, inspections (many of which were solicited by the complaints of workers themselves) regularly reported gross deficiencies in quantity, quality and hygiene of food. 'Daily menus are fictitious in that they do not list the food actually served.'[49] 'No variety of food was being served, with chili con carne served one day and carne con chili the next; meat was being served of less than utility grade.'[50] Workers were charged full subsistence fees for inedible food and often ended up spending additional money at the commissary, owned by the landowner or an associate, to buy their own food and cook their own meals. Eleanor Martin, a store clerk interviewed for the Braceros History Archive, noted down the expenditures to be deducted from paycheques. At the end of the contract, *braceros* were asked to stay, and work unpaid, if they still owed money to the employer.[51] Worker Ignacio Nájera recalled that he owed his employer $10 a week for the daily meals. This constituted roughly a third of the earnings if one considers the account of another worker, Ismael Rodríguez Rico, who in 1952 received only $35 after working 70 to 80 hours picking cotton for a week.[52]

Another method to increase debt was to have contract workers purchase from the employer the tools necessary to perform their labour. For instance, carrot growers in Salinas Valley sold to farm workers the wire necessary to bundle the carrots. This amounted to a deduction of about 11 per cent from the workers' salary. The National Agricultural Workers Union complained that the arrangement was 'coercive' because *braceros* could not work without buying the wire.[53] The company replied that it was an effective method to cut waste and that workers would have purchased the wire at higher prices elsewhere. Yet, in effect, a production cost that was worth a sizeable fraction of the salary came out of the workers' pockets.

The simplest way for employers to steal the wages of contract workers was through the lack of transparency in the accounting. Sometimes employers tried to cow their workers into signing records that showed fewer hours than those effectively worked.[54] At other times, contrary to the mandates of the contract, employers instructed crew leaders, often of Mexican background themselves, not to record the hours worked in the field, but to reverse-calculate the hours on the basis of the pounds of cotton harvested. The book-keepers were then attributing hours to workers based on the amount of cotton, according to remuneration quotas decided unilaterally, 'without benefit of any information whatsoever as to the number of hours worked by the Mexican Nationals in the crew in question', as one investigator frustratingly reported.[55] Other reports offer similar judgments on worker management in the cotton fields. The actual hours worked were 'ignored', 'disregarded', 'erroneous', 'not accurate'.[56] The amount of unpaid wages dwarfed what employers deducted for the *mordida*.

These practices were so ingrained that when in 1959 an inspector of the Department of Labor visited a cotton farm in Hargill, Texas, to examine their records, he heard the book-keeper nonchalantly instruct the crew leader to alter the entries to show that every Mexican worker in his crew had earned at least $0.50.[57] After more than a decade of impunity in observing the Bracero agreement, this Texan book-keeper had simply assumed that the ultra-exploitation of the contract workers was condoned by the institutions – in fact, given the paucity of control that characterised the programme until the late 1950s, this could be considered a fairly accurate assessment of the situation. While complaints investigations were formally part of the bilateral agreement from the outset, it was only from the late 1950s onwards that activist exposés and political pressure prompted the government to activate such investigations.

In the case of the Heidrick Farms in California, the investigators spelled out in words a practice that could describe several hundred cases: 'The payrolls records ... clearly show erasures and alterations, misrepresentations ... discrepancies between employers' copies and the workers' copies.'[58] But what employers were attempting to erase here, together with the correct digits, was also the contract workers' broader ability to claim the fruits of their labour agreed on in the contract signed by both parties. As much as contracts were supposed to be rational, efficient and fair ways to regulate labour relations (compared to the plantation-style cultural legacy of labour relations between planters and freedmen), the ability of growers to dodge paying full wages undermined a key element of the 'free labour' ideology, predicated on the ability of workers to work for wages for employers of their choosing.

Conclusion

In the first half of the twentieth century, labour coercion, agricultural work and debt had become entangled in the US South. They underpinned the financial workings of the political economy, social practices, managerial practices, discourses of morality and normativity; they interlinked an official discourse (inscribed into practices of accountancy and jurisprudence) with a tacit discourse (embodied social behaviours that made racial violence and inequality legitimate).

The transformation of agriculture in scale and mechanisation and of the rural labour market in the course of the first half of the twentieth century brought with it an evolution of the role and understanding of debt as an enabler of coercion. In the framework of 'peonage', managerial practices were central to manufacturing debt; debt was concocted by employers, often in connivance with the State. In this framework, debt had a wider social function: if physical violence was the ultimate enforcer of unequal social relations, it was debt, in its symbolic as well as material dimensions (and as a discourse as well as a social practice), that kept the 'subalterns' in their place.

As the rural labour force changed through the influx of Mexican migrants subject to deportation, the manufacturing of debt became 'externalised'; it occurred elsewhere, in a different nation, beyond the borders, and with the autonomous choice of workers who invested a part of the future in changing their present. At this point, employers only had to prolong that state of indebtedness with various, rather creative, ploys. However, debt remained the foundation upon which employers could exert increased labour discipline. In the process, any form of reciprocity and social bonding between debtors and creditors disappeared: workers did not work any more, by and large, for the people to whom they owed money.

> As I was writing this chapter, I was reminded of several newspaper articles that I came across about the labour conditions of transnational migrants. The 2022 Qatar football World Cup has exposed to the wider public a phenomenon previously of interest mainly to the scholar: the thousands of migrants from south-east Asia who make up Qatar's exploited workforce pay exorbitant fees, between $1,000 and $4,000, to labour recruiters before their departure. *The Guardian* reported, 'Workers often have to take out high-interest loans or sell land to afford the fees, leaving them vulnerable to debt bondage – a form of modern slavery – as they are unable to leave their jobs until the debt has been repaid.'[59] This echoes for me David McNally's concept of 'predatory inclusion' of the poor and the marginalised into the global labour market in conditions of high insecurity, a process that is often attributed to the rise of neoliberalism and of policies like privatisation of public assets and cuts to welfare that have driven up inequality.[60] Through the externalisation of debt, employers have, over the course of the twentieth century, also externalised the violence of the predatory relationship, as workers are dispossessed before

the start of the labour relationship or even the migratory process. It is now back at home that migrants face 'imperilled livelihoods' by taking loans from moneylenders and 'coyote networks' and face the risks, not only economic, of not being able to repay their debts.[61]

One other example is the way scholars link wage theft to the erosion of labour standards enforcement since the 1980s, a problem strongly correlated with the conditions of immigrant workforces.[62] This scholarship has captured the rising phenomenon of the exploitative practice of withholding or denying remuneration to immigrants susceptible to deportation, typically Latino migrants.[63] However, it is clear that this is a phenomenon that predates the decline of organised labour or the shift from a Fordist to a neoliberal regulatory regime, or even the more draconian anti-immigration regulatory regimes of the 2000s that make immigrants easy prey. As the historical analysis shows, vulnerable workers in the US had consistently been targets of these practices, which started as both a way for employers to save money and a way to keep workers in check by narrowing their opportunity to pay their debts. Plunging into the project (wider than this chapter) of tracing the genealogy of the nexus between debt, labour and coercion in the US throughout the twentieth century has therefore allowed me to complicate the narrative that would see the social restructuring of neoliberalism as the origin story of the growth of spurious forms of debt bondage. As this chapter shows, it has been long in the making: the mechanism of debt as enabler of coercion has been integrated in the workings of capitalism in ever-changing forms, which have included the use of advance remuneration to foster indebtedness. While nongovernmental organisations, scholars and policy-makers have increasingly paid attention to the relationship between debt and coerced labour in the contemporary US, this needs to be put into historical perspective to understand how throughout the twentieth century debt has obfuscated, to all but the staunchest labour advocates, the coercive nature of work relations under the smokescreen of contractual consent.

Acknowledgements

I would like to express my gratitude for the support of the Library Grant of the JFK Institute, Freie Universität, Berlin, and the generous research grant of the Gerda Henkel Foundation, without which the archival research for this article would not have been possible.

Notes

1. Foner, *Nothing but Freedom: Emancipation and its Legacy*; Foner, *Reconstruction: America's Unfinished Revolution, 1863–1877*; Wiener, 'Class Structure and Economic Development in the American South, 1865–1955', 1979; Wright, *Old South, New South*; Berlin et al., 'The Terrain of Freedom: The Struggle over the Meaning of Free Labor in the US South', 1986; Hahn, *A Nation under our Feet*; Baker and Kelly (eds), *After Slavery*; Rodrigue, *Reconstruction in the Cane Fields*.
2. Daniel, *The Shadow of Slavery: Peonage in the South*; Woodruff, *American Congo*; Blackmon, *Slavery by Another Name*; Goluboff, *The Lost Promise of Civil Rights*.
3. Harold Preece, 'Peonage – 1940 Style Slavery', Abolish Peonage Committee, Pamphlet, 1940. Copy in Department of Special Collection, Stanford University.
4. Balkin and Levinson, 'The Dangerous Thirteenth Amendment', 2012.
5. US Constitution, Amendment XIII, §1.
6. Harris, *Deep Souths*; Cohen, *At Freedom's Edge*; Cohen, 'Negro Involuntary Servitude in the South, 1865–1940: A Preliminary Analysis', 1976, 33–5, 47–53; Blackmon, *Slavery by Another Name*.
7. Peonage Investigation, 12 September 1947, Archives of Labor and Urban Affairs Work Defense League, Box 128, Folder 01.
8. Affidavit attached to J. R. Butler to Workers Defense League, 7 June 1938, Archives of Labor and Urban Affairs, Workers Defense League Collection, Box 172, Folder 3.
9. The transition to sharecropping in the nineteenth-century American South has been the focus of a vast debate in the last quarter of the twentieth century. The broad lines of that debate can be grasped in Mandle, *The Roots of Black Poverty*; Ransom and Sutch, *One Kind of Freedom*; Royce, *The Origins of Southern Sharecropping*; Saville, *The Work of Reconstruction*.
10. For a clear discussion of the meaning and differences between these forms of labour in the agricultural ladder of the South, see Woodman, 'Post-Civil War Southern Agriculture and the Law', 1979, 324–8.
11. Rodrigue, *Reconstruction in the Cane Fields*.
12. For a discussion on the transition in the late nineteenth century to a racialised and coercive notion of domestic servitude, see Branch and Wooten, 'Suited for Service: Racialized Rationalizations for the Ideal Domestic Servant from the Nineteenth to the Early Twentieth Century', 2012; for a general framework on the question of coercion and care in the US, see Glenn, *Forced to Care*.
13. Stanfield II, *Historical Foundations of Black Reflective Sociology*, 143–59.
14. Thomas, *The Plight of the Sharecropper*; Venkataramani, 'Norman Thomas, Arkansas Sharecroppers, and the Roosevelt Agricultural Policies, 1933–1937', 1965.
15. Raper, *Preface to Peasantry*.
16. On fluctuation of cotton prices and overproduction crises, see, for instance, Daniel, *Breaking the Land*, 18.
17. Otken, *The Ills of the South*; Ransom and Sutch, 'Debt Peonage in the Cotton South after the Civil War', 1972.
18. Johnson, *Shadow of the Plantation*, 128.
19. Black men were, with some exception, the primary target of immobilisation in a rural setting, but the phenomenon indirectly concerned women, too, when the man was employed as head of household and the work (productive or reproductive) of his wife and children considered as part of the labour that he would bring into the sharecropping arrangement.
20. Johnson, *Shadow of the Plantation*, 124.
21. Johnson, *Shadow of the Plantation*, 120, 128.
22. Woodson, *The Rural Negro*, 88. The reference to 'families' points to the indirect dependency of the whole household of the sharecropper or tenant who contracted the debt.
23. Peonage Cases, 123 F. 671 (1903).
24. Samec, 'Discursive Construction and Materiality of Debt in Context of Housing'.
25. Lazzarato, *The Making of the Indebted Man*, 45–6.
26. Raper, *Preface to Peasantry*, 153.
27. Raper, *Preface to Peasantry*, 172.
28. Nietzsche, *On the Genealogy of Morality*.
29. For a full account of practical handbooks aimed at assisting freedmen in their transition from slavery to freedom, see Hartman, *Scenes of Subjection*, 125–63.

30 Raper, *Shadow of the Plantation*, 161.
31 Woodson, *The Rural Negro*, 68.
32 Marx, quoted in Thorup, 'The Promissory Self–Credit and Debt Rationalities', 95.
33 Raper, *Shadow of the Plantation*, 162.
34 For an introduction to the hacienda system in its colonial origin, see Van Young, *Hacienda and Market*. See also Lindley, *Haciendas and Economic Development*. For a comparison with Mexican peonage, see Knight, 'Mexican Peonage: What Was It and Why Was It?', 1986.
35 *Clyatt vs United States* (1905), https://supreme.justia.com/cases/federal/us/197/207/.
36 'Peonage in the United States' (1907), https://awpc.cattcenter.iastate.edu/2019/11/22/peonage-in-the-united-states-1907/.
37 'Peonage in the United States' (1907).
38 Holley, *The Second Great Emancipation*. On the African-American migration, see Grossman, *Land of Hope*; Marks, *Farewell—We're Good and Gone: The Great Black Migration*; Gottlieb, *Making Their Own Way: Southern Blacks' Migration to Pittsburgh, 1916–1930*; Phillips, *Alabama North: African-American Migrants, Community, and Working-Class Activism in Cleveland, 1915–45*.
39 Pizzolato, 'On the Unwary and the Weak'; Goluboff, 'Race, Labor, and the Thirteenth Amendment in the 1940s Department of Justice', 2006.
40 See, for instance, the cases of 'peonage' involving Mexican workers described in the Federal Bureau of Investigation report, 3 November 1943, Department of Justice, Peonage Files, Reel 23, page 0901–0923; Federal Bureau of Investigation report, 22 August 1944, Department of Justice, Peonage Files, Reel 24, page 0140.
41 Montejano, *Anglos and Mexicans in the Making of Texas*, 175.
42 For the broader context of this continuity, see Pizzolato, 'Harvests of Shame', 2018.
43 One of my favourite introductions to the complex labour issues raised by the Programa Bracero is Bernardi, 'Within the Factory of Mobility'. See also the classic Calavita, *Inside the State: The Bracero Program, Immigration, and the INS*.
44 'Statement of the Rev. James L. Vizzard', 11 June 1958, Stanford University ibraries, Special Collections. Coll. 324, Box 31, Series VI, Fol. 9.
45 Montejano, *Anglos and Mexicans*, 220–3.
46 Interview with Catalino Díaz Villa by Anais Acosta, 2008, 'Interview no. 1340', Institute of Oral History, University of Texas at El Paso for the Bracero History Archive.
47 Interview with Barnabé Álvarez Díaz by Alejandra Díaz, 2008, 'Interview no. 1331', Institute of Oral History, University of Texas at El Paso for the Bracero History Archive.
48 'Extension of Mexican Farm Labor Program', Hearings of the House of Representatives, March 22, 1960, 425.
49 In the matter of Yuma Producers Cooperative Association, Folder 'Joint Determinations, 1959 [1 of 2]', RG174, Department of Labor, Office of the Solicitor, Region IX, Records Relating to the Mexican Labor 'Bracero' Programme, 1950–1965, Container #4.
50 In the matter of Northern California Growers Association, Folder 'Joint Determinations, 1959 [1 of 2]', RG174, Department of Labor, Office of the Solicitor, Region IX, Records Relating to the Mexican Labor 'Bracero' Programme, 1950–1965, Container #4.
51 Richard Baquera, 'Eleanor Martin', in Bracero History Archive, Item #46, http://braceroarchive.org/items/show/46.
52 Myrna Parra-Mantilla, 'Ignacio Nájera', in Bracero History Archive, Item #17, http://braceroarchive.org/items/show/17; Mario Sifuentes, 'Ismael Rodríguez Rico', in Bracero History Archive, Item #409, http://braceroarchive.org/items/show/409.
53 Department of Industrial Relations, from Attorney Shore to Legal Section, January 8, 1953, Folder Special Problems, 1953–56 Interpretation Art. 21 of Agreement, RG174, Department of Labor, Office of the Solicitor, Region IX, Records Relating to the Mexican Labor 'Bracero' Programme, 1950–1965, Container #9.
54 In the matter of Martin Gandy, Joint Determination, 1959 [2 of 2], RG174, Department of Labor, Office of the Solicitor, Region IX, Records Relating to the Mexican Labor 'Bracero' Programme, 1950–1965, Container #4.
55 In the matter of A-A Harvesting Association, La Feria, Texas, Folder Joint Determinations, 1960 [1 of 2], RG174, Department of Labor, Office of the Solicitor, Region IX, Records Relating to the Mexican Labor 'Bracero' Programme, 1950–1965, Container #4.
56 In the matter of J-P Terrell, Navasota, Texas, Folder Joint Determinations, 1960 [1 of 2],

RG174, Department of Labor, Office of the Solicitor, Region IX, Records Relating to the Mexican Labor 'Bracero' Programme, 1950–1965, Container #4.
57 In the matter of Hargill Cooperative Association, Hargill, Texas. Folder: Joint Determinations 1959 [1 of 2]. RG174, Department of Labor, Office of the Solicitor, Region IX, Records Relating to the Mexican Labor 'Bracero' Programme, 1950–1965, Container #4.
58 In the matter of Yolo Growers Inc., Woodland California, Folder: Joint Determinations 1959 [1 of 2]. RG174, Department of Labor, Office of the Solicitor, Region IX, Records Relating to the Mexican Labor 'Bracero' Programme, 1950–1965, Container #4.
59 'Revealed: Migrant Workers in Qatar Forced to Pay Billions in Recruitment Fees', *The Guardian*, 31 March 2022, https://www.theguardian.com/global-development/2022/mar/31/migrant-workers-in-qatar-forced-to-pay-billions-in-recruitment-fees-world-cup [accessed 16 July 2022].
60 McNally, *Global Slump*; see also De La Barra, 'Who owes and who pays?', 2006.
61 Johnson and Woodhouse, 'Securing the Return', 2018.
62 Fine and Bartley, 'Raising the Floor', 2019; Bobo, *Wage Theft in America*.
63 Fussell, 'The Deportation Threat Dynamic', 2011.

Bibliography

Baker, Bruce E. and Kelly, Brian (eds). *After Slavery: Race, Labor, and Citizenship in the Reconstruction South*. Florida: University Press of Florida, 2013.
Balkin, Jack M. and Levinson, Sanford. 'The Dangerous Thirteenth Amendment', *Columbia Law Review* (2012): 1459–99.
Berlin, Ira, Hahn, Steven, Miller, Steven F., Reidy, Joseph P. and Rowland, Leslie S. 'The Terrain of Freedom: The Struggle over the Meaning of Free Labor in the US South', *History Workshop Journal* 22/1 (1986): 108–30.
Bernardi, Claudia. 'Within the Factory of Mobility: Practices of Mexican Migrant Workers in the Twentieth-Century US Labour Regimes'. In *Precarity and International Relations*, edited by Ritu Viji, Tahseen Kazi and Elisa Wynne-Hughes, 253–77. Cham: Palgrave Macmillan, 2021.
Blackmon, Douglas A. *Slavery by Another Name: The Re-enslavement of Black Americans from the Civil War to World War II*. New York: Doubleday, 2008.
Bobo, Kim. *Wage Theft in America: Why Millions of Americans Are Not Getting Paid—And What We Can Do about It*. New York: The New Press, 2014.
Branch, Enobong Hannah and Melissa E. Wooten. 'Suited for Service: Racialized Rationalizations for the Ideal Domestic Servant from the Nineteenth to the Early Twentieth Century', *Social Science History* 36/2 (2012): 169–89.
Calavita, Kitty. *Inside the State: The Bracero Program, Immigration, and the INS*. New York: Routledge, 1992.
Cohen, William, 'Negro Involuntary Servitude in the South, 1865–1940: A Preliminary Analysis', *Journal of Southern History* 42 (1976): 31–60.
Cohen, William. *At Freedom's Edge: Black Mobility and the Southern White Quest for Racial Control, 1861–1915*. Baton Rouge: Louisiana University Press, 1991.
Daniel, Pete. *The Shadow of Slavery: Peonage in the South, 1901–1969*. Urbana: University of Illinois Press, 1972.
Daniel, Pete. *Breaking the Land: The Transformation of Cotton, Tobacco, and Rice Cultures Since 1880*. Urbana: University of Illinois Press, 1986.
De La Barra, Ximena. 'Who Owes and Who Pays? The Accumulated Debt of Neoliberalism', *Critical Sociology* 32/1 (2006): 125–61.
Fine, Janice and Bartley, Tim. 'Raising the Floor: New Directions in Public and Private Enforcement of Labour Standards in the United States', *Journal of Industrial Relations* 61/2 (2019): 252–76.
Foner, Eric. *Nothing but Freedom: Emancipation and its Legacy*. Baton Rouge: Louisiana University Press, 2007.
Foner, Eric. *Reconstruction: America's Unfinished Revolution, 1863–1877*. New York: Harper & Row, 1989.
Fussell, Elizabeth. 'The Deportation Threat Dynamic and Victimization of Latino Migrants: Wage Theft and Robbery', *The Sociological Quarterly* 52/4 (2011): 593–615.

Glenn, Evelyn Nakano. *Forced to Care: Coercion and Caregiving in America*. Cambridge, MA: Harvard University Press, 2010.

Goluboff, Risa L. 'Race, Labor, and the Thirteenth Amendment in the 1940s Department of Justice', *University of Toledo Law Review* 38 (2006): 883–94.

Goluboff, Risa. *The Lost Promise of Civil Rights*. Cambridge, MA: Harvard University Press, 2009.

Gottlieb, Peter. *Making Their Own Way: Southern Blacks' Migration to Pittsburgh, 1916–1930*. Urbana: University of Illinois Press, 1987.

Grossman, James R. *Land of Hope: Chicago and the Great Migration*. Chicago: University of Chicago Press, 1989.

Hahn, Steven. *A Nation under our Feet: Black Political Struggles in the Rural South from Slavery to the Great Migration*. Cambridge, MA: Harvard University Press, 2005.

Harris, J. William. *Deep Souths: Delta, Piedmont, and Sea Island Society in the Age of Segregation*. Baltimore: John Hopkins University Press, 2001.

Hartman, V. Saidiya. *Scenes of Subjection: Terror, Slavery & Self-Making in Nineteenth-Century America*. New York: Oxford University Press, 1997.

Holley, Donald. *The Second Great Emancipation: Mechanical Cotton Picker, Black Migration & Modern South*. Fayetteville: University of Arkansas Press, 2000.

Johnson, Richard L. and Woodhouse, Murphy. 'Securing the Return: How Enhanced US Border Enforcement Fuels Cycles of Debt Migration', *Antipode*, 50/4 (2018): 976–96.

Knight, Alan. 'Mexican Peonage: What Was It and Why Was It?', *Journal of Latin American Studies* 18/1 (1986): 41–74.

Lazzarato, Maurizio. *The Making of the Indebted Man*. Los Angeles: Semiotext(e), 2012.

Lindley, Richard B. *Haciendas and Economic Development: Guadalajara, Mexico, at Independence*. Austin: University of Texas Press, [1983] 2014.

Mandle, Jay R. *The Roots of Black Poverty: The Southern Plantation Economy after the Civil War*. Durham, NC: Duke University Press, 1978.

Marks, Carole. *Farewell—We're Good and Gone: The Great Black Migration*. Bloomington: Indiana University Press, 1989.

McNally, David. *Global Slump: The Economics and Politics of Crisis and Resistance*. Oakland: PM Press, 2010.

Montejano, David. *Anglos and Mexicans in the Making of Texas 1836–1986*. Austin: University of Texas Press, 1987.

Nietzsche, Friedrich. *On the Genealogy of Morality*. Second Treatise. Translated by Maudemarie Clark and Alan J. Swensen. Indianapolis, IN: Hackett Publishing, 1998.

Otken, Charles. *The Ills of the South or Related Cases Hostile to the General Prosperity of Southern People*. New York: G. P. Putnam's Sons, 1894.

Phillips, Kimberley L. *Alabama North: African-American Migrants, Community, and Working-Class Activism in Cleveland, 1915–45*. Urbana: University of Illinois Press, 1999.

Pizzolato, Nicola. 'Harvests of Shame: Enduring Unfree Labour in the Twentieth-Century United States, 1933–1964', *Labor History* 59/4 (2018): 472–90.

Pizzolato, Nicola. 'On the Unwary and the Weak: Fighting Peonage in Wartime United States: Connections, Categories, Scales'. In *Micro-Spatial Histories of Global Labour*, edited by Christian G. De Vito and Anne Gerritsen, 291–312. Cham: Palgrave Macmillan, 2018.

Ransom, Roger L. and Sutch, Richard. 'Debt Peonage in the Cotton South after the Civil War', *The Journal of Economic History* 32/3 (1972): 641–69.

Ransom, Roger L. and Sutch, Richard. *One Kind of Freedom: The Economic Consequences of Emancipation*. Cambridge, UK: Cambridge University Press, 1977.

Raper, Arthur, F. *Preface to Peasantry: A Tale of Two Black Belt Counties*. Chapel Hill: The University of North Carolina Press, 1936.

Rodrigue, John C. *Reconstruction in the Cane Fields*. Baton Rouge: Louisiana State University, 2001.

Royce, Edward. *The Origins of Southern Sharecropping*. Philadelphia: Temple University Press, 1993.

Samec, Tomáš. 'Discursive Construction and Materiality of Debt in Context of Housing', PhD dissertation, Charles University, Prague, 2018.

Saville, Julie. *The Work of Reconstruction: From Slave to Wage Laborer in South Carolina, 1860–1870*. New York: Cambridge University Press, 1994.

Stanfield II, John H. *Historical Foundations of Black Reflective Sociology*. New York: Routledge, 2016.

Thomas, Norman. *The Plight of the Sharecropper*. New York: League of Industrial Democracy, 1934.

Thorup, Mikkel. 'The Promissory Self: Credit and Debt Rationalities in the Work and Life of Karl Marx'. In *History of Economic Rationalities*, edited by Jakob-Bek Thomsen, Christian Olaf Christiansen, Stefan Gaarsmand Jacobsen and Mikkel Thorup, 95–102. Cham: Springer, 2017.

Van Young, Eric. *Hacienda and Market in Eighteenth-Century Mexico: The Rural Economy of the Guadalajara Region, 1675–1820*. Lanham: Rowman & Littlefield Publishers, 2006.

Venkataramani, M. S. 'Norman Thomas, Arkansas Sharecroppers, and the Roosevelt Agricultural Policies, 1933–1937', *The Arkansas Historical Quarterly* 24/1 (1965): 3–28.

Wiener, Jonathan M. 'Class Structure and Economic Development in the American South, 1865–1955', *The American Historical Review*, 84/4 (1979): 970–92.

Woodman, Harold D. 'Post-Civil War Southern Agriculture and the Law', *Agricultural History* 53/1 (1979): 319–37.

Woodruff, Nan Elizabeth. *American Congo: The African American Freedom Struggle in the Delta*. Cambridge, MA: Harvard University Press, 2003.

Woodson, Carter Goodwin. *The Rural Negro*. Washington, DC: The Association for the Study of Negro Life and History, 1930.

Wright, Gavin. *Old South, New South: Revolutions in the Southern Economy since the Civil War*. New York: Basic Books, 1986.

OBLIGATORY CONTRIBUTIONS TO SOCIETY 301

OBLIGATORY CONTRIBUTIONS TO SOCIETY 303

13
Obligatory contributions to society: student foreign-language guides as seasonal wage workers in socialist Bulgaria, 1970s–1980s

Ivanka Petrova

With the establishment of socialism as a political system in the People's Republic of Bulgaria after the Second World War, wage labour was assigned a central role in the creation of the new socialist person. After all, labour was considered a duty in the service of society[1] and it became a central protagonist of the socialist way of life. Within the socialist paradigm, young people are seen as the age group that must be included in the system of socially useful labour from their early years. In economic life in socialist Bulgaria, similar to that in the USSR, labour coercion and labour control were integrated as principles of the socialist economy, closely intertwined with labour relations mediated by remuneration.

In this chapter, I will present one of the forms of temporary employment of students during socialism in Bulgaria: the job of seasonal foreign-language guides in the sphere of international tourism. This type of employment was desirable for young people; however, it involved the use of acquired excellent language skills in foreign languages, and this requirement severely limited young people's access to it. It was available only to high school students from the final two classes of the few foreign language schools and to students who were alumni of these high schools or were studying a relevant philological specialty at the universities. The permission to perform it was obtained after successfully passing an entrance exam, completing specialised training and passing exams for acquired skills for a specific type of work.

My research object is the Youth Travel Bureau (YTB) Orbita, established in 1958 with headquarters in Sofia and branches in some Bulgarian district towns.[2] It was established as a specialised division of the Central Committee of the Communist Youth Union for Youth and Tourism. The bureau's target market was primarily students and young people up to the age of 30 in Bulgaria and abroad: it sent Bulgarian youth groups abroad as tourists and organised visits of foreign youth groups to Bulgaria as well as excursions of Bulgarian groups within the country. For three decades, the structure of Orbita gradually grew, as the enterprise managed the tourist facilities it owned (hotels, restaurants, sports complexes). The Black Sea resort International Youth Center (IYC) 'Georgi Dimitrov' near Primorsko, whose bungalows, hotels, restaurants, discos, stadium and summer theatre were managed by the bureau, enjoyed a great reputation in the country and abroad. Other youth tourist complexes were built in the capital Sofia, in the towns of Varna, Veliko Tarnovo, Pleven, Lovech, Vratsa and Rila and in the Tsigov Chark area near the town of Batak in the Rhodope Mountains. The head office of the bureau was located in a large new building in the city centre of Sofia.[3] Besides managers and the financial department, one of the most important departments was located there, the guiding department. The tour and translation services were provided by the employees of this department, the staff tour guides. They were divided into sectors according to the foreign languages involved and each sector was led by a head.

Established as one of the first tourist organisations in socialist Bulgaria, by the mid-1960s Orbita began to experience a dire need for seasonally working guides to serve the numerous youth tourist groups coming during the summer season, mainly from European socialist countries. The groups from the former Union of Soviet Socialist Republics (USSR) and German Democratic Republic (GDR) were the most numerous, while the number of groups from Poland, Hungary and the former Czechoslovakia was much smaller. The employees in the guiding department were tasked with recruiting applicants to be seasonal guides, conducting entrance exams and training approved candidates. About 50–60 young seasonal guides were trained annually in the 1970s and 1980s, and about 200–250 seasonal employees were needed for each season. According to the foreign languages used, the young seasonal guides reported directly to the respective staff guides and were subordinated to the head of the sector.

The job of foreign-language guide as a form of wage labour was accompanied by and linked with labour coercion. This chapter sets out to explore whether, why and how the young students employed as tourist guides perceived this type of seasonal work as a form of labour coercion. The chapter presents the working norms and duties set through the bureau's training, explores their application in the daily working life of the young tour guides and analyses students' labour practices and perceptions thereof. It also explores whether or not these practices were in line with the intended goals of the ruling elite, in particular the bureau's managers.

My hypothesis is that the socialist government deliberately created the opportunity for this kind of work for this small, selected group of highly educated young people. First, in economic terms, the aim was to make maximum use, at relatively low cost, of the language skills acquired by young people in their current training for the needs of international tourism. Second, from the youth policy perspective, the government intended to discipline them early through special training and keep them under control in a formal structure that tried to bring them into the ideological framework of the regime. Young people were perceived as an important target group to be educated ideologically. And third, beyond their specific job tasks, seasonal guides were used as intermediaries to convey official ideological messages of socialism among tourists from foreign countries, which could also be seen as a kind of coercion. Although mainly coming from socialist countries, young foreign tourists were seen as targets of ideological work by the bureau, which is another reason why young guides were assigned these kinds of duties.

Over six summer seasons I participated in this programme, working as a foreign-language guide for tourists from the former GDR when I was a student at the German language high school in Sofia and later at Sofia University. Now I have decided to share my personal story. I rely on the method of reflective anthropology; I will analyse the object of my study by refracting it through the lens of my personal experiences and by using 16 biographical interviews with former tour guides, men and women aged between 50 and 65, which I conducted in 2019 and 2020. I know all of the respondents personally, and have maintained relationships with some of them over the years. I tried to select former guides who had worked with tour groups from different countries, yet most of my interviewees had accompanied German or Russian groups. I am exploring the respondents' memories and present-day attitudes towards their everyday working lives in order to discover what role this kind of work played in constructing their identities and whether and how it contributed to their perception and evaluation of coercion and remuneration in wage labour during socialism.

It should be noted that my interlocutors stated in the interviews that they did not feel exploited, although they recalled and commented on several examples of coercion in labour relations. In order to understand their attitude, we need to consider their work within the framework of student and youth labour during socialism and the mechanisms of control and coercion exercised.

Youth labour brigades

An important part of the People's Republic of Bulgaria's state policy was the temporary engagement of young people as unpaid physical workforce in the Youth Brigadier Movement, organised in so-called 'youth labour brigades' in various sectors of the economy.[4] The Brigadier Movement, led by the Central Committee of the Communist Youth Union, was established in 1945 as 'a mass movement for the voluntary undertaking of socially useful labour by the youth in solving economic and social tasks in the building of socialism'.[5]

The establishment of state socialism as a political system was associated with radical changes in the economic, social and cultural structure of the country. The ruling Communist Party set out on a course of forced industrialisation and reconstruction (collectivisation) of agriculture with the aim of transforming the country from a predominantly agrarian to a developed industrial state in a few decades. The Communist Party's efforts were directed towards the construction of large-scale industrial facilities, which would lay the foundations of heavy industry as the leading economic sector. Rapid industrialisation also meant urgent urbanisation. To accomplish these grandiose tasks, however, there was a shortage of available workforce, especially during the immediate post-war years. This was precisely the reason for the establishment of the Youth Brigadier Movement. Indeed, the members of youth brigades, regardless of their gender, worked on sites where the state did not have sufficient funds to pay regular construction workers.

The first youth brigades were set up in the mid-1940s to help build roads, railways and dams, which involved heavy manual labour. The initial period until the late 1940s was characterised by mass mobilisation of the youth workforce based on enthusiasm and youthful impulses.[6] The Youth Union appealed to the youth, who were charged with a duty to participate in the reconstruction and development of a modern industrial society in Bulgaria. Part of the new government's ideology was the claim that the communist utopia was achievable with enormous efforts and that the youth were called to be its builders.[7] During the first period of the Brigadier Movement, young people from the villages participated in the spring and autumn for two months each, and students took part in the summer for 35–45 days. For their daily work of eight hours in a six-day work week, the youth received no pay, only food. Many participants joined of their own volition and shared the enthusiasm that gripped the youth of that time.[8] Gradually, however, during the late 1940s and early 1950s, the number of participants began to decrease, so from the mid-1950s voluntarism was replaced by labour coercion, with penalties for non-participation in the brigades.[9]

During the second period of the Brigadier Movement (1956–1989), each year the Central Committee of the Youth Union proposed where brigadiers should be sent to work in the summer and the proposals were approved by the Council of Ministers. The local youth committees concluded contracts with the enterprises where the youth would work and began to form brigades. No individual wages were provided for the young people in this period either, although the enterprises paid a certain amount to the Youth Union. During this time, typical participants were young individuals of the intelligentsia,[10] students from high schools (over 16 years of age) and universities, and young employees with higher education (between 25 and 30 years old). The latter were forced by the Youth Union's leadership in the respective enterprises or establishments to temporarily leave their jobs and perform physical work in a production crew for about 30–45 days, which usually happened relatively soon after the beginning of their professional careers.[11] The participants in the youth labour brigades during the second period also performed relatively hard physical labour for one or two months during school-free summer and autumn weeks. Students were not subject to prior training for the respective physical work; they were usually trained on the spot by the hired workers. The Bulgarian ethnologist Radost Ivanova, who first explored the Brigadier Movement, notes in her study of youth construction brigades that this phenomenon, which was characteristic of the Bulgarian version of socialism, left lasting traces in the economic and social life of the country both during and after the socialist regime.[12] Brigades were formed throughout the entire socialist period in Bulgaria (1945–1989), making participation in them a permanent part of the individual biographies of high school and university students.[13]

In most cases young people in the brigades were forced to live in poor living conditions. Usually they were housed in barracks with 20–30 beds and no sanitary facilities or in frugal workers' dormitories; they were provided with uncomfortable work clothes and fed in canteens with poor sanitary conditions and poor food quality; their daily regime and the general organisation of work and life was modelled on the military. The historian Ulf Brunnbauer notes that this structure was intended to provide a specific form of discipline that would represent society according to the vision of the party leadership: a unified population that was isolated from the outside world and sacrificed itself for the common good by exhibiting as little individuality as possible.[14]

Thus, young people were forced to work every year for at least one month, to experience humble working and living conditions and understand that only through collective work can prosperity be achieved. However, this often became a means of enforcing obedience in practice. Their labour was mainly manual and the means of work were usually primitive. In the construction sites, for example, they worked with shovels, picks and wheelbarrows; in the food industry they prepared fruit and vegetable preserves by hand; in agriculture they helped to harvest the crops in the fields mainly through manual physical labour. The brigadier's workday was described by the researchers as hard, exhausting and stressful.[15]

The deliberate deployment of the young intelligentsia outside their areas of skill and training to perform low-skilled and unpaid labour was part of the state policy of denigrating the role of the intelligentsia in building socialism. Ivanova notes that in the labour brigades, young, highly educated people were placed in a dependent and subordinate position in relation to the workers and were forced to conform to their way of life and work.[16] The workers usually assigned them the most unskilled work involving the heaviest physical labour. Like the workers, brigadiers also had to fulfil daily and weekly work norms and participate in competitions. The temporary status of the young brigadiers did not oblige the administration of the enterprises to provide the same care for them as it usually did for its permanent workers.

The Bulgarian folklorist Anatol Anchev draws similar conclusions in his study of everyday working life in a sewage canal brigade, where he was forced to work temporarily, detached from his duties as a young, highly qualified philologist.[17] Young professionals with higher education not only received neither remuneration nor food in the brigade, but were often ridiculed by the workers for their lack of skills for physical work, and their higher education and aptitude for intellectual work were symbolically belittled through jokes and anecdotes. Although educated forces were needed, the ideology of the regime was characterised by a general disparagement of mental labour, which was also expressed in a material aspect. Almost throughout the entire socialist period in Bulgaria, workers' wages were higher than those of employees with higher education. This was in line with the view that the working class should play a leading role in society and create the social base of socialism as its main social force.[18] Ivanova also argues that 'the brigades helped to establish and perpetuate in society a stereotype of a dismissive attitude towards the intelligentsia'[19]. The reason is that in the brigades the young intelligentsia was put in a regime of coerced labour and dependence: on the leaders of the local Youth Union, on the management of the enterprises, even on the wage workers with a much lower level of education.

Participation in the brigade during the second period of the Brigadier Movement was compulsory; otherwise students were not allowed to continue their education in the next school or academic year. The state-issued certificate of work in the one-month brigade of newly admitted students was a prerequisite for the commencement of their higher education at the respective university. It was possible to be exempt for health reasons, which was allowed after submission of a medical certificate stating that the person could or should not perform heavy physical work. In such a case, however, the student was required to carry out unpaid administrative work at the high school or university for the same period of time. Thus, during most of their free extracurricular time, young people were used as unpaid workforce and controlled by the heads of the brigades or the management of the educational institutions. This was in line with the prevailing socialist ideology and the government's aspirations to impose control over all spheres of public and private life and to achieve a rationalisation of society.[20] The brigades were to serve the purpose of disciplining the young intelligentsia and educating them in work habits even before they began their professional careers.[21]

After the 1960s, the temporary employment of young seasonal language guides at the YTB Orbita was accepted, officially recognised and promoted as an equal substitute for the youth labour brigade. Unlike the physical low-skilled labour of the brigadiers, this type of work involved mentally highly skilled labour and was not done for free as was the unpaid brigadier labour. Thus, guiding tourists emerged as a small island within a system of labour coercion that only a small and selected group of young people could access. While guides were still forced to work, they saw themselves as privileged in comparison to thousands of other young people and their working and living conditions in the brigades.

Recruitment and training of seasonal guides

The entrance exam for seasonal guides was held in September before the beginning of each school and academic year. No official campaign was announced for it. The candidates were recruited in two ways. The first was very popular and often practised in enterprises and establishments: it was the access to a workplace through family and friendship 'connections'.[22] Some of my respondents said they had been encouraged to apply for this work by relatives or friends of their parents who worked at the Youth Travel Bureau in various positions. Such young people, who were also required to be studying philology or to be studying at or have graduated from a foreign language high school, formed the first contingent of applicants. Usually they were all accepted, regardless of their performance in the entrance exam.

The second group of candidates who registered for the exam had learned about this opportunity from their classmates or fellow students who were already working as seasonal employees at Orbita. Of these candidates, not all were accepted for training, and it was common practice that those rejected were not even told the reasons for this decision by the examination board. As a classmate of mine who failed the entrance exam recalls, 'I didn't even understand why I wasn't accepted as a tour guide, I didn't get a grade or anything. And on the exam they didn't correct me, they didn't ask me, they just listened. It was just that my name was not on the board with the accepted ones' (A. D., male, b. 1963).

Thus, access to seasonal work was provided mainly through informal channels and networks. This is not unusual because access to prestigious permanent employment at that time usually operated in the same way. I belong to the second group of young people: my older cousin, who had graduated from the German language school in Sofia and had worked as a seasonal tour guide at Orbita, recommended that I sign up for the entrance exam.

The training of the seasonal guides lasted about 20 days. It took place at the headquarters in Sofia during the winter and spring vacations for high school students and during the semester vacation for university students, and included lectures and practical training seminars. The young people (the majority aged between 17 and 21) were trained to work with tourist groups and with financial and accounting documents, and they studied the Guidebook on their own.[23] The 10-day study trip along the country's tourist routes during the April vacation was organised and conducted by the staff guides, with the trained young people being divided into groups according to their knowledge of the respective foreign languages (Russian, German, Czech, Polish and Hungarian). During this trip, practical exams were taken in a foreign language for routes, settlements and tourist sites. None of the respondents remembered that they had been graded on this practical exam; on the contrary, the stories of the study trip emphasised the good mood, the emotions, the exploration of natural and cultural sites. At the end of the training, the young people took an exam with few questions on Bulgarian history and geography and with a predominant number of questions on Bulgaria's foreign and domestic policy, economy, state and political structure, health, social policy and education.

Among the young trainees, this exam was called the 'political training exam'. I remember that the two examiners asked me questions about Balkan politics and the work of the Council for Mutual Economic Assistance[24] and I was not very confident in my answers. Finally they advised me to pay attention to 'current political events' and did not even tell me what my assessment was. I was quite worried about it, but the next day I found out that my grade was very good. It turned out that there were no trainees who had not passed the 'political exam'; my respondents did not remember any such cases either. Probably once the bureau accepted the young people for training, it took care to keep them and get them to work as quickly as possible. The entrance exam can also be defined as a test of loyalty to the system. Once that was proven, the next exams functioned only as 'controlling' mock exams.

The tour guide was the first local resident whom the foreign tourists met in Bulgaria, the one with whom they had the most contact and from whom they learned the most facts about the country and life there, which is why the bureau burdened the young employee with great responsibilities. In each arriving tourist group, there was a person in charge called a 'group leader' who organised the group members for participation in the planned activities, helped the local tour guide and monitored the behaviour and discipline of the tourists. The guide, along with the group leader, had to make sure that the group members spent as much time together as possible. In this way, it was part of the work tasks of the tour guide to prevent the young tourists from being out of supervision and control, even in their free time. This normative requirement, which was also extended to young tourists from other socialist countries from the Warsaw Pact, fully coincided with the ideology of the socialist government in terms of establishing inspection of people's private lives.

In specifying the content and type of tour guide services offered by the bureau, ideological goals stood out as primary, above the purposes of providing recreation and leisure entertainments during the vacation. New guides were trained to provide services in which the main emphasis was put on conveying the principal ideological messages of the Bulgarian socialist regime, such as the progressive nature of state socialism, the solidarity and friendship between socialist countries, and loyalty to the ruling Bulgarian Communist Party and to the Communist Party of the Soviet Union. Such was the nature of the lectures given during the training and such were the basic guidelines in the Guidebook. During visits to museums and memorials, the guides were obliged to offer tourists information about the heroic past of Bulgaria and the Bulgarians, emphasising the long-standing ties and cooperation with the peoples of socialist countries, drawing tourists' attention to the role of Russia/the USSR as a dual 'liberator' and highlighting the role of Bulgarian–Russian and Bulgarian–Soviet 'friendship'.

In talks and conversations with tourists, the young guides had to present the country and the population as 'exemplary' in the building of state socialism on the Soviet model, emphasising the successes of the socialist planned economy, social policy, health, education and cultural development. Last but not least, the seasonal guides were entrusted with the task of creating sustainable ties between young people from different socialist countries during the obligatory bilateral 'friendship meetings' and other mass events organised by them. This ideological orientation of the guide services was frequently mentioned in the interviews and is still remembered by my respondents. They often talk about their failure to comply with these norms and comment on the ways in which they circumvented or rejected them. One respondent recalled:

> All the ideology we were taught and tested on, I didn't apply it. What German who came on holiday was interested in our history? Or in the victories of the Soviet army. I wanted to entertain them, to keep them happy, and when I saw they were tired, I just let them rest and didn't bother them with history or politics. And very often I organised games and quizzes for them instead. (S. G., male, b. 1963)

We can hardly speak of a fully conscious resistance of the young tour guides to the ideological norms of the work. Rather, it was a question of taking into account the interests of young tourists and their desires for spending their leisure time, which tour guides as young people also shared. Such circumvention of the ideological orientations of the services testifies that the tour guides experienced some leeway in their work, and also that the young employees at Orbita did not have 'infinite' respect for their superiors and in general for the socialist regime.

Conditions for and forms of remuneration

Working with foreign tourist groups required 24-hour availability of the guides, who also acted as translators. They met the group at the airport, accompanied it by bus throughout the itinerary and were responsible for the implementation of all parts of the tour programme. During the bus tours, the guides had to tell the group about the history and geographical features of the respective region, while showing them the sights. They led city tours, organised visits to museums and memorials, and took care of the meals, ordering from the menus in the restaurants and paying for the group's accommodation and meals with cheques they filled out. At the end of the stay, they sent the group to the airport or to the 'Friendship Bridge' before signing, together with the group leader, the two copies of the most important document, the so-called 'voucher', which certified the completion of the tourist programme and the tour guide's duties and detailed the mandatory tour programme of the group.

The programme usually covered two weeks and most often included a seven-day stay on the Black Sea coast and a seven-day tour of the country (or a seven-day stationary stay in a mountain resort or in a city where the bureau had hotel facilities). Less often, the group spent two weeks at the IYC near Primorsko. In the latter case, the seasonal guides were often assigned to work with two or three groups at the same time; however, they received the usual payment for accompanying only one group and were not paid extra. At the IYC, the responsibilities of the students were greater: they attended mandatory briefings three times a week early in the morning and were obliged to mobilise their groups daily for sports games and competitions on the beach, to organise and conduct afternoon 'friendship meetings' and to stimulate tourists to participate in public ideological lectures and discussions in the afternoons, where they had to provide simultaneous interpretation into the respective languages. They also had to offer additional entertainment outside the programme, which was paid for by willing tourists, such as a visit to a restaurant with a folklore programme, a disco outing or an attractive excursion. Considering the main tasks of the guides, they were intermediaries and translators for the guests in their interactions with local authorities, health services, law enforcement agencies and other institutions. In assigning them this role, there was an attempt to make the guides indebted to the tourist sector and even to a temporary group of tourists.

The terms and conditions of the seasonal guides' remuneration were determined by the bureau's management. The young guides could work during the summer months with no time limit, according to their request at the beginning of each season. Most often they accompanied four to six tourist groups per season, which meant they worked for two to three months. However, the payment for their labour during these months was different. Students who worked as seasonal tour guides at Orbita for one month instead of participating in the mandatory labour brigade received a daily wage for that month at a very low rate, BGN (Bulgarian levs) 2 per day or BGN 60 for the month. It was two or three times lower than the remuneration they received when they worked as seasonal guides at the bureau during the other weeks of the vacation – BGN 4 for high school students and BGN 6 for university students, up to BGN 120 and BGN 180 respectively per month – even though the type of hired work and responsibilities were the same. For comparison, the salary of a newly hired young specialist with a university degree at that time was BGN 175 per month.

Apart from the low salary, students received a document that they had worked as seasonal tour guides and this document was compulsory for enrolling in the next school or university year. The participants in the labour brigades received only a document, and no payment. The same applied to those exempt from brigades for medical reasons who performed unpaid labour in the high school or university administration. This expressed the social aspect of labour coercion in relation to the seasonal tour guide work. One month's work as a seasonal guide, replacing participation in the labour brigade, was an attractive alternative to the unpaid brigades, although the pay was low. In fact, it could be argued that the function of these low wages was to disguise coercion, but in reality it could not be disguised. Rather the coercion was reinforced, as the certificate was required of students until the end of the socialist period and the wages did not justify the forced recruitment to youth work.

The quality of work and the initiative involved in the student guides' work were neither taken into account nor rewarded by the bureau. For example, in the voucher signed by the leader of the tourist group, there was no column for noting the quality of the services provided by the tour guide. In contrast to the staff guides, who received monthly bonuses, there were no additional financial incentives for good work performance by young guides. Despite the lack of such incentives, guides were forced to offer additional services to tourists. When I asked what motivated them to be active in offering such services, the respondents mainly pointed out the consumer side of the services, which they enjoyed equally with tourists, but without paying for them: they visited diverse and attractive tourist sites, enjoyed free entrance to discos and dined in expensive restaurants, which they could not afford on their own. Thus, coercion was combined with the possibility of consuming services and goods that were luxurious and sometimes difficult to access for young people during socialism. Moreover, during these additional events, someone else took over the main responsibility for the tourists' entertainment (such as a DJ, folk band or local paid guide) and the young guides had the opportunity for a short break and more relaxed consumption.

Everyday working life practices

The work put a heavy workload on the young people – there were no days off, nor a set time for rest on working days; they had to be as focused as possible during the day and always ready for work at night. Some young guides could not withstand the demands and pressure, and worked only one season. However, they were a minority; those who worked two or more seasons predominated. Most seasonal guides were highly motivated to do this work instead of working in the brigade.

Labour relations at Orbita were formally carried out at a vertical level, involving the guide management, staff guides and seasonal guides. In my conversations with respondents, they pointed out that their relations with the staff tour guides at the higher level were entirely formal and that the distance between the two levels remained too great to overcome this. My interlocutors had no memories of crossing the hierarchical boundaries in the working environment and establishing closer, informal friendly relations between seasonal and staff employees. Even if there were such cases, they were too few to talk about or remember.

Some of my respondents pointed out that, as beginners, they were even afraid of the senior staff guides on whom they depended to obtain the equivalent of a brigadier's work document. 'The first year I went to Primorsko and there I watched S., the senior tour guide, who led our training,' an interlocutor told me. 'He had been sent on a mission to be in charge of the seasonal guides at the IYC. I was very worried all the time, lest I messed something up, lest I get embarrassed, because he was supposed to sign our notes for the university later' (I. D., female, b. 1964). So dependency relations were at stake here.

Guide work did not imply competition among young employees, as was the case in other enterprises and establishments during socialism in Bulgaria.[25] While vertical hierarchical relationships were highly formalised, horizontal relations between seasonal guides often blurred the boundaries between official formal and private informal relationships. In the working environment of young guides, along with professional relations, interpersonal friendly relations were established, which played an important role in helping them cope with work duties. Solidarity and mutual help among the young employees stood out as key features in the seasonal guides' working life. Very often, they joined forces when they accompanied groups with the same tourist programme, by sharing common tasks or replacing each other.

For example, when I and a former classmate of mine, both then university students, were leading two parallel groups of German tourists in the Tsigov Chark resort near the town of Batak, we agreed between ourselves that she would take over the visit and guided tour in Batak for both groups at the same time, and the next day I would accompany all the tourists to the Snezhanka cave. In this way each of us had a day off. Of course, our superiors were not informed. I am convinced that they knew about this, but did not react, as it was important for the bureau to provide the services to the tourists, and implicitly to give the young guides the opportunity for some kind of rest. This was not an official condoning; rather, this leniency should be traced back to the individual people working at the bureau.

There were cases when a young colleague's absence was deliberately concealed from superiors by having another seasonal guide take over the colleague's work with the group for a few hours. Temporary absence from work was not common and was mainly related to overwork of young people. Services rendered by colleagues were usually returned with reciprocal favours or a treat. A respondent said:

> I had to send my group from IYC to the airport in Burgas, their charter was at night. I barely went to the reception, there the bus already came, and they loaded the suitcases. And I can't look up from tiredness; I hardly slept the night before. The driver feels sorry for me when he looks at me. There was another group with the same charter, and N. was its guide. And he shouts to me, 'You go to sleep, I'll send them both groups'. I wasn't comfortable, to tell you the truth, but he was very insistent, he even got along with the leader of my group. I remember that later I bought him a *Pliska* brandy from the bar, just to thank him. (I. D., female, b. 1964)

There were also rare cases of deliberate evasion of duties. Sometimes, the guides did not talk about the sights along the route throughout the bus rides, as required of them. This occurred most often during night transfers from the airport: the guides would leave the newly arrived tourists to rest after the tiring flight. Occasionally, the guided tours were shortened if the guide noticed a lack of interest among tourists. I remember that when I took a group of German tourists to the restored church on the historic Tsarevets Hill in the old capital Veliko Tarnovo, most of the young people did not want to visit the Orthodox church or listen to my lecture. Thus I took the liberty of giving a very short talk so as not to bore the tourists. Such flexibility in the programme was not desired at all by the bureau but there was no way it could be controlled. My respondents also told me about similar cases. Their statements point to a common practice: providing tourists with opportunities to satisfy their individual desires for spending their vacation. The guides sought and found ways to pay attention to the interests of tourist groups and provide niches of free time for them, thus avoiding the perception of international tourism as a kind of serial production.[26]

Respondents' memories: responsibility and punishment

Respondents' stories often pointed out that tour guiding work entailed too much workload for them. They said that they not only worked without days off, but also worked nonstop for weeks in the summer – sending one group to the airport to catch the plane and welcoming the next, who had just arrived on the same plane. It was not unusual for tourists to get involved in brawls and fights or to suffer from acute illnesses at night, and then the tour guide had to be available throughout the night to provide assistance. My respondents still remembered such cases:

> The Germans did not tolerate the sea climate very well and neither our food, especially the alcohol. They regularly woke me up at night: some with abdominal pains, some with fever or sunburnt from the beach. And I kept my guard up, though I watched them all to warn them. ... I had a case, one had forgotten his jacket in Primorsko with the passport in its pocket, and now we are on our way to Rila mountain. He remembered, but too late. I took them to Rila, and I – back by train and then by bus for the passport. (N. N., male, b. 1961)

Although it was not part of the job description, tour guides had to be 'everywhere' and to do 'everything' when needed by the tourists.

One of my negative memories is related to tourists' aggressive behaviour, which for me resulted in exhausting work throughout the night and the next day. In one of my groups staying in Michurin (now Tsarevo) at the Black Sea coast, a German tourist, after drinking alcohol, got into a fight with a young Bulgarian man at night, and I was called urgently around midnight to the city police station to translate. I was detained there until the morning. The police officer berated me viciously for the fact that a tourist from my group had been at the heart of the drunken brawl, repeating that all German tourists behaved in a similar way, that they abused alcohol all the time and that the guides, in particular me, were very much to blame for this. Finally, the official conclusion of the police was that the incident was caused by the German tourist and the Bulgarian was not at fault. Disagreeing with this conclusion and supported by the leader of the group, the young man insisted on being examined by a forensic doctor for his injuries. The tourist, the leader of the group and I had to travel to the district hospital in Burgas by bus, where a doctor examined him and issued a medical certificate. In the afternoon we travelled back to Michurin. My exhaustion was not only physical, but also mental.

This case illustrates how the local public, especially in smaller towns and resorts, perceived tour guides. They were often seen as personally responsible for the behaviour of all members of the tour group. Sometimes this created tensions with local residents, not just with institutions. For example, when I accompanied the same group to Michurin, there were two Russian tourist groups there at the same time, and almost every night one of the three guides was called to a house where the owners complained about drunken brawls between the tourists accommodated in their homes.

A negative aspect of the work often mentioned in the interviews was the control of labour and discipline imposed by a representative of Orbita in the locality or resort: seasonal guides reported to such representatives directly and relied on them for assistance in their work. The control at the IYC was perceived as particularly strict. Every day, staff guides monitored the seasonal guides' attendance at sports events on the beach and the mandatory briefings at 9.00 a.m.

In the interviews, respondents talked about how they were forced by staff employees to carry out activities outside their direct duties. One gave the following example:

> The most unpleasant thing for me was when I had to convince the Germans to play volleyball or football on the beach, and that every

> morning for two hours. Instead of sunbathing and swimming. If we didn't get a whole German team together, as a penalty we, the guides of German groups, had to complete the team and compete. (Yu. P., male, b. 1962)

I was also very burdened by the duty of exhorting the group leaders to gather their tourists to participate in beach team games and competitions. On several occasions I was unable to secure anyone from my group and was forced by the staff guides to replace a 'German' at volleyball or basketball so that the planned game could go ahead.

My respondents pointed out the lack of access to work with youth tourist groups from capitalist countries as another negative aspect of the labour. This concerned the work of German-speaking seasonal guides who, despite having successfully passed a 'political training' exam and even after several seasons of successful work, were not highly trusted by the bureau and deliberately not allowed to serve groups from the former West Germany. Although few youth tour groups from France and Great Britain visited the Black Sea, they, like those from West Germany, were served only by senior staff guides. The bureau acted cautiously and in full accord with the discourse about the high likelihood that young seasonal guides would be vulnerable to the ideological ideas and aims of 'Western propaganda'.

The bureau's penalties against seasonal tour guides are commented on in a negative light today. For example, the young guides were paid less if there was a signal from the group leader or a complaint from the senior guides. One respondent reported on such a case:

> I worked with three groups at the same time in Primorsko. Over 90 people, from different towns, with three group leaders. It was very difficult to communicate. They [the leaders] were staying in bungalows quite a distance away from the three groups and even in the evening I could barely get them together to discuss things and organise the next day. Finally the three leaders, when we met to sign the vouchers, wrote down that they had received 10 days of guide services instead of 14. This was not true, but they had already spoken. (E. M., female, b. 1964)

The consequences for her were that she was paid for only 10 days at the lowest rate (the daily rate of BGN 2) for serving these groups, despite the hard work. While not common, these types of penalties were in accord with regulations and possible to impose. My respondent shared that as a reason for doing so, the three group leaders highlighted their rare daily meetings with her. They expected her to give more attention to each of the groups. For them, writing fewer days of guided services on the voucher was a way to alert the bureau to the problem of guiding three groups at the same time. The tour guide was paid for as many days as the group leaders had written on the voucher, instead of addressing the problem of serving so many tourists with only one guide.

During the six seasons of my work, I was penalised once too. When we worked with tourist groups at the Black Sea resorts, it happened that our friends visited us and we accommodated them in our rooms for several nights, of course with the consent of our roommates (who were fellow guides). During one of my stays at Primarsko, I was exceptionally accommodated in a room with a staff tour guide, who did not seem to mind sheltering my friend for two nights, but immediately rushed to file a written complaint to the senior tour guide that I had sheltered a girl in the room who was not a tour guide. So, for those two days I was deprived of remuneration. The bureau had no fixed penalties for such cases, and the decision to impose them was negotiated in everyday working life by the heads of the guiding department.

In their recollections about the negative aspects of the work, my interlocutors often mentioned tension in relations with other staff from the tourist business. They drew attention to the fact that there were a number of occasions when tourists were not provided with good accommodation and food. They said that they had to argue with hotel managers over poor hygiene and bad rooms, complain to chefs about the poor quality of food or small portions and make remarks to waiters about the low level of service. From their early working years, young people were forced to confront the dislocations of the economy of shortages and issues in the quality of services, particularly in tourism. Many of them developed a critical approach towards employees of this industry:

> I was uncompromising there: when I saw that it was dirty, that they were lying to us on the scale, that they were serving yesterday's grilled food, I went straight to the manager. We can't expose ourselves like this, people have paid and what do they get? They come on holiday and they stay hungry. Is that how they remember us? I used to scold them, I didn't spare them. (I. P., male, b. 1958)

My observations and interview data allow me to argue that many seasonal guides took their tasks quite seriously, because they were sympathetic to the needs of young tourists, with whom they felt solidarity after spending 14 days together.

However, not all problems could be immediately resolved by the guides. While, for example, a hygiene issue could be quickly solved at check-in, problems with 'uneatable' food already served to the group were not so easily sorted out and often the seasonal guides felt powerless at such moments. This feeling was further reinforced by the fact that there was no practice in the bureau of submitting written complaints about poor service, and in fact all such problems were either verbally resolved on the spot or not resolved at all.

Unauthorised labour practices

Apart from reducing certain services from the mandatory tourist programme, the seasonal guides used some practices that were not part of the rules of work in Orbita and were therefore not always legal. Such practices, however, were established as socially acceptable for tour guides, and they found application and recognition in the social environment of the young employees. In bars or cafés, where 'friendship meetings' were held between two tourist groups from different socialist countries, a small part of the money allocated for the tourists' consumption was diverted and shared between the manager of the establishment and the two tour guides. The tourists did not notice this because they had no information about what budget was provided and what it should or should not be spent on. In other cases, the three would agree to receive a bottle of luxury alcohol each. I remember my amazement at my first 'friendship meeting' in Primorsko, when right at the beginning the bar manager very casually handed me a bottle of cognac and gave the same to my colleague who was leading a Russian group of tourists. When I asked what this was, they both explained that this was the usual practice, this alcohol was for us and if I wanted, I could get a bottle of vodka instead.

The young guides were not allowed to purchase alcoholic beverages from the group's budget for these friendship meetings, which were defined as mandatory ideological events for all group members. However, the young employees encouraged the tourists from the group to order and pay for such drinks with their own money. In this way, revenue was brought into the respective establishment beyond the modest budget allocated for soft drinks and snacks. The friendship meetings quite often did not even proceed according to the set ideological framework with speeches by the two leaders and the tour guides, but from beginning to end passed as entertainment with listening to music and dancing. By implementing this practice, the young guides were diverted from the task of being intermediaries for the transmission of ideological messages among foreign tourists.

Seasonal guides were also required to consume the same food they ordered for the tourist group in the restaurants. Often, however, they ordered for themselves an extensive lunch and evening menu, different and more expensive than that of the group, and paid for from the budget. They also used money from the budget to provide the bus driver with alcohol in the evening in gratitude for helping them. Diverting even a small part of the common resources in order to meet personal needs was a strategy inherent to working life during socialism.[27] Those strategies were not 'visible' in the accounting because in the cheques, the tour guides covered up the expensive meals and alcohol through, for example, a fictitious record of the consumption of slightly more expensive meals or soft drinks by all tourists. The guides, even today, consider that such practices served as compensation for the lack of additional financial incentives and as a 'reward' for hard work.

There were other practices which could be described as close to illegal commercial activities during socialism, including unregulated currency exchange, most often involving the exchange of Bulgarian levs for East German marks. On foreign tourist trips, citizens of socialist countries were allowed to purchase currency only in bank offices for a very small amount (BGN 30), which would hardly cover their necessary personal expenses. Tour guides offered illegal currency exchange to tourists from their groups, calculating a profit for themselves, and then usually managed to sell the purchased currency, again at a profit, to friends, relatives and acquaintances travelling to the GDR. Thus, they became participants in the 'black market' of currency, with personal entrepreneurial activity also playing a role here. One respondent reported as follows in the interview:

> There was a great demand for levs, right, from Germans when they came to the seaside on holiday. And I, you know, have been a risk taker since I was young, so to speak. I exchanged them, they were happy, I was too. And from the exchange of German marks, well, I used to earn so much money in those two or three months every summer, which then when I started working as a young professional, I managed to earn it for the whole year.

Currency trade developed because of the disadvantages of the economy of shortages and the lack of certain consumer goods in some countries that could be bought in others.

Another similar practice was the purchase of bottles of vodka with Bulgarian currency from Russian groups who carried them in their buses for personal consumption and for sale. The tour guide sold the vodka to managers of local restaurants for a profit. In that way the tour guides became participants in the 'black market' of goods.

Practices such as circumventing or seemingly following the rules, 'outsmarting' superiors and changing the content of labour norms were not uncommon; they were part of the cultural resources created and used during socialism in order to cope with the problems and challenges of everyday life, including the labour sphere. Researchers have discovered and analysed similar responses when examining everyday practices during socialism. They explain them as strategies of resistance and resilience, of ingenious circumvention of the laws and of apparent adherence to norms.[28] These approaches have been described as protective, even defensive, and as subordinates' vacillation against any form of control.[29] I argue that through the implementation of such practices, young tour guides from their early working years attempted to elude the government's efforts to turn them into a homogeneous mass of wage labourers in line with the ideology of social homogenisation of the population. Probably this behaviour was also connected with the 'inner' building of solidarity among the young tour guides.

In carrying out their working tasks, the young guides tried to reconcile duties with entertainment. Despite the long and busy working days, they usually managed to create free spaces for themselves and find time to unwind. They often stayed up late at discos, or spent time communicating with their groups or other guides around campfires or in hotel rooms. Such entertainments were not encouraged by their superiors; yet, they were not officially prohibited and the guides were rarely sanctioned.

The provision of entertainment was explained by my interview partners as a successful attempt to slip away from the day-to-day control of superiors as well as to circumvent the rules. Informal social communication created an opportunity for cohesion, for better bonding of young employees with each other, which in turn helped them to cope with problems at work and made their busy working lives more bearable. Friendship bonds and emotional contacts were created with both other guides and tourists.

Although such entertainments were considered legitimate by everyone, they could have some negative consequences: they exhausted the tour guides and sometimes led to poor performance of professional work, which was actually detrimental to the state labour organisation.

Conclusion

During socialism, a small proportion of young, highly educated people in Bulgaria were recruited as seasonal employees in the tourist sector at relatively low cost. The excellent knowledge of languages acquired by students of foreign language schools and universities was successfully used by the government to meet the growing demand for seasonal tour guides. Through this state policy, these young people were 'won over' to participate in the economy, and wage labour in international tourism was recognised as an alternative to the compulsory participation in unpaid labour brigades.

In socialist Bulgaria, labour was a prerequisite for continuing education, which facilitated the social and ideological coercion in wage labour. The bureau saw the job of the guide as a practice through which young people would 'grow up', learn to take responsibility and then also build up cooperation on the ideological level. However, the formal structure failed to bring the guides within the ideological framework, and the attempts to use them as intermediaries to convey official messages of socialism to foreign tourists also failed. Young guides often emptied the events of their intended ideological content, conducting them according to the set form but giving them a completely different meaning.

This chapter has emphasised the discrepancy between the ideological expectations and intentions of the provided tourist services and the actual practices of young people. The examples are indicative of the changes 'from below' through everyday strategies. Young seasonal employees applied unauthorised practices that deviated from the intended goals of the tourist organisation. These practices, however, can be evaluated as constant, common ways of 'tackling' restricting working conditions. They became established as legitimate and useful among the young employees, and today former tour guides see them as successful ways of coping with the difficulties of everyday (working) life during socialism. Orbita allowed some leeway; the practices of improvising and subversion were accepted by the bureau in most cases, even though they were sometimes penalised.

Respondents explained that their seasonal work as tour guides was seen as prestigious by teachers, university professors, classmates and fellow students. Compared to the conditions in the youth labour brigades, peers perceived the tour guiding work as privileged: the seasonal employees of Orbita performed intellectually skilled work for which they received remuneration, visited numerous tourist destinations or spent several weeks at the seaside, and enjoyed the same good accommodation and food as foreign tourists. These assessments are fully shared by my respondents, who, however, also draw attention to the great responsibilities they had for the lives and health of tourists. These, as well as their financial and organisational obligations, were not comparable to those of the young people participating in the brigades, who performed labour without any personal responsibilities. Unlike the brigadiers, the seasonal guides did not disparage their own work and social status.

Yet, there is some ambivalent perception of the labour coercion experienced by the seasonal employees. On the one hand, they often spoke about the heavy workload and the small amount of remuneration, giving examples of ideological and social coercion. On the other hand, they stated they had never felt exploited – not even from today's perspective. Participation as seasonal guides at Orbita has been and continues to be a source of pride and is perceived as valuable cultural capital – it is included, for example, in the publicly available CVs of famous Bulgarian scientists, politicians, lawyers and other public figures. For most of my respondents, the memories of guiding work during their student years nowadays evoke positive emotions. Here we have to address the issue of experience in the years of youth and memory. From a researcher's point of view, there was social, ideological and labour coercion. From the point of view of the interlocutors, coercion was indeed experienced in concrete situations, but after many years, the actual experiences of coercive situations were no longer remembered.

My interview partners appreciated spending their free time earning money, being away from parental control, improving their language skills and gaining work and life experience. The interlocutors stressed, however, that in the formal organisation of Orbita they always found themselves under the social control of the senior guides and dependent on them. Mutual help and solidarity at work were remembered by respondents, and they often mentioned the importance of these features. During their work, the guides established emotional contacts, friendships and lasting relationships with other young people, seasonal guides or foreign tourists, which in many cases continue to the present day. These trust-based relationships formed an important part of their social networks and often led to successful economic partnerships in later years.

Notes

1. Roth, 'Arbeit im Sozialismus – Arbeit im Postsozialismus. Zur Einführung', 10.
2. The bureau was privatised in the 1990s.
3. The building currently houses the headquarters of a Bulgarian political party.
4. A brigade is a tactical unit of the armed forces. This term, along with other terms to denote the structures (camp, commander, headquarters, detachment), was borrowed from military terminology characteristic of the barracks (Иванова, 'Строим за народната република', 60). The military form of brigade organisation is characterised by strict rules, discipline and a clear military hierarchy; see Брунбауер, *Социалистическият начин на живот*, 100.
5. *Енциклопедия България*, 316.
6. Брунбауер, *Социалистическият начин на живот*, 86.
7. Брунбауер, *Социалистическият начин на живот*, 87.
8. Брунбауер, *Социалистическият начин на живот*, 88.
9. Иванова, 'Строим за народната република', 61; Брунбауер, *Социалистическият начин на живот*, 86; Раева, 'Детството и бригадирското движение (1946–1950)', 135.
10. The intelligentsia during socialism was defined as a social stratum which was assigned an auxiliary role in the building of socialism and which was located on the periphery of the two main classes, the workers and the peasants.
11. Анчев, *Фолклорът на работниците от едно звено на каналджийска бригада*, 5.
12. Иванова, '*Строим за народната република*', 61.
13. Брунбауер, *Социалистическият начин на живот*, 85.
14. Брунбауер, *Социалистическият начин на живот*, 100.
15. Иванова, 'Строим за народната република', 56–8; Анчев, *Фолклорът на работниците от едно звено на каналджийска бригада*, 4–10; Брунбауер, *Социалистическият начин на живот*, 84–8.
16. Иванова, 'Строим за народната република', 60.
17. Анчев, *Фолклорът на работниците от едно звено на каналджийска бригада*, 4–6.
18. This view had already begun to take hold in Bulgarian society at the formation of the socialist state and was normatively enshrined in the Constitution adopted in 1971. According to Article 1, (1) of the Constitution, 'People's Republic of Bulgaria is a socialist state of the working people of the city and the village led by the Working Class'; see *Конституция на Народна Република България* of 1971; see also Иванова, 'Строим за народната република', 58.
19. Иванова, 'Строим за народната република', 62.
20. Petrova, 'Betriebsfeste im sozialistischen Bulgarien', 73.
21. Иванова, 'Строим за народната република', 59; Брунбауер, *Социалистическият начин на живот*, 99.
22. Benovska, 'Social Networks, Coalitions, and Clientelism at the Workplace in Bulgaria', 121; Петрова, *Трудов свят и етнология*, 102.
23. Until 1980 the Guidebook of the Tour Guide, published in 1964 for the needs of the largest Bulgarian tourist organisation, Balkantourist, was used, and since 1980 the newly published Guidebook of the Tour Guide in four parts has been studied. The first part contained material on the geography, history, contemporary politics, economy and culture of Bulgaria. Part 2 presented the main routes and tourist sites in the country, Part 3 the Bulgarian Black Sea coast and Part 4 the capital, Sofia.
24. The Council for Mutual Economic Assistance is a former economic organisation of socialist countries that existed from 1949 to 1991. Among the main factors behind the founding of the Council was the desire of the USSR to strengthen its influence over the neighbouring countries of Eastern Europe and to neutralise the interest in the Marshall Plan. Unity was ensured by political and ideological factors. All countries were 'united by a commonality of fundamental class interests and the ideology of Marxism-Leninism' and had common views on economic

ownership (state rather than private) and governance (planned rather than market); see Dragomir, 'The Creation of the Council for Mutual Economic Assistance as Seen from the Romanian Archives', 2014, 356.
25 Беновска-Събкова, 'Социализмът като модернизация', 2009, 8.
26 Иванова, *Туризъм под надзор*, 25.
27 Benovska, 'Social Networks, Coalitions, and Clientelism at the Workplace in Bulgaria', 124.
28 Рот, 'Практики и стратегии за овладяване на всекидневието в едно село на социалистическа България', 1998, 227–9.
29 Волф, '"Власт" и "своенравие"'; Крийд, *Опитомяване на революцията*.

Bibliography

Анчев, Анатол. *Фолклорът на работниците от едно звено на каналджийска бригада* [The Folklore of the Workers of One Unit of a Canal Brigade]. София: Издателска къща 'Тип-топ прес', 2017.

Беновска-Събкова, Милена. 'Социализмът като модернизация (наблюдения върху България)' [Socialism as Modernization (Observations on Bulgaria)], *Българска етнология*, 4 (2009): 5–22.

Брунбауер, Улф. *'Социалистическият начин на живот'. Идеология, общество, семейство и политика в България (1944–1989)* ['The Socialist Way of Life'. Ideology, Society, Family and Politics in Bulgaria (1944–1989)]. Русе: МД 'Елиас Канети', 2010.

Волф, Габриеле. '"Власт" и "своенравие". Към анализа на реалния постсоциалистически жизнен свят' ['"Power" and "Self-will". Towards the Analysis of the Real Post-socialist Life World']. В *Социализмът: реалност и илюзии. Етнологични аспекти на всекидневната култура* [Socialism: Reality and Illusions. Ethnological Aspects of Everyday Culture], ред. Радост Иванова, Ана Лулева и Рачко Попов, 120–32. София: ЕИМ, 2003.

Енциклопедия България [Encyclopedia Bulgaria]. София: БАН, 4, 1984.

Крийд, Джералд. *Опитомяване на революцията. От социалистическата реформа към противоречивия преход в едно българско село* [Domesticating the Revolution. From Socialist Reform to the Controversial Transition in a Bulgarian Village]. София: Апострофи, 2007.

Иванова, Мая. *Туризъм под надзор. Балкантурист – началото на международния и масов туризъм в България* [Tourism under Supervision. Balkanturist – the Beginning of International and Mass Tourism in Bulgaria]. София: Сиела, 2018.

Иванова, Радост. 'Строим за народната република'. Младежките строителни бригади – школа за комунистическо възпитание ['Building for the People's Republic'. The Youth Construction Brigades – School for Communist Education]. В *Социализмът: реалност и илюзии. Етнологични аспекти на всекидневната култура* [Socialism: Reality and Illusions. Ethnological Aspects of Everyday Culture], ред. Радост Иванова, Ана Лулева и Рачко Попов, 54–62. София: ЕИМ, 2003.

Конституция на Народна република България 1971 [Constitution of People's Republic of Bulgaria 1971]. Accessed 2 September 2022. https://bg.wikisource.org/wiki/Конституция_на_Народна_Република_България_(1971).

Петрова, Иванка. *Трудов свят и етнология* [Labour World and Ethnology]. София: ИЕФЕМ, 2010.

Раева, Биляна. 'Детството и бригадирското движение (1946–1950). Разпределение на времето в бригадата (по материали от Димитровград)' [Childhood and the Brigadier Movement (1946–1950). Distribution of Time in the Brigade (Based on Materials from Dimitrovgrad)]. В *Детството при социализма. Политически, институционални и биографични перспективи* [Childhood in Socialism. Political, Institutional and Biographical Perspectives], състав. Иван Еленков и Даниела Колева, 131–63. София: Рива, 2010.

Рот, Клаус. 'Практики и стратегии за овладяване на всекидневието в едно село на социалистическа България' [Practices and Strategies for Mastering Everyday Life in a Village of Socialist Bulgaria]. *Социологически проблеми*, 3–4 (1998): 225–37.

Янчева, Яна. *Колективизацията в българското село (1948–1970)* [Collectivization in the Bulgarian Village (1948–1970)]. София: ИК 'Гутенберг', 2015.

Benovska, Milena. 'Social Networks, Coalitions, and Clientelism at the Workplace in Bulgaria'. In *Arbeit im Sozialismus – Arbeit im Postsozialismus. Erkundungen zum Arbitsleben im östlichen Europa*, edited by Klaus Roth, 109–28. Münster: LIT Verlag, 2004.

Dragomir, Elena. 'The Creation of the Council for Mutual Economic Assistance as Seen from the Romanian Archives', *Historical Research* 88 (2014): 355–79.

Petrova, Ivanka. 'Betriebsfeste im sozialistischen Bulgarien – Ideologie und soziale Praxis'. In *Sozialismus: Realitäten und Illusionen. Ethnologische Aspekte der sozialistischen Alltagskultur*, edited by Klaus Roth, 73–86. Wien: Verlag des Instituts für Europäische Ethnologie, 2005.

Roth, Klaus. 'Arbeit im Sozialismus – Arbeit im Postsozialismus. Zur Einführung'. In *Arbeit im Sozialismus – Arbeit im Postsozialismus. Erkundungen zum Arbitsleben im östlichen Europa*, edited by Klaus Roth, 9–22. Münster: LIT Verlag, 2004.

14
To put a human face on the question of labour: photographic portraiture and the Australian-Pacific indentured labour trade

Paolo Magagnoli

Can photography picture coerced labour? Such a fundamental question admits no easy answer. We are faced with two problems. One has to do with the object or process that we are trying to understand: labour coercion and its complexities. Coercion in labour relations is often hard to pin down. Historians regard the dichotomy between free and unfree labour as fraught with ambiguities.[1] As Marcel van der Linden has suggested, there seems to be a 'continuum or spectrum of forms of labour with differing degrees of autonomy and different statuses merging seamlessly into one another'.[2] Furthermore, in labour relations, coercion may manifest in a variety of subtle ways. It can be exerted not only through overtly punitive actions but also through complex forms of remuneration and regulations that significantly curtail the freedom of workers under the pretence of protecting it. In other words, coercion in labour is a proteiform phenomenon. How can the photographic image, with its concreteness and specificity, account for the elusive but no less real nature of labour coercion under capitalism?

The other problem has to do with the material technology of representation, the photographic camera. When photographs documenting labour history can be found in the archive, these are, for the most part, portraits of workers which were made on behalf of bosses, without the intention of exposing the violence and exploitation of labour. Likewise, when they were commissioned by workers, these images were meant to be consumed privately, in the space of the family and kin networks; the primary function of these images was to reinforce those social networks, not to provide a testimony for the duress of work conditions. This makes it difficult to use archival photography to understand retrospectively the dynamics of labour coercion.

And yet, pictures are an extraordinary tool that can be deployed to narrate stories about work. Consider the Queensland State Library's use of photography to recount the history of the Pacific indentured labour trade. Spanning half a century (1863–1907), the trade involved the migration of over 60,000 young women and men from Melanesian islands to Australia to provide cheap labour for the burgeoning sugar industry of Queensland and New South Wales. South Sea Islanders, also called Melanesians, Polynesians or Kanakas, planted, weeded and cut sugar cane in the large plantations of the tropical north.[3] The trade epitomises the hybridity of waged work: Melanesian labour was contract work and entailed the payment of wages; however, these wages, which were embedded in a very restrictive legislative framework, were also used to discipline South Sea Islanders. The Pacific indentured labour trade was a system of laws and remuneration that was designed to tie workers to their employees and prevent them from leaving or negotiating better wages and conditions. Despite repeated calls for abolition, voiced by liberal politicians as well as humanitarian associations, Melanesian indentured labour in Australia lasted well into the early 1900s, as rural capitalists strenuously lobbied the Queensland parliament to grant its continuation.[4]

This long and complex history was courageously addressed by the Queensland State Library in the 2019 exhibition Plantation Voices: Contemporary Conversations with Australian South Sea Islanders.[5] Curated by Imelda Miller, the show relied on the evocative power of images to recount the experiences of coerced labourers and today's South Sea Islander community. Importantly, archival portraiture of Melanesian workers dominated the materials displayed in the exhibition. Blown up to mural size, rarely seen poignant pictures from the library collections filled the walls of the gallery. The show also included works commissioned from four young Australian artists of Melanesian ethnic background.[6] Two of them, Dylan Mooney and Jasmine Togo-Brisby, appropriated and manipulated portraits of workers drawn from private collections and the library's archive. These artistic practices possessed significant affinities.

Mooney's *Stop and Stare* (2018) comprised two large charcoal drawings each based on a photographic image: one of his great-great-grandmother Fanny Togo, who was taken from Santo Island of Vanuatu and brought to Tweed Heads, and another of an unnamed South Sea Islander man working in Mackay (Figure 14.1). By magnifying the

Figure 14.1 Dylan Mooney, *Stop and Stare*, 2018 (showing one of the two images forming the artwork). Pencil and charcoal on paper. © John Oxley Library, State Library of Queensland (Accession no. 31872). Reproduced under the Creative Commons Licence CC BY-NC 4.0.

images and translating them into a pictorial medium, Mooney reworked the cold anonymity of the mugshot, highlighting the subjects' eyes and physiognomies. As the artist declared, the aim of this series was to reconnect with his forebears: 'By drawing a family member and stranger I make a personal connection and reclaim them here in the present, bringing them to the foreground and acknowledging them both as my ancestors.'[7]

Also drawing from archival photographs of South Sea Islanders, Togo-Brisby's project *The Past is Ahead, Don't Look Back* (2019) conjoined past and present in the same image. In her series, the artist rephotographed three pictures of Melanesian workers from the library collection. She used the collodion wet plate process, commonly deployed in the mid-nineteenth century at the time of South Sea Islanders' migration to Australia, to produce manipulated photographs that project likenesses of herself into the realities represented in the original archival pictures. One image in the series shows Togo-Brisby and her daughter on the backyard verandah of a sugar cane farm, posing for the camera together with a group of Islanders and their master (Figure 14.2). 'I insert myself and my daughter into the image using projection,' Togo-Brisby remarked,

Figure 14.2 Jasmine Togo-Brisby, South Sea Islanders with sugar plantation owner, from the series *The Past is Ahead, Don't Look Back*, 2019. Collodion on glass. This work was one of three photographs by the artist displayed in the exhibition Plantation Voices at the State Library of Queensland, 16 February–8 September 2019. © John Oxley Library, State Library of Queensland (Accession no. 31843). Reproduced under the Creative Commons Licence CC BY-NC-SA 4.0.

'we then step into the archive, we stand with them and them with us, we are creating a space that we hold together, past, present and future.'[8]

Both Togo-Brisby and Mooney's projects reflected contemporary South Sea Islanders' desire to reclaim their history and, more importantly, identity. Their striking and poignant images aimed to bring the artists in touch with their ancestors. This desire was also at the centre of Plantation Voices' curatorial framework. As Miller put it in her introductory statement to the exhibition, old photographs of South Sea Islanders were more than simple didactic tools. For Miller, the pictures held an affective dimension whose meaning transcended their mere informational value. As she explained:

> What a privilege it has been to sit here in front of images that were taken over 150 years ago. I am curious about the people in the photos, the names in books, names on papers and I wondered if they thought I would sit here 150 years on and look at their faces and think about their story. Their faces seem familiar and I feel a connection like I know them, but yet they are all strangers. I exist because they do and

now they exist because I do. This is a personal story about people, family, some we know and some we don't know. It's difficult and it's emotional. I have felt more connections with these images through this exhibition than I have in the last two decades; and in some way I have seen the people in these images for the first time.[9]

Like Mooney and Togo-Brisby, Miller extolled photography's ability to build emotional connections between contemporary Islanders and their ancestors. The curator successfully mobilised the capacity of photography to act as a 'certificate of presence'.[10] As Eelco Runia has suggested, '"Presence," … is "being in touch" – either literally or figuratively – with people, things, events, and feelings that made you into the person you are.'[11] In other words, presence is linked to personal and social identity. By using photography to make past South Sea Islander labourers 'present', Plantation Voices fulfilled contemporary Australian Islanders' need to reclaim, affirm and celebrate their unique identity.

This focus on identity and the politics of recognition led curators to stress the resilience of Islander workers in the face of labour coercion and social discrimination. Mooney and Togo-Brisby's art was displayed in the room of the exhibition entitled 'Resilience'. As the wall text read, 'Australian South Sea Islanders' resilience to overcome adversity is evident in the strength, determination and the humility of the people and the community in its entirety.' This capacity to resist extreme hardship and coercion owed much to Islanders' oral storytelling practices: 'Such storytelling', the wall text continued, 'strengthens the connection between Elders and younger generation, and inspires the Australian South Sea Islander community to reclaim their history, stories and cultural identity.' In the attempt to emphasise Melanesians' capacity to preserve their unique identity in the face of extreme hardship, however, the exhibition tended, perhaps inadvertently, to downplay the powerful system of coercion underpinning the Pacific labour trade.[12] By foregrounding the ability of photography to connect distinct generations of South Sea Islanders, the curators of Plantation Voices seemed to reduce the function of visual documents to identity or community building. What was forgotten in this approach was the role that photography played in the construction and preservation of coercion at the time of the labour trade.

In order to understand labour coercion *in* photography, we need an approach that is attentive to pictures' original context of use. Does it matter by whom and for whom the portrait was taken? Does it matter whether it was commissioned by Islanders or by the plantation owners and government officials? To whom was it given? How was it circulated, and with what effects? These questions are particularly challenging since most archival pictures of South Sea Islanders are, unfortunately, unsigned and undated, and the sitters of the portraits are, usually, unnamed, making it hard to establish the specific cultural and historical context in which they were made. Nevertheless, addressing these questions enables us to illuminate the rhetoric of the photograph and the way photographic culture mediated the coercion underpinning the indentured labour system. As we will see, even when not representing labour relations directly, photography affected those relations insofar as it helped to normalise the racial ideologies and hierarchies that informed labour coercion. And yet, at times, photography could destabilise the social order. If unaccompanied by dismissive captions, honorific photographic portraits of South Sea Islanders could pose a threat to the coercive labour system as they implicitly asserted equality between European workers and Melanesians.[13] Like other historical sources, photographs of Islanders are ambivalent documents, which need to be carefully scrutinised and interpreted.

This chapter is based on an analysis of photographs of sugar industry indentured labour printed in Australian newspapers and illustrated periodicals from the 1860s to 1906. The case studies selected and discussed here have been chosen as paradigmatic examples of the discursive framing of photography of Melanesians in nineteenth-century Australia. Importantly, the analysis focuses on photography of Islanders circulating in the public sphere rather than on pictures circulating in private photo albums. Considering the relation between pictures, layout and text, the analysis of press photography of South Sea Islanders provides insight into the medium's ability to affirm and reinforce the racist ideology supporting labour coercion.[14] Before turning to the visual analysis of the case studies, I will provide a summary of the complex history of the Australian-Pacific labour trade. The focus on the forms of remuneration, working conditions and regulations that structured the trade helps to place the photographic works into their original historical context. In this way, we can more fully grasp the multilayered meanings and functions of the archival photographs analysed in the remaining part of the chapter.

Coercion and contract: a short history of the nineteenth-century Pacific labour trade

The coercion within South Sea Islanders' indentured labour relations manifested itself in a form of 'slow violence'. It was exerted and normalised less through spectacular physical gestures than through the technicality, if not even banality, of legal contracts, remuneration methods and state regulations. To use Tracey Banivanua-Mar's words, indentured labour's impact on Melanesians 'did not attract the sensational cry of atrocity, kidnapping or massacres'.[15] Labour in the sugar cane field was paid and regulated through contracts signed by Melanesian workers; however, these were highly disadvantageous to them and tended to tie them to their employers. As Kay Saunders has remarked, 'whilst Islanders in Queensland were never slaves (that is the *legal* property of another person, to whose will they were totally subject and who could coerce their labour), they comprised a form of highly unfree labour, subject to stringent legal and social discrimination'.[16] The coercion of the trade can be ascertained from the methods of recruitment as well as from the particularly restrictive forms of remuneration used to subordinate Melanesians to their employers.

As to the methods of recruitment, in the early years of the trade, approximately from 1863 to 1875, Islanders were brought to Australia by force, trickery or fraud (a practice called 'blackbirding' – 'blackbird' was another word for slave).[17] 'Blackbirding practices included the enticing of islanders onto ships on the pretence that the crew wanted to barter or to offer them a short pleasure cruise, or ambushing villages and seizing the inhabitants.'[18] Additionally, recruiters tricked Melanesians by impersonating a missionary and seizing any Islanders who approached them by inviting them to visit the ship's cabin. Before 1875, there were 'few returning labourers to explain the nature of service in Queensland, and interpreters were scarce', hence there was 'blatant misrepresentation about the period of service'.[19] The Islanders recruited were mostly boys and men aged between 16 and 32. Their youth and limited knowledge of the English language made them more susceptible to deception and manipulation. After the arrival of the first cargoes of indentured workers at the port of Brisbane in 1863, missionaries in Britain and Australia raised the question of whether labourers arrived in Queensland because of their own free will, or because they had misread the terms of their engagement.[20] In 1872, the accusations made about the methods of recruitment deployed by traders led the Imperial Government to draft the Pacific Islanders Protection Act, also called the Kidnapping Act. This specified stricter licensing procedures for agents on British recruiting vessels, and enhanced the Admiralty's powers to seize ships suspected of being engaged in abductions of Melanesians, whether by deception or force.

Called 'Kanakas' (from a Hawaiian word meaning 'man'), South Sea Islanders worked under a three-year contract. The aim behind this fixed time period was to stabilise the workforce and prevent the mobility of workers. The 1868 Queensland Polynesian Labourers Act stipulated that all first-contract workers should work for three years and be paid £6 per annum with food, clothing, housing and medical attendance provided by the employer. This salary was significantly lower than for Anglo-Europeans working in the plantations. For instance, the yearly salary of an overseer was £30 while a junior chemist working for the Colonial Sugar Refinery in 1898 received £50.[21]

Work conditions in the plantations were harsh. In several plantations and farms, Islanders faced very long work hours and a poor diet. According to government records, almost 15,000 Melanesians died in Queensland between 1868 and 1906 due to the poor conditions in which they had to live and to frequent diseases. This is by far the highest death rate for any group of immigrants in Australia. In addition, 'the supervisory staff used severe violence to force unwilling servants to toil or to maintain a faster pace as they weeded the large cane fields'.[22] Islanders were prevented from forming unions, and from choosing different employers if they were dissatisfied with their contracts. Furthermore, the conditions of indentured labour were imposed through a complex system of legislation and regulations, which Melanesians – for the most part illiterate and unaccustomed to European mores – could barely understand.[23] The Queensland Masters and Servants Act of 1861, for example, established severe penalties for offences committed by workers (including Melanesians as well as labourers of other races). The act prescribed a penalty of three months' jail or forfeiture of wages for offences such as absconding or leaving hired service without permission. It also instituted that servants' attempts to raise wages or otherwise improve conditions of work were a misdemeanour. The only protection afforded to employees was the right to sue for outstanding wages, but this involved high legal costs and the collaboration of several witnesses, and the court was often biased towards the masters.[24]

The immobilisation of workers was strongly linked to the remuneration strategies adopted by employers, which constituted a system of deferred payments. Melanesians were not paid monthly or fortnightly but only at the end of their contracts, making absconding and labour mobility very difficult.[25] This coercive dimension of indentured labour was compounded by the truck system, involving 'the payment of wages in goods or in money with a view to its being spent in shops in which the employer has either a direct or indirect interest'.[26] Each worker owned a box that stored a variety of goods – tobacco, weapons, dynamite, steel implements, ironmongery, cloth and various adornments – purchased from the company store, often at inflated prices. Building on the functions of the Melanesian gift economy, the truck system was a particularly effective tool used by farm owners in keeping the labourers docile and at their place of work. As Adrian Graves has argued, 'first, islanders were tied to their employers because the immigrants could not achieve the ultimate objective of filling their trade box until the end of their contracts' and 'secondly, the system contributed to the lengthening of the immigrants' labour cycle. Increasingly workers had to make new contracts in the colony in order to accumulate sufficient commodities.'[27]

Some of the most restrictive measures against Melanesians came with the Queensland Pacific Island Labourers Act of 1880 (amended in 1884). The act significantly curtailed the upward social and spatial mobility of South Sea Islanders as 'they were expressly forbidden to work as mill operatives, carriers, domestic servants and tradesmen'.[28] Finally, according to the legislation, Islanders could not be recruited for pastoral work, could not strike or join a union, and could only be employed within 30 miles of the coast. The legislation also introduced inspectors commissioned to monitor the recruitment of Islanders and prevent kidnapping. In addition, it divided Melanesians into three categories: those on first contracts, who were still required to serve an initial term of three years; 'time-expired' workers, who had already served a term and were allowed to work for shorter terms; and a very small minority of 'exemption tickets': Melanesians who had lived in Queensland since before 1879 and who were not subject to the restrictions of the act.

Coercion in photography: portraiture of South Sea Islander workers in context

Photographs of South Sea Islanders in the plantations resisting or protesting against their work conditions cannot be found in the archive. This makes it very difficult for the critic to find clear and visible evidence of coercion in photography of Melanesians. In fact, most of the pictures now accessible in museums and libraries tend to be group or individual portraits, mostly taken in photographers' studios or by amateurs. What do we make of this enigmatic imagery? How do these photographs convey the reality of labour coercion? It is impossible to provide a conclusive answer to this question given the different contexts in which photographic images of Melanesians were used and circulated. It is only by attending to the complexity and specificities of each photographic practice that we can evince the role of the image in either concealing or resisting labour coercion.

One of the risks of interpreting commercial portraiture of Melanesians is to read it as an unequivocal sign of the agency of the depicted individual. Consider, for example, a photograph taken by studio photographer Harriett Pettifore Brims in the late 1890s (Figure 14.3). Taken in Ingham, in the north of Queensland, the site of an important sugar cane plantation, it shows a bare-breasted Melanesian man wearing European trousers as well as traditional ornaments such as feathers and a pearl necklace, and staring proudly at the viewer. It would be tempting to take this picture of a worker as evidence of the benevolence of the indentured labour system and the capacity of workers to preserve their ethnic and cultural traditions. However, can this picture be read as evidence of the absence of coercion in the plantation system? I would

Figure 14.3 Harriett Pettifore Brims (1864–1939), untitled, late 1890s, negative glass. Taken in Ingham, north Queensland, this portrait shows an anonymous South Sea Islander wearing a pearl necklace, feathers and other traditional ornaments. © John Oxley Library, State Library of Queensland (Accession no. 31054). Reproduced under the Creative Commons licence CC BY-NC 4.0.

say 'no'. As Tom Brass has pointed out, the experience of coercion in indentured labour relations could coexist with some degree of autonomy in the cultural, private sphere. 'On specifically *cultural* matters,' Brass has declared, 'planters and/or landholders can indeed afford to be "generous", and concede varying degrees of autonomy without threatening their own economic power.'[29] In other words, in interpreting photography of proud Melanesians wearing symbols of ethnic identity as evidence of agency and resistance, we might end up supporting the revisionist historiographic strand, prominent in the 1980s and 1990s, so heavily criticised by Brass for its tendency to portray colonialism as a benevolent enterprise.[30] In fact, one could also argue that pictures of Melanesians wearing traditional outfits could have been used by racist groups to reinforce prejudices about the tribalism and primitiveness of Pacific native people.

And yet, although it would be an exaggeration to interpret the portraits of South Sea Islanders as evidence of the egalitarian nature of the plantation system, these portraits may reveal Islanders' aspirations towards equality and upward social mobility. Here I am suggesting that we look at portraiture of South Sea Islanders as 'sites of articulation and aspiration'.[31] Archival photographs of Melanesian indentured labourers might reflect how they wanted to be seen. They can be read as projections of a desired social identity, or, following Tina Campt's analysis of family photographs of Black European communities, these vernacular pictures can be interpreted as 'personal and social statements that express how ordinary individuals envisioned their sense of self, their subjectivity, and their social status'.[32]

In the mid-to-late nineteenth century, the photographic portrait symbolised social respectability. As Allan Sekula remarked in 1986, the function of the portrait was 'that of providing for the ceremonial presentation of the bourgeois *self*'.[33] Importantly, this new notion of the self, which can be said to have taken its early modern form in the seventeenth century, included the freedom of alienating one's labour on the capitalist market. By the end of the nineteenth century, a petite bourgeoisie of Australian South Sea Islanders – who had been living in the country for decades – had started to appear.[34] These were small farmers, shopkeepers and boardinghouse owners, who had the means to purchase photographic portraits from local studios. While a very small minority of the total population of South Sea Islanders, this group posed a substantial threat to the indentured labour system and the colonial social order. This emerging petite bourgeoisie – not yet organised politically but still potentially dangerous, especially for the White labour movement – could use photography to signal their equal status to the coloniser. They could use this powerful technology of representation to stake revolutionary claims for their right to freely access, enter and exit the labour market.[35]

Given the symbolic threat to the labour system that portraiture of South Sea Islanders carried at the turn of the century, it is thus no coincidence that only very few honorific portraits of South Sea Islanders appeared in the public sphere and that most photographic portraits of Melanesians now held by museums and libraries were circulated privately. In fact, as we will see, most periodicals and newspapers that published portraits of Melanesians tended to undermine their authenticity, describing Islanders themselves as con artists, bad imitators of the 'civilised' White race. An examination of Australian periodicals and newspapers printed from the 1860s to 1906 shows that the language and layout used by editors work to contain subversive readings of the photographs. Hence, the coercion of the indentured labour system can be detected in photography in the ways the medium shaped and reinforced the racial order of Australian society, which also impacted the power relations of the workplace. Most of the time, photography participated in legitimising the racial order and concealing labour coercion; and yet, the instability of photographic meaning also made the medium a potentially subversive tool.

A look at the illustrated tabloids and periodicals of the time shows that the conventional way of representing Kanaka workers in the public sphere was through pictures that deprived them of individuality. Consider, for instance, a feature from the *Queensland Agricultural Journal* published in 1897. Devoted to the sugar cane of the Gibson Bros at Bingera, near Bundaberg, the feature contains several photographs of Melanesian workers cutting cane, planting seeds in the field, and loading cane onto tramway trucks. The anonymous author of the article commends the pictures, taken by F. C. Wills, artist of the Queensland Department of Agriculture, as they 'give an excellent idea of the method of working a plantation'.[36] One photograph in the series epitomises the conventional way to depict scenes of Melanesian labour in the field (Figure 14.4). Placed at a distance from the bodies and faces of workers, the camera provides a sense of the scale of the operation but reduces the Kanaka labourer to generic types. 'Gangs of Kanakas are busily engaged in the various operations of cutting, topping, and trimming ready for loading.'[37] So reads the caption. There is no intimacy in these staged images. Only the figures in the foreground are busy working. They seem to have been told to ignore the camera. The purpose of the image is, simply, to illustrate the process of production.

Figure 14.4 F. C. Wills, 'Kanakas Planting Cane (Bingera)', *Queensland Agricultural Journal*, 1 September 1897, 248. The photograph depicts a gang of Melanesian workers in a sugar cane field. While those in the background are inactive, those in the foreground seem to have been instructed by the operator to ignore the cameraman. Reproduced courtesy of the National Library of Australia and under the Creative Commons licence CC BY-NC 4.0.

Coercion is vaguely hinted at by the presence of an overseer monitoring Melanesians. However, he can be seen only in the far distance and the composition tends to blend workers with the tall sugar canes in the background, foregrounding the product over the producer. The worker is presented not as an individual but as a member of 'a gang' – a kind of visual translation of the 'average worker' discussed by Marx.[38] This mode of representation epitomises the conventional way in which scientific journals as well as the general press depicted South Sea Islanders at work.

And yet, sometimes individual portraits of South Sea Islanders made their appearance in newspapers and gazettes. The way in which these were discursively and visually framed is indicative of the potentially dangerous connotations that portraits of Islanders carried for contemporary Australian audiences. When the Melanesian worker was photographed in combination with props, backgrounds or clothing that too closely drew on the conventions of bourgeois honorific portraiture, editors used captions and text that aimed to cordon off the elevation of Melanesians' personhood and class status. A sense of these anxieties triggered by the portrait of a Kanaka worker can be evinced from an 1886 article in the popular weekly *Queensland Figaro*. Written in response to a Christian progressive society's call for the abolition of the labour trade, the anonymous author of the article states:

> If the Creator made me like unto Himself, and if He also made that thick-lipped, wooly-polled, bandy-legged Kanaka like unto Himself, how many likenesses has He? This is a question for the Photographic Society to deal with. As for myself I wouldn't marry a Kanaka's sister; I wouldn't visit a Kanaka and expect him to return the visit on equal terms; and I don't call Kanaka my brother.[39]

Not all newspapers were as crude as the *Figaro* in their defence of racial inequality and their attack on humanitarian discourse; nevertheless, the violence of the writer's language is symptomatic of the fear provoked by honorific portraiture of Melanesians. The vehement tone of the passage suggests that, for many White settlers, visual depictions of Melanesians that presented them as assimilated or 'civilised' people were taboo.

An article published in the *North Queensland Register* in 1892 encapsulates very well the problematic nature of Melanesian portraiture. The article presents three portraits of the same couple of young South Sea Islanders working in the Pioneer Plantation in Lower Burdekin. The pictures were taken by Mr D. McFarlane, an accountant for the plantation and, according to the newspaper, 'an exceedingly clever amateur photographer'.[40] In one image the couple stare self-assuredly at the cameraman, wearing contemporary European clothing (Figure 14.5). In the remaining pictures – a diptych that occupies a separate spread – the same individuals are presented partially naked wearing traditional Melanesian necklaces and beads (Figure 14.6). The young woman holds a perfectly shaped banana leaf, which resembles the shape of her exposed breasts. There is something contrived in these sexually charged and well-composed images, which suggests that the photographs were highly directed. As typical of contemporary photographers aspiring to be professional artists, in these pictures McFarlane blends the sobriety of anthropological records with overt theatricality, trading on a deliberate lack of distinction between authenticity and outright fabrication. Commenting on the diptych, the text indulges in a fantasy of primitiveness and savagery, a fantasy which is nevertheless presented as truth:

> The figures in native attire are splendid specimens of the kanaka race, the man being as sturdy a fellow as we remember to have seen. As he stands, he is a good representation of what the reader fancies is the type of man chosen by Rider Haggard as his Zulu hero, Umslopogaas, and the axe (inkosikasi) increases the verisimilitude.[41]

Figure 14.5 D. McFarlane, 'South Sea Islanders', *North Queensland Register*, 21 December 1892, 41. This double portrait depicts a South Sea Islander man and woman wearing Western clothing and posing for the camera. Reproduced courtesy of the National Library of Australia and under the Creative Commons licence CC BY-NC 4.0.

Figure 14.6 D. McFarlane, 'South Sea Islanders', *North Queensland Register*, 21 December 1892, 44. These portraits show the same Melanesian couple as in Figure 14.5, this time dressed in their 'authentic' traditional costumes. Reproduced courtesy of the National Library of Australia and under the Creative Commons licence CC BY-NC 4.0.

More importantly, the *North Queensland Register* deployed a mix of condescension and humour to ridicule Melanesians' portrayal as 'civilised' subjects. 'While considerable trouble was experienced in inducing the kanakas to pose in native attire,' so reads the article, 'the contrary was the case in "calico and civilization," dozens of couples eagerly presenting themselves as candidates.'[42] Melanesians' westernised identity is described as nothing more than pretence (as Homi Bhabha explained, the coloniser has a 'desire for a reformed, recognizable Other, as a subject of a difference that is almost the same, but not quite'[43]). The *North Queensland Register* article continues as follows:

> The great ambition of a kanaka is to be taken 'white' – attired in the dull prosaic garments of civilization. It will be noticed that they have been taken of the complexion desired. When they go back to the islands, they will triumphantly carry with them their photographs, one of which may form the nucleus of an art gallery in Tanna or Malicolo.[44]

The notion of Melanesians as a vain and superficial race appears in several commentaries circulating in the press in the late nineteenth century. 'The Kanaka is', wrote Harry Blake in *The Antipodean*, 'a vain personage, much given to adding to his personal appearance by strange ornaments.'[45] The correspondent for the *Sydney Mail* in 1906 declared:

> Now, the wants of the kanaka are few, although he is as imitative as a monkey, trying to do all that a white man does, from getting his photo taken in boxing costume or in student attitude with impressive book in hand, to dressing like a dandy and riding his free-wheel bicycle downhill, arms folded and head held haughtily erect.[46]

The *Mail* included a series of studio likenesses of Melanesians, most probably 'time-expired' or 'ticket-exempt' Kanakas, that follow the aesthetic conventions of bourgeois portraiture (Figure 14.7). Posed in front of decorated backdrops, wearing suits and holding props such as bicycles and books, the men in these photographs look more like educated petits bourgeois rather than humble farmhands. Yet, with their ironical tone, the captions tend to devalue, if not even mock, these workers' projected social identities ('in student attitude, with impressive book in hand'). By comparing Melanesians with monkeys, the article not only dehumanises them, but also mocks and invalidates their social aspirations.

Figure 14.7 'Before the Exodus: A Kanaka Wedding', *The Sydney Mail*, 31 October 1906, 563. Part of a feature narrating the experience of a Christian wedding among South Sea Islanders, the article includes various portraits of assimilated Melanesians accompanied by sneering captions. Reproduced courtesy of the National Library of Australia and under the Creative Commons licence CC BY-NC 4.0.

As these examples demonstrate, nineteenth-century Australian print culture used a variety of devices to contain Melanesian portraiture's 'socially dangerous implications'. Editors used a veneer of humour to undermine photography's claim for the citizenship and equality of South Sea Islanders. These articles demonstrate the potential of apparently harmless jokes to become avenues for the dehumanisation of Melanesian workers and the assertion of White supremacy. As Margaret Olin has remarked, commenting on America's early twentieth-century visual culture, 'this veneer of humour, its presumed light-heartedness, can paper over some of the same assumptions that underlie violence, making light of the perceived danger coming from the other race and offering a more palatable vision to the spectator than does a photograph of a lynching.'[47] Olin's analysis is valid for Australian print and visual culture as well. Through humour and derisive language, the Australian press tempered the dangerous claims for individuality and personhood that underpinned portraiture of Melanesians, offering, at the same time, a more acceptable version of its racist ideology. This ideology, in turn, provided a justification for the coercive labour system of the plantation.

McFarlane's photograph of the South Sea Islander couple was to reappear nine years later in *The Queenslander*'s pictorial supplement (Figure 14.8). Whereas this time the feature did not express any explicit negative remarks about the couple's identity, it nevertheless inserted the picture into an imagined narrative of civilisation that subtly undermines Melanesians' agency. The photographic sequence begins with a picture of a group of newly recruited Islanders (captioned as the 'raw material') and ends with a group of Melanesians in European attire at a Sunday picnic (the 'finished article'). The layout and the language used in the captions serve a larger ideological function: namely, to contain the Melanesian workers' claims of social mobility and equality asserted through the images. Even though Melanesians are depicted as respectable middle-class subjects, their citizenship, instead of being represented on its own terms, is tethered to their previous status as 'primitive' people and manual workers. Through the sequencing of the pictures, agency is placed back onto the White man, whose 'civilising' mission has managed to transform Melanesian workers into proper subjects. In other words, in this illustrated feature, labour coercion is presented as a benign system. South Sea Islanders' place within the body politic is bounded by the submissive terms of their 'primitive' past, which serves to differentiate them and thus deny them full access to Australian freedom, including the freedom to sell one's work to the highest-bidding employer on the labour market.

Figure 14.8 'The Evolution of the Plantation Kanaka', *The Queenslander*, 23 March 1901, 563. Drawing on the photographs published by the *North Queensland Register* a decade earlier, the article arranges collective and individual portraits of Melanesians in a sequential manner to suggest the benign effects of coerced labour. Reproduced courtesy of the National Library of Australia and under the Creative Commons licence CC BY-NC 4.0.

This cursory analysis of photography of South Sea Islanders shows that workers experienced coercion not only through punitive laws, binding modes of remuneration and various forms of surveillance, but also through culture. While photographic portraiture might seem alien to the question of labour, it nevertheless intersects with it insofar as portraiture could act as a powerful discursive platform through which Melanesian workers could make claims against the state's restrictive legislation. In the public sphere, honorific individual portraits of Islanders had the potential to reclaim their identity as different from 'uncivilised' others. Hence, as the coercive nature of the Pacific labour trade was being questioned by social groups within and outside the colony, it was key for plantation owners to control the public interpretation of portraiture of Melanesian workers that presented them as assimilated individuals. In other words, even photographs that did not directly depict coercive labour relations, such as portraits of labourers showing intellectual skills and moral virtues, were connected to those relations and could have potentially impacted them. Photography mattered for the coercion of Islanders as it expressed, reinforced and, at times, questioned the racial order that constantly conditioned and shaped their labour relations.

Conclusion: the ambiguities of the portrait and the ambiguities of indentured labour

Historians of the Pacific indentured labour trade who want to recover Islanders' voices have to face significant challenges. Not only was the labour coercion often 'quiet', inscribed in complex forms of contracts and legislation that merely gave a superficial appearance of protecting Melanesian labourers; in addition, the language barrier between English colonisers and Islanders prevented the clear expression of workers' grievances within the police and judicial system. 'The colonial world,' Banivanua-Mar remarked, 'with all its reams of paper and wells of ink, when it mattered was incapable of recording or hearing Islanders' story and was not equipped with the language and words to do so.'[48] If written documents do not adequately capture the experience of South Sea Islanders, is photography a better medium? In other words, to return to the opening question raised by this chapter: can photography picture coerced labour? Can it provide us with access to the authentic experience of indentured labourers?

The question is of great relevance, especially for contemporary museums that rely on photographic archives to tell South Sea Islanders' history. Like the written word, photography poses a methodological challenge as the medium was largely controlled by the White hegemonic class. In fact, all the photographers mentioned in this chapter who took pictures of Kanakas were White: government artists, amateurs who also happened to work as accountants or chemists for the plantation, including Harriett Pettifore Brims. Likewise, the journalists who published Islanders' pictures in the press were White middle-class men. Melanesians did not have the chance to use photography to expose their harsh work conditions. Consequently, it is fair to say that photographic documentation of Melanesians provides only scant access to evidence of labour coercion. Like official police and bureaucratic reports, photography, to a significant extent, was not capable of recording Islanders' traumatic experiences.

Nevertheless, the neglect of the photographic archive would be an oversight. Fragmented and distorted, the voices of Islanders, while not always recorded by the camera, were never completely silent. Portraits of Islanders can offer entry points into the aspirations of workers and the racist ideology of late nineteenth-century Australia, an ideology that legitimised the need for coerced labour. Photography's ability to act as a social leveller somehow posed a threat to the racist social order that informed the system of the plantation. The portrait's honorific function made an implicit claim about Melanesians' social status. By presenting them as equal to White 'civilised' men, honorific portraits of Islanders implicitly asserted their right to sell their labour without restrictions. Countering these claims, newspapers tended to re-signify portraits of Melanesians through captions and layout. They deployed a variety of discursive and visual strategies that tended to mock Islanders' social aspirations. In other words, photographic portraiture of plantation workers is a useful platform for reconstructing the mentality that shaped coerced labour.

Photography, for South Sea Islanders, was both a threat and a promise. It was a threat because it tended to sanitise indentured labour, presenting it as a form of 'desirable' work. Pictures of Islanders working in sugar cane fields, published in newspapers and periodicals of the time, aimed to illustrate the productivity of the sugar plantation. They show Melanesians not protesting against their conditions but as active and ordered participants in the plantation system. Photography of this kind tended to conceal the coercion of indentured labour. But photography also offered a promise: the symbolic space where a fantasy of freedom from labour could be enacted. I want to stress the term 'fantasy' on purpose: I am not suggesting that, because Islanders had the chance to buy and own portraits, they should be considered to have been empowered, a familiar revisionist trope. Certainly, the emancipation offered by the portrait was only symbolic. Yet, it mattered somehow, given the complex ways in which, in the press, these pictures were editorialised, and their potentially subversive meanings contained.

Addressing the traumatic past of South Sea Islanders, the exhibition Plantation Voices represented a first important step towards the recovery of a history of labour in Australia.[49] For a long time, official Australian historiography has reduced the Pacific labour trade to a minor footnote in a glorious national narrative of development and progress. As Lorenzo Veracini has pointed out, Australian historiography has tended to perpetuate the myth of Australia as the 'Quiet Continent', the notion of Australia as a harmonious society lacking class conflicts and divisions.[50] Plantation Voices certainly challenged this myth and provided an antidote to the general amnesia of educational institutions and the media. The exhibition capitalised on the power of photographic documentation to address contemporary Australian South Sea Islanders' desire for identity and belonging. The exhibition curator and the artists deployed photographic portraiture to resurrect and connect with their ancestors. They devoted scant attention to the ways in which photography also worked to conceal and perpetuate the oppression of indentured labour. To return to the initial question, photography can convey coerced labour when we look at this material technology of representation with a kind of double vision, that is to say, when we envision it as either an instrument of oppression or one of liberation, neither reducible to the other, neither existing without the other.

Notes

1. For an introduction to the theme of coerced labour, see Müller, 'Introduction: Labour Coercion, Labour Control, and Workers' Agency', 2019.
2. van der Linden, 'Dissecting Coerced Labour', 321–2.
3. Indentured workers came from more than 80 Pacific Islands, including Vanuatu and the Solomon Islands, with distinct cultures and economies. Although I am aware of the perils of homogenising them under one label, in this article, for convenience, I use the terms 'Melanesian' and 'South Sea Islander' as synonyms. The southwest Pacific Islands operated as a vast labour reserve not only for Australia but also for other European colonies. Pacific Islanders also worked in Fiji, Samoa, Hawai'i, New Caledonia, French Polynesia, Nauru, Peru, Guatemala and Mexico.
4. The Commonwealth's 1901 Pacific Islanders Labourers Act banned the import of indentured workers from the Pacific and imposed their deportation to their native lands. The act made all Melanesian workers who had arrived after 1879 illegal and gave the federal authorities the power to deport any Islander found in Australia after December 1906, except for a small minority of Islanders who were given exemption. As Stefanie Affeldt has pointed out, the deportation and repression of Islanders would not have been possible without the activity of an emerging labour and trade union movement. This deployed a variety of methods – including

cultural propaganda through a plethora of publications and printed media – to persuade the government that Islanders represented a threat to White Australia. In opposition to the 1901 Pacific Islanders Labourers Act, Melanesian migrants formed political organisations, such as the Mackay Pacific Islanders' Association and the Nambour South Sea Island Cane Growers, to lobby parliament against their deportation. For a discussion of the trade union movement's vilification of Melanesian labour, see Affeldt, 'Making Black White: Sugar Consumption and Racial Unity in Australia', 2017.
5   Over the last 10 years, the State Library of Queensland has digitised and made public part of its vast photographic archive of South Sea Islander labourers through internet sharing platforms like Flickr.
6   Besides works by Mooney and Togo-Brisby, Plantation Voices included a performance work by Joella Warkill and a series of documentary photographs by LaVonne Bobongie. As my focus in this chapter is the use of archival photography to represent coerced labour, I will limit my analysis to Mooney and Togo-Brisby's projects as they appropriated and made direct reference to the archive.
7   Mooney, 'Stop and Stare'.
8   Togo-Brisby, 'The Past is Ahead, Don't Look Back'.
9   Miller, 'Plantation Voices'.
10 Barthes, *Camera Lucida*, 87.
11 Runia, 'Presence', 2006, 5.
12 As Michael Roth has noted, the promise of presence offered by photography is ultimately illusory. 'The desire for presence is so strong in the face of loss, of death, and photography conveys *both* this desire *and the fact that it cannot be gratified*. Photography stokes the desire for fullness or presence, but this also means that the photographic image never satisfies this desire. The photograph points to and accentuates this ambivalence' (Roth, 'Photographic Ambivalence and Historical Consciousness', 2009, 89).
13 On the relation between colonialism and photography, there is a vast bibliography. See, for instance, Ryan, 'Photography and Empire'; Ryan, *Picturing Empire: Photography and the Visualization of the British Empire*; Pinney, *Exposures: Photography and Anthropology*; Pinney, *Camera Indica: The Social Life of Indian Photographs*; Pinney and Peterson (eds), *Photography's Other Histories*; Hight and Sampson (eds), *Colonialist Photography: Imag(in)ing Race and Place*; Landau and Kaspin (eds), *Images and Empires: Visuality in Colonial and Postcolonial Africa*; and Gartlan and Behdad (eds), *Photography's Orientalism: New Essays on Colonial Representation*.
14 While this essay does not follow a strict semiotic approach to press photography, it is nevertheless indebted to Stuart Hall and Roland Barthes's pioneering studies of photojournalism and advertisement. See Hall, 'The Determination of News Photographs'; and Barthes, 'Rhetoric of the Image'.
15 Banivanua-Mar, *Violence and Colonial Dialogue: The Australian-Pacific Indentured Labour Trade*, 13.
16 Saunders, 'The Black Scourge', 168.
17 Saunders estimated that up to 1,000 Melanesians officially brought into Queensland had been abducted by force or trickery. As she wrote, 'the traffic was to undergo radical changes from 1863 to 1904. At first, in "low contact" areas in which Melanesians had experienced little intercourse with Europeans or had minimal knowledge of European culture, the enlistment process was consistently illegal, at times having some aspects of genuine slave-trading. These methods declined to a significant degree in the transitional period as the Pacific Islanders came to understand better what enlistment entailed, until, in the "high contact" era, the process became almost totally one of legal recruitment. By this time, Melanesians made conscious decisions to enlist for colonial servitude' (Saunders, *Workers in Bondage*, 20).
18 Mortensen, 'Slaving in Australian Courts', 2009, 9.
19 Mortensen, 'Slaving in Australian Courts', 2009, 9.
20 In 1868 a group of missionaries hinted at the coercive nature of the recruitment process. They described its questionable nature on the pages of the *Sydney Morning Herald*: 'It is clear that the Act contemplates the deportation of the civilised or semi-civilised only, since the uncivilised could not be made to understand the nature of a contract and would only be brought to regular work by the unreasoning and arbitrary lash. But the commissioned skippers will not read the Act in this light; it will be little matter to them whether the natives are civilised or uncivilised; one man will bring as much head money as another, and what has been defective in training

at home will be left for the stock-whip and stock-drivers of Queensland to accomplish' ('Polynesian Labourers in Queensland', *Sydney Morning Herald*, 1869, 2).
21 Miller, 'Sugar Slaves'.
22 Saunders, 'The Workers' Paradox', 225.
23 'Polynesian Labourers in Queensland', *Sydney Morning Herald*, 1869, 2.
24 Saunders, 'The Black Scourge', 169.
25 The same system of deferred payment was used by farmers in the 1890s with the rise of the 'butty gang' method of production, which involved the outsourcing of work to a team of cane cutters contracted on short term and agreed price. See Saunders, 'The Workers' Paradox', 235.
26 Graves, 'Truck and Gifts', 1983, 87.
27 Graves, 'Truck and Gifts', 1983, 90.
28 Saunders, 'The Workers' Paradox', 227.
29 Brass, 'The Return of "Merrie Melanesia"', 1996, 220–1.
30 In the 1980s, in Australia, a strand of scholarship – called 'revisionist' – emerged as a response to the scathing historical accounts published in the previous decade. This scholarship emphasised the capacity of Melanesians to resist their oppressive work conditions through a variety of strategies such as absconding, malingering and sabotage, and the retention of indigenous cultural practices. The new strand argued that the indentured labour trade would not have been possible without a substantial degree of voluntary participation from Melanesians. Specifically, revisionists downplayed the phenomenon of blackbirding, dismissed as myth or European folklore, and emphasised workers' ability to preserve parts of their cultures and cosmologies as mechanisms of resistance against colonial and state power. See Moore, *Kanaka: A History of Melanesian Mackay*; Lal, Munro and Beechert (eds), *Plantation Workers: Resistance and Accommodation*; Finnane and Moore, 'Kanaka Slaves or Willing Workers? Melanesian Workers and the Queensland Criminal Justice System in the 1890s', 1992; Corris, *Passage, Port and Plantation: A History of Solomon Islands Labour Migration, 1870–1914* (and Corris, 'Pacific Island Labour Migrants in Queensland', 1970; Scarr, 'Recruits and Recruiters: A Portrait of the Pacific Islands Labour Trade', 1967; Scarr, *Fragments of Empire: A History of the Western Pacific High Commission*, 137–60). For an overview of the revisionist historiography, see Munro, 'The Pacific Island Labour Trade: Approaches, Methodologies, Debates', 1993; Munro, 'The Labour Trade in Melanesians to Queensland: An Historiographic Essay', 1995. For a critique of revisionist historiography, see Brass, 'Contextualizing Sugar Production in Nineteenth-Century Queensland', 1994.
31 Campt, *Image Matters: Archive, Photography and the African Diaspora in Europe*, 7.
32 Campt, *Image Matters*, 7.
33 Sekula, 'The Body and the Archive', 1986, 6–7.
34 Saunders, *Workers in Bondage*.
35 On the relation between the *carte de visite* and bourgeois subjectivity, see Batchen, 'Dreams of Ordinary Life'; Tagg, 'A Democracy of the Image'.
36 'Sugar at Bundaberg', *Queensland Agricultural Journal*, 1897, 244.
37 'Sugar at Bundaberg', *Queensland Agricultural Journal*, 1897, 244.
38 Marx, *Capital: A Critique of Political Economy*, 440–1.
39 'Some Anti-Slavery Reflections', *Queensland Figaro*, 1886, 5.
40 'South Sea Islanders', *North Queensland Register*, 1892, 41.
41 'South Sea Islanders', *North Queensland Register*, 1892, 41.
42 'South Sea Islanders', *North Queensland Register*, 1892, 41.
43 Bhabha, 'Of Mimicry and Man', 86.
44 'South Sea Islanders', *North Queensland Register*, 1892, 53.
45 Harry I. Blake, 'The Kanaka: A Character Sketch', *The Antipodean*, 1892, 82.
46 'Before the Exodus: A Kanaka Wedding', *The Sydney Mail*, 1906, 563.
47 Margaret Olin, 'Study in Black and White', 2021, 139. See also Sheehan, *Study in Black and White*.
48 Banivanua-Mar, *Violence and Colonial Dialogue*, 4.
49 The exhibition was propelled by the Commonwealth recognition of South Sea Islanders as a unique minority group in the late 1990s. One of the actions taken after recognition has been the development of a curriculum on the history and culture of Australian South Sea Islanders to be taught in Queensland schools.
50 Veracini, 'Historylessness', 2007.

Bibliography

Affeldt, Stefanie. 'Making Black White: Sugar Consumption and Racial Unity in Australia', *Zeitschrift für Australienstudien/Australian Studies Journal* 31 (2017): 87–110.

Banivanua-Mar, Tracey. *Violence and Colonial Dialogue: The Australian-Pacific Indentured Labour Trade*. Honolulu: University of Hawai'i Press, 2007.

Barthes, Roland. 'Rhetoric of the Image'. In *Image Music Text*, 32–51. New York: Hill and Wang, 1977.

Barthes, Roland. *Camera Lucida: Reflections on Photography*. New York: Hill and Wang, 2006.

Batchen, Geoffrey. 'Dreams of Ordinary Life: Cartes-de-Visite and the Bourgeois Imagination'. In *Photography: Theoretical Snapshots*, edited by Jonathan Long, Andrea Noble and Edward Welch, 80–97. London: Routledge, 2009.

'Before the Exodus: A Kanaka Wedding', *The Sydney Mail*, 31 October 1906.

Bhabha, Homi. 'Of Mimicry and Man: The Ambivalence of Colonial Discourse'. In *The Location of Culture*, 85–92. London: Routledge, 1994.

Blake, Harry I. 'The Kanaka: A Character Sketch', *The Antipodean: An Illustrated Annual*, 1892, 80–85.

Brass, Tom. 'Contextualizing Sugar Production in Nineteenth-Century Queensland', *Slavery and Abolition* 15/1 (1994): 100–17.

Brass, Tom. 'The Return of "Merrie Melanesia": A Comment on a Review of a Review', *The Journal of Pacific History* 31/2 (1996): 215–23.

Campt, Tina. *Image Matters: Archive, Photography and the African Diaspora in Europe*. Durham: Duke University Press, 2012.

Corris, Peter. 'Pacific Island Labour Migrants in Queensland', *Journal of Pacific History* 2 (1970): 43–64.

Corris, Peter. *Passage, Port and Plantation: A History of Solomon Islands Labour Migration, 1870–1914*. Melbourne: Melbourne University Press, 1973.

Finnane, Mark and Moore, Clive. 'Kanaka Slaves or Willing Workers? Melanesian Workers and the Queensland Criminal Justice System in the 1890s', *Criminal Justice History* 13 (1992): 141–60.

Gartlan, Luke and Behdad, Ali (eds). *Photography's Orientalism: New Essays on Colonial Representation*. Los Angeles: Getty Publications, 2013.

Graves, Adrian. 'Truck and Gifts: Melanesian Immigrants and the Trade Box System in Colonial Queensland', *Past and Present* 101 (1983): 87–124.

Graves, Adrian. *Cane and Labour: The Political Economy of the Queensland Sugar Industry, 1862–1906*. Edinburgh: Edinburgh University Press, 1993.

Hall, Stuart. 'The Determination of News Photographs'. In *Manufacture of News*, edited by Stanley Cohen and Jock Young, 226–43. Beverly Hills: Sage, 1973.

Hight, Eleanor M. and Sampson, Gary D. (eds). *Colonialist Photography: Imag(in)ing Race and Place*. London: Routledge, 2002.

Lal, Brij V., Munro, Doug and Beechert, Edward D. (eds). *Plantation Workers: Resistance and Accommodation*. Honolulu: University of Hawai'i Press, 1993.

Landau, P. S. and Kaspin, D. D. (eds). *Images and Empires: Visuality in Colonial and Postcolonial Africa*. Berkeley: University of California Press, 2002.

Marx, Karl. *Capital: A Critique of Political Economy, Vol. 1*. London: New Left Books, 1976.

Miller, Imelda. 'Sugar Slaves', *Queensland Historical Atlas: Histories, Cultures, Landscapes*, The University of Queensland, 22 October 2010. Accessed 20 March 2023. https://www.qhatlas.com.au/content/sugar-slaves

Miller, Imelda. 'Plantation Voices: Contemporary Conversations with Australian South Sea Islanders', 19 March 2019. Accessed 3 September 2021. https://www.slq.qld.gov.au/discover/exhibitions/plantation-voices-contemporary-conversations-australian-south-sea-islanders

Mooney, Dylan. 'Stop and Stare', State Library of Queensland Blog, 23 May 2019. Accessed 15 September 2022. https://www.slq.qld.gov.au/blog/stop-and-stare

Moore, Clive. *Kanaka: A History of Melanesian Mackay*. Port Moresby: Institute of Papua New Guinea Studies and University of Papua New Guinea Press, 1985.

Mortensen, Reid. 'Slaving in Australian Courts: Blackbirding Cases, 1869–1871', *Journal of South Pacific Law* 13/1 (2009): 7–37.

Müller, Viola F. 'Introduction: Labour Coercion, Labour Control, and Workers' Agency', *Labour History* 60/6 (2019): 865–8.

Munro, Doug. 'The Pacific Island Labour Trade: Approaches, Methodologies, Debates', *Slavery and Abolition* 14 (1993), 87–108.
Munro, Doug. 'The Labour Trade in Melanesians to Queensland: An Historiographic Essay', *Journal of Social History* 28/3 (1995), 609–27.
Olin, Margaret. 'Study in Black and White: Photography, Race, Humour by Tanya Sheehan', *The Art Bulletin* 103/4 (2021): 138–40.
Pinney, Christopher. *Camera Indica: The Social Life of Indian Photographs*. London: Reaktion, 1997.
Pinney, Christopher. *Exposures: Photography and Anthropology*. London: Reaktion, 2012.
Pinney, Christopher and Peterson, Nicolas (eds). *Photography's Other Histories*. Durham: Duke University Press, 2003.
'Polynesian Labourers in Queensland', *Sydney Morning Herald*, 9 February 1869.
Roth, Michael. 'Photographic Ambivalence and Historical Consciousness', *History and Theory* 48 (2009): 82–94.
Runia, Eelco. 'Presence', *History and Theory* 45/1 (2006): 1–29.
Ryan, James. *Picturing Empire: Photography and the Visualization of the British Empire*. Chicago: Chicago University Press, 1997.
Ryan, James. 'Photography and Empire'. In *The Encyclopedia of Empire*, edited by N. Dalziel and J. M. MacKenzie, 1–9. New York: Wiley, 2016.
Saunders, Kay. 'The Black Scourge'. In *Race Relations in Colonial Queensland*, edited by Kay Saunders, Raymond Evans and Kathryn Cronin, 147–234. St Lucia: The University of Queensland Press, 1975.
Saunders, Kay. *Workers in Bondage: The Origins and Bases of Unfree Labour in Queensland, 1824–1916*. St Lucia: University of Queensland Press, 1982.
Saunders, Kay. 'The Workers' Paradox: Indentured Labour in the Queensland Sugar Industry to 1920'. In *Indentured Labour in the British Empire, 1834–1920*, edited by Kay Saunders, 213–59. London: Croom Helm, 1984.
Scarr, Deryck. *Fragments of Empire: A History of the Western Pacific High Commission, 1877–1914*. Canberra: Australian National University Press, 1967.
Scarr, Deryck. 'Recruits and Recruiters: A Portrait of the Pacific Islands Labour Trade', *Journal of Pacific History* 2 (1967): 5–22.
Sekula, Allan. 'The Body and the Archive', *October* 39 (1986): 3–64.
Sheehan, Tanya. *Study in Black and White: Photography, Race, Humor*. University Park, PA: Penn State University Press, 2018.
'Some Anti-Slavery Reflections', *Queensland Figaro*, 12 June 1886.
'South Sea Islanders', *North Queensland Register*, 21 December 1892.
'Sugar at Bundaberg', *Queensland Agricultural Journal*, 1 September 1897.
Tagg, John. 'A Democracy of the Image: Photographic Portraiture and Commodity Production'. In *The Burden of Representation: Essays on Photographies and Histories*, 34–65. London: Macmillan, 1988.
Togo-Brisby, Jasmine. 'The Past is Ahead, Don't Look Back', State Library of Queensland Blog, 29 July 2019. Accessed 3 September 2022. https://www.slq.qld.gov.au/blog/past-ahead-dont-look-back
van der Linden, Marcel M. 'Dissecting Coerced Labour'. In *On Coerced Labour: Work and Compulsion after Chattel Slavery*, edited by Marcel M. van der Linden and Magaly Rodríguez García, 321–2. Leiden: Brill, 2016.
Veracini, Lorenzo. 'Historylessness: Australia as a Settler Colonial Collective', *Postcolonial Studies* 10/3 (2007), 271–85.

Afterword

15
Word and image in communication: 'translation loop' as a means of historiographical research
Anamarija Batista

The methodology of this volume brings to mind the figure of thought of a 'translation loop'. Characteristic of this loop process is the exploration of the common topic – coercive relations in the context of gainful employment – based on the method of an intermedial translation of reflections and interpretations. Accordingly, the interplay of the textual and the visible is analysed by continuously correlating, linking and, in doing so, also distorting the reflections on and interpretations of a text or a picture. In an interactive loop, the mechanisms of coercion are recomposed linguistically as well as visually. The commentary, contextualisation and supplementation of both conceptual topologies and visual motifs take place through interactive referencing.[1] At the same time, this type of translation goes hand in hand with the formation of an intermedial hybridity.[2]

Following Marshall McLuhan, intermedial hybridity can create a line between forms that ultimately results in a 'moment of freedom and release from the ordinary trance and numbness imposed by them on our senses'.[3] The numbness that McLuhan refers to emanates from the representation of contexts in the form of subject-specific motifs and models, around which lines of arguments are drawn continuously. Thereby, necessary deepening and explaining of structures oscillate between the tension of procedural logics of the own discipline and the own medium. In doing so, however, we enter a certain framework that is marked by its own normativity for the development of lines of argumentation. The intermedial production chain proposed here aims to expand mediation formats of the network of historical relations and to put the normativities of the 'offered' interpretation into a state of tension. In this process, we did not, however, lay down a guideline for a fixed repertoire of situations or tools for interpretation. Both texts and pictures are considered producers of a common hybridity, which sees the intermedial difference as a potential for questioning and expansion.[4]

The role of pictures in exploring historical relations: a historical review

For some time, pictures have been collaborators of historical research. We find illustrations as protagonists of historiography in book paintings from antiquity and the Middle Ages.[5] Pictures act as narrators in picture and nonfiction books, conveying and designing historical artefacts – one only needs to think of history paintings, graphic novellas with historical depictions, nonfiction books with historical source material such as photos or maps.[6] For historiographical practice in areas such as restoration and cultural heritage preservation, illustrations without art as a reference frame, such as natural scientific pictures or diagrams, play an important role. Their visualisations are the result of decisions made during the research process and operational steps of conservators and conservationists as well as the tools used in the process.[7] It is exactly the crucial role of the technology used that results in a relativisation of 'the bodily experience of perception and the body as an observation and measurement tool'.[8] Images produced in this way can be interpreted by certain groups as visual evidence.[9]

Diagrammatic visualisations (such as bar charts and pie charts) that ostensibly collect, evaluate and present statistical and accounting data are also important in the context of the exploration of historical labour conditions.[10] Stating numerical relationships in this way abstracts local and cultural circumstances to make them comparable with each other across epochs. The abstract form of the curve or the bar allows us to think in proportions and ratios, but it seems to inadequately represent other relations such as spatial atmospheres, human perception, bodily inscriptions, local contexts and so on. The abstraction does indeed facilitate categorisation; however, specific formations and inscriptions, the shaping of everyday working practices and its embedding in other networks of relationships as well as the subjectivity of the working people become more difficult to recognise in the course of this subsumption. As a result, knowledge formation about the interplay of norm, order and emotion is also made more difficult. In the context of coercive relations, the proposed number of quantitative indicators may reflect, for example, the amount of the wage or the number of cases affected by a certain practice, but the perception of workers, their living conditions, previous histories and scope for decision-making can only be inferred from them to a limited extent.

Since the 1980s, historiography has started to include pictures such as paintings, photographs and film as sources and reference points in order to close this gap.[11] For example, Heike Talkenberger and Rainer Wohlfeil focus on the exploration of prints from the Middle Ages and the early modern period, while Sybil Milton uses contemporary photographs as sources in the context of research on the Holocaust.[12] Talkenberger proposes a functional analytical approach for analysing historical pictures. The picture and its social effects are considered elements of a historical communication process. Based on a quantitative image analysis, larger quantities of pictures are examined for their contexts as well as deviant and typical characteristics. As a result, assumptions are made about the visual interpretation made by the recipients.[13] Sybil Milton also points to an important gain in knowledge through including as many photographic sources as possible, because the analysis of photographic source material – such as the photographs of anti-youth violence in villages and small towns during the Nazi regime – leads to information and insights that may not be available in written sources.[14] Following Rainer Wohlfeil, the evaluation of existing photographic material could be carried out based on the picture analysis developed by the art historian Erwin Panofsky,[15] which can be adapted to different research purposes.

As a consequence, historiography challenges the primacy of text- and number-based sources within its practice and attempts to expand its landscape of sources through other medial forms of expression.[16] Including pictures as sources also requires us to scrutinise the concept of sources within historiography.[17] If a source is seen as a metaphor of historical development, it 'has entered but not immersed the stream of history', symbolising significant meaning in the historical discourse. In order to grasp both the meaning and the sensuality of a historical situation, images are also added as sources. The change of perspective thus introduced opens up the possibility of studying the image as well as its relationship to text and number in the historical context. This is the point of departure of this volume.

Coercion and remunerated work: intermedial and interdisciplinary perspectives

Some of the chapters (those by Eva Kuhn, Paolo Magagnoli and Eszter Őze) examine and explore visual contributions – such as the film work *Maquilápolis*, nineteenth-century portrait photography of Pacific Islanders or the exhibitions of the Budapest Museum of Social Health – as sources that describe, shape and reflect on labour relations and labour conditions as well as the idea of labour and the body. Whether it is Mexican female workers who participate in the production of the film *Maquilápolis* in order to narrate their history and the history of labour conditions and its background through their own 'voices' to make them audible and visible; or the photographic portraits of workers, whose mode of picture taking and historical reception make an important contribution to the discussion of the role of Pacific Islanders in Australia; or the ideological ideas of the Hungarian state about work, health and the body in the first half of the twentieth century, represented by and conceptualised in exhibition formats such as exhibition posters: all these visual, or rather visual-audio formats, as well as their content and aesthetic form, contribute to the analysis of the volume's topic: paid labour and coercion.

In these cases, the picture, the audio track and the exhibition display are understood as self-reflexive and actively influencing media that are taken as points of reference and primary sources for the interpretation within the framework of art historical text production. Historical events are analysed based on visual and audio material. In doing so, pictures, intertwined with textual sources, are used as sources in historical research on the topic of coercion and paid labour.

Furthermore, this book makes a plea for an interdisciplinary research practice and for commitment to the importance of intermedial methodological approaches in the field of coercion and labour, with members of the editorial team coming from various disciplines (history, art studies, literary studies and economics). The editorial work was marked by continuous reflection on the compatibility, objectives and application of the methodologies and approaches involved.

The interdisciplinary research process will be illustrated using the example of portrait photography by Pacific Islanders who migrated to Australia to work on sugar plantations. During this time, they had their photos taken by portrait photographers. The 2019 exhibition Plantation Voices: Contemporary Conversations with Australian South Sea Islanders[18] focuses on these portrait photographs. Its potential for reflection regarding historical circumstances is explicitly considered, and the artworks of this exhibition address and reflect on photography's potential for conveying meaning. In his contribution, art historian Paolo Magagnoli comments and reflects on how the artworks presented in the exhibition address the social role of Pacific Islanders in Australia. He notes that the crucial aspect of the exhibition – namely the world of labour – is given little attention. During our work, the editorial team and Magagnoli intensively discussed the interwovenness of issues around the medium of photography and its reception with historical labour conditions such as the pay and contract terms of Pacific Islanders.

The consequence of such a close cooperation is the shared responsibility for historiography and teaching history – shared by illustrators, art scholars, historians, artists, economists, sociologists and other scholars – and the reconstruction of everyday history and its social framing through the lens of certain disciplines and their interconnectedness. This interplay, however, is not, first and foremost, the affirmation or complementation of knowledge. Rather, the goal is to critically examine and scrutinise forms of knowledge production.[19]

'Translation loops'

As already mentioned, this book not only focuses on primary sources of historical research but also pays greater attention to their interplay with secondary literature. We have invited the illustrators Dariia Kuzmych, Monika Lang and Tim Robinson to visualise and conceptualise the lines of argument developed by historians, anthropologists and sociologists. Research contexts formulated in the text are translated into images to establish further references to historical facts and test further facets of interdisciplinary work. The visual drafts inspired the researchers to include further questions in their research design. For example, Akın Sefer uses Tim Robinson's collage, which visualises the competing demand for workers in agriculture and industry, as an impulse to elaborate on this tension in his textual contribution.

It must be noted that it is particularly characteristic of the production of illustrations to discuss the challenges of interdisciplinary collaboration from the outset. In contrast to artistic practice that focuses on novelties and thus individual forms of expression, the illustrator's work requires the intensive perception, reflection and addressing of the largely textual production in the context of the text–image composite production. The framing strategies of both media forms merge with each other in a process of interaction.

To illustrate something means to illuminate it, or to process an event or a fact by using a visualisation so that a certain content is conveyed pointedly and allegorically. The illustration is both a conveyor and producer of knowledge, criticism and fiction. The performativity of the body that is described and introduced by the text is translated into a visual form and redefined. Just like Adorno's 'expert listener', who is able to hear music when reading a score, a reader of the text can picture the performativity of the body.[20] The illustration picks up the impulse laid out in the text and sets itself the goal of further examining and discussing the ways in which the space and the body are presented. It looks for compositions that reflect and deconstruct the inscription of body politics and labour relations in the social space of time.[21] However, alongside the text, images in the form of primary or secondary sources are also included in the process, to create imagination. Through the form of illustration, the coding and marking of the 'working body' (factory workers, domestic workers, tour guides and so on) and its interwovenness in labour processes and labour relations in its environment are culturally reflected. Dariia Kuzmych and Monika Lang (situational embedding) and Tim Robinson (collage-style constructions) discuss realities of labour and its backgrounds. Both the mechanisms of coercion and subjective experiences become visible through the illustration and can thus be imagined. Assumptions about modes and forms of payment can be made implicitly. The degree of collaboration as well as that of autonomy of the illustration's narrative potential in relation to the text is created in the tension between accompanying, being parallel and acting as counterpoint.

In this book, we see the illustration as one of the players in the circular process of translation and interpretation. In this process, the illustration explores its own compositional possibilities, in this case to encompass, depict and, at the same time, transform both the reception and the citation of historical events through its own composition. It uses forms, motifs, symbols and structural solutions from spatial and figurative repertoires for depicting and interpreting coercive mechanisms of paid labour relations. The question is: how can the conditioning, control and coercion of workers that occurred in a locally and historically specific manner be visualised?

In order to achieve this, depictions, citation and interpretations from archival documents and secondary literature – and thus created historical reality of mechanisms such as indebtedness, control, immobility, punishment, honour – that are described in the textual contributions of the volume are used as references for the illustrative process afterwards.

One step back: contextualising and conceptualising primary sources

If we pause for a moment, we realise that several different steps have already been taken to conceptualise everyday working life in history. The preservation of archived material (primary sources) is in itself an abstracted process. By examining archival material, secondary literature develops its own interpretation and analysis with its own focus and intention, its own concepts, terminology and ideas of contexts. Even quotations in a text can be seen as a textual hybridisation.[22] The contributions in this volume follow the idea of 'translation loop' (as described above) and the development of intermedial hybridity with the means of 'own' lines of argument.

Anamarija Batista and Corinna Peres wrote textual scenarios that were given to the illustrators. While Batista focused on spatial scenes, Peres developed literary narratives in which historical actors took the leading roles. In the scriptwriting process, the element of fiction formed an integral part of the composition. Intensive discussions and further research followed, which seemed necessary for visual representation – capturing landscapes, people, fashions, designs and so on. As mentioned above, primary sources were consulted. Ideas of space and body, plausible relationships between historical characters, archival documents and their surroundings as well as possibilities and mechanisms of coercion in labour relations were searched for.

Intermedial micro-histories questioning macro-historical models

This search is in line with the trend of current research practice in global labour history, which increasingly focuses on the study of micro-histories of individuals and groups and their interdependencies with macro-historical developments (see the Introduction to the volume). The precise analysis of these aspects is intended to lead to further insights into the mechanisms of coercion. How were individual workers and their families, as well as groups of workers, recruited and retained through coercive measures in order to generate production and higher productivity? These practices, as argued in the contributions, took place precisely in interaction with paid work, which challenges the assumption that this is a form of work with a high degree of autonomy.

Often, the allegedly newly gained independency resulted from changes in ownership structures or the legitimisation of political-economic ideas – for example in seventeenth-century agrarian capitalism, in the period of the abolition of slavery or during the first decades of the implementation of socialist societies in the 1950s. As a result, new legislation was issued, in many cases on the grounds of increased productive capacities. The ways in which 'old' formats and relations were shaped, how their conditions of transformation were designed and manifested themselves were often overshadowed, overplayed and overwritten by 'new' regulations and practices. John Locke, for example, justified the privatisation tendencies in the agricultural sector in seventeenth-century England with the assumption that privatisation equalled higher productivity. One's own labour or that of others was to be used for this purpose.[23] Changes in the structure of ownership brought new categorisations and determinations of roles and mechanisms, which from then on began to reproduce and become independent through application.

Privatisation, which followed the logic of more efficient management, resulted, for example, in the ban on collecting dead wood, leaves and fruits in nineteenth-century Germany, which had been common practice before. The right of the poor to freely use forests of which they were not the owners was transformed into a 'monopoly of the rich' through the process of expropriation.[24] It is precisely the spatial and situational contextualisation of labour relations and their social transformations that is examined and elaborated through the illustrations in this volume, which provides references to coercive practices, relations and ideas.

The case studies specify, describe and reflect on coercion through legislative changes and their impacts. Visual representations focus on and intensify selected relationships of coercion (see Tim Robinson's illustrations for Sigrid Wadauer's chapter, pp. 47–50), link labour relations and labour goals of the pre-industrial and industrial ages (see Tim Robinson's illustrations for Akın Sefer's chapter, pp. 22–3), visualise mechanisms of the capitalist relationship between centre and periphery (see Dariia Kuzmych's illustration for Mohammad Tareq Hasan's chapter, p. 201) and show the ambivalence of certain labour relations in terms of privilege and coercion (see Monika Lang's illustrations for Ivanka Petrova's chapter, pp. 301–3).

Binding the workforce

Tim Robinson's collage-style illustrations, consisting primarily of archival photo material, depict the role of state control and applied coercive mechanisms in labour conditions. The use of the collage technique can also be seen as revealing the strong constructivist mechanisms of a political-economic decision, which is itself conceived as an idea and an imagining, and its impact on working life, labour relations and work situations. For it is precisely the state that assumes the role of organising property structures and contracting in terms of capitalist requirements. The Austro-Hungarian monarchy, for example, introduced labour booklets to record the mobility, identity and work history of workers. This information was, among other uses, used by employers to control workers, as discussed in Sigrid Wadauer's chapter. Robinson makes the labour booklet the main protagonist of his collages for this chapter (pp. 47–50). It encloses the workers, forms the ceiling of the imaginary prison and contains data that frame and standardise the workers. From the 1920s onwards, the requirement for papers gradually disappeared and the labour booklet was abolished.

Robinson also produced illustrations for two other texts. Akın Sefer's contribution on the nineteenth-century Ottoman Empire discusses the state's intention to become an employer in the shipping industry and increase the construction of military ships. In order to recruit workers, the state made use of mechanisms of community commitment and demanded that communities make workers available at fixed time intervals. Workers were paid, but below market value. The communities challenged the state's demand as they were convinced that their new duty to pay taxes exempted them from providing workers. The first collage (p. 22) shows the workers framed by two rulers, one of them looking directly at the viewer of the picture. The red circles around workers in turn mark the possibility and the ambivalence of the new arrangement. In general, the workers would have been free to decide for themselves at what price they were willing to work. Here, however, they were recruited in the name of the community. At the same time, the second collage (p. 23) shows that state recruitment of workers made it more difficult to cultivate the fields because it resulted in a shortage of agricultural labour. The performativity of representations of the body in the context of agrarian production differs from the representation of disciplined bodies in the shipping industry, based on changes in the organisation of work and the relation of working time and leisure time.

The third set of collages, relating to the chapter by Nataša Milićević and Ljubinka Škodrić, is concerned with a state of emergency, namely the Second World War, when Nazi Germany occupied Serbia and tried to introduce a new administrative structure with the help of collaborators on the ground. Robinson depicts this story in three collages (pp. 79–81), the first showing German officers obsessed with the idea of imposing their ideology on the whole world. They proudly stand in front of the territories they imagine will be ruled by their ideological ideas in the future. A large colourful map unfolds behind them that signals the territorial desire for conquest. It is also clear that governing such large areas and transforming existing administrative structures would be a major undertaking. Their desire is matched by the challenge. The transformation can only take place by means of coercion. The second and third collages show collaborators and representatives of the Third Reich who are already stationed in Serbia. They no longer look at the map but at civil servants whose working lives have changed completely since the arrival of the new rulers. As the collages show, they work hard, earn meagre wages and must carry out physically demanding work in addition to their actual jobs – cultivating land, clearing snow and so on. State decrees categorise civil servants into 'new' groups: women, pensioners, Jews, communists and so on (p. 81), who are drawn into the tension between low pay, high perseverance and new systematisation of the administrative apparatus.

Confronting coercion

Dariia Kuzmych's illustrations are in watercolour, depicting the selected situations and protagonists in one picture for each chapter. She simultaneously presents several scenographic moments of everyday working life, its coercive mechanisms and the chances for resistance considered and practised by the workers themselves. In the medieval literary story *Yvain ou le Chevalier au Lion* by Chrétien de Troyes, women discuss their pay and labour conditions. In his contribution, Colin Arnaud takes up and analyses these discussions. In her illustration for the chapter (p. 141), Kuzmych shows a door in a fence 'shaped' by ribbons, referring to the possibility of changing one's own labour conditions through reflection. The women work inside the fence, and also sleep and eat there. Despite being paid, they are by no means free to decide how they work, at what and how much.

Similarly, the protagonist in Müge Özbek's chapter, Emine (in Ottoman Istanbul of 1910) wanted to leave her employer but was prevented from doing so by her own family, the economic situation and the cultural code of gender roles. Kuzmych shows the young woman trying to escape, but struggling as her dress becomes caught in the door (p. 185). The attempt to escape exposes her position: the naked legs symbolise her desire for emancipation. She wanted to be freed from her current labour situation (domestic work) and the coercion that she experienced, and have power over her will and her body. But although the law in theory provided for this, realising this goal was difficult. The protagonist's posture represents the young woman's struggle and her motivation to escape the existing constraints. The bush behind Emine whose leaves turn into flames of fire, also indicates that the situation is revolutionary and thus coercive. In the public space we can only see men. It is a borderline situation, an in-between space between the law and routine.

The artwork depicting a German miner searching for precious metals (for the chapter by Gabriele Marcon; p. 165) also shows an in-between space. Through penetration and intervention, the worker's hand deforms layers of soil to discover the source of precious metals, the quantity of which determines his employer's wealth. The path to wealth is long, labour-intensive and uncertain, as revealed by the path travelled and the engineer's working body, which has been burned by the sun. Relying on the help of tools and his experience, the man is caught in the in-between until he finds the treasure he seeks. The fourth image, which depicts current everyday working conditions in Bangladesh's textile industry (p. 201, illustrating the chapter by Mohammad Tareq Hasan), links the cause of labour conditions – the ship waiting for cargo to sail to Europe – with the manifestation of these conditions in the production process itself. The colour red signifies danger and the problem itself: coercion.

Textile materiality is used as an important compositional motif in all four of Kuzmych's illustrations. In the twelfth-century story, the ribbons form the spatial structure for the working women who are held 'captive' to produce and be financially rewarded for their labour. In the case of the mining engineer, the fabric serves to protect him from the sun and, at the same time, conceals the gaze backwards, to what remains, to what is overlooked. Emine's dress that is stuck in the door symbolises the ties that prevent her escape. And in the case of the workers in Bangladesh, it is precisely the mass production of textiles and its demands that result in their precarious working situation.

Manipulating labour relations

Monika Lang works with the graphic novel method. The visual stories are characterised by dense narrative strands. This can be seen in the story of the foreign language guide in socialist Bulgaria (chapter by Ivanka Petrova). The scenic representation (pp. 301–3) visualises a guided tour and the togetherness of young people. One of the pictures, however, shows a person with a raised index finger. This gesture raises the question of who is actually disciplining and controlling the situation. This is the moment when the viewer starts to reinterpret the idyllic image of holiday, leisure and cultural tour.

The visual representation of the historical situation in nineteenth-century Brazil (chapter by Marjorie Carvalho de Souza; pp. 249–51) is very similar. Initially, the viewer sees the researcher entering the archive to create textual descriptions, reflections and argumentations based on the sources stored there. She selects the sources, combines them with other primary and secondary sources, and develops a textual structure to convey the features and specificities of the historical relationships and events. This approach is outlined in the image on p. 249 by simultaneously presenting a writing hand and the historical scenography. The way in which contract negotiations took place in nineteenth-century Brazil depended on social standing and legal status, although legal innovations between 1830, when the first Brazilian law on labour contracts was enacted, and 1888, when slavery was abolished, attempted to level out differences between migrants, slaves and so on in a rudimentary way. The paradox of the social situation is illustrated by Lang. The black female slave – who was no longer enslaved – was forced to continue to obey her old or new 'mistress', despite her new legal status, by running after her and working for her to pay off the debt for her own liberation.

The US South of the early twentieth century (chapter by Nico Pizzolato; images on pp. 272–3) saw a similar situation, and here, through the shadow with the ball and chain, Lang's illustration suggests that the granting of loans to free indebted Black people in fact imposed debt and thus new dependency. The question of debt was placed in a somewhat different context in socialist Bulgaria in the 1940s and 1950s, as shown by Lang's series of illustrations following this Afterword (pp. 373–6). These are based on Ana Luleva's research on labour camps in socialist Bulgaria.[25] The Bulgarian state defined work as a duty of the new 'socialist' man. Lang presents the 'new' man against the backdrop of the new social order – factory work, the fathers of the socialist idea, work as a source of freedom. Everyone had to make a contribution to the collective in the form of work performance. People who, for certain reasons, were not considered honourable in this context – and were constructed as drunkards, gamblers and so on – were forced to work in labour camps, as the next illustration shows. The person depicted in the opening illustration is caught in a circulating stream and cannot escape from the new idea. They are forced to join in, otherwise they will be punished. Only the 'ideal worker' in the first illustration has a face. All others are depicted without facial features. As a series of illustrations without a direct textual partner, this last visual contribution mobilises the viewers' engagement to a greater extent and confronts us more clearly with the potentialities and limits of images as conveyors of history.

Conclusion

The method of the 'translation loop' presented in this volume is characterised by intermedial translations of previous interpretations and reflections. The formation of a difference is based on the 'incomplete' repetition and 'additions'. The selected lines of argumentation of the reference work are taken up, but the decision on how they are 'translated' in terms of motif, colour and scenery depends on the specific history of one's own approach, methodology and ways of conceptualisation. And it is precisely through the juxtaposition of the successive processes and the focus on one's own 'proposals', which also lie in the processual logics and peculiarities of the specific medium, that the ability to create an in-between space unfolds. This in-between space has the potential to symbolise, question and engage with research tools, promising the inclusion of locally specific inscriptions in and effects on the space, the body and social relations.

Notes

1. See Deleuze, *Foucault*, 86.
2. It is important to note at this point that intermedial hybridity is understood here as an ongoing, one-after-another process of interpretation. In its 'own' mode of media-specific translation, interpretation itself embodies the potential of hybridity by weaving the pictorial into the textual and the textual into the pictorial. In doing so, it forms itself neither in the sense of an affirmation nor in the sense of an alliance, but aims to secure the field for a deepening contextualisation through the inclusion of body and space. See, for example, Bhabha, 'The Third Space: Interview with Homi Bhabha'; Bachtin, *Die Ästhetik des Wortes*; Ette and Wirth (eds), *Nach der Hybridität: Zukünfte der Kulturtheorie*; Kristeva, *Die Revolution der poetischen Sprache*.

3   McLuhan, *Die magischen Kanäle*, 66.
4   Mitchell, 'Über den Vergleich hinaus: Bild, Text und Methode'.
5   See, for example, Lirer, *Schwäbische Chronik / Gmünder Chronik*, 1485/6; Burgkmair der Jüngere, *Turnierbuch*, c.1540; Kal, *Fechtbuch*, second half of the 15th century.
6   See, for example, Kirchner, 'Historienbild'; Beckstette, 'Das Historienbild im 20. Jahrhundert'; Anderson and Offermann, *Yvain: The Knight of the Lion*.
7   See Werner, 'Bilddiskurse. Kritische Überlegungen zur Frage, ob es eine allgemeine Bildtheorie des naturwissenschaftlichen Bildes geben kann', 32–4.
8   Werner, 'Bilddiskurse. Kritische Überlegungen zur Frage, ob es eine allgemeine Bildtheorie des naturwissenschaftlichen Bildes geben kann', 34.
9   Werner, 'Bilddiskurse. Kritische Überlegungen zur Frage, ob es eine allgemeine Bildtheorie des naturwissenschaftlichen Bildes geben kann', 34.
10 See, for example, Alfani and Di Tullio, *The Lion's Share: Inequality and the Rise of the Fiscal State in Preindustrial Europe*; Piketty, *Capital in the Twenty-First Century*.
11 Becker, 'Historische Bildkunde – transdisziplinär', 2008; Zierenberg, 'Die "Macht der Bilder". Infrastrukturen des Visuellen im 20. Jahrhundert', 2010; Burke, *Eyewitnessing: The Uses of Images as Historical Evidence*; Jordanova, *The Look of the Past: Visual and Material Evidence in Historical Practice*.
12 Talkenberger, 'Von der Illustration zu Interpretation: Das Bild als historische Quelle. Überlegungen zur Historischen Bildkunde', 1994; Wohlfeil, 'Das Bild als Geschichtsquelle', 1986; Wohlfeil, 'Methodische Reflexionen zur Historischen Bildkunde', 1991; Milton, 'Argument oder Illustration: Die Bedeutung von Fotodokumenten als Quelle', 1988.
13 Talkenberger, 'Von der Illustration zu Interpretation: Das Bild als historische Quelle. Überlegungen zur Historischen Bildkunde', 1994, 300.
14 Milton, 'Argument oder Illustration: Die Bedeutung von Fotodokumenten als Quelle', 1988.
15 Wohlfeil, 'Methodische Reflexionen zur Historischen Bildkunde', 1991; Panofsky, 'Ikonographie und Ikonologie. Eine Einführung in die Kunst der Renaissance'.
16 Hamann, *Visual History und Geschichtsdidaktik*.
17 Stoellger, 'Bild als Quelle – Quelle als Bild: zur symbolischen Funktion von Bildern im wissenschaftlichen Diskurs'.
18 Curated by Imelda Miller, State Library of Queensland, 16 February–8 September 2019.
19 See, among others, Scholtz, *Die Interdisziplinarität der Begriffsgeschichte*; Joas and Vogt, *Begriffene Geschichte. Materialien zum Werk Reinhart Kosellecks*; Kollmeier, 'Begriffsgeschichte und Historische Semantik'.
20 Adorno, *Der getreue Korrepetitor*, 205; Adorno, *Einleitung in die Musiksoziologie*, 325–6.
21 Butler, 'Performative Akte und Geschlechterkonstitution. Phänomenologie und feministische Theorie'.
22 Derrida, 'Signature événement contexte', 32.
23 Čakardić, *Sablasti Tranzicije. Socijalna Historija Kapitalizma*, 43–4, 177–9.
24 Bellamy Foster, 'Marx, Value, and Nature', 2018.
25 Luleva, 'Commemorating the Communist Labour Camps: Is a New Memory Culture Possible?'.

Bibliography

Adorno, Theodor. *Einleitung in die Musiksoziologie*, GS XIV, edited by Rolf Tiedemann, Gretel Adorno, Susan Buck-Morss and Klaus Schultz. Frankfurt am Main: Suhrkamp, 1997.
Adorno, Theodor. *Der getreue Korrepetitor*, GS XV, edited by Rolf Tiedemann, Gretel Adorno, Susan Buck-Morss and Klaus Schultz. Frankfurt am Main: Suhrkamp, 1997.
Alfani, Guido and Di Tullio, Matteo. *The Lion's Share: Inequality and the Rise of the Fiscal State in Preindustrial Europe*. Cambridge: Cambridge University Press, 2019.
Anderson, M. T. and Offermann, Andrea. *Yvain: The Knight of the Lion*. Somerville, MA: Candlewick, 2017.
Bachtin, Michail. *Die Ästhetik des Wortes*. Frankfurt am Main: Suhrkamp, 1979.
Bauman, Zygmunt. *Moderne und Ambivalenz. Das Ende der Eindeutigkeit*. Frankfurt am Main: Fischer, 1995.

Becker, Frank. 'Historische Bildkunde – transdisziplinär', *Historische Mitteilungen* 21 (2008): 95–110.
Beckstette, Sven. 'Das Historienbild im 20. Jahrhundert'. Dissertation, Freie Universität Berlin, 2008.
Bellamy Foster, John. 'Marx, Value, and Nature', *Monthly Review* 70/3 (July–August 2018). Accessed 20 February 2022. http://monthlyreview.org/2018/07/01/marx-value-and-nature/.
Bhabha, Homi K. 'The Third Space: Interview with Homi Bhabha'. In *Identity: Community, Culture, Difference*, edited by Jonathan Rutherford, 207–21. London: Lawrence & Wishart, 1990.
Burgkmair der Jüngere, Hans. *Turnierbuch*, Cod.icon. 403. Augsburg, c.1540.
Burke, Peter. *Eyewitnessing: The Uses of Images as Historical Evidence*. New York: Ithaca, 2001.
Butler, Judith. 'Performative Akte und Geschlechterkonstitution. Phänomenologie und feministische Theorie'. In *Performanz. Zwischen Sprachphilosophie und Kulturwissenschaft*, edited by Uwe Wirth, 301–20. Frankfurt am Main: Suhrkamp, 2002.
Čakardić, Ankica. *Sablasti tranzicije. Socijalna historija kapitalizma*. Rijeka/Zagreb: Jesenski i Turk, Drugo more, 2020.
Cetina Knorr, Karin. '"Viskurse" der Physik: Konsensbildung und visuelle Darstellung'. In *Mit dem Auge denken. Strategien der Sichtbarmachung in wissenschaftlichen und virtuellen Welten*, edited by Bettina Heintz and Jörg Huber, 305–20. Wien: Springer, 2001.
Deleuze, Gilles. *Foucault*. Frankfurt am Main: Suhrkamp, 1992.
Derrida, Jacques. 'Signature événement contexte'. In *Marges de la Philosophie*, edited by Jacques Derrida, 365–93. Paris: MINUIT, 1972.
Ette, Ottmar and Wirth, Uwe (eds). *Nach der Hybridität. Zukünfte der Literaturtheorie*. Berlin: Verlag Walter Frey, 2014.
Hamann, Christoph. *Visual History und Geschichtsdidaktik. Bildkompetenz in der historisch-politischen Bildung*. Herbolzheim: Centaurus Verlag, 2007.
Joas, Hans and Vogt, Peter (eds). *Begriffene Geschichte. Materialien zum Werk Reinhart Kosellecks*. Frankfurt am Main: Suhrkamp, 2011.
Jordanova, Ludmilla. *The Look of the Past: Visual and Material Evidence in Historical Practice*. Cambridge: Cambridge University Press, 2012.
Kal, Paul. *Fechtbuch*, Cgm 1507, Bavaria, second half of the 15th century.
Kirchner, Thomas. 'Historienbild'. In *Handbuch der politischen Ikonographie*, Vol. 1, edited by Uwe Fleckner, Martin Warnke and Hendrik Ziegler, 505–12. München: C. H. Beck, 2011.
Kollmeier, Kathrin. 'Begriffsgeschichte und Historische Semantik', *Docupedia-Zeitgeschichte*, 29 October 2012. Accessed 20 September 2022. http://docupedia.de/zg/kollmeier_begriffsgeschichte_v2_de_2012.
Kristeva, Julia. *Die Revolution der poetischen Sprache*. Frankfurt am Main: Suhrkamp, 1992.
Lirer, Thomas. *Schwäbische Chronik / Gmünder Chronik*, Cgm 436, 1485/6.
Luleva, Ana. 'Commemorating the Communist Labour Camps: Is a New Memory Culture Possible?'. In *Contested Heritage and Identities in Post-socialist Bulgaria*, edited by Ana Luleva, Ivanka Petrova and Slavia Barlieva, 60–89. Sofia: Gutenberg Publ. House, 2015.
McLuhan, Marshall. *Die magischen Kanäle*. Düsseldorf/Wien: Econ-Verlag, 1968.
Miller, Imelda. 'Plantation Voices: Contemporary Conversations with Australian South Sea Islanders', 19 March 2019. Accessed 8 September 2022. https://www.slq.qld.gov.au/discover/exhibitions/plantation-voices-contemporary-conversations-australian-south-sea-islanders.
Milton, Sybil. 'Argument oder Illustration: Die Bedeutung von Fotodokumenten als Quelle', *Fotogeschichte* 28 (1988): 1–90.
Mitchell, W. J. T. 'Über den Vergleich hinaus: Bild, Text und Methode'. In *Bildtheorie*, 136–170. Berlin: Suhrkamp, 2018.
Palonen, Kari. *Die Entzauberung der Begriffe. Das Umschreiben der politischen Begriffe bei Quentin Skinner und Reinhart Koselleck*. Münster: LIT-Verlag, 2004.
Panofsky, Erwin. 'Ikonographie und Ikonologie. Eine Einführung in die Kunst der Renaissance'. In *Sinn und Deutung in der Bildenden Kunst*, edited by Erwin Panofky, 36–67. Köln: DuMont, 1996.
Picketty, Thomas. *Capital in the Twenty-First Century*. Cambridge, MA: Harvard University Press, 2014.
Scholtz, Gunter (ed.). *Die Interdisziplinarität der Begriffsgeschichte*. Hamburg: Felix Meiner Verlag, 2000.

Stoellger, Philipp. 'Bild als Quelle – Quelle als Bild: zur symbolischen Funktion von Bildern im wissenschaftlichen Diskurs'. In *Mit Klios Augen*, edited by Kornelia Imesch and Alfred Messerli, 21–43. Oberhausen: Athena-Verlag, 2013.

Talkenberger, Heike. 'Von der Illustration zu Interpretation: Das Bild als historische Quelle. Überlegungen zur Historischen Bildkunde', *Zeitschrift für Historische Forschung* 3 (1994): 289–313.

Werner, Gabriele. 'Bilddiskurse. Kritische Überlegung zur Frage, ob es eine allgemeine Bildtheorie des naturwissenschaftlichen Bildes geben kann'. In *Das Technische Bild. Kompendium zu einer Stilgeschichte wissenschaftlicher Bilder*, edited by Horst Bredekamp, Birgit Schneider and Vera Dünkel, 30–5. Berlin: Akademie-Verlag, 2008.

Wohlfeil, Rainer. 'Das Bild als Geschichtsquelle', *Historische Zeitschrift*, 243/1 (1986): 91–100.

Wohlfeil, Rainer. 'Methodische Reflexionen zur Historischen Bildkunde', *Zeitschrift für Historische Forschung* 12 (1991): 17–35.

Zierenberg, Malte. 'Die "Macht der Bilder". Infrastrukturen des Visuellen im 20. Jahrhundert', *ZeitRäume. Potsdamer Almanach des Zentrums für Zeithistorische Forschung 2009* (2010): 219–27.

Graphic novel © Monika Lang, 2021

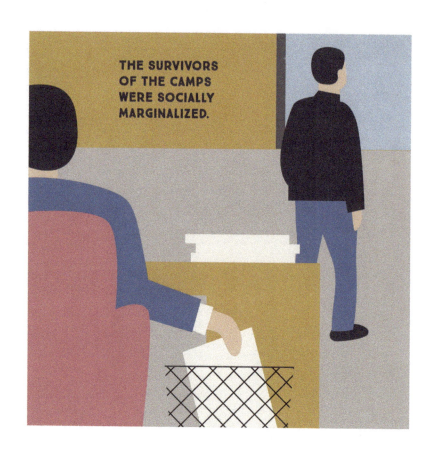
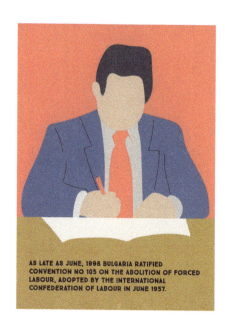

Index

Aćimović, Milan, 87
African-Americans, *see* Black people
Ağa, Hasan, 191, 195
agricultural workers, 289ff, *see also* rural labour
alcohol, 123, 124
Âli Pasha, Mehmed Emin, 33–4
al-Makhzūmī, 157
al-Maqrīzī, 153–4
angarya (compulsory service), 31–3, 36, 42
apprentices/apprenticeships, 52, 53, 55–9, 111, 195
arrest (of workers), 57, 59, 65, 67, 89, 193–4, 196, 237, 259, 278, 288
Austria, Habsburg Empire, 51–69, 88, 110
Avramović, Mihailo, 97, 103

Bangladesh, 203–20, *see also* garment factories
Benoist, Philippe, 253, 254
biopolitics, 108–9, 117, 126
'blackbirding', 337, *see also* recruitment
Black people, 257, 258, 260, 278, 281, 288, 368
border plants, *see Maquilápolis: City of Factories*
bourgeoisie, 117, 119, 341–2
Bracero Program, 229, 289, 290–2
Brazil, 253–65
Brims, Harriett Pettifore, 340
Budapest Museum of Social Health, 107–9, 114–25, 126, 128, 130–2
Bulgaria, 305–28
bureaucracy, 25–34, 40–1, 68, 95

capitalism, 2–3, 25, 35, 52, 107ff, 116ff, 130–1, 144, 191, 226, 227, 229, 232–3, 240, 241, 283, 287, 331, 341, 364

Capitulare De Villis, 145–6, 151, 159
Charlemagne, 145, 151
Chilpancingo Collective, 237–9, 241
child health, 124–5
child labour, 36, 188, 195
civil servants, 83–5
    dismissals, 90–3, 102–3
    grades and promotion, 85–6, 101
    Tim Robinson (illustrations), 79–81, 366
    occupation, collaboration and administration, 85–8
clothing industry, 203–20, *see also* textile production
collage, 22–3, 33–6, 365–6
collective action, 213–15, 218, 220
colonialism, 117, 260, 341, 353n13, 354n30, *see also* indenture
communal obligation, 38
conscription, 30–1, 36–7
consent (of workers), 31–2, 192, 196, 294
consumption, consumer, 3–4, 205, 290–1, 338–9
contracts, *see* labour contracts
corruption, 94–5, 236
Cosimo I de' Medici (future Grand Duke of Tuscany), 171–2, 174–5, 177–8
Cota, Jaime, 235–6
Council for Mutual Economic Assistance, 313, 328–9
credit, 285–6
Cruz, Sor Juana Inés de la, 236

Danzinger, Ignaz, 66
debt, 158, 172, 255, 256–65, 275–93, 368, *see also* guilt
    Monika Lang (illustrations), 272–3, 276, 282, 368

Deeds of the Abbots of St Truiden, 148–9
desertion, 31, 38, 39, *see also* escape
Deutsch, Julius, 66
discourses, 204–5, 217–18
domestic work, 187–97
Dragačevac, Svetolik, 89

Eckbert of Schönau, 146–7
Egypt, Fatimide Caliphate, 153–4, 155–8
enslaved people, *see* slavery
eugenics, 125–30
escape (of workers), 39, 192–6, 284, 287, 367, *see also* desertion
exhibitions, 109, 332–6, 352, 360–1, *see also* Budapest Museum of Social Health

family, 127, *see also* household work
factories/factory workers, 36, 60, 111, 120, 154, 203–21, 225–42, 362, 368, *see also* clothing industry; industrialisation
fieldwork, 204, 205, 206
film, 225–42
folklore, 170
Frond, Jean-Victor, 253, 254

Garcia Lepe, Manuel, 239
garment industry, *see* textile production
 Dariia Kuzmych (illustrations), 201, 203, 367
gedik (institution to protect craftsmen), 27–9, 42
genitium, 145–7, 151
German miners in Medici Tuscany, 167–79
German occupation of Serbia, 83–100
Germany, 145–7
globalisation, 226, 230, 231, 233, 234, 236, 240
Glöggl, Hans, 173, 176, 177, 178
Gortvay, György, 116, 117

graphic novels, 249–51, 368
guilt, 284, 285, 286–7, *see also* debt

Hanusch, Ferdinand, 67
Hoffmann, Géza, 127–8
Holek, Wenzel, 66
household work, *see* domestic work
Hungary, 107, 110–13, 117, 124, 126, 127, 131

Ibn Mammātī, 156–7
identity documents *see* labour booklets
identity of South Sea Islanders, 334–5, 341, 346
ideologies and/of labour, 26, 40, 52, 84–6, 95–7, 99, 212, 217, 292, 307, 308, 310, 311, 313–14, 321, 323–4, 326–7, 336, 348, 351, 366
illegality, 56, 95, 114, 288, 290, 324
immigrants, *see* migrants
immobility, *see* labour immobility
Imperial Arsenal (Tersane-i Amire, Ottoman state), 26, 27–9, 30–1, 32–3, 34–5, 37, 38, 39–40
Imperial Yarn Factory (İplikhane/ Riştehane-i Amire, Ottoman state), 26, 36, 38
indenture, 331–52
industrialisation, 25, 40
 in Bulgaria, 308
 in Hungary, 110, 112, 113
Ingwer, Isidor, 57–8, 68
intermediality, 7–10, 357–8, 360–1, 363–4
International Labour Organization (ILO), 4
irregular workers in Ottoman state, 25–6, 27–8, 29, 41

Jodlbauer, Josef, 66–7

Kahn, Jose, 237
Khitat, 153–4
kinship networks (fictitious), 212
Knežević, Desanka, 92

kuluk (mandatory duties), 97–8, 103–4
Kuzmych, Dariia (illustrations), 361, 362, 364
  garment factories in Bangladesh, 201, 203, 367
  German miners in Medici Tuscany, 165, 169, 367
  medieval textile production, 141, 159, 366, 367
  runaway domestic worker, 8–9, 185, 190, 366–7

labour booklets, 51–69
  Tim Robinson (illustrations), 47–50, 365
labour camps, 368–9
  Monika Lang (illustrations), 373–6
labour contracts, 55–63, 255, 257–9, 261–5, 368
  Monika Lang (illustrations), 249–51, 368
labour immobility, 26, *see also gedik*
labour movements, 2, 54, 120
Landerl, Adolf, 67
Lang, Monika (illustrations), 361, 362, 364
  debt and labour coercion in US South, 272–3, 276, 282, 368
  labour camps in socialist Bulgaria, 368–9, 373–6
  labour contracts as tools of coercion and opportunity in Brazil, 249–51, 368
  obligatory contributions to society (student guides in socialist Bulgaria), 301–3, 368
legal action against companies/ employers, 235–6
Loyola, Teresa, 228
Luján, Lourdes, 227, 233, 237, 238, 241

managers/management
  agricultural, 288–9
  garment factories, 207–20
  mines, 173, 175, 177
  museums, 117

tirāz factories, 154
tourist facilities, 306, 307, 311, 315, 317, 322, 323
manumission, 261, 264, 265
maquiladora workers, *see Maquilápolis*
Maquilápolis: City of Factories (2006) (film), 225–30
Marschan, Dr Géza, 115
Marx, Karl, 4, 143, 285
McFarlane, D., 344–5, 348–9
McLuhan, Marshall, 357
Medici (rulers in Tuscany), 168–79
Metales y Derivados, battery recycling factory, 237–8, 241
Mexican migrants, 225ff
Mexico
  peonage and hacienda system, 287
  See also Maquilápolis: City of Factories (2006) (film)
migrants, migration, internal, 126–7, 128, 204
Mijangos, Vianey, 236–7, 240–1
military
  German, in Serbia, 83, 86, 87, 90
  Ottoman, 25–40, 192
minimum wage, 203–4, 206
miners/mining, 167–79
mobilisation (of workers/economy), 26, 31, 32, 98, 308, *see also* recruitment
Mooney, Dylan, 332–3, 334, 335
multinational companies, *see Maquilápolis* (film)
museums, *see* Budapest Museum of Social Health; exhibitions

Nāṣi-i-Khusraw, 155
natalism, 127–8, 130
naval industry, 22–41
Nedić, General Milan, 87
newspapers, 342–4, 351
Nizam-ı Cedid (New Order), 25, 41
nizam (order), 25, 27
North Queensland Register, 344–6
notary office, Brazil, 256, 261, 266

Olin, Margaret, 348
Orbita/Bulgaria, 305–7, 311–312, 316–317, 320, 326–7
Ottoman state, 25–41

Pacific, indentured labour in the, 332, 336–52
Paşa, Ishak Cevdet, 190–1, 192–3, 194–5
Pasha, Sadık Rıfat, 33–4
patriarchy, 191, 196–7, 235
peonage, 275–6, 279, 280, 282, 286–8, 293
people of African descent, *see* Black people
people of colour, *see* Black people
petitions, 36, 37, 190, 191, 192–4
Petzold, Alfons, 67
photography, 9, 34, 331–52
piece rates, 5, 207, 213, 215
planters/plantations
　Australia, 331–52
　Brazil, 260–1, 266n10
　US South, 275–94
police, 55, 65, 66, 193–4, 320, 350, 351
pollution, 237–9, 241
Popp, Adelheid, 67
Portugal, as place of emigration, 256–7, 259, 261, 266, 267
poverty, 33, 113, 131, 150, 192
power relations
　debates on, 2–6
　in garment factories, 206ff
　museums and, 108–9, 119
　self-empowerment, 226–7, 235, 237
　sharecroppers, 280–1
privatisation, 293, 364
promotoras, 227, 231, 235–6, 236–7
protest, 89, 175, 203, 213–16
public health, *see* Budapest Museum of Social Health
public history and art, 8, 15
punishment, threats/fear of, 65, 86, 89, 98, 99, 209, 220, 277

Qatar, World Cup (2022), 293
Queensland Agricultural Journal, 342–3
Queenslander, 348–9
Queensland Figaro, 343–4

Raper, Arthur F., 279–80, 283, 284, 286
recruitment, *see also* mobilisation
　Australian-Pacific indentured labour, 337, 353–4
　Bangladeshi garment factories, 218
　Mexican migrants, 290
　Ottoman domestic workers, 188, 191
　Ottoman naval, 27, 31, 33
　student guides in socialist Bulgaria, 311–12
　Tuscan mines, 171–2
reproductive labour, 14, 226–7, 231–2
resistance, 12, 30, 89, 92, 97, 100n6, 204–6, 216ff, 219–20, 228–9, 235ff, 314, 325, 341, 354n30, 366
Rio de Janeiro, 253–65
Robinson, Tim (illustrations), 361, 362, 364
　civil servants in occupied Serbia (1941–4), 79–81, 366
　labour booklets in the Habsburg Monarchy/Austria, 47–50, 365
　labour immobility in Ottoman state, 22–3, 33–7, 41, 365
Roth, Michael, 353
rural labour (US South), 278–94

Sanyo, 235–6
Saunders, Kay, 337, 353
self-employment, 11, 169, 172, 174–5
Serbia, 83–100
sharecropping, 278–89
Shatzmiller, Maya, 154–5
slave, slavery
　abolition of, 6, 258
　domestic, 187, 188–9

380　COERCION AND WAGE LABOUR

new, US South in twentieth
    century, 277–8
  trade, 187, 256, 258, 260
socialism (Bulgaria), 305–28
Social Museum Review, 115–16
'social question', 112–14
solidarity, 6, 112, 204–5, 212, 220,
    228, 314, 318, 323, 325, 327
Soviet Union, 314, 328
Steinhardt, Karl, 65–6
Stop and Stare (2018), 332–3
strikes, 40, 57, 59, 339
student guides
  Monika Lang (illustrations),
    301–3, 368
  responsibility and punishment,
    319–23
  unauthorised labour practices,
    323–6
Sydney Mail, 346–7
Szántó, Menyhért, 115

Talkenberger, Heike, 359
Tanzimat (Reordering/
    Reorganisation), 25, 26–7, 31,
    32–3, 36, 41
taxation, 30, 32, 39, 155–6
Tegler, Cristof, 167–8, 172–3, 174,
    176
Terrell, Mary Church, 287
textile production, *see also* clothing
    industry
  medieval, 143–5
  archaeological evidence of textile
    labour, 145–7
  female silk weavers of *Yvain*, 143,
    150–3
  Dariia Kuzmych (illustrations),
    141, 159, 366, 367
Thirteenth Amendment (1865, US),
    277
Thomas, Albert, 118
Thompson, Floyd, 278
Togo-Brisby, Jasmine, 332, 333–4,
    335
Torre, Sergio de la, *see Maquilápolis:
    City of Factories* (2006) (film)
trade court, 58–61, 64

trade/labour unions, 61, 64, 65,
    110–11, 112, 120, 203–4,
    235–7, 338, 339, 352n4, *see
    also* labour movements
tramping, 64–6
'translation loop', 357, 361–3
Tribute, 143, 144, 155–6
Troyes, Chrétien de, 143, 150–3,
    159
truck system, 338–9
Turda, Marius, 126–7
Tuscany, 168–79

United States, 133n36, 229, 275–94
United States vs Reynolds (1914),
    286–7
universalism, 119, 133

vagrancy, vagrant, 64, 66, 193–4,
    277, 278
Vasić, Nataša, 92
voluntarism, voluntary labour, 197,
    220, 309, 354n30

welfare state, 3, 5
Wills, F. C., 342–3
Wohlfeil, Rainer, 359
Woodson, Carter, 281, 285
work documents, *see* labour
    booklets
Workers' Compensation Act (1907,
    Hungary), 120, 125
Workers Defense League (WDL),
    276–7, 279
World Bank, 236
World's Fairs, 119

youth labour brigades, Bulgaria,
    308–11, 316, 328
Youth Travel Bureau (YTB) Orbita,
    305–7, 311, 312, 316, 317,
    320, 326–7
Yugoslavia, 83, 87, 88, 100
Yvain ou le Chevalier au Lion, 143,
    150–3, 159

Zbor movement, 96

www.ingramcontent.com/pod-product-compliance
Lightning Source LLC
Chambersburg PA
CBHW042258240125
20677CB00034B/18